CHILDREN AND YOUTH IN
ARMED CONFLICT

SOCIOLOGICAL STUDIES OF CHILDREN AND YOUTH

Series Editor: David A. Kinney (from 1999)
Series Editors: David A. Kinney and Katherine Brown Rosier (2004–2010)
Series Editors: David A. Kinney and Loretta E. Bass (from 2011)
Outgoing Series Editor: Loretta E. Bass (from 2012)
Incoming Series Editor: Ingrid E. Castro (from 2024)

Previous Volumes:

Volume 22:	2016 Loretta E. Bass, Series Editor; Ingrid E. Castro, Melissa Swauger and Brent Harger, Guest Editors
Volume 23:	2017 Loretta E. Bass, Series Editor; Patricia Neff Claster and Sampson Lee Blair, Guest Editors
Volume 24:	2019 Loretta E. Bass, Series Editor; Magali Reis and Marcelo Isidório, Guest Editors
Volume 25:	2019 Loretta E. Bass, Series Editor; Doris Bühler-Niederberger and Lars Alberth, Guest Editors
Volume 26:	2020 Loretta E. Bass, Series Editor; Anuppiriya Sriskandarajah, Guest Editor
Volume 27:	2020 Loretta E. Bass, Series Editor; Sam Frankel and Sally McNamee, Guest Editors
Volume 28:	2022 Loretta E. Bass, Series Editor; Agnes Lux and Brian Gran, Guest Editors
Volume 29:	2022 Loretta E. Bass, Series Editor; Adrienne Lee Atterberry, Derrace Garfield McCallum, Siqi Tu and Amy Lutz, Guest Editors
Volume 30:	2022 Loretta E. Bass, Series Editor; Sabina Schutter and Dana Harring, Guest Editors
Volume 31:	2023 Loretta E. Bass, Series Editor; Marcelo S. Isidório, Guest Editor
Volume 32:	2023 Loretta E. Bass, Series Editor; Rachel Berman, Patrizia Albanese and Xiaobei Chen, Guest Editors
Volume 33:	2023 Loretta E. Bass, Series Editor; Katie Wright and Julie McLeod, Guest Editors
Volume 34:	2024 Loretta E. Bass (outgoing) and Ingrid E. Castro (incoming), Series Editors; Tamanna M. Shah, Guest Editor

EDITORIAL BOARD

Lars Alberth
Leuphana University Lüneburg, Germany

Sampson Lee Blair
The State University of New York, USA

Ingrid E. Castro
Massachusetts College of Liberal Arts, USA

Patricia Neff Claster
Edinboro University, USA

Tobia (Toby) Fattore
Macquarie University, Australia

Sam Frankel
King's University College at Western University, Canada

David Kinney
Central Michigan University, USA

Valeria Llobet
Universidad de Buenos Aires, Argentina

Sandi Nenga
Southwestern University, USA

Doris Bühler-Niederberger
Universität Wuppertal, Germany

Kate Tilleczek
York University, Canada

Yvonne M. Vissing
Salem State University, USA

Nicole Warehime
University of Central Oklahoma, USA

Katie Wright
La Trobe University, Australia

SOCIOLOGICAL STUDIES OF CHILDREN
AND YOUTH VOLUME 35

CHILDREN AND YOUTH IN ARMED CONFLICT: RESPONSES, RESISTANCE, AND PORTRAYAL IN MEDIA

EDITED BY

TAMANNA M. SHAH
Ohio University, USA

OUTGOING SERIES EDITOR

LORETTA E. BASS
The University of Oklahoma, USA

INCOMING SERIES EDITOR

INGRID E. CASTRO
Massachusetts College of Liberal Arts, USA

United Kingdom – North America – Japan
India – Malaysia – China

Emerald Publishing Limited
Emerald Publishing, Floor 5, Northspring, 21–23 Wellington Street, Leeds LS1 4DL.

First edition 2025

Editorial matter and selection © 2025 Tamanna M. Shah.
Individual chapters © 2025 The authors.
Published under exclusive licence by Emerald Publishing Limited.

Chapter 2, "Children of the Balkan Wars": Responses and Resistance to War-Related Media Content in Bosnia-Herzegovina, Kosovo, Montenegro, and Serbia, copyright © 2025 Eva Tamara Asboth and Michaela Griesbeck, is Open Access with copyright assigned to respective chapter authors. Published by Emerald Publishing Limited. This work is published under the Creative Commons Attribution (CC BY 4.0) licence. Anyone may reproduce, distribute, translate and create derivative works of this work (for both commercial and non-commercial purposes), subject to full attribution to the original publication and authors. The full terms of this licence may be seen at http://creativecommons.org/licences/by/4.0/legalcode

Reprints and permissions service
Contact: www.copyright.com

No part of this book may be reproduced, stored in a retrieval system, transmitted in any form or by any means electronic, mechanical, photocopying, recording or otherwise without either the prior written permission of the publisher or a licence permitting restricted copying issued in the UK by The Copyright Licensing Agency and in the USA by The Copyright Clearance Center. Any opinions expressed in the chapters are those of the authors. Whilst Emerald makes every effort to ensure the quality and accuracy of its content, Emerald makes no representation implied or otherwise, as to the chapters' suitability and application and disclaims any warranties, express or implied, to their use.

British Library Cataloguing in Publication Data
A catalogue record for this book is available from the British Library

ISBN: 978-1-83549-703-6 (Print)
ISBN: 978-1-83549-702-9 (Online)
ISBN: 978-1-83549-704-3 (Epub)

ISSN: 1537-4661 (Series)

INVESTOR IN PEOPLE

To my son, Qais
and
To the children who are our future

CONTENTS

List of Figures, Tables, and Appendices *xi*

About the Editor *xiii*

About the Contributors *xv*

Acknowledgments *xxi*

Children and Youth in Armed Conflict: Responses, Resistance, and Portrayal in Media
Tamanna M. Shah *1*

PART I
CHILDREN AND YOUTH RESPONSES AND RESISTANCE IN MEDIA

Chapter 1 Between Hope and Death: *Shaheed* as Equipment for Living Amid Palestine's Youth
Sophia Koleno *13*

Chapter 2 "Children of the Balkan Wars": Responses and Resistance to War-related Media Content in Bosnia–Herzegovina, Kosovo, Montenegro, and Serbia
Eva Tamara Asboth and Michaela Griesbeck *25*

Chapter 3 Diaries of War: Children's Narratives and Agency in Ukraine and Syria
Iuliia Hoban and Denise R. Muro *39*

Chapter 4 Children and Youth Art as a Form of Resistance in Conflict Zones
Raghu Yadav and Rose Williamson *55*

PART II
MEDIA PORTRAYAL OF NARRATIVES AND LIVED EXPERIENCES

Chapter 5 Media Intervention for Young Children During Mass Trauma Experiences: Promoting Theory of Mind and Resilience
Erin L. Ryan — *83*

Chapter 6 Children Throwing Stones as a Metaphor of Counter-Hegemony
Kazım Tolga Gürel — *101*

Chapter 7 Beginning of Life, End of Life: Examining Online Memorials of Children in Sites of Armed Conflict
Aya Diab and Danielle L. Johnson — *115*

Chapter 8 Capturing Resistance: Unveiling Visual Narratives of Youth Activism in the Israel–Palestine 2023 Conflict through Media Posted on Instagram
Sonali Jha and Mary-Magdalene N. Chumbow — *131*

Chapter 9 The Evolving Family and the Lyrical Child
Haoyue Zhang — *157*

Chapter 10 Loss of Naivety and Innocence: War Childhood in the Nineties Balkans
Julija Ovsec — *173*

Chapter 11 Children as Participants in Terrorism: Uche Aguh's *Sambisa* (2016) as a Paradigm
Stephen Ogheneruro Okpadah and Damilare Ogunmekan — *189*

Chapter 12 Resistance in Youth Literature
Omama Al-Lawati — *201*

PART III
EMOTIONS AND TECHNOLOGY

Chapter 13 Healing Through Empathy: Machine Learning for Adaptive Therapy for Children and Youth in Armed Conflict
Javed M. Shah and Tamanna M. Shah — *227*

LIST OF FIGURES, TABLES, AND APPENDICES

Figures

Fig. 4.1.	Handala.	56
Fig. 13.1.	Tracking In-Session Anxiety Triggers.	234
Fig. 13.2.	Emotional State Changes in Sample Therapy Session.	235
Fig. 13.3.	Algorithm 1: Training EmoGenPath Using A2C.	240
Fig. 13.4.	Sample EmoGenPath State-Action-Reward.	244
Fig. 13.5.	EmoGenPath Trial Episode Run.	246

Tables

Table 2.1.	Sub-categories of the Categories "Sender" and "Receiver."	32
Table 2.2.	Sub-categories of the Category "Media Content."	32
Table 8.1.	Workbook Showing Data Collection and Analysis.	142
Table 8.2.	Color Coding Scheme Used to Analyze Captions.	143
Table 8.3.	Scheme of Coded Captions.	144
Table 8.4.	Color Coding Scheme Used to Analyze Visual Content.	145
Table 12.1.	*The Hen of the House that Departs.*	208
Table 12.2.	*The Dragon of Bethlehem.*	210
Table 12.3.	*The Tale of the Secret Oil.*	213
Table 12.4.	*Lady of All.*	215
Table 12.5.	*Thunderbird.*	217

Appendix

Fig. A7.1.	Most Prevalent Topics in Memorials on r/SyrianCivilWar.	128
Fig. A7.2.	Prevalence Scaling of Individual Words.	129
Table A12.1.	Arabic Language Publications Targeted at Youth and Children.	222
Table A12.2.	Novels Analyzed for the Study.	223

ABOUT THE EDITOR

Tamanna M. Shah is an Assistant Professor of Instruction in the Department of Sociology and Anthropology at Ohio University, USA. She serves as an Experiential Learning Community-of-Practice Fellow at Ohio University and is the Book Reviews Editor for *Sociological Research Online (SRO)* and earned her PhD in Sociology from the University of Utah and holds a Master's degree in Sociology from Kansas State University and a Bachelor's degree in Economics. She has conducted field research in Kashmir, India, and East Timor. Her interests include comparative political sociology, gender and race, social change, and inequality. She has authored several publications, including "Adjustment to Divorce (Spouses)" for the *Wiley Blackwell Encyclopedia of Family Studies* and "Chaos and Fear: Creativity and Hope in an Uncertain World" in *International Sociology*. She is currently editing a book on *Gendered Identities in the Media* for Vernon Press. She has collaborated with the Asian Development Bank on water and sanitation policy papers (ORCID: 0000-0001-9609-0191).

ABOUT THE CONTRIBUTORS

Omama Al-Lawati, formerly an academic specializing in mass communication, has previously held roles as a Quality Assurance and Academic Accreditation Officer at Sultan Qaboos University in Oman. Holding a PhD in Communication and Media Studies from the Université de La Manouba, Tunisia (2021), and a Master's degree in Communication and Public Relations from the University of Westminster, London (2001), she possesses diverse interests, including writing and photography, with a particular focus on children's literature. She has authored around 15 storybooks with Arab publishers and contributed to short stories and articles. Her research primarily centers on children's literature and cultural issues, with numerous scholarly contributions. In 2016, she received the Omani Cultural Association Award in Children's Literature. Her children's book "A Man from China" made the long list for the Sheikh Zayed Book Award in 2019. Additionally, "Sandrani" was shortlisted for the Etisalat Award in 2022, and it was also a finalist for the Arab Forum Prize for Children's Books in 2023.

Eva Tamara Asboth is a Historian and a Communication Scientist. She works as a Postdoc Researcher at the Institute for Comparative Media and Communication Studies at the Austrian Academy of Sciences in Vienna. She is a Lecturer in the Department of Media and Communications at the University of Klagenfurt and teaches Historical Anthropology at Sigmund Freud University Vienna. Her research areas are historical communication and memory studies as well as transnational and oral history.

Mary-Magdalene N. Chumbow is a dedicated Communicator committed to tackling social disparities through storytelling. With extensive academic credentials and over a decade in communications, she focuses on global issues like health, gender-based violence, and community engagement. Her PhD in Media Arts and Studies from Ohio University, specializing in Health Communication and Communication for Social Change, anchors her work. Her dissertation, "Breaking the Silence," sheds light on survivors of female genital cutting in Kenya, reflecting her commitment to marginalized communities. She holds a Master's in Communication and Development, supplemented by a Graduate Certificate in Women's, Gender, and Sexuality Studies, all from Ohio University, shaping her expertise in Communication for Social Change and Development. Beyond academia, she actively advocates for underrepresented communities, evident in her roles with organizations like the Association of Cameroonians in Colorado. Her leadership in student unions underscores her dedication to inclusive communities. Her blend of academic rigor and practical experience positions her as a catalyst for positive change, amplifying marginalized voices and striving for lasting societal impact.

Aya Diab is a Doctoral Student studying political communication. She received her BA and MA from USF. While she is interested in political communication broadly, she is most interested in political communication as it intersects with Middle Eastern contexts. Her current research utilizes orientalist frameworks to investigate how elite structures portray and discuss the Middle East.

Michaela Griesbeck is a Semiotician and a Communication Scientist. She is currently employed as a Postdoc Researcher at the JKU in Linz, Austria, in the Department of Sociology, with a focus on Innovation and Digitalization. Her research deals with the topics of young people (adolescents and young adults), mediatization, and digitalization. Between 2016 and 2020, she worked on intercultural research projects with young adults in Southeast Europe.

Kazım Tolga Gürel was born in Istanbul in 1978. His first doctoral thesis, "Magazineisation in Turkey during the Economic Crisis," was not accepted by some universities in Turkey for political reasons. His second doctoral thesis, "LGBT+ Representation in Turkish Mainstream Newspapers," was accepted at a freer university, where he received his PhD. He has written 10 books, 1 of which he edited, which can be included in politics, communication, culture, and other studies. He produced around 40 articles. His subjects of interest are gender, communication, migration, and political issues. He writes in Turkey and lectures and conferences at universities, political parties, and associations.

Iuliia Hoban is an Assistant Professor at the Department of Emergency, Disaster and Global Security Studies, College of Arts & Sciences at Embry-Riddle Aeronautical University-Worldwide holds PhD in Global Affairs from Rutgers University. Her research centers on the politics of childhood and youth in conflict and peacebuilding, gendered responses to conflict, and the interplay between law and war. Her research has been published in such journals as *Cooperation and Conflict*, the *International Journal of Human Rights*, and the *Nordic Journal of Human Rights*. She has also contributed her scholarly expertise to book chapters and edited volumes. Prior to her role at Embry-Riddle, she held academic positions at Radford University and the College of New Jersey. She also applied her research skills in NGOs and think tanks such as Watchlist for Children and Armed Conflict (New York, NY), the Institute of World Policy (Kyiv, Ukraine), and the Laboratory to Combat Human Trafficking (Denver, CO) where her major responsibilities focused on analysis and research of multidimensional factors and aspects of human rights.

Sonali Jha is a PhD Student in the School of Media Arts and Studies at Ohio University. She holds a Bachelor's and a Master's degree in English Literature. She has two years of experience in the marketing industry working as a Content Writer. She focuses on unraveling media and social media usage inequalities, examining how it could help in creating an impact in society such as Human Trafficking. She explores the subjective nature of people's tech relationships, along with the significance of comedy in raising awareness. She is passionate about interpersonal communication, media's impact on daily life, digital inequalities, and international media.

About the Contributors xvii

Danielle L. Johnson (M.A. Coastal Carolina University) is a Doctoral Student at the University of South Florida researching interpersonal communication, computational communication science, fandom studies, and health. Broadly, she is interested in examining how computer-mediated communication is entwined with fandom. Specifically, she explores computer-mediated interpersonal communication among fans, and between fans and the person(s)/organization they are interested in. Her interest in health centers around how computer-mediated communication influences fans' understandings of and reactions to illness and end-of-life topics. Currently, her research focuses on how Korean popular music (K-pop) fans and artists curate parasocial intimacy during fan calls and to what degree of intimacy these calls reach. Her previous research looks at online reactions to the overturning of Roe v. Wade, COVID-19 disclosures by K-pop management companies, and social exchange theory in the Disney fandom during merchandise releases.

Sophia Koleno, Ohio University, United States, is a Muslim Doctoral Student within the Communication Studies program, specializing in rhetoric and cultural studies. She utilizes Islamic concepts, terms, and ideas to interpret both contemporary and classical rhetorical artifacts.

Denise R. Muro has over 10 years of experience working, advocating, and conducting research with immigrant and refugee communities in Colorado, Wyoming, Germany, and Massachusetts. Her research focuses on immigrant and refugee experiences, narratives, and community-building, centering their agency and voices. She also has a background in nonprofit and higher education settings, working on gender and racial justice, equity, and restorative justice. She has worked in various roles, supporting and creating opportunities for immigrant and refugee communities, women of color, first-generation students, and other historically marginalized and underrepresented groups. She is a first-generation student and holds a PhD from the Department of Conflict Resolution, Human Security, and Global Governance at the University of Massachusetts Boston's McCormack Graduate School of Policy and Global Studies.

Damilare Ogunmekan holds a Master's degree in Theatre Arts from the Department of the Creative Arts, University of Lagos, Lagos State Nigeria, and a BA (Hons) degree in Performing Arts from the University of Ilorin, Ilorin, Nigeria. Apart from being a Filmmaker, his areas of research include theater directing, playwriting, dramatic criticism, and eco-theater.

Stephen Ogheneruro Okpadah is a Chancellor International PhD Scholar at the University of Warwick, Coventry, UK. He is currently researching participatory theater and climate justice in the context of the Niger Delta region of Nigeria. His project draws on theater for development in creating community-based performances that advocate for climate justice. He won the 2021 Janusz Korczak/UNESCO Prize for Global South in emerging scholar category, and he is also Director of research at the Theatre Emissary International, Nigeria. He is a

Non-resident Research Associate at the Centre for Socially Engaged Theatre, University of Regina, Canada.

Julija Ovsec graduated with her Master's thesis on children's war literature from the University of Ljubljana. She is continuing her education as a PhD Candidate at Charles University in Prague, where she is writing a PhD thesis on female writers of the Second World War. She is working as a Literary Researcher at the Laboratory for Literature and Sociology at the Institute for Czech Literature at the Czech Academy of Sciences. Her research focuses mainly on two main groups – literature written by women and literature for children and youth. One of her most visible works in the ex-yu region is monitoring literary criticism. A group of feminist literary scholars called *Pobunjene čitateljke*, based in Belgrade, has been monitoring literary criticism in five countries (Slovenia, Serbia, Montenegro, Bosnia and Herzegovina, and Macedonia). They also organized workshops and podcasts on literary criticism.

Erin L. Ryan is Professor and Head of the Department of Communication at the University of Tennessee at Chattanooga. Her research focuses on children, adolescents, and the electronic media: the content and quality of children's media, how they use or are impacted by media, why they use media, advertising directed at the child/adolescent market, parental involvement and mediation, the regulation of children's media, and media literacy. Much of her current research revolves around preschool-aged children and how they use electronic media technology to learn new skills. She holds a BA in Psychology from the University of Georgia, a BS in Communication from Kennesaw State University, an MA in Mass Communication from Georgia State University, and a PhD in Mass Communication from the Grady College of Journalism and Mass Communication at the University of Georgia.

Javed M. Shah, University of Illinois, Chicago, USA, has over 20 years of experience in building software products for startups. He is currently pursuing a Master of Science in Computer Science from the University of Illinois, Chicago. He holds a BS in Computer Engineering from the University of Pune and an MBA from the University of California, Berkeley. He is passionate about research in permissionless systems, incentive design, computational science, and machine learning. His work on the multifaceted role of agency in shaping political landscapes has been published in the *International Political Science Abstracts*. He is a versatile technologist and researcher with deep empathy for building socially responsible innovation.

Rose Williamson holds a Master's degree in experimental psychology from Ohio University and is currently finishing her Doctorate in the same field. Her work primarily focuses on emotional responses to making decisions, as well as how socioeconomic status influences self-perception, particularly regarding goal attainment. She also has many years of experience creating, as well as academic knowledge of, both poetry and art.

Raghu Yadav is a Doctoral Student of Experimental Psychology at Ohio University. His general research interest is human cognition with a core focus on attention, emotion, concept formation, and categorization. At present, he is working on a project on relational similarity assessment. He also has an engineering background and passionately engages in poetry, art, and philosophy.

Haoyue Zhang is a film producer and scholar who specializes in the production and research of children's films, or the films about children and for children. Haoyue finished her master degree on Children's Literature in China, and pursued her doctoral degree of Film Studies in Southern Illinois University in the United States. Her dissertation was the first thorough theorization of the representations of childhood in the Fifth Generation filmmakers in China's New Wave in the 1980s. Her experiences interwove between theoretical exploration of childhood and children's film in China, and diverse industrial expertise spanning from film production to distribution. Her latest production was a co-produced children's film between China and Holland, the first achievement since the two countries signed the co-production treaty in 2015. (IMDB link: https://www.imdb.com/name/nm7491644/?ref_=fn_al_nm_2.).

ACKNOWLEDGMENTS

This volume is curated to serve as a resource for scholars and practitioners dedicated to advancing policies for the rights of children and youth. I want to applaud the authors and the reviewers for their unwavering commitment to bringing the narratives and experiences of children to the forefront. A heartfelt thank you goes to the contributors who painstakingly documented and analyzed the stories of children and youth embroiled in conflict. While it brings us joy to share this volume with the world, it was no small feat. As we wrote the chapters, we lived through the adversities faced by these young individuals. I am also grateful for the support and encouragement from the Editorial Staff at Emerald Publishing, particularly Katy Mathers and Lauren Kammerdiener, whose guidance was invaluable throughout this project. A special note of thanks to Professor Loretta Bass from the University of Oklahoma, the Series Editor of *Sociological Studies of Children and Youth (SSCY)*.

As the editor, I am inspired by a collective sense of hope and dedication to advocating for children's experiences.

Lastly, I want to acknowledge all those who helped me assemble this volume which gives voice to the struggles of millions of children worldwide. I extend my sincere appreciation to our reviewers, whose thorough and timely feedback significantly enhanced the quality of our chapters.

Dr. Holly Ningard, Ohio University (Special thanks for your support and encouragement)
Sonali Jha, Ohio University
Dr. S. A. Welch, Professor Emerita University of Wisconsin-Whitewater
Dr. Jodie Jones, Salt Lake Community College
Nikhil Reddy, Ohio University
Cameron Graham, University of Tennessee-Knoxville

CHILDREN AND YOUTH IN ARMED CONFLICT: RESPONSES, RESISTANCE, AND PORTRAYAL IN MEDIA

Tamanna M. Shah

Ohio University, USA

ABSTRACT

This volume explores the intersection of youth agency, media representation, and conflict, urging a reevaluation of the roles of youth in contemporary socio-political contexts. Media serves as a tool for and a site of resistance. Chapters in this volume highlight ways in which children and youth leverage digital platforms to reshape narratives around conflict and peace. The compilation draws from a wide range of contexts, from the Balkan Wars to the current conflicts in Syria and Ukraine, offering in-depth analyses of the transformative potential of the (re)imagining of youth experiences, thus shifting from passive subjects to active narrators. This reorientation emphasizes the role of new technologies, including digital media and artificial intelligence, in supporting these endeavors, especially in enhancing mental health and psychological resilience among children affected by conflict.

Keywords: Media portrayals; everyday resistance; peacebuilding; digital narratives; youth agency; social activism

INTRODUCTION

While Volume I of the book, *Children and Youth as 'Sites of Resistance' in Armed Conflict*, informed us about celebrating the agency and the stories of survival, resistance, and spirit of children and youth, this volume shifts focus to the outward projections of these lived experiences. It aims to bridge the gap between individual experiences and societal perceptions by examining how these narratives are portrayed and perceived in the media. Simultaneously, it seeks to capture the "responses, resistance, and portrayal" of the narratives in the media. This volume examines how media shapes public perception of conflict and resilience by analyzing its portrayal and reception across various platforms. As part of the *Sociological Studies of Children and Youth*, this compilation critically explores the complex interplay between media representation and youth agency in armed conflict. The chapters gathered here provide critical insights into how children and youth endure conflict and how their stories are told and retold in the public sphere, influencing advocacy, policymaking, and community responses worldwide.

Historically, the integration of new technologies has opened unparalleled opportunities for shaping the discourse of marginalized groups and facilitating decentralized communication during crises. Digital technologies have played a critical role in escalating tensions, exposing the brutality of authoritarian regimes, and strengthening calls for international support during times of war. These dynamics are particularly pronounced in a global political landscape marked by nationalism, racism, and neoliberalism, which influence the daily lives of young people. Media not only consumes the attention of children and youth but also shapes the portrayal of their experiences and narratives. This volume delves into how digital media provides avenues for young people to navigate and contest their experiences of social injustice (Shah, 2019), turning media platforms into spaces of active resistance (e.g., Curwood & Gibbons, 2010; Price-Dennis, 2016; Shah, 2021).

Scholars have extensively researched how young individuals produce digital media within community settings and family environments to articulate their identities and undertake social action (e.g., Ellison & Kirkland, 2014; Shah, 2020). Another body of work focuses on how the youth utilize media platforms to participate in political activities (Jenkins et al., 2016; Kahne et al., 2016). The chapters in this volume seek to redirect attention to how young people actively reshape their narratives, countering the usual marginalization or silencing of their voices (Thomas & Stornaiuolo, 2016). This act of *restorying* empowers youth to utilize digital tools to manifest their lived experiences and challenge dominant narratives (Stornaiuolo & Thomas, 2018). These acts of cultural production help young people voice their perspectives and display a potential to impact the broader discourse on peacebuilding, infusing it with a deeper sense of structural equity.

The compilation investigates deep-seated issues such as trauma and online memorialization, examining their implications for human rights in these challenging environments (Shah, 2013). It scrutinizes the role of social media in youth activism within India and Israel–Palestine, including how poetry serves as a medium to express trauma. An in-depth analysis of the impact of Boko Haram on girls, portrayed through media, and social media narratives in the Israel–Palestine conflict underscores the resilience and coping mechanisms that young individuals develop in response to traumatic events. Furthermore, the exploration of Yugoslavian literature through feminist lenses, and the study of children's art and poetry that arise from conflict, serves to amplify the voices of affected youths. This nuanced exploration aims to inform policies and shape programs that prioritize the well-being and rights of children and youth post-conflict, offering insights into their roles as agents of change within their communities. As we reflect on these varied and intricate roles, it is imperative to recognize the necessity for further research that listens to and prioritizes these young voices in policymaking and community engagements.

(RE)MAKING THE *SELF* AND IDENTITY

Identity and the *self* are concepts that have been used – and perhaps abused – across various contexts and for numerous purposes. The notions of *self* and what it means to possess an *identity* are often contested in spaces where collective claims of belonging are made. In these dominant political narratives, the *self* can become obscured as assumptions about identity prevail, dictating how it should be understood or defined. This often leads to the uniqueness of an individual's identity being overshadowed, or individuals facing the arduous task of validating their identity (Shah, 2023, 2024b). Similarly, there is a struggle in how one envisions oneself within the broader discourse of a national identity promoted by the state.

Our identity is something uniquely our own; it is what distinguishes us from others. Yet, identity also implies a connection to a broader collective or social group. Discussing national identity, cultural identity, or gender identity, for instance, suggests that our identity is partly defined by what we share with others. In this context, identity is about aligning with others who we believe are similar to us – at least in significant ways.

An assertion of identity by the youth, particularly from subordinate social groups, is often constructed as a "social problem," "at risk," or "naïve" to be peacebuilding agents. This legitimizes state-driven narratives pushing the experiences of children and youth as deficient to make any significant contributions (Shah, 2024a). On the contrary, through the power of their stories and art, children and youth echo Walter Benjamin's (1986) idea that violence should neither be exercised nor be naively tolerated in our everyday lives. Yet, the reality of postwar recovery across various nations often reveals a "violence continuum" that spans a spectrum of aggressive behaviors, including domestic violence, sexual offenses, and more severe crimes like armed theft and abduction, as well as systemic injustices (Scheper-Hughes & Bourgois, 2004; Whitehead, 2007).

Youth, significantly impacted by these harsh realities, find themselves bearing the burden, with families and societal institutions increasingly leaving them to devise their own coping mechanisms. The contributors of this volume highlight how narratives from young individuals in conflict settings reveal their interpretations of conflict within their everyday experiences and how they relate their stories to broader, adult-centric narratives prevalent in mainstream media. Restorying or reimagining narratives assert one's existence and experiences in a space that frequently silences subaltern voices (Thomas & Stornaiuolo, 2016).

YOUTH CONFLICT NARRATIVES AND THE MEDIA

In contemporary societies, access to diverse mass media fosters new ways of imagining the communities and the broader world (Appadurai, 1996). Media, therefore, enables the construction or the imagining of a self while the outside world is co-constructed. This process of imagination is identified as "a constitutive feature of modern subjectivity" (Appadurai, 1996, p. 3) that acts as a "form of negotiation between sites of agency (individuals) and globally defined fields of possibility" (Appadurai, 1996, p. 31). However, the transmission and reception of mass media messages are complex and not merely passive (Spitulnik, 1993, p. 296). Denov (2012) argues that media is akin to an "ideological tool" that molds our perceptions and values, often echoing the dominant worldviews that media entities aim to propagate (Kellner, 2011). The portrayal of youth and children in media is frequently simplified and sensationalized (Booker, 2007). Such simplistic portrayals marginalize their experiences and obscure their active participation in shaping their environments.

The humanist approach to media representation often unintentionally evokes pity rather than empathy for conflict victims, casting them solely as passive sufferers (Bleiker & Kay, 2007). In contrast, pluralist approaches allow individuals to document their own stories through media, validating diverse local knowledge and practices and challenging established power hierarchies often perpetuated by mainstream Western media (Bleiker & Kay, 2007, p. 151). Participatory media empowers individuals to actively engage in the construction of social meanings (Debrix, 2003, p. ix; Bleiker & Kay, 2007, p. 151), fostering a broader spectrum of voices and enriching our understanding of conflict scenarios (Gregory, 2006). As Appadurai (1996) argues, engagement with mass media can spark resistance and open up new possibilities for agency.

By engaging with participatory media, young people can break through constraints, reasserting their agency and altering perceptions of their role in society. In participatory media environments, children and youth are consumers and creators of content that reflects their unique perspectives and experiences. This shift from invisibility to visible agents of change allows them to challenge the narratives that have traditionally defined them. Their stories, once made visible, reveal a resilience that contests and transcends the reductive portrayals often found in conventional media (Denov, 2012). Narratives are expressed by youth and children in different forms: action, expression, rational, or moral tales. Through digital platforms, blogs, social media, and other forms of participatory media, they articulate their struggles and triumphs, contributing actively to the discourse on conflict and resistance. Art, poetry, and songs serve as powerful platforms for resistance, transcending mere esthetic appeal to act as formidable tools for social and political change (Shah, 2012). These forms of cultural expression provide marginalized voices a canvas to articulate their grievances and aspirations, often challenging oppressive systems and advocating for transformative shifts in society. This participation enriches the media landscape and empowers them, offering a counter-narrative that emphasizes their strength and resilience as potent forces in the pursuit of peace and justice.

SCOPE OF CONTRIBUTIONS

This volume is structured into three distinct parts. The first section presents youth voices of resistance as they interact with various forms of media. Here, young individuals articulate their everyday realities and desires for how their traumatic experiences should be understood by others. The second section shifts focus to how the media interprets and portrays the experiences of children and youth, examining the narratives that are constructed around them. The final part of the volume looks forward, to exploring the potential for hope and healing through the application of artificial intelligence for children and youth impacted by the traumas of war and conflict.

In Part I, Sophia Koleno starts us off with *Between Hope and Death: Shaheed as Equipment for Living Amid Palestine's Youth*, which critically examines the complex meanings associated with the concept of *shaheed* (martyrdom) among Palestinian youth. By integrating the Islamic concept of *ayah* with Kenneth Burke's notion of narratives as "equipment for living," Koleno reframes *shaheed* not as a glorification of death but as a deep source of resilience and a means to navigate the challenging realities of conflict. This analysis reveals how youth in Gaza utilize *shaheed* as a form of resistance, countering the negative stereotypes often perpetuated in Western media to reposition it within a broader existential and spiritual context.

In Chapter 2, Eva Tamara Asboth and Michaela Griesbeck analyze *"Children of the Balkan Wars": Responses and Resistance to War-related Media Content in Bosnia–Herzegovina, Kosovo, Montenegro, and Serbia*, where they explore the intricate relationship between post-war generations in Bosnia–Herzegovina, Kosovo, Montenegro, and Serbia and the media content related to the conflicts experienced during childhood. They highlight how young lives engage with media as a form of everyday resistance, opting to sidestep traditional media narratives that often perpetuate nationalistic and ethnopolitical ideologies. Instead, the youth actively seek out and distribute alternative narratives and historical facts through digital platforms, thus redefining their roles from passive recipients to active shapers of media discourse. Such narratives underscore their role in challenging and reshaping the collective memory and national narratives prevalent in their respective societies.

Chapter 3 is a journey into the civil war in Syria and the full-scale war in Ukraine. Iuliia Hoban and Denise R. Muro, in a heart-wrenching comparison, provide first-hand accounts of Ukrainian and Syrian children, utilizing diaries as a medium to explore their experiences of conflict and resistance. By focusing on the children's written words, the chapter illustrates how these young individuals document their lives amid the chaos and actively engage in the narrative construction and resistance against the militarization of their everyday lives. Their stories underscore the children's agency in shaping the discourse around their experiences, challenging dominant narratives, and offering nuanced insights into the complexities of life in war-torn regions. The last chapter in this section examines the role of creative expression and the use of art and poetry by children and youth as coping mechanisms and forms of resistance (Chapter 4). Raghu Yadav and Rose Williamson present an intersection of trauma, resilience, and creative expression. They emphasize the transformative power of art, highlighting how the genuine and raw outputs from young individuals facilitate personal healing and function as powerful tools for social change and resistance.

In Part II of the volume, Dr. Erin L. Ryan draws attention to the media portrayal of young children during mass trauma experiences. This analysis contributes uniquely to the themes of "responses, resistance, and portrayal in media" by emphasizing how strategic media use can foster resilience and a theory of mind in children amidst conflicts (Chapter 5). Dr. Erin L. Ryan explores the delicate balance of exposure and protection that media offers, presenting media as a dual force that can either exacerbate trauma or aid in healing and resilience. Through an in-depth examination of how media shapes the experiences and perceptions of young children during wartime, this chapter highlights the potential vulnerabilities and the powerful agency of children in conflict zones. Dr. Erin L. Ryan's emphasis on using media strategically to support children's development and well-being offers a hopeful perspective on intervention strategies that can be utilized in conflict and post-conflict settings.

After a unique take on media, we are presented with the metaphor of children throwing stones, analyzed as symbols of counter-hegemony, reflecting the complex interaction between local struggles and global media narratives by Dr. Kazım Tolga Gürel (Chapter 6). This analysis presents how Kurdish children, represented through their resistance in stone-throwing, are often portrayed in the media under frameworks that serve state or corporate interests, overshadowing their agency and the socio-political context of their actions. On a related note, it also explores the role of state policies in perpetuating certain narratives while silencing others, thereby contributing to a broader discourse on the intersection of media portrayal, youth activism, and resistance in conflict settings.

In Chapter 7, Aya Diab and Danielle L. Johnson focus on how children trapped in armed conflict are memorialized in online spaces, using the Syrian Civil War as a context. This analysis unveils a dual theme of visibility and blame within these digital memorials. Children, although central to the narratives of war and conflict, often remain underrepresented in memorials, highlighting a concerning trend of their absence in discussions where they should be prominently featured. This omission underscores a broader issue of their marginalization in conflict narratives and as overlooked agents within media portrayals. Furthermore, the chapter discusses the allocation of blame for the children's deaths, demonstrating how online platforms serve as arenas for both grief and political expression.

Sonali Jha and Mary-Magdalene N. Chumbow explore the complex interplay between social media and youth activism in the context of the 2023 Israel–Palestine conflict, particularly focusing on Instagram's role as a crucial platform for resistance and dissemination of unfiltered frontline perspectives (Chapter 8). Their analysis through the Textual–Visual Thematic Analysis of Instagram content reveals how youth leverage digital platforms to document events and rally international support, shaping public discourse and contributing to the narrative of resistance. This goes to show that youth not only experience conflict but actively engage in shaping perceptions and responses through media portrayal.

The youth demonstrate their roles as significant agents in contemporary forms of activism and resistance.

Continuing with an exploration of media portrayals, Haoyue Zhang showcases the interplay between cinema and the shifting perceptions of childhood within the context of China's dramatic socio-economic transformations over the decades (Chapter 9). Zhang's analysis focuses on two seminal films by director Chen Kaige, *Yellow Earth* and *Together*, which reflect the evolution of family structures from a collective, state-oriented system to a more individualistic and neoliberal framework. The films portray children as central figures whose experiences and voices challenge and resist the imposed narratives of authority and tradition. Through the lens of these narratives, Zhang articulates how the children's roles evolve from passive participants to active agents who both question and redefine their identities within the changing landscapes of family and society.

Julija Ovsec's chapter in the volume delves into the harsh realities faced by children during the Balkan wars of the 1990s (Chapter 10). Ovsec's work is grounded in the analysis of literary portrayals, particularly focusing on novels like *Ukulele Jam* by Alen Mešković and *Hotel Zagorje* by Ivana Simić Bodrožić. These narratives offer insights into how war accelerates the coming of age for its youngest participants, casting light on their rapid loss of innocence and the intense, often violent upheavals that redefine their identities and social roles. By examining how these young characters navigate contentious spaces, Ovsec highlights their resilience and the transformative potential of their stories, aligning closely with the broader themes of resistance and identity reshaping within the context of armed conflict.

Uche Aguh's *Sambisa* (2016) serves as a poignant case study illustrating the complex roles of children in the mechanisms of terrorism within Nigeria, particularly under the influence of Boko Haram (Chapter 11). Stephen Ogheneruro Okpadah and Damilare Ogunmekan discuss the psychological impact and the instrumentalization of children within these violent networks, emphasizing the critical role children play and challenging the traditional narratives of victimhood by highlighting their agency in situations of armed conflict and terrorism. In Chapter 12, Omama Al-Lawati reflects on the resistance literature by the Palestinian writer Ghassan Kanafani. This genre depicts experiences of resistance and resilience amidst colonization, often investigating the personal struggles of writers within contexts of injustice and oppression. When created for children and youth, the literature of resistance diverges from that intended for adults for many reasons. Mustafa employs a dual analytical approach to offer a comprehensive understanding of how resistance is conveyed in the chosen narratives and the extent to which these stories fulfill their intended objectives.

The final chapter of the volume brings together ideas and solutions to encourage the use of Artificial Intelligence (AI) in the detection of emotions (Chapter 13). Javed M. Shah and Tamanna M. Shah introduce the *EmoGenPath* model – an AI-driven approach designed to offer adaptive therapy tailored to children and youth impacted by war. *EmoGenPath* utilizes advanced machine-learning techniques to provide a personalized therapeutic experience that respects the cultural and emotional diversity of its users. The innovative use of AI in therapy underscores a progressive step in leveraging technology to address the complex psychological needs of young survivors in conflict zones, emphasizing the importance of ethical implementation and culturally sensitive interventions to foster resilience and recovery.

BEYOND SURVIVAL: ENACTING TRANSFORMATIVE CHANGE

The inspiration behind this volume was to bring to the fore the adversities young people face in war zones and to spotlight their capacity for resistance. While exploring their trauma, hardships, and resilience and how these experiences shape the self was crucial, an equally important focus was the portrayal and influence of these narratives in the media. Several chapters challenge the dominant narrative that portrays children and youth as victims or passive bystanders, highlighting instead their active participation in shaping their circumstances and engaging in resistance, whether through direct action or cultural and digital expressions.

Scholars contributing to this volume critically assessed how young people's struggles and resilience are depicted across various media platforms, acknowledging the empowering aspects of media that allow youth to voice their stories and the potential for misrepresentations or oversimplifications. Another important theme is the use of new technologies, including artificial intelligence and digital platforms, to support children's mental health and well-being affected by conflict. This includes developing adaptive therapies sensitive to the users' cultural and emotional contexts, highlighting a forward-thinking approach to humanitarian aid. There is a strong emphasis on ethical considerations when deploying technologies in sensitive environments, advocating for culturally appropriate approaches that prioritize young individuals' safety and privacy.

By focusing on the active roles of children and youth in conflict and peace processes, this volume contributes to a broader understanding of them as critical political and social actors, rather than passive entities. Through these chapters, which span diverse conflict contexts, we bridge sociology, political science, psychology, and media studies to offer a comprehensive view of the challenges and potential of studying youth in conflict zones. There are valuable lessons for everyone in this volume. The in-depth analyses of various case studies and technological interventions provide actionable insights for policymakers, practitioners, and NGOs to address children's rights, mental health, and conflict resolution issues. Overall, the book positions children and youth not merely as survivors of conflict but as essential and influential contributors to societal change and peacebuilding, urging a reevaluation of their roles in international discussions about war, peace, and recovery.

REFERENCES

Appadurai, A. (1996). *Modernity at large*. University of Minnesota Press.
Benjamin, W. (1986). *Critique of violence*. In P. Demetz (Ed.), *Walter Benjamin: essays, aphorisms, autobiographical writings* (pp. 277–300). Schocken.
Bleiker, R., & Kay, A. (2007). Representing HIV-AIDS in Africa: Pluralist photography and local empowerment. *International Studies Quarterly, 51*, 139–163.

Booker, M. K. (2007). *From box office to ballot box: The American political film*. Bloomsbury Publishing USA.

Curwood, J. S., & Gibbons, D. (2010). 'Just Like I Have Felt': Multimodal counternarratives in youth produced digital media. *International Journal of Learning and Media*, *1*(4), 59–77.

Debrix, F. (2003). Rituals of mediation. In F. Debrix & C. Weber (Eds.), *Rituals of mediation: International politics and social meaning* (pp. 69–96). University of Minnesota Press.

Denov, M. (2012). Child soldiers and iconography: Portrayals and (mis) representations. *Children & Society*, *26*(4), 280–292.

Ellison, T. L., & Kirkland, D. E. (2014). Motherboards, microphones and metaphors: Re-examining new literacies and Black feminist thought through technologies of self. *E-Learning and Digital Media*, *11*(4), 390–405.

Gregory, S. (2006). Transnational storytelling: Human rights, WITNESS, and video advocacy. *American Anthropologist*, *108*(1), 195–204.

Jenkins, H., Shresthova, S., Gamber-Thompson, L., Kligler-Vilenchik, N., & Zimmerman, A. (2016). *By any media necessary: The new youth activism*. New York University Press.

Kahne, J., Hodgin, E., & Eidman-Aadahl, E. (2016). Redesigning civic education for the digital age: Participatory politics and the pursuit of democratic engagement. *Theory and Research in Social Education*, *44*(1), 1–35.

Kellner, D. (2011). Cultural studies, multiculturalism, and media culture. *Gender, Race, and Class in Media: A Critical Reader*, *3*, 7–18.

Price-Dennis, D. (2016). Developing curriculum to support Black girls' literacies in digital spaces. *English Education*, *48*(4), 337–361.

Scheper-Hughes, N., & Bourgois, P. (2004). *Violence in war and peace*. Blackwell.

Shah, T. M. (2012). *Collective memory and narrative: ethnography of social trauma in Jammu and Kashmir* [Doctoral dissertation]. Kansas State University.

Shah, T. M. (2013). Chaos and fear: Creativity and hope in an uncertain world. *International Sociology Reviews*, *28*(5), 513–517.

Shah, T. M. (2019). Social justice and change. In S. Romaniuk, M. Thapa, & P. Marton (Eds.), *The Palgrave encyclopedia of global security studies* (pp. 1–4). Springer Nature.

Shah, T. M. (2020). Children of Kashmir and the meaning of family in armed conflict. In S. Frankel, S. McNamee, & L. E. Bass (Eds.), *Bringing children back into the family: Relationality, connectedness, and home* (pp. 213–216). Emerald Publishing Limited.

Shah, T. M. (2021). Women as "sites of gendered politics." In D. Aikat, B. Beamer, M. K. Biswas, B. Bowen, L. F. Brost, S. Fatima, & S. Srivastav (Eds.), *Misogyny across global media*. Lexington Books.

Shah, T. M. (2023). *Global patterns of decolonization and the right to self-determination: A comparative-historical analysis of East Timor and Kashmir* [Doctoral dissertation]. The University of Utah.

Shah, T. M. (2024a). Decolonization and peacebuilding: The case of Timor Leste and Kashmir. In P. Pietrzak (Ed.), *Dealing with regional conflicts of global importance* (pp. 262–278). IGI Global.

Shah, T. M. (2024b). Emotions in politics: A review of contemporary perspectives and trends. *International Political Science Abstracts*, *74*(1), 1–14.

Spitulnik, D. (1993). Anthropology and mass media. *Annual Review of Anthropology*, *22*, 293–315.

Stornaiuolo, A., & Thomas, E. E. (2018). Restorying as political action: Authoring resistance through youth media arts. *Learning, Media and Technology*, *43*(4), 345–358.

Thomas, E. E., & Stornaiuolo, A. (2016). Restorying the self: Bending toward textual justice. *Harvard Educational Review*, *86*(3), 313–338.

Whitehead, N. (2007). Violence and the cultural order. *Daedalus*, *136*, 40–50.

PART I

CHILDREN AND YOUTH RESPONSES AND RESISTANCE IN MEDIA

CHAPTER 1

BETWEEN HOPE AND DEATH: *SHAHEED* AS EQUIPMENT FOR LIVING AMID PALESTINE'S YOUTH

Sophia Koleno

Ohio University, USA

ABSTRACT

The narrative surrounding shaheed, *or martyrdom, among Gaza's youth, unfolds against the backdrop of intensified Israeli–Palestinian conflicts. In this piece, the author explores the layers of meaning that* shaheed *carries within this community, moving beyond the Western interpretations and stereotypes that often frame it within a solely negative light. Drawing from the Qur'anic concept of* ayah *and Kenneth Burke's framework of narratives as "equipment for living," the author offers an alternative viewpoint by showcasing how Palestinian youth, through the analytic of* ayah, *understand* shaheed *not as an endorsement of death but as a profound source of resilience and a scaffold for navigating the turbulent realities of conflict. In doing so, the author's rhetoric analysis unveils the youth's active role in shaping a narrative that bridges their immediate survival and broader existential beliefs, challenging the monolithic portrayal of their experiences and beliefs in mainstream media. This understanding positions* shaheed *within a broader existential and spiritual framework, revealing the complex relationship between cultural narratives, religious beliefs, and the lived realities of conflict.*

Keywords: *Ayah* analytic; rhetorical analysis; *Shaheed*; resilience and resistance; Gaza and Palestine; equipment for living; Kenneth Burke

INTRODUCTION

In the throes of conflict, the youngest among us face a reality rife with insurmountable hurdles and pervasive uncertainty. Children and adolescents are thrust into an existence besieged by violence, death, displacement, scarcity, and the persistent presence of grief. This has been especially evident during the recent escalation in the Israeli–Palestinian conflict, which commenced in another epoch of violence beginning on October 7, 2023, and quickly escalated into the most lethal clash in the history of this longstanding struggle. By the new year, the Ministry of Health in Gaza reported that over 10,000 children had been killed by Israeli airstrikes and ground operations in Gaza (Save the Children, 2024). This means that since October 7, 2023, 1% of the child population in Gaza, which amounts to 1.1 million children, has died. The United Nations has subsequently somberly described the Gaza Strip as a "graveyard for thousands of children" (Al Jazeera, 2023). The dire situation in Gaza, exacerbated by the increased risk of further casualties, presents numerous adversities that the youth must navigate and comprehend.

Moreover, amid this critical state and the variety of narratives circulating, one particularly contentious criticism accuses Palestinian society at large and Gaza specifically of glorifying martyrdom to its youth. Such narratives have circulated amid news outlets and social media platforms which profess that mothers are "[expressing] joy over their children's martyrdom and willingness to sacrifice all their children to the cause" (Memri, 2023). Prominent YouTube political and cultural commentators, such as Timcast IRL (2023a, 2023b), echo sentiments of Palestinian leadership glorifying martyrdom to children through cartoon characters and school programs. Senator Ron Latz, representing St. Lous Park, Minnesota, further promulgated this narrative during a Capitol press conference, stating that "Palestinian youth dream of the opportunity to achieve glory and even martyrdom by killing as many Jews as possible" (Griffith, 2023). This narrative has been given further traction on social media platforms, such as X, where users like AmirPars_ (2023) perpetuate critical stereotypes, claiming that becoming a martyr is the fundamental ideological and theological objective of Palestinian society and that "their death is their life! !!" (Alex [@alexbnk], 2023). Such framing and portrayals, without adequate context, tend to feed into and reinforce existing negative stereotypes in Western news and media outlets that too often depict the populace of Gaza and Palestine, and by extension, Muslims, as barbaric, brutal, and extreme.

Though I do not dispute the presence or elevation of the martyr, *shaheed*, in Palestine and the Gaza Strip amid its youth (Palestinian Media Watch, 2021a, 2021b), I do seek to question and reshape the understanding of *shaheed*. Specifically, I posit that the term *shaheed* rhetorically functions as a symbolic site of resilience and resistance for the youth residing and Gaza and Palestine which is a stabilizing influence and fosters a comprehensive narrative logic to their contextual surroundings. To substantiate my argument and mode of interpretation, I utilize rhetorical analysis as a methodological and theoretical approach that examines how language, symbols, and narratives are used to influence, shape, and convey meanings within specific contexts. This approach not only reveals how communicative acts influence audience perceptions and actions but also brings to light how those communicative and symbolic instances embed and propagate cultural values and societal norms.

My analysis is further informed by the analytical concept of *ayah* – commonly understood as a (Divine) warning, sign, or proof – and Kenneth Burke's (1957) notion of "equipment for living" (pp. 253–262). Throughout my analysis, I demonstrate that *shaheed* rhetorically functions on two fronts. First, it is a cognitive scaffold for the youth, a method to comprehend, explain, and cope with the incessant violence and despair that encroach upon their daily lives that allows them to find resilience and resist the horror of their positionality. Second, by using *ayah* as an analytical tool, *shaheed* additionally functions as a transcendent narrative that offers solace and a sense of purpose in the face of corporeal sufferings. It reassures believers with a vision of a life to come – an eternal existence devoid of the material world's pain and restrictions – with an explicit focus on witnessing and, by extension, justice. I will begin by redefining *shaheed*, setting the stage with essential theoretical frameworks to guide the subsequent rhetorical analysis. This analysis will traverse different public spheres within both the specific context of the Gaza Strip and the broader Palestinian landscape before closing with future implications.

AYAH, *SHAHEED*, AND EQUIPMENT FOR LIVING

The word *ayah* (plural *ayat*) comes from the Arabic root ه-ي-أ ('-y-h), which has various meanings related to signifying, marking, or evidencing something. Tracing back to its roots, the initial ا (a/ay) in *ayah* conveys a sense of direction or orientation, suggesting that an *ayah* possesses an inherent purpose – a telos – aiming to guide or direct one toward a specific end or understanding (Khan, 2016). Within the Qur'an, *ayah/ayat* fundamentally designates the verses of the Islamic holy text, which Muslims consider as manifestations, evidence, warnings, or prompts of divine existence, insight, and omnipresence (Neuwirth, 2014, pp. 41 & 81). Each verse, each *ayah*, is, thus, perceived as a reflection of Allah's wisdom which has the *potential* to offer guidance and insight into the complexities of existence. The ontological perspective in Islam considers life as a divinely orchestrated test (The Qur'an, 18:7), rather than a punishment, suggesting that, epistemologically, Allah provides *ayat* as directions to shape human understanding, orientation, and actions. For example, the Qur'an's *surah* Al-Baqarah points to the marvels of creation – the universe, the cycle of day and night, the ships at sea (2:164) – as signs for those who contemplate and seek understanding, whereby emphasizing the idea that the natural world is filled with *ayat* meant to reorient individuals.

However, the scope of *ayah* is far more expansive than its textual or oral manifestation. As Khan (2016) elucidates *ayat* is present not only in the text of the Qur'an but also in every facet of human experience – from emotions and historical events to the broader strokes of knowledge and revelation and even in the tangible world of nature that surrounds us. This, as aforementioned, encompasses the stars in the night sky, the geological wonders of the earth, and every element of the natural world. The Qur'an presents *ayah* as an embodied framework through which all reality is to be viewed, positioning it as a cornerstone for a unified understanding of our existence. Thus, the notion of *ayah* transcends mere textual interpretation, serving as a rhetorical vehicle through which the Qur'an positions humanity amidst the trials and tribulations of life, providing guidance, reminders, and direction across life's varied landscapes. It interlaces our understanding of the universe, pivotal life events such as birth, family dynamics and disintegration, and mortality, along with our interaction with the natural world, into a cohesive framework. This means that, for a reflective Muslim, the ethics governing one's business practices are deeply intertwined with faith, and the way one engages with a challenging family member reflects teachings and advice on domestic relations. Similarly, the understanding of martyrdom and death, especially in times of conflict or war, transcends mere despair, guided instead by a Divine structure. Thus, utilizing *ayah* as an embodied analytical framework offers a different set of interpretative schemata through which to view life, granting an additional layer of context and directionality.

Considering the word *shaheed*, in class Arabic etymologically it is derived from the root ش-ه-د (sh-h-d), which encompasses the acts of witnessing, testifying, or bearing witness, and can function as both a verb and a noun – indicating the role of one as a witness (Ibn Manzur, 2003). This notion parallels, to some extent, the English "martyr" but is more specifically applied in Islamic contexts to individuals who die under certain circumstances, such as from illness, drowning, childbirth, defending property, family, or faith (Suleiman, 2021). In the context of the Qur'an, this term takes on further significance. Allah addresses the notion of *shaheed* by proclaiming, "Do not say that those who are killed in [Allah]'s cause are dead; they are alive, though you do not realize it" (Abdel Haleem, 2004, 2:154). In Islam, moving beyond the physical life, it's believed that on the Day of Judgment those who are *shaheed* transition into a state where they will be testifying or witnessing, embodying a deeper spiritual testimony as *shahaada* – the one who is testifying or witnessing. The belief in the transition from the temporal existence of being a witness – *shaheed* – to eternal witnessing – *shadaada* – before Allah in Islam illustrates a profound spiritual journey. This journey signifies a metamorphosis, where earthly life's limitations are transcended, allowing the soul to bear witness in a Divine, everlasting realm.

Currently, the concept of *shaheed* is integrated into the fabric of daily life in Palestine and the Gaza Strip, finding expression in various public and private spheres. Interviews and media reports frequently address *shaheed* and its function amid the youth (Palestine Culture [@PalestineCultu1], 2024; Pietromarchi, 2023), while social media platforms amplify its significance across digital landscapes (Gaza_Shaheed, 2024a, 2024b). Beyond the public eye, the notion of *shaheed* permeates personal spaces such as educational environments and healthcare facilities, manifesting in classroom discussions and even in children's games within hospital wards (@belalfadl, 2023). This widespread rhetorical presence underscores *shaheed's* role not just as a religious or cultural symbol but also as an integral element of Palestinian lived reality.

Within the contemporary discourse, conversations surrounding *shaheed* are multifaceted, delving into the spaces of private, public, cultural, religious, and political life. Current scholarship has explored the complex emotions of Palestinian mothers, who grapple with personal grief even as society exalts the idea of their martyred children (Habiballah, 2004). Publicly, *shaheed* has been posited to foster a "culture of martyrdom" (Loadenthal, 2014, p. 183), visible in the political and performative aspects of funerals and *shaheed* posters, which mirror discourses on national unity and individual mourning, imbued with cultural and religious significance (Allen, 2006; Whitehead & Abufarha, 2008). Positioned within a global context, Khalili (2007) argues that these commemorative acts of *shaheed* are not unique to Palestine, thus emphasizing their universal implications within the space of mnemonic practices and devices in relation to those that have been killed amid social and political turmoil. These scholars paint a picture of *shaheed* that weaves through the personal, societal, and global spheres yet their perspectives, I contend, do not fully encapsulate the term's role as a dynamic mechanism for coping and meaning-making – as equipment for living, as mental schemata that structures and orientates both an individual and a collective social body.

Literary theorist Kenneth Burke (1957) first introduced the innovative concept that literature and, more broadly, a human's use of language and symbol systems serve a rhetorical purpose as a form of equipment for living. He posited that social structures generate recurring types of situations with each necessitating its own mode of engagement or strategy. Burke encouraged the reintroduction of individual, personal, and poetic aspects into scholarly examination, highlighting their significance (Anders, 2011). In doing so, Burke's literary approach additionally centered on lived, physical reality whereby "[enhancing] our awareness of man as a social, political actor with mixed motives and reality as contingent verisimilitudes staged through communication" (Zhang et al., 2012, p. 187). Using proverbs as a specific literary example, Burke contends that they encapsulate collective wisdom in succinct and memorable phrases, words, or expressions, providing guidelines for expected behavior or attitudes in certain circumstances. In this view, proverbs emerge not just as cultural expressions but also as practical responses to life's challenges, serving as "strategies for dealing with *situations*" (Burke, 1957, p. 256).

These strategies extend beyond texts to become tools for navigating life, emblematic of the idea that "rhetoric serves as 'equipment for living' to help people confront present and future perplexities and risks" (Olson, 2020, p. 382). They are functional narrative tools often crafted in response to cultural or political realities that help people navigate the complexities of social life, living through life's trials and providing them with a sense of direction and patterns to follow (Katsion, 2013; Lewis, 2020). Expanding on Kenneth Burke's concept, Aden

(2018) introduces foundational memory spaces as essential equipment for living that offer a "temporal foundation" and address critical spatial needs such as identity and belonging. Brigham et al. (2017) further illustrate how metaphorical narratives can reduce death anxieties, positioning religious beliefs and communications as practical tools for navigating life and death. Their work underscores the practical application of narrative and memory in managing existential challenges, linking Burke's ideas with contemporary analyses of memory and metaphor in shaping human experience and understanding.

ANALYSIS

The concept of *shaheed* in Palestine, particularly in Gaza, among its youth serves as a potent tool that operates as a mode of resilience and resistance. The subsequent analysis will present an alternative view on the role of *shaheed*, one not stooped in barbarism, brutality, or extremism, but one that is understood as a stabilizing, and transcendent, narrative logic. In a context marked by the daily reality of gunfire and sirens, where the skyline is often marred by missile trails and smoke, *shaheed* serves as a bulwark against despair and a deep stated declaration of dignity.

In interviews conducted by Al-Jazeera with teenagers from Palestine in the West Bank, a prevailing sentiment surfaces a conditioned acceptance and even expectation of becoming a *shaheed*. Seventeen-year-old Araf, reflecting on the frequent Israeli attacks and the omnipresent danger of death, asserts on behalf of his group, "we are not afraid. We are used to this" (Pietromarchi, 2023). Earlier in the discussion, Araf and his friends express their future aspirations distinctly: they aim to become martyrs, to embrace the role of a *shaheed*. This response, potentially startling to those unfamiliar with their circumstances, reflects a deep adaptation by the youth of the West Bank to their tumultuous environment. Contextualizing the aspiration of Araf and his friends through Burkes's concept of "equipment for living," their desire to become *shaheed* is not merely a longing for death or brutality but, rather, a form of resilience and resistance. Recalling that Burke's theory suggests that narratives and symbol systems serve as tools enabling individuals to confront life's complexities and adversities, the youths' declaration of wanting to become *shaheed* represents a narrative strategy, a symbolic mechanism they utilize to navigate their turbulent reality marked by conflict and occupation. Rather than succumbing to a myopic sense of eminent death, this narrative acts as psychological armor, enabling them to face their circumstances with resilience and dignity.

Simultaneously, when viewed through the embodied literary analytic of *ayah* – as that which provides guidance, direction, and insight – this aspiration gains further depth. *Ayat*, as Divine signs, provides Muslims with a framework for interpreting their experiences and existence within a larger order. In this context, the Qur'anic *ayah*, "Do not say that those who are killed in [Allah]'s cause are dead; they are alive, though you do not realize it" (Abdel Haleem, 2004, 2:154), resonates profoundly. This principle enriches the young Palestinians' aspiration

Between Hope and Death

to become *shaheed*, situating it within the Divine narrative – the equipment for living – articulated by the Qur'an, which extends solace and purpose beyond the confines of the material world. This alignment with *ayah* empowers them to imbue their potentially tragic ends with spiritual significance, recasting their actions and possible martyrdom not as mere cessation of life but as meaningful testimonies of faith, dedication, and an unwavering commitment to their community and beliefs.

In a different iteration, the children of Gaza, particularly through their enactment of the "*Shaheed* game" recorded within a hospital hall, illustrate a significant method for confronting and interpreting the harsh realities of their conflict-ridden environment (Fadl, [@belalfadl], 2023). Captured on camera, children role-play scenarios where one assumes the role of a deceased peer, symbolically carried in a blanket, mimicking the rituals of burial and martyrdom. While acknowledging the inherently morbid nature of the "*Shaheed* game" – a sentiment echoed by social media users like Abdullatif, who observed the game's weighty sadness (@muhaabdu07, 2023) – it is essential to recognize its deeper function within the children's social environment. This activity extends beyond mere grim child's play, serving instead as a vital coping mechanism and a schema for processing their complex reality. Through this form of engagement, the children of Gaza find a way to articulate and manage the overwhelming experiences of loss and conflict surrounding them, thus transforming a narrative of despair into one of resilience and collective understanding. This game represents a direct engagement with the themes of death and sacrifice, transitioning the abstract concept of *shaheed* from a mere symbol of loss to an active part of their collective processing and social learning. Through such interactions, they are not only acknowledging the pain and reality of loss but are also learning to navigate and make sense of their experiences in a context saturated with violence, thereby converting a narrative of despair into one of collective resilience and personal growth.

In this context, the act of playing the *Shaheed* game represents an application of Kenneth Burke's concept of "equipment for living." Here, symbolic resources, in this case, the narratives and roles associated with *shaheed*, are utilized by children to navigate the adversities presented by their environment. This transformation through play enables them to not just passively witness the chaos around them but actively engage with it, reconstructing their reality within a framework they can understand and manage. Moreover, this engagement with the concept of shaheed within the play can be seen as aligning with the Qur'anic notion of *ayah*. *Ayah*, as Divine signs, guides Muslims to find meaning and purpose beyond their immediate material circumstances. Through play, children in Gaza are not merely acting out scenarios of death; they are embodying narratives that provide them with a sense of continuity, community, and moral grounding. The narrative framework of *shaheed*, when viewed through the prism of *ayah*, offers a spiritual dimension to their play, allowing them to position their experiences within a larger narrative of faith and endurance. The integration of *shaheed* into their play serves several crucial psychological and social functions.

First, it empowers the children to confront and manage their fears related to ongoing violence and loss, providing them with a sense of agency and resilience.

Rather than being passive victims of their circumstances, they become active narrators of their own stories of struggle and survival. Second, by adopting the narrative of *shaheed*, these children process complex emotions and situations, transforming their understanding of death from an absolute end to a part of a broader, collective story of resistance and dignity. Last, through these shared narratives, children in Gaza communicate their experiences, contributing to a collective memory and identity. This shared narrative practice not only fosters solidarity among them but also strengthens communal bonds, ensuring that the values and lessons encapsulated in the concept of shaheed are perpetuated and reinforced within their community. Thus, the *Shaheed* game, underpinned by the concepts of Burke's equipment for living and the Qur'anic *ayah*, becomes a powerful tool for Gaza's youth, providing them with a means to navigate, understand, and find resilience in their tumultuous reality.

Transitioning from personal and enacted experiences to compilations of collective narratives, the stabilizing logic of *shaheed* can additionally be seen within the digital landscape, particularly through platforms such as Gaza_Shaheed on X. This transition highlights how digital spaces serve not just as repositories of memory but as active sites where the youth of Gaza and Palestine can engage with, reinterpret, and contribute to the communal narrative of resistance and resilience. Far from promoting a simplistic view of *shaheed* as revered by external misconceptions, these platforms challenge the reductionist perspectives often portrayed in Western media. They provide a nuanced space where the concept of *shaheed* is reframed not as a call to die but as a testament to the spirit of living with dignity, resisting oppression, and maintaining a sense of community amidst ongoing conflict.

Exemplifying this is the account of Elia Al-Khalidi, a three-year-old described as "the dainty one" (Gaza_Shaheed, 2024a), highlights not just her tragic end but the vibrancy of her life, her gentle nature, and her close bond with her brother. Similarly, Jude Jamal Al-Hasayna, known as "The Fruit of the House" (Gaza_Shaheed, 2024b), is remembered for his laughter, aspirations, and the ordinary, yet profoundly human, details of his life before it was cut short. These stories underscore the concept of *shaheed* not as a glorification of death or extremism but as an acknowledgment of the life that was lived and unjustly taken. They stand as testimonies to what was lost, narrating, and conveying not just the end but a more holistic encapsulant of their existence. These accounts, more than mere stories, function as practical mechanisms enabling the youth to interpret and contend with their daunting realities. By framing their experiences within the context of *shaheed* and utilizing the guidance of *ayah*, these stories transform from simple recounts into profound narratives imbued with divine significance. By presenting the *shaheed* as individuals full of aspirations, relationships, and humanity, the concept of *shaheed* transcends mere tragedy to become a beacon of resilience. This perspective shift enables the youth of Gaza to see themselves and their *shaheed* counterparts not merely as casualties of conflict but as integral characters in a larger narrative of resistance and survival. This aligns with Burke's (1957) notion that narratives are not passive stories but active strategies for dealing with life's adversities.

Between Hope and Death 21

Additionally, the act of sharing and recounting stories of *shaheed* contributes to building a collective memory and identity among Gaza's communities. This collective recounting ties individual grief to the broader historical and cultural narrative of the region, a foundational memory place (Aden, 2018), reinforcing communal bonds and a shared sense of destiny. It anchors personal experiences within the broader collective story, ensuring that individual losses are seen as part of the larger struggle and history of the Palestinian people. Moreover, these shared narratives foster a strong sense of continuity and belonging among the youth, crucial for maintaining morale and communal identity amidst ongoing turmoil. Platforms like Gaza_Shaheed allow individuals to see reflections of their own experiences in the stories of others, thereby reducing feelings of isolation and alienation. This shared narrative space offers a form of solace and solidarity, reinforcing a communal identity that persists despite the challenges of conflict and occupation. In essence, the narratives of *shaheed* serve as a vital component in the collective psyche, offering both a lens to interpret the chaos of the present and a bridge to the enduring spirit of the community's past and future. In exploring the transcendent qualities of *shaheed*, its rhetorical function emerges as a profound narrative that not only offers solace amidst the conflict but also enriches the experience of resistance with a deeper, spiritual resonance. Through the lens of *ayah* as an embodied framework, *shaheed* evolves beyond a mere term into a significant component of spiritual testimony, or *shahada*, underscoring its role as both equipment for living and an avenue for transcendent meaning.

A poignant and final example of this can be found in a video post by @PalestineCultu1, where a young girl recounts to a camera crew the overwhelming loss of life in Gaza, including her classmates and relatives. Specifically, she states:

> The children of Palestine have died. There aren't any children left. All the girls in my class died, they all died, they all died. All my relatives died. There's no one left! There's no one left! From the girls in my class, only… They all died and I'm the only one who's left. I'd like to tell them all not to be upset because you've left this world. No, on the contrary, you are very much happier than us, God willing. You are in the highest paradise; you are in the greatest paradise. It means you are very, very, very happy in your spirits. That you have escaped from this oppression. And rose above this dirty life. I wish I could be where you are. I, I wish I could be in your place, to go up and be with God in heaven (2024).

Following her account, it becomes apparent that the girl's reflections extend beyond mere expressions of grief and shed light on a deeper spiritual and rhetorical transformation. For instance, her reflection, "I'd like to tell them all not to be upset because you've left this world…You are in the highest paradise, you are in the greatest paradise…That you have escaped from this oppression," illuminates the transformation of *shaheed* into *shahada*. This narrative leap from *shaheed*, the martyr who dies in the cause of Allah, to *shahada*, the act of bearing witness to one's faith and Allah's promise of eternal peace, encapsulates a significant spiritual and rhetorical shift. It suggests that those who have become *shaheed* have not merely ceased to exist but have transitioned to a state of eternal witnessing (*shahada*) before Allah. This belief in transcending the temporal confines of earthly existence to attain a form of eternal witnessing in the presence of Allah illustrates a significant spiritual journey within the Islamic faith. It represents a metamorphosis from the physical limitations and sufferings of life to a state where the soul transcends to bear witness in an everlasting Divine realm. The girl's longing, "I wish I could be where you are...to go up and be with God in heaven," echoes this transformative vision, portraying *shaheed* not as an end but as a beginning of a Divine testimony – *shahada*.

Within the Islamic faith, the concept of *shaheed*, when viewed through the prism of *ayah* as an embodied framework, transcends the immediate context of earthly conflict, evolving into a profound narrative of *shahada* – the act of witnessing or testifying. This transformation imbues the term *shaheed* with a profound rhetorical function as equipment for living, offering solace and a pathway to navigate loss and suffering. This narrative not only affirms life's value and dignity in the face of death but positions martyrdom as a sacred passage to a higher plane of existence. Such a perspective provides those grappling with the pain of loss a framework to find continuity and meaning amid turmoil.

Crucially, the journey from *shaheed* to *shahada* encompasses a significant eschatological dimension, anticipating the Day of Judgment when those who have died as martyrs will testify before Allah. They will bear witness not only to their faith but against those who persecuted, harmed, and killed them. This act of testifying transforms the concept of *shaheed*, elevating it from a testament of faith to a potent form of Divine accountability. On the Day of Judgment, where truth and justice are absolute, unlike the often ambiguous and unjust earthly realm, the martyrs' *shahada* becomes a testimony of their experiences and a denouncement of their oppressors.

CONCLUSION

This eschatological promise shifts the cognitive and emotional landscape for those left behind and those who contemplate martyrdom. The anticipation of absolute justice in the afterlife, where the *shaheed* plays a crucial role in testifying against injustice as a *shahada*, alters the dynamics of power and accountability. It suggests that the sorrow and fear associated with loss are not only burdens for the bereaved but also foreshadow the accountability awaiting those who perpetrated such losses. Viewing *shaheed* and its transcendent extension, *shahada*, as equipment for living, and utilizing *ayah* as an analytical lens, thus, offers a cognitive scaffold to reorient the youth of Gaza and Palestine amid conflict. It embeds in the communal consciousness the belief that ultimate justice awaits beyond this life, providing a source of comfort and strength. This belief in the eventual Divine adjudication and the martyrs' role therein reinforces the dignity of those who have passed and instills a sense of moral and spiritual resilience among the survivors. Therefore, the narrative of *shaheed*, enriched by the scriptural depth of *ayah*, serves not merely as a coping mechanism but as a transformative belief system. It assures the community that the sacrifices of their loved ones transcend temporal suffering, contributing to a Divine ledger of justice and righteousness. This understanding fosters a sense of solace and continuity, offering those affected by conflict a spiritual framework to navigate their grief and affirm their resilience, rooted in the conviction that their loved ones' voices will resonate in the ultimate pursuit of truth and justice.

In this light, the concept of *shaheed* moves past its immediate association with death and martyrdom, becoming a source of spiritual solace and existential affirmation. It reassures the living that their loved ones have achieved the highest honor in Islam – entrance into the greatest paradise (@PalestineCultu1, 2024) – and in doing so, it imbues the lived experiences of those who resist with a transcendent narrative of hope, dignity, and eternal peace. This spiritual perspective, deeply rooted in the Islamic tradition and articulated through the language and narratives of the Qur'an, exemplifies how *shaheed*, as both a concept and a lived reality, serves as a critical tool for navigating life's trials, providing not only a framework for understanding but also a source of eternal hope and spiritual resilience.

REFERENCES

Abdel Haleem, M. A. S. (2004). *The Qur'an: A new translation*. Oxford University Press.

Abdullatif, M. [@muhaabdu07]. (2023, October 23). *An influential scenery for children from Gaza playing a game known as the "Shaheed" martyr game; Which is waiting for death for "Allah" God, these are the children of Gaza killed by Israel with its fighter aircraft at night and day* [Post]. X. https://twitter.com/muhaabdu07/status/1716548383601508588

Aden, R. C. (2018). *Childhood memory spaces: How enduring memories of childhood places shape our lives*. Lang Publishing.

Alex, B. [@alexbnk]. (2023, December 14). *Arabs chanted and teach their children to kill the Jews and become martyrs and their death is their life! !! Allah heard you and fulfilled your wish … ya Isma-il you should be happy, may Allah make you all martyrs #FAFO #GAZA #HappyHamasSupporters* [Tweet]. Twitter. https://twitter.com/alexbnk/status/1735274123222221041

Al Jazeera. (2023, October 31). *Gaza has become a graveyard for thousands of children: UN*. Al Jazeera. https://www.aljazeera.com/news/2023/10/31/gaza-has-become-a-graveyard-for-thousands-of-children-un

Allen, L. A. (2006). The polyvalent politics of martyr commemorations in the Palestinian "Intifada". *History & Memory*, *18*(2), 107–138.

AmirPars_. (2023, December 30). *So, your attempt to draw parallels is just desperate and laughable. Like, have you seen what they teach their children in schools in Gaza? Are you familiar with the concept of Shaheed? What are you even talking about?? Everything – and I mean everything – you said was wrong 10/*[Post]. X. https://twitter.com/AmirPars_/status/1741064847754731821

Anders, A. (2011). Pragmatisms by incongruity: "Equipment for Living" from Kenneth Burke to Gilles Deleuze. *KB Journal*, *7*(2).

Brigham, M. P., Harvell-Bowman, L. A., & Szendey, O. R. (2017). Metaphorical re-framing as "Equipment for Living": Confronting death with exuberance in the exit interviews of Heaven's Gate followers. *Journal of Communication & Religion*, *40*(5), 72–90.

Burke, K. (1957). *The philosophy of literary form*. Vintage Books, Inc.

Fadl, B. [@belalfadl]. (2023, October 23). ما فيش كلام يتقال [Post]. X. https://twitter.com/belalfadl/status/1716529322251493851

Gaza_Shaheed. (2024a, February 4). الشهيدة إيلياء الخالدي بلغت من العمر 3 سنوات، كانت أول حفيدة في عائلة أمها، وكانت "الدلوعة" كما يحبون تسميتها. كانت رقيقة جدًا، ورغم صغر سنها تعلقت بأخيها كثيرًا [Post]. X. https://twitter.com/Gaza_Shaheed/status/1754224049599697036

Gaza_Shaheed. (2024b, February 4). الشهيد جود جمال الحساينة بلغ من العمر 7 سنوات، كان لقبه بين أفراد عائلته "فاكهة البيت وفرفوش البيت"، كان محبوبًا من الجميع، ضاحكًا دائمًا، مُبتسمًا في جلساته مع جدّه وأعمامه. [Post]. X. https://twitter.com/Gaza_Shaheed/status/1754025113836491074

Griffith, M. (2023, November 30). *13 DFL senators criticize Sen. Latz for saying Palestinian children 'dream' of killing Jews*. Minnesota Reformer. https://minnesotareformer.com/2023/11/30/13-dfl-senators-criticize-sen-latz-for-saying-palestinian-children-dream-of-killing-jews/

Habiballah, N. (2004). Interviews with mothers of martyrs of the Aqsa Intifada. *Arab Studies Quarterly*, *26*(1), 15–30. http://www.jstor.org/stable/41858470

Ibn Manzur, A. F. J. A. M. A. (2003). *Lisan Al-Arab* [Linguistic database]. IslamWeb. https://www.islamweb.net/ar/library/content/122/4453/%D8%B4%D9%87%D8%AF

Katsion, J. (2013). The hymn "Amazing Grace:" The grace anecdote as equipment for living. *Journal of Communication & Religion*, *36*(2), 134–150.

Khalili, L. (2007). *Heroes and martyrs of Palestine: The politics of national commemoration*. Cambridge University Press.

Khan, N. A. [Bayyinah Institute]. (2016, February 29). *What's an Ayah? – Nouman Ali Khan – Malaysia Tour 2015* [Video]. YouTube. https://www.youtube.com/watch?v=HKjUgJD0Tw4

Lewis, C. K. (2020). From sousaphones to Superman: Narrative, rhetoric, and memory as equipment for living. *Journal of Aesthetic Education*, *54*(4), 6–18.

Loadenthal, M. (2014). Reproducing a culture of martyrdom: The role of the Palestinian mother in discourse construction, transmission, and legitimization. In D. Cooper & C. Phelan (Eds.), *Motherhood and war: International perspectives* (pp. 181–206). Palgrave Macmillan

Memri. (2023, November 3). *Hamas indoctrination of children to jihad, martyrdom, & hatred of Jews*. Memri. https://www.memri.org/reports/hamas-indoctrination-children-jihad-martyrdom-hatred-jews#_edn1

Neuwirth, A. (2014). *Scripture, poetry, and the making of a community: Reading the Qur'an as a literary text*. Oxford University Press.

Olson, K. (2020). Barry Goldwater's 1981 critique of intolerance in American public policy deliberations. *Western Journal of Communication*, *84*(4), 379–399.

Palestine Culture [@PalestineCultu1]. (2024, February 4). *Listen to her words* [Post]. X. https://twitter.com/PalestineCultu1/status/1754134841283526835

Palestinian Media Watch. (2021a, May 19). *"We'll return to our land Palestine from the [Jordan] River to the [Mediterranean] Sea... Israel will be destroyed" – Hamas spokesman's young daughter*. https://palwatch.org/page/23855

Pietromarchi, V. (2023, July 14). Why do some Palestinian teens in Jenin dream of martyrdom. *Al Jazeera*. https://www.aljazeera.com/news/2023/7/14/why-do-some-palestinian-teens-in-jenin-dream-of-martyrdom

Palestinian Media Watch. (2021b, May 25). *Children in Gaza taught to seek martyrdom-death and chant: "Millions of martyrs are marching to Jerusalem"*. https://palwatch.org/page/23875

Save the Children. (2024, January 11). *Gaza: 10,000 children killed in nearly 100 days of war*. https://www.savethechildren.net/news/gaza-10000-children-killed-nearly-100-days-war

Suleiman, O. (2021, January 26). *Ep. 10: Are the considered shaheed? For those left behind*. Yaqeen Institute. https://yaqeeninstitute.org/watch/series/ep-10-are-they-considered-shaheed-for-those-left-behind

Timcast IRL. (2023a, October 16). *US Marines deployed io Israeli waters, may enter, Biden advocates war w/Josie TRHL* [Video]. YouTube. https://www.youtube.com/watch?v=2P78lmB2dvc&list=PLErukX1W1OYjFx2pG8zjWiMuPMG0F-LbI&index=72&t=5765s

Timcast IRL. (2023b, October 17). *Biden Goes to Israel, US surges 19k troops, protests erupt at US Embassy w/Riley Moore* [Video]. YouTube. https://www.youtube.com/watch?v=YDXJQF5YuUg&list=PLErukX1W1OYjFx2pG8zjWiMuPMG0F-LbI&index=71&t=5757s

Whitehead, N. L., & Abufarha, N. (2008). Suicide, violence, and cultural conceptions of Martyrdom in Palestine. *Social Research*, *75*(2), 395–416.

Zhang, P., Yi, Z., & Yang, X. (2012). The rhetorical–theatrical sensibility as equipment for living. *ETC: A Review of General Semantics*, *69*(2), 186–196.

CHAPTER 2

"CHILDREN OF THE BALKAN WARS": RESPONSES AND RESISTANCE TO WAR-RELATED MEDIA CONTENT IN BOSNIA–HERZEGOVINA, KOSOVO, MONTENEGRO, AND SERBIA

Eva Tamara Asboth[a] and Michaela Griesbeck[b]

[a]*Austrian Academy of Sciences, Austria*
[b]*Johannes Kepler University, Austria*

ABSTRACT

The Children of the Balkan Wars, *as a post-war generation in Bosnia–Herzegovina, Kosovo, Montenegro, and Serbia, share similar childhood war experiences, grew up in post-socialist societies, and live in comparable political and media systems. In our study about their practices relating to war-related media content based on qualitative interview data, we discovered that knowledge about the recent wars is very important for them. By interpreting the data against the background of everyday resistance theory, we argue that the findings show two main practices of media use: (1) avoidance of traditional media, which is perceived as distributing the official hegemonial narratives that are also transmitted within the family. (2) "Accommodating" as a form of everyday resistance: when it comes to war-related media content, members of the post-war generation become active media users. They expose historical facts or disseminate their own knowledge mainly online; they create their own content as a way of coping with the unsatisfying traditional (nationalistic, ethno-political) media offerings.*

Keywords: Post-Yugoslavia; post-war generation; childhood memories; war memories; media use; everyday resistance; collective memory; qualitative interviews; qualitative secondary analysis

INTRODUCTION

On a sunny day in October 2019, we walked through the streets of Pristina and discovered a few interesting and intriguing things in the city that has been Kosovo's capital since the country's independence in 2008. The main boulevard in the inner city of Pristina is called Bill Clinton Boulevard, and at the end of it stands a statue of Bill Clinton on a pedestal. NATO, with the United States of America at its forefront, is perceived as having rescued the Kosovo Albanian population from the Serbs, and this story of the Albanian majority is still visible in their capital and burned into their collective memory (Baliqi, 2017).

The walk continued to our interview appointment with Nora. Nora is a young woman who was born in 1997, shortly before the NATO bombardment ended the Kosovo War in 1999. She grew up in post-war Pristina and was nine years old by the time of Kosovo's independence. Although the war is over, Nora feels the consequences and the hostility even today, and she names one institution that she believes supports the division between Kosovo Albanians and Kosovo Serbs: "As I said, media has a very bad, great, great influence like it's huge but a very bad one" (Nora, Pristina, Kosovo, born in 1997). Nora is not the only member of the post-war generation who blames television, radio, and newspaper companies in Serbia and Kosovo for hindering reconciliation processes among the population by preserving national narratives like the one of the US rescuers.

A POST-WAR GENERATION: THE "CHILDREN OF THE BALKAN WARS"

Nora was one of our interview partners for the research complex "The Children of the Balkan Wars," which was established in 2014 by communication scientist and historian Rainer Gries. He was head of the *Franz Vranitzky Chair for European Studies* (*FVC*) at the *University of Vienna (Austria)* until 2023 and worked with a transdisciplinary research team on three interrelated projects[1] that aimed to research the post-war generation in Bosnia–Herzegovina, Kosovo, Montenegro, and Serbia.

All three research projects focused on this generation, on their experience of the same crisis and their coping strategies, as well as on their communicative practices in relation to their historical heritage (see, e.g., Asboth, 2023; Asboth et al., 2017). The first armed conflict on European soil after World War II, the Yugoslav wars of secession, took place in the 1990s. As the Socialist Federal Republic of Yugoslavia dissolved, there were territorial fights, ethnic cleansing, and genocide (Calic, 2018). The independent countries of Bosnia–Herzegovina, Croatia, Serbia, Montenegro, and Kosovo emerged in the 1990s and 2000s, and the post-war and post-socialist generation consequently did not grow up in a common Federal Republic, but in separate states. We refer to this generation as "Children of the Balkan Wars," first of all to highlight that their common heritage did not start with Yugoslavia but is based on a centuries-old historical legacy (Todorova, 2005). Second, they share childhood experiences of crisis situations, such as witnessing atrocities, experiencing (ethnic) hostilities, and flight. Last, they have interconnected prospects for the future: they need to deal with reconciliation and help to establish political sustainability for their countries in preparation to join the European Union.

Focusing on a generation means gaining insight into the members' everyday lives: where do they work, what do they study, what are their (ethno-)political views and activities? What about their free time or their media use? Also, do they feel that they lack opportunities or options for their future, or that they have unequal (ethno-political) positions within this social group? (Gries, 2008). According to theories on social generations, they share spaces of experience (Bohnsack & Schäffer, 2002), such as growing up in a (post-)war and post-socialist society. Due to shared experiences and expectations, they feel connected by comparable political, social, and cultural challenges, they react in similar ways, and they are able to recognize each other (Gries, 2008; see also Gries & Ahbe, 2006; Jureit, 2017; Jureit & Schneider, 2010; Mannheim, 1928). Generation as an analytical category for research, thus, enables the discovery of social groups within transregional contexts and spaces, such as those of post-war Yugoslavia.

Based on the assumption that the post-war generation's shared traumatic and crisis experiences shaped their self-image and world views as well as forming the foundation of their political dispositions, speaking with members of this generation was of central importance in all three projects (Gries, 2016). Therefore, as part of the research team working on these projects, we took several field trips to post-Yugoslavia between 2016 and 2020 and collected over 80 qualitative interviews with members of the post-war generation. We were eager to collect these young adults' childhood memories, war experiences, family narratives, and historical legacies, and to find out how they live today and how they feel about the past.

Accessing their childhood experiences was not an easy task (Asboth & Griesbeck, 2024), but there was one point that the post-war generation was noticeably eager to discuss: the media (system) in their countries, the negative political influence it had on them, and how (ethno-)politics are trying to place "their" historiographical view of the Yugoslav wars of secession in the national media. The members of the post-war generation often told us that at some point in their lives, they started to doubt what media channels told them about the wars, the former enemy parties, or their own "national" state. During an interview, one young woman stated:

> In a sense it's, I think, it's quite evident that it's controlled by the government, most of the media is controlled by the government. ... that's terrible, and this is not just that it's controlled by the government, it's just that the system, the content that's placed on the market, that is presented to people is terrible. (Female, Belgrade, Serbia, born in 1990)

With this observation in mind, we formulated new research questions that we aimed to answer with the qualitative data gathered for the abovementioned three research projects during our field trips: How are the "Children of the Balkan Wars" responding to war-related media content? How are they talking about and remembering, but also dealing with the wars in the context of media activities? Which intragenerational practices – formed transregionally and independently, no matter where in post-Yugoslavia they are living – can we observe in their handling of war and war-related media content? The secondary analysis presented in this chapter focuses on researching the attitudes of the post-war generation toward war-related media content. The scholarly concepts of "Collective Memory" (Assmann, 2005; Assmann, 2016) and "Everyday Resistance" (Vinthagen & Johansson, 2013) turned out to be pivotal for explaining the patterns of media use uncovered in the interviews, and are presented below.

"COLLECTIVE MEMORY" AND FAMILY NARRATIVES – THE POST-YUGOSLAV MEMORY LANDSCAPE

In order to research the attitudes of the post-war generation toward war-related media content, we needed to evaluate their level of history knowledge about Yugoslavia and the 1990s and identify their (media) sources for gaining this knowledge within the corpus of interview transcripts. Consequently, in preparing the basis for coding the transcripts, we defined war-related media content as well as history knowledge not only in reference to the 1990s but also to World War I and World War II, the Balkan Wars (1912/1913), and wars and uprisings against the Ottoman Empire (14th–19th centuries). It is evident that the media discourse in the 1990s was influenced by historical narratives from the previous wars (Calic, 2018); hence, the transmission and re-interpretation of past conflicts play a crucial role within the post-Yugoslav societies and their current collective memory.

Jan (2005) and Aleida Assmann (2016) divided the collective memory into a communicative or social memory based on a communicative network that, on the one hand, has a time span of one generation. According to them, the family and media narratives of the wars of the 1990s and World War II were transmitted to the post-war generation through a communicative memory; the witnesses to these events are the parents or grandparents. On the other hand, there is cultural memory, which stores the historical legacy from a distant past, such as the Kosovo myth that is rooted in the 14th century. Unsurprisingly, we found that the communicative memory is the more prevalent one and that World War II is present as a frame of reference in addition to the secession wars. Some interviewees gave us insight into their cultural memory when talking about their country or Yugoslavia. One young woman immediately referred to her history classes, where she learned "what happened when Serbia got free from [unclear whether Ottoman or Austrian] occupation." Then, she remembered another historiographic event: "Yeah, or well three years ago, I think, it was the anniversary of Serbia becoming a kingdom, like 800 years ago" (Female, Požarevac, Serbia, born in 2001).

Being aware of the generation's cultural memory, of the historical narratives and events stored within it, helped us define interview paragraphs that referred to a war-related discourse. One must consider that this study is a secondary analysis of qualitative interviews that we conducted, but for other projects, it is a reconstruction of the generation's media attitudes and habits that came up incidentally in the interview. In some cases, members of the post-war generation activated their cultural memory when talking about media or other representation forms, which was one reason to broaden our search for corresponding text paragraphs. The (sub)public negotiation of war-related media content does not happen solely in newspapers, TV, or radio, but also comes across during commemorations, such as "Srebrenica Memorial Day," which is broadcasted by Bosnian TV channels as a national media event. It also comes across in the classroom, in history books, and on the streets in the form of graffiti or protests. Hence, the war-related media content was not bound to a certain media type, channel, or genre but can be found in different (sub)public spheres.

"EVERYDAY RESISTANCE" – MEDIA USE BETWEEN AVOIDANCE AND ACCOMMODATION

When talking about media or war-related media content, our interviewees never used the word "resistance." This is explained within the concept of "everyday resistance," where Stellan Vinthagen and Anna Johansson (2013) point out that "actors themselves are not necessarily regarding it as 'resistance' at all, but rather a normal part and way of their life, personality, culture and tradition" (p. 10). The authors understand everyday resistance as a practice that is *done routinely*, and they exclude organized forms of resistance, such as demonstrations, from their definition (Vinthagen & Johansson, 2013, p. 10). Based on their theory, we scrutinized the interviewees' *practice* (Vinthagen & Johansson, 2013, p. 18; see also Picone et al., 2019) of media use regarding war-related content, which exhibited both diversity and a homogeneous (hidden) culture of resistance, and organized the findings according to the techniques that Vinthagen and Johannson (2013) elaborated.

Vinthagen and Johannson (2013, p. 25) name four key techniques of resistance practices: coping, survival technique, accommodation, and avoidance/escape. In our analysis, we found that our interview partners mainly employed the avoidance or accommodation technique, as we will present in our results section. In our case, the avoidance of certain war-related media content or certain (traditional) media channels can be interpreted as a form of resistance since avoidance makes the exercise of power impossible.

The accommodation technique can be described as a disguised form of resistance, in which a subject seems to show subordination while acting out within the available possibilities – as if offering accommodation. This became visible mainly in the use of social media platforms by the post-war generation, where they carefully decide what to reveal or conceal based on the circumstances, topic, and audience they are addressing. According to Vinthagen and Johansson (2013), the coping, surviving, and accommodation techniques are quite often found in combination because they all target the dominant power (system) by which people are repressed, with the goal of undermining it.

The comprehension of power and hegemonial structures is another key factor in resistance theory. We argue that the "Children of the Balkan Wars" share not only similar childhood experiences and past events, but also similar current power structures, like national(istic) politics or Yugoslav traditions. By acting within the prevailing power structures, they take position somewhere along the axis of obeying and resisting; hence everyday resistance can be observed through their individual practices. For our goal of approaching resistance theory in combination with the post-war generation's media use, the density of interview transcripts collected for the *FVC* was, thus, an ideal departure point.

RESEARCH DESIGN: A STUDY BASED ON QUALITATIVE INTERVIEW TRANSCRIPTS

This secondary analysis is based on the qualitative interviews we conducted with young people on our field trips that happened in the context of our work at the *FVC*. In one-on-one, pair, and group (3–4 people) interviews, we asked people about their current living situation, their childhood memories, and their war and post-war experiences. We wanted to ensure our young interview partners felt comfortable being with and talking to us, so we used different stimuli, including narrative and drawing stimuli (Asboth & Griesbeck, 2024; Fujii, 2018; Lindlof & Tayler, 2018). In total, we spoke to 95 "Children of the Balkan Wars" in 82 interviews about growing up and living in a post-war and/or post-socialist country.

Studying the post-war generations' use of the media in relation to war-related content was not the original goal of our interviews, so we first had to ensure a practical solution for filtering the relevant interviews, text phrases, and paragraphs for additional analysis. We developed a list of trigger words (e.g., media, TV, and Internet) for a full-text search of all our interview transcripts and conducted a test round to see if we could find (a) a sufficient number of referring paragraphs and (b) information on their knowledge about the history of (the dissolution of) Yugoslavia. The final sample consisted of 58 interviews (single, pair, and group) with 67 "Children of the Balkan Wars" (30 women and 37 men, aged between 16 and 38, most in their 20s) who met these criteria, which we analyzed in MAXQDA following a qualitative content analysis (Kuckartz, 2018).

To distinguish between media use and media content, we designed the deductive main categories (Kuckartz, 2018) for the qualitative content analysis based on a robust but simplified communication model. According to sociologist and political scientist Harold Lasswell (1966), "a convenient way to describe an act of communication is to answer the following questions: Who says what in which channel to whom with what effect?" (p. 178).

For our analysis, we concentrated on three elements: "who" (the sender), "says what" (content), and "to whom" (receiver). "Receiver," in our case, was coded when the interviewees talked about media consumption, that is, their own habits and even more often the media use of others. Sometimes they talked about it very generally, but in certain cases, the media channels that were (not) used were associated with war-related content, and the interviewee specifically explained why it was avoided or used.

"Sender" was coded for paragraphs in which we found out about their participatory and active media use, especially social media activities. These practices include engaging with existing content, such as through likes, shares, and comments, as well as creating content like video or art productions or spontaneous posts. Based on this system, we coded the speaker as "sender" and/or "receiver," adding the category "content," which provided information about what was talked about in the paragraph. Hence, after this first round of deductive coding, we introduced sub-categories for "content" such as "Yugoslavia," "wars of the 1990s," and "World War II," as well as sub-categories for "receiver" and "sender," by using an inductive coding approach (Kuckartz, 2018). It turned out that these two main categories of "receiver" and "sender" have similar sub-categories, because many media services are used by a sender as well as a receiver, especially in the social media context. Under the category of "receiver," we introduced two additional sub-categories. The first sub-category is "family narratives," which were identified as a source of knowledge about the wars. Second, the category of "politics" contains paragraphs in which the post-war generation talked about the connection between the media system in their country and political parties or government. Nora explained to us what she and her friends talk about when the topic of war comes up:

> But more than talking about ex-Yugoslavia, we talk about the relation between Kosovo and Serbia, the politics and the image that is being put on TV, and the influence that politics has on media in general. (Nora, Pristina, Kosovo, born in 1997)

Table 2.1 offers an overview of the sender and receiver codes with their sub-categories and gives insight into which media services are used and talked about.

Table 2.2 shows the media content that was mentioned by senders and receivers.

Using MAXQDA to analyze the content of 58 qualitative interviews, we found that the post-war generation responds similarly to war-related media content. More importantly, the analysis showed that their responses can be understood as an act of resistance. This *resistance*, which Vinthagen and Johansson (2013) define as an individual's disguised or hidden everyday *practice or activity* within the prevailing discourse, will be discussed in the following results section in relation to young people's media use.

The concept of media use stems from the discipline of communication science, where it is deeply rooted in the subfield of audience studies (Das & Ytre-Arne, 2018). Media use can be understood as all possible media habits and activities: the consumption or production of content or infrastructure, or activities between consumption and production (Bruns & Schmidt, 2011; see also Picone, 2011), which are highly relevant in the context of social media use. In the following first results section, we focus on media use and non-use in the sense of media consumption, whereas in the second results section, we concentrate on active media use, understood as active engagement with and production of media content.

Table 2.1. Sub-categories of the Categories "Sender" and "Receiver."

Sender	Receiver
Media Services/ channels used	Media Services/ channels used
Public sphere & media in general	Public sphere & media in general
TV	Documentaries
Videos and movies	Videos and movies
Magazines & newspapers	Magazines & newspapers
Radio	The news on traditional media in general (radio, TV, press)
Internet	Internet
Social media platforms	Wikipedia
Websites	Online newspapers
Twitter	Twitter
Instagram	Instagram
Facebook	Facebook
Skype	YouTube
Online games	Books
Demonstrations & protests	Commemorations & memorials
Art (e.g., Street Art, Music)	School & official knowledge
Peers & siblings	Peers & siblings
Family narratives	
Politics	

Table 2.2. Sub-categories of the Category "Media Content."

Media Content	1990s
	The (political) news
	Present (ethnic) conflicts, based on the 1990s
	Peer group exchange online and offline
	Youth exchange project
	Ethno-politics
	Yugoslavia
	Srebrenica
	World War II
	LGBTQI
	Ottoman period and Turkish heritage/history
	Nationalism
	Fake news and hate speech
	Media/media system
	Human rights and women's rights
	ICTY trials

RESULTS I: MEDIA USE AND NON-USE AS AVOIDANCE TECHNIQUE

The majority of the "Children of the Balkan Wars" reject official media content, especially as a way of dissociating from elderly generations. They argue that the news, reports, and stories of the wars in the 1990s are dominated by the ruling political party. The post-war generation encounters those war stories critically as part of their *everyday technique* (Vinthagen & Johansson, 2013, p. 11).

However, the traditional media is not the first encounter with war-related content; rather, the family is often the initial setting where children consume stories of war, as previously stated. These family narratives, stored in the communicative memory, play a significant role in shaping the perception of the Yugoslav wars of secession among the post-war generation. Vita Yakovlyeva (2020), who studied the post-Chernobyl generation of children in Ukraine, states, "children's lives are heavily influenced by the structures of collective memory they are born into, available to children through the complex system of inter- and intragenerational relationships from very early on." (p. 57). Dealing with family narratives gets the young people personally engaged in the memories and contributes to their emotional intensity (Sindbæk Andersen & Törnquist-Plewa, 2016). They were fed with their own family stories, learning where their parents and grandparents had spent the wartime, how other relatives were doing, and who to blame for the outbreak or atrocities. The family narratives set the basis of knowledge about war-related topics for the "Children of the Balkan Wars," as their own memories are fragile or even non-existent (Gries et al., 2016).

Equipped with the family narratives, the post-war generation processed the war-related content that was available in the public sphere, starting with traditional media. By traditional media, we mean the offline media services of TV and radio broadcasting and the printing media. One must acknowledge that the media is highly influenced by (ethno-) politics in Bosnia and Herzegovina, Kosovo, and Montenegro, and it is perceived as a major power structure by the post-war generation. The situation is highly problematic in Serbia because the media system is under the control of the ruling government (Bajić & Zweers, 2020). Watching the news on TV is often one-sided and, due to reporting on the relations with neighboring countries or on the minorities in their own country, it perpetuates ongoing conflicts or tensions among the communities resulting from the 1990s. As a matter of fact, this generation shows a significant tendency to mistrust the government system, in general, and especially party politics with a nationalistic background (Lavrić et al., 2019).

It seems that the offerings of traditional and often state-sponsored channels and newspapers, which, according to the interview partners, are mainly consumed by their parents and grandparents, had triggered some practices of resistance within the post-war generation. All of them show skepticism toward the news or other formats on TV or in the press. One of our interviewees, an 18-year-old man living in Sarajevo, referred to information in the traditional media as catastrophic:

> But RTRS (i.e. Radio Televizija Republike Srpske) is catastrophic. You wouldn't believe what kind of stuff they show their viewers and everything. It's horrible. There inside, that people, I think, they still believe that if you go to Sarajevo, Muslims will kill you. (Male, Sarajevo, Bosnia–Herzegovina, born in 2001)

Another aspect of the post-war generation's knowledge sources for war-related content shows that the uncertainty of information from traditional media leads to an exchange among peers. This tends to occur at schools, mostly among individuals with comparable social backgrounds (schools are often mono-ethnic in the post-Yugoslav countries), and, therefore, does not bring much new information, but rather repeats the stereotypes already familiar from the media. The school, as another official channel of the state, contributes to a contra-hegemonic attitude within the post-war generation. One woman from a small city in Montenegro explicitly reveals her doubts: "I came across the fact that I was reading a history book that was not objective at all, it was clear that the book was written in such a way that some things were written that were not true" (Female, Bar, Montenegro, born in 1997).

The mixture of these traditional media reports perceived as dubious; the emotional, often incomplete family stories; and the unsatisfactory exchanges with peers led the young people to use additional sources like documentaries, movies, books, blogs, and information on the Internet to build their own perception of the recent past and to reflect on stories about the war and its causes. However, searching the Internet may lead to even more ambiguous information in some cases:

> I really like the theme, '90 to '95 war. So, I searched all on the internet and I found the like two websites that talk about one thing in two different ways and how they look among guys as hero or as criminal. So, I wasn't there, so I will never know the truth. (Male, Sarajevo, Bosnia–Herzegovina, born in 2000)

On the other hand, some of the interviewees did research and found informative websites, such as the **YIHR** (Youth Initiative for Human Rights) regional network and the **BIRN** (Balkan Investigative Reporting Network), which provide reliable information. Furthermore, many national and local initiatives aim to inform young people in the region through various online channels.

Throughout our interviews in all of the Yugoslav secession countries, we found a profound skepticism toward traditional media, which we call an everyday practice of "resistance": "If I was just watching the news, I would like be, 'Serbians are bad. They did genocide. They killed many people'" (Male, Sarajevo, Bosnia, and Herzegovina, born in 2001). By avoiding the consumption of traditional media, the post-war generation weakens the omnipresence of nationalistic political parties, family narratives, and national or ethno-national myths:

> I would never read one article and say 'Hey, Croats are right, or Serbs are right, or Muslims are right.' I will always read several different articles, separately, so I can give certain judgment of my own about it. In most cases, it is the Internet, and sometimes a book, since I have a lot of books. (Male, Vrbanja, Bosnia–Herzegovina, born in 2001)

Departing from this standpoint of questioning the family narratives in their adolescent years distributed through traditional media channels, the members of the post-war generation became active and especially used the possibilities of the World Wide Web to distribute their own created content.

RESULTS II: ACTIVE MEDIA USE AS ACCOMMODATION TECHNIQUE

The everyday decision not to consume TV, radio, or newspapers for news or war-related topics, and the general mistrust in political institutions, could give the impression that the post-war generation is politically lethargic and uninformed. However, we learned that their media avoidance is a form of resistance, a way to challenge the political parties in power that control the official media system in their countries. Moreover, their resistance practices toward (ethno-)politics, national narratives, and family narratives show a broad range of public participation. Though these observed practices of public participation contain a "nondramatic, nonconfrontational or *non-recognized* way" (Vinthagen & Johansson, 2013, p. 37) of acting against the actors in power, we argue that they are coping strategies for an ongoing conflict that dates to the 1990s. Only in a few cases do we have examples of resistance in the form of protesting. Nevertheless, the "Children of the Balkan Wars" are trying to *accommodate* (p. 25) themselves to this political situation (Vinthagen & Johansson, 2013).

Over the years, the "Children of the Balkan Wars" have become active media users (Picone et al., 2019). They show a variety of producing activities: posting and commenting on selected Internet platforms, on the streets (graffiti), through youth exchange programs, and by questioning some (family) narratives within the collective memory. They are starting to disseminate their research results, their opinions, their life stories, and other puzzle pieces in different ways in the public sphere. The interviewees talked about their broad spectrum of social media activities: they might share a call for protests, for instance, or a call for (mostly NGO) projects. They use social media platforms as distribution channels and for peer group contact.

Some of our interviewees take advantage of anonymity on social media platforms, where they can perform as disguised users. Although they actively share and produce war-related content, their personal information remains hidden. Others use those platforms as self-presentation, to give insights into their personal life or professional field of expertise, but they put the message in the background. One of our interview partners, for example, was a young man in his 20s from a small town in Bosnia and Herzegovina, in which he was running for political office. On Facebook, he always appeared in photos as a family father and religious person, but his political program was not featured. Nevertheless, his political agenda was contrary to the dominating one. Both methods of *everyday resistance* use social media platforms, hiding as well as highlighting, were approached (Vinthagen & Johansson, 2013).

The post-war generation shows resistance toward several actors who, in their eyes, are powerful players that determine either the consequences of the wars or their historiographical presentation. As the main actors that dominate the hegemonial discourse, they define the party politicians and media producers – not the individual journalists working within the system, but rather the media system itself, which is dependent on ethno-political and state institutions. Depending on their viewpoint, they counter the power discourse dominated by the political and media system at home or/and abroad or the communicative memory. As active media users, they publicly cast doubt on what these systems and memories distribute. Although they do not organize a rebellion against the government or the media/political system, we consider their media productions as a form of resistance.

Their role as active media users is manifold: one young woman from Kosovo wrote an article about the Serbian-Kosovar relationship that was removed from the website by the provider after a few days. Two young people proudly told us about the high school magazine they were working on. Other interviewees told us they attend youth initiatives that deal with war-related topics. Commemoration festivities were often mentioned. One young man from Sarajevo managed to establish an exhibition based on submissions from his age cohort: He asked for childhood memories relating to the Bosnian war, and he got so many responses that he collected them, published a book, and created an exhibition in Sarajevo: the "War Childhood Museum." (https://warchildhood.org). The resistance of narratives, archived in collective memory and upheld by the political and media system, shows a variety of practices. Although some of them are organized and lead to a protest, many are part of the interviewees' everyday actions that have no certain intent. Nevertheless, they reveal the discontent with the hegemonic system and discourse and must be seen as a valuable source for democratization and anti-nationalism in post-Yugoslavia.

CONCLUSION: EVERYDAY RESISTANCE THROUGH VARIOUS MEDIA USES

The results of the study based on qualitative data show that knowledge about the recent wars is very important for the "Children of the Balkan Wars," and conversely, they feel the need to pass along their own knowledge and re-interpretations of certain historical narratives about it. The post-war generation is commonly characterized by their skepticism toward media reports on war-related topics, which can affect their trust in news reporting as a whole. They observed and criticized the intersection of political issues with war-related narratives from the collective memory in traditional media channels.

We can organize our findings into two main practices of media use: (1) Selective Media Consumption: Historical knowledge is sought and processed. This starts with intergenerational transfers within the family narratives and includes more and more external sources, along with the avoidance of traditional media use. (2) Active Media Use: Once historical facts are exposed, this generation aims to inform the public and disseminate knowledge through various channels and formats. They intend to bring topics or perspectives to the surface that are usually silenced by more traditional or nationalistic media.

In short, this generation mistrusts war-related media reports and tries to resist official media channels by creating their own perspective of the past, re-interpreting the narratives found in the collective memory. The past is perceived differently from one generation to the next, and the communication and exchange in media discourse about historical heritage play a major role in identity formation (Welzer,

2010), as was also reflected in the story of Nora, the then 22-year-old woman we met in Pristina who talked about the problematic media system in Kosovo.

ACKNOWLEDGMENTS

The Open Access publication costs were funded by the OA-Fonds of the Austrian Academy of Sciences.

NOTE

1. The Children of the Balkan Wars: Getting to know a crucial generation for Europe (2015); 2. How civic engagement leads to political participation. Learning from young active Europeans in Bosnia–Herzegovina, Kosovo, and Serbia (2016–2017); 3. Youth in the Balkans. Their cultures of communication and non-communication, and their notions of reconciliation (2019–2020).

REFERENCES

Asboth, E. T. (2023). Inherited border regions: Remembrance strategies among young adults in post-Yugoslavia and their multi-layered perspective on the past. *Oral History (Colchester)*, *51*(2), 67–79.

Asboth, E. T., & Griesbeck, M. (2024). Junge Lebensgeschichten aus Post-Jugoslawien: Reflexion über die Rolle der Forschenden im lebensgeschichtlichen Interview. Young life stories from post-Yugoslavia: reflection on the role of the researcher in life story interviews. *SWS-Rundschau*, *64*(1), 77–94.

Asboth, E. T., Griesbeck, M., & Nadjivan, S. (2017). "My milk lasts longer than my visa". The longings of the "Generation on the Move" in Kosovo. *Zeitgeschichte*, *44*, 19–31.

Assmann, A. (2016). *Shadows of trauma. Memory and politics of postwar identity*. Fordham.

Assmann, J. (2005). Der Begriff des kulturellen Gedächtnisses. In T. Dreier & E. Eule (Eds.), *Kulturelles Gedächtnis im 21. Jahrhundert. Tagungsband des internationalen Symposiums* (pp. 21–29). KIT Scientific Publishing. https://doi.org/10.5445/KSP/1000003721

Bajić, D., & Zweers, W. (2020). *Declining media freedom and biased reporting on foreign actors in Serbia. Prospects for an enhanced EU approach*. Clingendael Institute. https://www.jstor.org/stable/resrep25690.1

Baliqi, B. (2017). The aftermath of war experiences on Kosovo's generation on the move – Collective memory and ethnic relations among young adults in Kosovo. *Zeitgeschichte*, *44*, 6–19. https://d-nb.info/1128234440/04

Bohnsack, R., & Schäffer, B. (2002). Generation als konjunktiver Erfahrungsraum. Eine empirische analyse generationsspezifischer Medienpraxiskulturen. In G. Burkart & J. Wolf (Eds.), *Lebenszeiten. Erkundungen zur Soziologie der Generationen* (pp. 249–273). Leske+Budrich. https://doi.org/10.1007/978-3-663-10626-5_15

Bruns, A., & Schmidt, J. H. (2011). Produsage: A closer look at continuing developments. *New Review of Hypermedia and Multimedia*, *17*(1), 3–7.

Calic, M.-J. (2018). *A history of Yugoslavia*. Purdue University Press. https://directory.doabooks.org/handle/20.500.12854/35114

Das, R., & Ytre-Arne, B. (Eds.). (2018). *The future of audiences. A foresight analysis of interfaces and engagement*. Palgrave Macmillan.

Fujii, L. A. (2018). *Interviewing in social science research: A relational approach*. Routledge.

Gries, R. (2008). Kommunikationshistorie aus generationengeschichtlicher Perspektive. Ein kursorischer Überblick. In K. Arnold, M. Behmer, & B. Semrad (Eds.), *Kommunikationsgeschichte. Positionen und Werkzeuge. Ein diskursives Hand-und Lehrbuch* (pp. 235–258). Lit Verlag.

Gries, R. (2016). Franz Vranitzky lecture: A "Lost Generation"? In R. Gries, E. T. Asboth, & C. Krakovsky (Eds.), *Generation in-between. The children of the Balkan wars. Getting to know a crucial generation for Europe* (pp. 13–24). Erste Stiftung Studies. https://www.erstestiftung.org/wp-content/uploads/2020/02/generation-in-between_2016.pdf

Gries, R., & Ahbe, T. (2006). Generationengeschichte als Gesellschaftsgeschichte. Theoretische und methodische Überlegungen am Beispiel der DDR. In T. Ahbe et al. (Eds.), *Die DDR aus generationengeschichtlicher Perspektive. Eine Inventur* (pp. 475–571). Leipziger Universitätsverlag.

Gries, R., Asboth, E. T., & Krakovsky, C. (2016). *Generation in-between. The children of the Balkan wars. Getting to know a crucial generation for Europe*. Erste Stiftung Studies. https://www.erstestiftung.org/wp-content/uploads/2020/02/generation-in-between_2016.pdf

Jureit, U. (2017). Generation, generationality, generational research. *Docupedia-Zeitgeschichte*. http://dx.doi.org/10.14765/zzf.dok.2.1110.v2

Jureit, U., & Schneider, C. (2010). *Gefühlte Opfer: Illusionen der Vergangenheitsbewältigung*. Klett-Cotta.

Kuckartz, U. (2018). *Qualitative inhaltsanalyse. Methoden, Praxis, Computerunterstützung* (4th ed.). Beltz Juventa.

Lasswell, H. D. (1966). The structure and function of communication in society. In B. Berelson & M. Janowitz (Eds.), *Reader in public opinion and communication* (2nd ed.) (pp. 178–190). Free Press.

Lavrić, M., Tomanović, S., & Jusić, M. (Eds.). (2019). *Youth study Southeast Europe 2018/2019*. Friedrich-Ebert-Stiftung. https://library.fes.de/pdf-files/id-moe/15274-20190408.pdf

Lindlof, T. R., & Taylor, B. C. (2018). *Qualitative communication research methods* (4th ed.). SAGE Publications.

Mannheim, K. (1928). Das problem der generationen. *Kölner Vierteljahrshefte für Soziologie*, 7(2), 157–185.

Picone, I. (2011). Produsage as a form of self-publication. A qualitative study of casual news produsage. *New Review of Hypermedia and Multimedia*, 17(1), 99–120. https://doi.org/10.1080/13614568.2011.552643

Picone, I., Kleut, J., Pavlíčková, T., Romic, B., Møller Hartley, J., & De Ridder, S. (2019). Small acts of engagement: Reconnecting productive audience practices with everyday agency. *New Media & Society*, 21(9), 2010–2028. https://doi.org/10.1177/1461444819837569

Sindbæk Andersen, T., & Törnquist-Plewa, B. (Eds.). (2016). *Disputed memory: Emotions and memory politics in Central, Eastern and South-Eastern Europe*. De Gruyter.

Todorova, M. (2005). Spacing Europe. What is a historical region? *East Central Europe*, 32(1–2), 59–78. https://doi.org/10.1163/18763308-90001032

Vinthagen, S., & Johansson, A. (2013). Everyday resistance: Exploration of a concept and its theories. *Resistance Studies Magazine*, 1(1), 1–46. https://resistance-journal.org/wp-content/uploads/2016/04/Vinthagen-Johansson-2013-Everyday-resistance-Concept-Theory.pdf

Welzer, H. (2010). Re-narrations: How pasts change in conversational remembering. *Memory Studies*, 3(1), 5–17. https://doi.org/10.1177/1750698009348279

Yakovlyeva, V. (2020). Children's agency in remembering: An intergenerational approach to social memory. *Sociological Studies of Children and Youth*, 27, 57–71.

CHAPTER 3

DIARIES OF WAR: CHILDREN'S NARRATIVES AND AGENCY IN UKRAINE AND SYRIA

Iuliia Hoban[a] and Denise R. Muro[b]

[a]*Embry-Riddle Aeronautical University-Worldwide, USA*
[b]*University of Massachusetts Boston, USA*

ABSTRACT

The prolonged civil war in Syria and the full-scale war in Ukraine have significantly impacted the nations' children, yet Ukrainian and Syrian children found ways to express their agency. This comparative study centers on children's first-hand accounts of conflict through a feminist geopolitical approach and interpretive textual analysis methods to explore common themes children express in diaries, how resistance is articulated, and how other actors mediate these narratives. Informed by feminist geopolitics, the authors investigate how the everyday practice of narrating their experiences provides children with a space to articulate their perspectives on war-related experiences. This research employs thematic analysis to explore four Ukrainian and four Syrian children's diaries. In this chapter, the authors discuss three salient themes from the diaries: (1) trauma and fear; (2) loss of normalcy; and (3) coping, hope, and resilience. The authors argue that these themes demonstrate children's agency and that diaries can be read as a medium of resistance. This chapter also pays attention to how such narratives are mediated, commodified, and even controlled by adults for political objectives. This chapter, thus, contributes to the discussion of the nature of children's experiences in armed conflict. Furthermore, it explores how children's agency is potentially articulated, manipulated, and restricted in everyday sites.

Keywords: Children; childhood; Syria; Ukraine; armed conflict; feminist geopolitics; militarization; resilience; thematic analysis

INTRODUCTION

The prolonged civil war in Syria and the full-scale war in Ukraine have significantly impacted the nations' children. Ukrainian and Syrian youngest citizens have been directly affected by the conflicts as they were displaced, wounded, and even killed. Still, Ukrainian and Syrian children created spaces to express their agency, narrating their experiences through diaries, poems, and art and engaging in political activities. Diaries have been recognized as an impactful medium for allowing children to process trauma, providing them with a space to articulate perspectives on their war-related experiences. Emerging research in sociology's engagement with armed conflict highlights how the evolving tactics of warfare affect the experiences of children in these settings marked by a complex interplay of violence, displacement, and societal disruptions (DiPietro, 2016; McGarry & Walklate, 2019; Shaw, 2015).

First-hand narratives of Ukrainian and Syrian children who have lived through large-scale political violence "register the commonplace, the mundane, the ordinary as it is lived within an extraordinary moment" (Tyner & Henkin, 2015, p. 300). Though these firsthand accounts might be dismissed as apolitical due to the authors' ages or personal nature, we argue that they represent an important site of geopolitics and offer insights into meaning-making and forms of resistance. By investigating how children bear witness to armed conflict and interpret their experiences, we approach children as "bona fide political subjects in their own right, not merely as repositories for politics issuing from other subjects" (Beier, 2022, p. 117).

This comparative analysis examines interrelated research questions: (1) What are common themes across Ukrainian and Syrian children's diaries that respond to two different conflicts? (2) How do these narratives illustrate children's resistance to war? (3) How do other political actors in these conflicts assign meaning to these narratives, thus potentially commodifying children's trauma and further weaving militarism in children's lives?[1] Following feminist theorizing, this study engages with the texts critically, allowing us to examine the diffusion of militarization from the everyday to the geopolitical and back again (Henry & Natanel, 2016). This research employs thematic analysis as a primary interpretive textual analysis method that focuses on meaning-making and allows one to examine power through language and discourse (Farnell & Graham, 2015; Hall, 2013).

This comparative study significantly contributes to the research on the complex and ambivalent nature of children's experiences in armed conflict, delving into the articulation, manipulation, and restriction of their agency in the everyday. The first-person narratives of Syrian and Ukrainian children provide valuable insights into how they interpret, adapt, disengage, and resist in the face of war. Additionally, the study's examination of how political actors use children's narratives to advance their political objectives is an important contribution to the field.

In the next section, we situate this study with the debate on the positionality of children and childhoods in global politics with specific attention to children's agency. We follow with an overview of our methods and a comparative analysis of key themes of trauma and fear, the loss of normalcy, and coping and resilience in Ukrainian and Syrian children's diaries. The chapter then discusses how children's voices are mediated, remediated, and collaboratively circulated. We conclude by reflecting on the importance of recognizing children as active participants in the complex geopolitical landscape.

LITERATURE REVIEW

The literature demonstrates that the institutional architecture concerned with children and war often silences children's voices (Berents, 2019, p. 464; see also Beier, 2020; Hook & Hoban, 2023; Horschelmann, 2016). Scholars have illustrated that in the context of armed conflict, children are often perceived in binary terms – either as subjects of security to be rescued or as objects to be feared, corrected, or regulated (Baines, 2009; Beier, 2018; Berents, 2015; Hoban, 2019; Lee-Koo, 2017; Macmillan, 2015; Rosen, 2005, 2015; Wagnsson et al., 2010). The characterization of child soldiers as "exaggerated deviants" (Macmillan, 2015, p. 41) reflects these constructions of childhood, particularly evident in the Western discourse. This characterization pathologizes children's agency, hindering its recognition as a legitimate form of political subjecthood (Beier, 2015).

Sociologists have contributed to this debate in their discussion of childhood as a social construction and plurality of childhoods determined by "exigencies of gender, ethnicity, race, class, location, and more" (James & Prout, 2015, p. 4; see also James & James, 2004). Expanding the scope of sociological inquiry into the study of war, recent scholarship has offered valuable insights into the evolving nature of conflict and its repercussions for civilians living in active war zones (McGarry & Walklate, 2019; Shaw, 2015). Our interdisciplinary study contributes to this emerging discussion on connecting sociological literature to the subject of war and examining how war enters and shapes the lives of children in active war zones. When children's agency is ignored or overlooked, considering their everyday life experiences during a war offers an opportunity to validate and amplify their voices (Berents, 2019). Moreover, research shows that children have demonstrated resilience through meaning-making practices despite their proximity to armed conflict (Hook & Hoban, 2023). Scholars demonstrated that children's life narratives, such as diaries, memoirs, and digital storytelling, articulate their experiences of war, offering valuable insights into their lives during conflicts and enhancing our understanding of how to address violence (Berents, 2019; Douglas, 2020; Douglas & Poletti, 2016; Hynd, 2021; Nasie & Bar-Tal, 2012).

This study also engages in the conversation on how children's narratives and their interpretation by adults in political spaces elicit the tensions of children's agency "as [children are] both potentially autonomous and a valued object of capture by other actors" (Beier, 2020, p. 13). Scholars have shown that various political actors (e.g., government officials, media outlets, and non-governmental organizations) view children as either objects of security in need of rescue and protection or as subjects to be feared, disciplined, and controlled in the interest of maintaining security (Beier, 2020; Horschelmann, 2016; Wagnsson et al., 2010). Applying Douglas and Poletti's (2016) framework for analyzing children's diaries in the Ukrainian and Syrian contexts, we provide insights into how these life narratives serve as sites of resilience and resistance, examining their transformations across different mediums. From the first-hand accounts of children to translation (when applicable) and publication, the journey of these stories is significant. Research notes that examining changes made to children's diaries through mediation is salient. These alterations limit childhood perspective, permitting only specific information deemed essential by adults (Wahlstrom, 2012). The analysis of the journey of diaries from the Ukrainian and Syrian contexts illustrates the evolution of stories and how they interact with geopolitics.

This research, taking a feminist geopolitical stance, explores how children's first-person narratives, as an everyday practice, both impact and are impacted by geopolitics (Henry & Natanel, 2016; Hook & Hoban, 2023). Importantly, this focus recognizes that armed conflict has become increasingly dangerous for civilians (McGarry & Walklate, 2019; Shaw, 2015), including children. Influenced by Ahall's (2019) observation that militarization practices dance their way into everyday life, this chapter examines performative meaning-making practices in children's diaries and their subsequent interpretation by political actors. We argue that the engagement with children's diaries provides insight into experiences of everyday militarized violence. Simultaneously, these first-hand narratives demonstrate "interconnections between day-to-day living and the broader, geopolitical practices" (Tyner & Henkin, 2015, p. 300). Through this lens, the analysis shows how, through their diaries, children connect to geopolitical events, such as Russia's full-scale invasion of Ukraine and the civil war in Syria, with their own everyday lives and experiences of conflict (Horschelmann, 2016). Informed by Woodward's insights (2007), we examine how these narratives allow us to understand how children pursue "mundane routine acts of daily living in circumstances of extreme physical danger" (p. 4). This project, thus, investigates how children's diaries become "significant sites for the animation of the geopolitical" (Basham, 2015, p. 9).

DATA SELECTION AND METHODOLOGY

This research focuses on children's diaries as "intentional, ultimately public texts and a vehicle for expression, growth, rebellion, and creation" (Wahlstrom, 2012, p. 44). These artifacts hold value for insights into armed conflicts in Syria and Ukraine and for revealing children's war experiences and how they narrate them (Douglas & Poletti, 2016; Hynd, 2021). Peri (2017) notes that first-person narratives, as articulations of experience, are mediated by the writing process and self-censorship (p. 15). It is essential to recognize that these narratives do not encompass the experiences of all children or fully reflect the Russian–Ukraine war or Syrian civil war.

Interestingly, while collecting sources for this project, the researchers encountered several mediums that referred to themselves as diaries. *The War Diaries* exhibition featured documentary elements like statistics and a conflict timeline. Other "diaries" took various forms, such as poetry, visual art, epistolary fiction, extensive quotes in the media, and narratives like memoirs, often written retrospectively. While these other forms provide insight into children's everyday experiences of war, for this study, we rely on first-hand accounts that were written "in the moment." The selected diaries differ in structure, style, dissemination, and translation methods.

Ukrainian diaries consist of three first-hand accounts featured in the *War Diaries* exhibition held in Amsterdam. The diaries were written by young authors of varying ages, genders, and regions of residence during the onset of the war. Yegor Kravtsov (2022), 8 years old, wrote a diary chronicling his experience of living for 96 days through one of the worst battles of the Russian–Ukrainian war, the Battle of Mariupol. Violetta Gorbachova, a 15-year-old from Nova Kakhovka in southern Ukraine, chronicled the first months of the Russian invasion and the challenges of living under occupation. The third diary from the exhibit is authored by Arina Pervunina, a 13-year-old girl who fled Odesa and was trapped under Russian occupation in the Kherson region. Arina started keeping her diary following the death of her father in March 2022 and used it as a space to grapple with this loss. The diary from Yeva Skalietskaa, "You don't know what war is," was officially published in Dublin in 2022. In her diary, Yeva chronicles her experience of living through the first day of war in native Kharkiv in eastern Ukraine and then her journey as a refugee to Ireland.

The Syrian diaries are from four girls and were published in different formats. The first is by 16-year-old Amira, published by *TearFund and CommonLit* in 2013. Although not dated, the diary spans at least three episodes, as Amira describes the night her family left her house, her experience crossing a border and her day-to-day life in a refugee camp. *TearFund* also published a resource kit with activities to accompany the diary. The second diary is by Marah (her pen name), who was 15 years old when the war began. Her entries started in April 2014 and ended in July 2016 after she fled her country; for this project, diary entries through 2014 are included. Marah's diary was published online in collaboration with *Syria Deeply* and *Rookie*. The third diary is by 12-year-old Mayar and features in a collection titled *While the Earth Sleeps We Travel: Stories, Poetry, and Art from Young Refugees Around the World*. Photographs of three pages of Mayar's diary appear in the book beside translations, and the author translated the diary from Arabic. The fourth diary, authored by Myriam Rawick at age 8, spans from June 2011 to March 2016 and is published as a book. Initially written in Arabic, it was translated into multiple languages, including French, Spanish, Portuguese, Italian, German, and Catalan.

This collection of Ukrainian and Syrian diaries allows us to explore various mediation forms for children's firsthand narratives, ranging from inclusion in exhibits or anthologies to individual book publications. The study investigates the circulation, mediation, and commodification of children's voices by analyzing newspaper articles, utilizing open-source data, and examining official statements by policymakers referencing children's firsthand narratives.

This study employs thematic analysis to engage with the texts critically. Braun and Clarke (2006) and others identify the challenge that thematic analysis needs to be better defined compared to other methods but can be useful for the systematic analysis of qualitative data investigating patterns across a dataset (Riger & Sigurvinsdottir, 2016, p. 33). Braun and Clarke (2006) emphasize the method's adaptability for extracting meaningful insights from qualitative data across diverse research contexts. Riger and Sigurvinsdottir (2016) note that thematic analysis may be done inductively or deductively. While our approach is inductive, allowing themes to emerge from the coding process rather than relying on a predetermined set, we also find alignment with themes discussed in existing literature.

Scholars identify six stages of thematic analysis that we follow in our study (Braun & Clarke, 2006; Riger & Sigurvinsdottir, 2016). The researchers began by immersing themselves in the data with close reading and notetaking on diaries. This stage was followed by generating initial codes where the research team identified, discussed, and consolidated codes. Subsequent stages involved exploring, examining, refining, and labeling themes. In the final stage, we synthesized our findings and presented a comprehensive analysis in the following section. The research team regularly engaged in collaborative discussions throughout the iterative process of searching for, reviewing, defining, and naming themes. The thematic analysis of the diaries revealed three main themes: (1) trauma and fear; (2) loss of normalcy; and (3) hope, coping, and resilience.

FINDINGS AND DISCUSSION

Trauma and Fear

War and conflict have devastating impacts on children, including post-traumatic stress disorder (PTSD), fear and anxiety, and other adverse mental health experiences (Macksoud et al., 1993; Shaw, 2003; Slone & Mann, 2016). In a systematic review of over 4,000 children exposed to war, Slone and Mann (2016) note that children experience dire circumstances, enduring injuries, displacement, orphanhood, and even death. Children witnessing injuries, deaths, and immediate dangers during war face trauma, developmental issues, mental and behavioral challenges, including PTSD, and revealing the profound impact of political violence on them. Moreover, conflict may generate uncertainty about the future. In their study on the Israeli–Palestinian conflict in Palestinian youth writings, Nasie and Bar-Tal (2012) highlight fear as a prevalent theme in children's diaries, describing it as the "expression of personal or collective threats and dangers" (p. 10). Masten et al. (2015) note that children's age and cognitive skills impact their experience of fear during the war. Adolescents, in particular, demonstrate a better understanding of the consequences of an unfolding crisis, displaying "more abstract and also more realistic fears about the meaning and lasting consequences of war" (p. 15).

In discussing the Syrian conflict, Pearlman (2016) explains different types of fear among refugees: "silencing fear" due to the coercive authority of the state, "personalized fear," "semi-normalized fear," and "nebulous fear" of an uncertain future (pp. 24–29). The Ukrainian and Syrian children's diaries illustrate witnessing traumatic events and experiencing various types of fear, both personal and collective, immediate and future-oriented.

The diaries' authors sometimes describe details of the trauma that they are witnessing. For example, Yegor Kratsov (2022) notes, "I have a wound on my back, my sister's skin was torn out. She had a head wound. My mother's flesh was torn out of her arm, and now she has a hole in her leg." Marah (2014) also describes the physical trauma and suffering of her community:

> Today, my city's familiar face has been replaced by the suffering of its residents: the young boy who has been exposed to chemical weapons and is unable to receive treatment. An old man feels powerless after he loses his legs. A young man wears black sunglasses as if to hide a severely scarred face that frightens children.

These human scars evoke strong emotions and cause emotional distress in the authors.

Perhaps, in part, due to witnessing these dire outcomes, the children's diaries also feature vivid descriptions of the immediate fear they experience during shellings and shootings. For example, during a morning missile strike, Yeva Skalietskaa (2023) writes, "I felt my heart go cold in my chest" (p. 10) and "My hands were shaking, my teeth rattling. I felt fear all around me. I realized I was having my first-ever panic attack." Myriam Rawick (2018) describes hearing shots throughout the night and writes, "This morning, there were more shots. At first, we counted them, but then there were a lot, and I lost count. […] I was a little scared, even though they were far away." Many of the authors write about hearing the sounds of bombs and shooting and experiencing physical manifestations of fear.

The children's diaries depict concerns for loved ones and instances of family members' deaths. Both Arina Pervunina (2022) and Marah lost their fathers, and both girls' diaries include missing and longing, along with observations of the sadness and changes in their mothers. Yeva Skalietska (2022) writes about how her grandmother's husband was killed, saying, "Bomb fragments had cut his entire body. We had just spoken to him only a few days ago, and today he's gone. It's terrifying" (p. 43). Similarly, Myriam Rawick (2018) describes her and her mother's worry for her cousin Fadi, noting, "since he went to the army, mom is afraid for him, and she just hopes that everything that is happening will soon be over" (p. 26). She later recounts when her uncle told her family that Fadi had been kidnapped and the fear, sadness, devastation, and confusion this brought to her and her family (pp. 27–28).

Finally, fear is also expressed through uncertainty and worry about the future. Yeva Skalietska (2022) writes, "What's going to happen next? Will they survive? Will our homes?" (p. 20). Marah, who was preparing for her final exams in high school in 2014, often expressed her concerns about the future, writing, "Will I achieve my dream and go to college? Or will I end up drifting off to where our country's current circumstances take me? I don't know where my destiny will lead." While not directed at immediate danger, this future-oriented fear is salient across the diaries.

The diaries portray various fears discussed in the literature. The authors detail personalized and collective fear for their families and communities. They also express immediate fear during shelling, alongside a more abstract, future-oriented fear regarding what will happen to them, their families, and their countries.

Loss of Normalcy

While fear may become normalized, children often experience a loss of sense of normalcy as their everyday drastically changes under conditions of war. Conflict disrupts regular routines, including access to school, food and water supplies, and other necessities, significantly impacting children (Dupuy & Peters, 2009). Urman et al. (2001) find that among children aged 9–13 years who had experienced a traumatic event, significant "negotiation" occurred between the trauma and their pre-traumatic experiences of "normal." For children living through war, schools can help retain a sense of normality with opportunities to learn and engage with peers (Dupuy & Peters, 2009, p. 34); however, children are often in IDP or refugee camps without the capacity to offer education, armed forces may target schools, and children may also be forced to abandon their education and become involved with armed forces (Dupuy & Peters, 2009, p. xiii). Additionally, the militarization of everyday spaces contributes to the loss of normalcy children as well as others in conflict zones may experience. Following Natanel's insight (2016) on the pervasive nature of military practices that result in the blurring of boundaries "including military/civilian, public/private, and political/intimate" (p. 901), we explore how children observe and engage with the militarization of space that seeps into part of their everyday.

Ukrainian and Syrian children capture stark contrasts between their pre-war lives and their current realities. Children reflect on how their familiar places, schools, and memories are destroyed. Yeva Skalietskaa (2023) notes how her neighborhood in the east of Kharkiv city "is being practically erased [.] all the little streets I used to play in, the little courtyards, my favorite pizza place, and my school! It was all so beautiful" (p. 21). Not only have physical spaces been affected by the onset of war, but explosions have replaced the sounds of birds singing, rain falling, and the tranquility that marked their lives before conflict erupted. As Yeva Skalietska (2022) notes, "I really want to hear the sounds of peace-time again – birds singing and the sound of rain. It was so nice before the war. I want to go back to my old life" (p. 35). Marah (2014) resonates with Yeva's writing:

> My city was once magnificent. In spring, it bloomed. We used to wake up to the sound of birds chirping and the fragrant scent of flowers. Today, spring is here again. But what kind of spring is this? We now wake up to the sound of falling bombs.

These changes in their surroundings signify physical destruction and the erasure of the sensory elements that once created a sense of normalcy.

Nostalgia, the profound desire to return to normalcy, permeates Ukrainian and Syrian children's diaries. The narrators, amidst the chaos and destruction, express a yearning for the ordinary routines that once defined their lives. Marah (2014) notes:

> I never wondered what I would have because our table was full of everything I liked: meat, vegetables, fruits, and desserts. But where are those nowadays? We fantasize about food, reminiscing over the well-stocked fridge we once had.

In a longitudinal study on the well-being of war-affected youth, Betancourt et al. (2013) acknowledge that disruptions to routines can significantly impact children's health. The yearning for ordinary routines becomes a coping mechanism – an attempt to reclaim control and stability in a world uprooted by war. The diaries also provide firsthand accounts of how the militarization of everyday spaces has become normalized. Children's references to the presence of "soldiers at every meter, in the market, on the embankment" and "an infinite number of armored personnel carriers" (Gorbachova, 2022) and "hear[ing] shots [that] hardly scare me anymore" (Rawick, 2018, p. 33) illustrate the pervasive militarization that permeates their daily lives. The diaries reflect profound changes to children's surroundings, erasing and transforming their neighborhoods. For example, Marah (2014) observes:

> Every day, we open our eyes to our bleak reality: to the mortar shells that bring fear, death, disease, and destruction.

Violetta Gorbachova (2022) also notes:

> My mother, sister, and I walk along the main street parallel to the bank of the Dnipro [...] We descend and hear the sound of a collision in the sky, a bright spot. [.] The sound is similar to the bomb falling and buildings crashing. We run in the opposite direction in panic.

These and other narratives from Syrian and Ukrainian children illustrate how militarization can unfold in a variety of ways, not only physically transforming the environment but also contributing to a profound sense of displacement, emphasizing the loss of the familial and sense of home.

Hope, Coping, and Resilience

We follow Anne Masten's (2001) definition of resilience as the ability of individuals to adapt to adverse situations to overcome difficulties. We do not envision resilience as either a negative or positive attribute as it is "entirely contingent on who is wielding it, and for what political purposes" (DeVerteuil et al., 2021, p. 144). The emphasis on the relational nature of resilience allows us to investigate how it "is constructed, negotiated, and resourced" (DeVerteuil et al., 2021, p. 87). The concept of resilience, viewed as a result of "multi-scalar relationships" (DeVerteuil et al., 2021, p. 86) embedded within larger socio-political structures, aligns with feminist geopolitics. This perspective acknowledges that war, as portrayed in children's diaries, is experienced simultaneously as a personal crisis and a societal catastrophe (Ahall, 2019; Natanel, 2016; Woodward, 2007). For example, Mayar's diary (2020) vividly illustrates this multi-scalar relationship in describing sacrifices made by her mother during the Syrian conflict to provide more opportunities for her children (Badr, 2020). Simultaneously, Yeva Skalietskaa

(2023) provides a poignant reflection on her struggle with the term refugee, reflecting the embodied experience of displacement following armed conflict.

Reading across the diaries, we notice how children engage in various activities to cope with the reality of armed conflict. For instance, amidst intensive shelling in her city, Yeva Skalietska (2022) paints a seascape in the kitchen, Marah (2014) enjoys playing with local first graders taught by her mom, and Violetta Gorbachova (2022) finds happiness during the occupation when going to a picnic, celebrating her birthday, and spending time with family. Children also express hope as a way to cope with ongoing conflict. Family, close friends, and community often become crucial elements in fostering resilience (Linklater, 2020). Violetta Gorbachova (2022) describes how learning to knit from a grandmother fills her days with joy. Marah (2014) conveys that her mother teaches her the lyrics of an old song, "This is my life. Life is beautiful. Life is a song," to encourage her children through the everyday evidence of violence. Hope involves "expectation and aspiration for a goal, as well as positive feelings about the anticipated outcome" (Nasie & Bar-Tal, 2012, p. 15). Badr (2020) and Marah (2014) share their dreams of pursuing education and career aspirations that allow these children to imagine a better future without specifying the details. Lear (2006) notes that this hope is radical because it involves anticipating a positive outcome that we may not yet have to comprehend.

FORMS OF MEDIATION

Mediation, remediation, and collaboration are inevitable processes in the circulation of life narratives (Douglas, 2020; Douglas & Poletti, 2016). Political leaders, organizations, media, and others have mediated Ukrainian and Syrian children's diaries. Initially, we analyzed the mediation of the diaries through news media. Using the NexusUni database, we followed the same procedures to search for articles related to selected children's diaries from Syria and Ukraine. However, our search yielded only five relevant articles for Syria, while we discovered 47 for Ukraine, despite the latter covering a shorter timeframe. Western media focuses more on Ukrainian children's diaries than Syrian ones, perhaps reflective of greater attention to the war in Ukraine versus conflicts in the Global South. Still, the Syrian diaries were subjected to mediation in the media and by other actors as well.

Syrian diaries entered public discourse through different mediums. Marah's diary was published online in collaboration with online news platforms *Syria Deeply*, and *Rookie* and seemingly underwent little to no mediation. The sites do not articulate any specific purpose behind posting her diary entries; instead, her entries are allowed to speak for themselves. Myriam Rawick's diary has been published in multiple languages and received media attention from Arab News (2017), France24 (2017), Business Insider (Bondarenko, 2024), and others. It also appears on Goodreads and Amazon. These news sources primarily quote from Rawick's diary, and both Arab News and France24 refer to how Myriam's childhood was "shattered by 'grown-up stuff.'"

We observe greater mediation with Amira's and Mayar's diaries. Amira's diary was published with *TearFund*, "a Christian charity which partners with churches in more than 50 of the world's poorest countries" (2024). *TearFund* published an accompanying guide (2015) that includes links to Amira's diary, which is being read aloud. The activities involve writing an encouraging letter to Amira, blindfolding children, and using animal noises to locate each other. These are designed to illuminate the circumstances surrounding Amira and her family's reunion in a refugee camp. While ostensibly aimed at fostering children's understanding of refugee experiences, this publication's approach appears disconnected and, at times, offensive.

In contrast, Mayar's diary, featured in an anthology that included art, poetry, and stories from young refugees from different contexts, undergoes a different mediation. Actor Ben Stiller contributes the foreword, and editor Ahmed M. Badar, a refugee, introduces the book, intending to humanize refugees and amplify their voices. Badar notes, "Together, we are speaking up and proclaiming to the world that our existence is worthy of its attention" (p. xvii). While *TearFund* heavily mediates the understanding of Amira's diary through their guide, Badar allows the stories and art to speak for themselves.

Similar to Mayar's narrative, diaries authored by Yehor, Violetta, and Arina became part of a greater exhibit. The exhibit represents what Kate Douglas (2019) defines as "a collaborative archive: a cumulative series of life narrative texts" (p. 297). Like anthologies in the Syrian case, exhibits serve as a method of curation and distillation, offering us fragmented narratives of children's experiences; these fragments, however, can be meaningfully interpreted and understood (Douglas & Poletti, 2016). For diaries like Yehor Kravtsov's, the exhibit was not the initial form of mediation; instead, it was re-mediated after photographer Sosnovsky first shared it with the broader public on his Facebook page. These three diaries have also entered the larger political discourse of the Russia–Ukraine war when politicians directly quoted the excerpts in the public arena to support their claims. For example, Ukraine's Minister of Foreign Affairs (2023) and President (2023) referenced these diaries in international forums like the United Nations. Referencing and directly quoting children's narratives, these political statements aim to mobilize global support for Ukraine in its struggle against Russian aggression. The goal is to emphasize that such support is crucial to ensuring the safety and well-being of children amid conflict.

Yeva Skalietska's diary has been published as a stand-alone book that describes Yeva's experience during the war in Ukraine and showcases her journey as a refugee to Ireland. Compared to the three diaries featured in the exhibit, Yeva's book appears in book rankings and reviews (Evelhoch, 2022; Hardyment & Nicol, 2022) and articles about the release of an audiobook featuring celebrity narrators (Bowman, 2022). Like Myriam's diary, Yeva's firsthand narrative is readily available on popular platforms like Amazon and Goodreads. These forms of mediation enhance accessibility for a wider audience, but concurrently, they also transform the personal narrative into a marketable and consumable product.

The mediation of children's diaries also reveals the inherent tension that while each diary shows a slice of the reality of an individual child in a particular moment in history, the media and the publishing industry tend to universalize these experiences, thus potentially restricting children's agency (Anderson, 2007; Douglas & Polleti, 2016; Smith, 2006). In the context of life narratives of Ukrainian children, there is a deliberate attempt to draw parallels with Anne Frank's diary (Bowman, 2022; Corder, 2023; Crowley, 2023). To make these stories universally relatable, the media articles and statements from politicians draw direct comparisons or, as seen in the exhibit held in Amsterdam, establish connections to Anne Frank's experiences. This approach creates a symbolic connection that resonates with the Western audience. However, this may oversimplify the realities faced by Ukrainian children.

CONCLUSION

The three prominent themes across these diaries – fear and uncertainty; loss of normalcy; and hope, coping, and resilience – offer insight into how children construct, navigate, and regulate everyday spaces during the war (Natanel, 2016). Ukrainian and Syrian children witnessed traumatic events and articulated fear of immediate circumstances such as bombings as well as a more nebulous fear and uncertainty about the future. The diaries encapsulate the stark contrast between the pre-war time and the current harsh realities and exemplify the simultaneous existence of multiple times and spaces where the boundaries between past and present, civilian and military, become blurred. These diaries serve as testimonials to the physical destruction and as windows into multiple ways war has affected children's everyday lives. Examining the diaries, we observe diverse coping mechanisms children employ, ranging from artistic expressions to finding joy in everyday routines. Family, close friends, and community emerge as crucial elements fostering resilience. These relationships form a foundation for the children to navigate the challenges of living through war and emphasize the interconnectedness of personal and collective resilience.

The mediation and remediation of children's diaries demonstrate how these accounts are curated, exhibited, and commodified, with deliberate efforts to draw parallels with universally recognized narratives like Anne Frank's diary. While this mediation allows for broader awareness, it also raises questions about potential depoliticization and oversimplification of the children's experiences. In exploring the journey of these narratives from personal accounts to their interpretation by political actors, the research highlights the complexities of children's agency.

This study explores performative meaning-making practices in the diaries of Ukrainian and Syrian children, contributing to our understanding of how children navigate daily life amid danger and disruptions. Ultimately, exploring these narratives as significant sites for the animation of the geopolitical (Basham, 2015) adds to discussions on militarized violence and calls for a more inclusive approach that considers children as active participants in the complex geopolitical landscape.

NOTE

1. Following Douglas's and Poletti's (2016), we understand the potential impact of our mediation as we incorporate these diaries into a broader discourse on life narratives authored by children.

REFERENCES

Ahall, L. (2019). Feeling everyday IR: Embodied, affective, militarising movement as the choreography of war. *Cooperation and Conflict*, *54*(2), 149–166.
Amira. (2013). *Diary of a teenage refugee*. CommonLit.
Anderson, M. M. (2007). The child victim as witness to the Holocaust: an American story? *Jewish Social Studies*, 2007, 1–22.
Badr, A. M. (2020). *While the earth sleeps we travel: Stories, poetry, and art from young refugees around the world*. Andrews McMeel Publishing.
Baines, K. E. (2009). Complex political perpetrators: Reflections on Dominic Ongwen. *The Journal of Modern African Studies*, *47*(2), 163–191.
Basham, V. M. (2015). Gender, race, militarism, and remembrance: The everyday geopolitics of the poppy. *Gender, Place & Culture*, *23*(6), 883–896.
Beier, J. M. (2015). Children, childhoods, and security studies: An introduction. *Critical Studies on Security*, *3*(1), 1–13.
Beier, J. M. (2018). Ultimate tests: Children, rights, and the politics of protection. *Global Responsibility to Protect*, *10*(1–2), 164–187.
Beier, J. M. (2020). Decolonizing childhood in international relations. M. Beier (Ed.). *Discovering childhood in international relations*. Palgrave Macmillan.
Beier, J. M. (2022). Governing conflict through childhood. *Georgetown Journal of International Affairs*, *23*(1), 52–58.
Berents, H. (2015). Children, violence, and social exclusion: Negotiation of everyday insecurity in a Colombian barrio. *Critical Studies on Security*, *3*(1), 90–104.
Berents, H. (2019). "This is my story": Children's war memoirs and challenging protectionist discourses. *International Review of the Red Cross*, *101*(911), 459–479.
Betancourt, T. S., Meyers-Ohki, M. S. E., Charrow, M. A. P., & Tol, W. A. (2013). Interventions for children affected by war: An ecological perspective on psychosocial support and mental health care. *Harvard Review of Psychiatry*, *21*(2), 70–91.
Bondarenko, V. (2024, January 30). *"The war was my childhood left among the ruins": Through her diary, this young girl chronicled her escape from the Syrian civil war*. Business Insider. https://www.businessinsider.com/myriams-diary-rawick-aleppo-syrian-civil-war-2017-6
Bowman, V. (2022, November 5). Keira Knightley narrates a memoir of the war written by a Ukrainian schoolgirl. *The Sunday Telegraph*. https://www.telegraph.co.uk/world-news/2022/11/05/ukrainian-schoolgirls-diary-warzone-gains-celebrity-narrator/
Braun, V., & Clarke, V. (2006). Using thematic analysis in psychology. *Qualitative Research in Psychology*, *3*(2), 77–101.
Corder, M. (2023, August 18). Ukrainian children's war diaries are displayed in Amsterdam, where Anne Frank wrote in hiding. *AP News*. https://apnews.com/article/ukraine-children-war-netherlands-diaries-4b910bfe045e754bcf2764ae134d36e
Crowley, E. (2023, June 12). 13-year-old charts her journey out of war-torn Ukraine. *Irish Examiner*. https://www.irishexaminer.com/lifestyle/people/arid-41165569.html
DeVerteuil, G., Golubchikov, O., & Sheridan, Z. (2021). Disaster and the lived politics of the resilient city. *Geoforum*, *125*, 78–86.
DiPietro, S. M. (2016). Criminology and war: Where are we going and where have we been? *Sociology Compass*, *10*(10), 839–848.
Douglas, K. (2019). Malala Yousafzai, life narrative and the collaborative archive. In D. McCooey & M. Takolander (Eds.), *The limits of life writing* (pp. 21–35). Routledge.
Douglas, K. (2020). @Alabedbana: Twitter, the child, and the war diary. *Textual Practice*, *34*(6), 1021–1039.

Douglas, K., & Poletti, A. (2016). *Life narratives and youth culture: Representation, agency and participation*. Springer.

Dupuy, K. E., & Peters, K. (2009). *War and children: A reference handbook*. Bloomsbury Publishing USA.

Evelhoch, Z. (2022, November 4). Review. *Library Journal*. https://www.libraryjournal.com/review/you-dont-know-what-war-is-the-diary-of-a-young-girl-from-ukraine-1794459

Farnell, B., & Graham, L. R. (2015). Discourse-centered methods. In H. R. Bernard & C. C. Gravlee (Eds.). *Handbook of methods in cultural anthropology* (2nd ed.). (pp. 391–438). The Rowman & Littlefield Publishing Group, Inc.

"Girl chronicles Aleppo terror in "Myriam's Diary."" (2017, June 14). *France 24*. https://www.france24.com/en/20170614-girl-chronicles-aleppo-terror-myriams-diary

"Girl chronicles Aleppo terror in 'Myriam's Diary.'" (2017, June 15). *Arab news*. https://www.arabnews.com/node/1115276/offbeat

Gorbachova, V. (2022). *Diary. War diaries exhibit*. Amsterdam. https://wardiariesukraine.org/violetta_ua/

Hall, S. (2013). *Representation: Cultural representations and signifying practices* (2nd ed.). Sage Publications Ltd.

Hardyment, C., & Nicol, P. (2022, December 16). The best audiobooks of 2022. *The Times*. https://www.thetimes.co.uk/article/best-audiobooks-2022-bk0k6w9wl

Henry, M., & Natanel, K. (2016). Militarisation as diffusion: The politics of gender, space and the everyday. *Gender, Place & Culture*, *23*(6), 850–856.

Hoban, I. (2019). Children, conflict, and the detention of 'child soldiers' in Canada and the United States: How framing contests shape policies. *Journal of Human Rights*, *18*(5), 597–618.

Hook, K., & Hoban, I. (2023). Children's agency and co-construction of everyday militarism(s). In H. Berents & M. Beier (Eds.), *Children, childhoods and global politics* (pp. 193–209). Bristol University Press.

Horschelmann, K. (2016). Crossing points: Contesting militarism in the spaces of children's everyday lives in Britain and Germany. In M. C. Benwell & P. Hopkins (Eds.), *Children, young people and critical geopolitics* (pp. 29–43). Newcastle University Press.

Hynd, S. (2021). Trauma, violence, and memory in African child soldier memoirs. *Culture, Medicine, and Psychiatry*, *45*(1), 74–96.

James, A., & James, A. L. (2004). *Constructing childhood*. Palgrave.

Kravtsov, Y. (2022). *Diary. War diaries exhibit*. Amsterdam. https://wardiariesukraine.org/yehor_ua/

Lear, J. (2006). *Radical hope: Ethics in the face of cultural devastation*. Harvard University Press.

Lee-Koo, K. (2017). Children, conflict, and global governance. In A. Burke & R. Parker (Eds.), *Global insecurity* (pp. 159–174). Palgrave Macmillan.

Linklater, R. (2020). *Decolonizing trauma work: Indigenous stories and strategies*. Fernwood Publishing.

Macksoud, M. S., Dyregrov, A., & Raundalen, M. (1993). Traumatic war experiences and their effects on children. In J. P. Wilson & B. Raphael (Eds.), *International handbook of traumatic stress syndromes* (pp. 625–633). Springer US. https://doi.org/10.1007/978-1-4615-2820-3_52

Macmillan, L. (2015). Children, civilianhood, and humanitarian securitization. *Critical Studies on Security*, *3*(1), 62–76.

Marah. (2014). My Syrian diary. *Syria Deeply*.

Masten, A. S. (2001). Ordinary magic: Resilience processes in development. *American Psychologist*, *56*(3), 227–238.

Masten, A. S., Narayan, A. J., Silverman, W. K., & Osofsky, J. D. (2015). Children in war and disaster. *Handbook of Child Psychology and Developmental Science*, *4*, 1–42.

McGarry, R., & Walklate, S. (2019). *A criminology of war?* Policy Press.

Ministry of Foreign Affairs of Ukraine. (2023). *Statement at the UN general assembly meeting on the situation in the temporarily occupied territories of Ukraine*. https://mfa.gov.ua/en/news/statement-minister-foreign-affairs-ukraine-dmytro-kuleba-un-general-assembly-meeting-situation-temporarily-occupied-territories-ukraine

Nasie, M., & Bar-Tal, D. (2012). Sociopsychological infrastructure of an intractable conflict through the eyes of Palestinian children and adolescents. *Peace and Conflict: Journal of Peace Psychology*, *18*(1), 3.

Natanel, K. (2016). Border collapse and boundary maintenance: Militarisation and the microgeographies of violence in Israel–Palestine. *Gender, Place & Culture*, *23*(6), 897–911.

Pearlman, W. (2016). Narratives of fear in Syria. *Perspectives on Politics, 14*(1), 21–37. https://doi.org/10.1017/S1537592715003205

Peri, A. (2017). *The war within: Diaries from the Siege of Leningrad.* Harvard University Press.

Pervunina, A. (2022). *Diary. War diaries exhibit.* Amsterdam. https://wardiariesukraine.org/arina_ua/

President of Ukraine Volodymyr Zelensky. (2023, June 31) *Speech at "UA: War. Unsung Lullaby" conference on international children's day.* https://www.president.gov.ua/en/news/usi-462-dobi-mi-byemosya-za-nashe-majbutnye-znachit-za-nashi-83269

Prout, A., & Alison, J. (Eds.) (2015). *Constructing and reconstructing childhoods.* Routledge.

Rawick, M. (2018). *El diario de Myriam* (Spanish ed.). AbeBooks.

Riger, S., & Sigurvinsdottir, R. (2016). Thematic analysis. In L. A. Jason & D. S. Glenwick (Eds.), *Handbook of methodological approaches to community-based research: Qualitative, quantitative, and mixed methods* (pp. 33–41). Oxford University Press.

Rosen, M. D. (2005). *Armies of the young: Child soldiers in war and terrorism.* Rutgers University Press.

Rosen, M. D. (2015). *Child soldiers in the Western imagination: From patriots to victims.* Rutgers University Press.

Shaw, J. A. (2003). Children exposed to war/terrorism. *Clinical Child and Family Psychology Review, 6*(4), 237–246. https://doi.org/10.1023/B:CCFP.0000006291.10180.bd

Shaw, M. (2015). *War and genocide: Organized killing in modern society.* John Wiley & Sons.

Skalietskaa, Y. (2023). *You don't know what war is.* Union Square & Co.

Slone, M., & Mann, S. (2016). Effects of war, terrorism and armed conflict on young children: A systematic review. *Child Psychiatry & Human Development, 47*(6), 950–965. https://doi.org/10.1007/s10578-016-0626-7

TearFund. (2015). *The journey of a refugee: Amira's story.* TearFund.

TearFund. (2024). *About us.* Tearfund. https://www.tearfund.org/about-us

Tyner, J., & Henkin, S. (2015). Feminist geopolitics, everyday death, and the emotional geographies of Dang Thuy Tram. *Gender, Place & Culture, 22*(2), 288–303.

Urman, M. L., Funk, J. B., & Elliott, R. (2001). Children's experiences of traumatic events: The negotiation of normalcy and difference. *Clinical Child Psychology and Psychiatry, 6*(3), 403–424. https://doi.org/10.1177/1359104501006003009

Wagnsson, C., Hellman, M. A., & Holmberg, A. (2010). The centrality of non-traditional groups for security in the globalized era: The case of children. *International Political Sociology, 4*(1), 1–14.

Wahlstrom, R. L. (2012). Be here now: Young women's war diaries and the practice of intentionality. *The English Journal, 102*(2), 44–50.

Woodward, R. (2007). Narratives of destruction and survival: Writing and reading about life in urban war zones. *Theory & Event, 10*(3), 1–14.

CHAPTER 4

CHILDREN AND YOUTH ART AS A FORM OF RESISTANCE IN CONFLICT ZONES

Raghu Yadav and Rose Williamson

Ohio University, USA

ABSTRACT

Sites of armed conflict produce significant human suffering. Children are some of the most tragic victims of these conflicts, and their suffering is often used as a colloquial measure of suffering at large. Children in conflict zones are likely to experience trauma and associated negative mental and physical health consequences such as post-traumatic stress disorder (PTSD). One way that children and youth cope with their circumstances in these environments is through creative outlets such as art and poetry. Not only does trauma influence the content of children's art, but the creation of art also influences children's responses to trauma and conflict. Furthermore, in the same way that children may humanize those living in conflict zones, so too does their art. While the art of children typically lacks the sophistication of high art or classic poetry, there is a genuineness to their work that resonates with others and allows them to see the conflict through a child's eyes. This chapter covers the relationships between armed conflict, trauma, and children, followed by art as a form of resistance generally, then finally the role of art and poetry as a form of children's resistance.

Keywords: Armed conflict zones; children and youth; art and poetry; resistance; trauma; healing; resilience

Art is our weapon. Culture is a form of resistance. (Shirin Neshat, 2011)

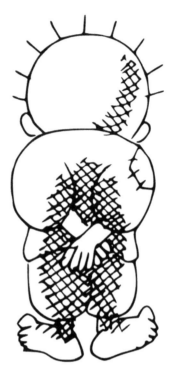

Fig. 4.1. Handala. *Source*: Naji al-Ali, Wiki Creative Commons (n.d.).

Do you know what this is about?

No, I don't. What's it about?

Well, it's about Handala. Handala is a 10-year-old boy.

Okay, but why he is hiding his face?

He is not hiding his face, he is turning his back to "outside solutions".

Outside solutions to what?

Solutions to the Israel-Palestine conflict. Handala was forced to leave his home at the age of 10, when the state of Israel was created in 1948.

So, you are showing me an old cartoon?

It's old, but it's new as well.

But Handala should be very old by now. Right?

Not really. He doesn't grow old.

How is that even possible?

Well, believe it or not, Handala defies the laws of nature. He is suspended in time. Only when he returns to his home will he start growing again.

But that's just crazy.

Source: Raghu Yadav

INTRODUCTION

Throughout human history, across nations and societies, armed conflict zones have witnessed immense human suffering. Children and youth are perhaps the most tragic victims of these conflicts. Their age makes them particularly vulnerable to trauma that may leave long-lasting effects and compromise their physical and psychological well-being. For example, rates of PTSD among children in Palestine have been shown to range from 30% to 70% (Dimitry, 2012), which mirror findings from children in other active combat zones. Handala has become a symbol for many of these children (Shahad, 2008).

Moreover, children, being especially susceptible to violence, can be victimized by both sides of conflicts – in Syria, both Bashar al-Asad's party and the rebels used children as a means to achieve their political ends (al-Natour, 2012). Female children are at a higher risk for other forms of trauma and downstream consequences as well (Chen & Gueta, 2016). For example, in the Syrian revolution, many young girls/women were subjected to sexual assault (sometimes referred to as "sex jihad") by the Syrian security forces; even when parents married their daughters off to save them from assault, those child marriages led to exploitation of girls by their husbands (al-Natour, 2012).

Sites of armed conflict are characterized by violence, chaos, uncertainty, and other negative conditions. Yet at the same time, amid death and destruction, signs of life and creativity emerge in these sites imbued with compassion, humanity, resilience, and striving. The artistic expressions of children and youth capture these experiences in their purest forms.

This chapter provides an overview of the relationships between armed conflict, trauma, and art followed by a discussion of how children's art can be a form of resistance in conflict zones. It also explores various useful functions art can serve in response to the negative conditions of armed conflict. We will illustrate these points from a broad social, psychological, and philosophical perspective. Lastly, we provide suggestions as to how the power of art can be harnessed to relieve suffering in children and youth.

ARMED CONFLICT AND TRAUMA

Armed conflict has a direct relationship with trauma. The Geneva Convention specifies two forms of armed conflict, international and non-international. International armed conflict occurs between two states. This is seen in traditional warfare between at least two states, such as World War II. Non-international armed conflict occurs between a state and an armed group, or between armed groups within a state. Most armed conflicts fall under this category.

Broadly defined, trauma is an emotional response to extremely distressing events that can be acute, chronic, or complex in nature. Acute trauma can arise from singular events such as natural disasters, whereas chronic trauma develops from repeated and prolonged exposure to distressing events. Finally, complex trauma develops in response to the experience of multiple, varied traumatic events. Armed conflict can produce circumstances where any or all forms of trauma may arise.

People, including children, who live in combat zones may not only experience acute threats to their safety, but lasting psychological harm from the constant state of living in fear and uncertainty or witnessing the suffering of others. For example, a single bombing may be an acute traumatic event. However, living under a bombing campaign would be a source of chronic trauma for both the threat to one's own life as well as through regularly witnessing the aftermath and worsening circumstances (Fasfous et al., 2013).

The consequences of experiencing trauma can be lifelong. While the quintessential consequence of experiencing trauma is often characterized as PTSD, it is certainly not the only negative consequence. Trauma can negatively impact physical health, mental health, and one's relationships with others in ways that are both immediate and across the lifespan (Sowder et al., 2018). While people typically associate trauma and its consequences such as PTSD with combatants returning from war, the impacts of armed conflict are much farther-reaching. Parents lose children, children become orphaned, and families lose their homes or ways of life. In Gaza's hospitals, some children are marked WCNSF: Wounded Child, No Surviving Family (Haidar, 2023). This label is given to children who are the only remaining members of their family. Armed conflict produces trauma through both explicit danger and destabilization on a broad scale.

Trauma and Children

Children and youth may experience trauma from many sources, both during and outside of armed conflict (Fasfous et al., 2013). The impacts of trauma on children are myriad and have been the subject of considerable research. Traumatized children, like adults, can experience the consequences of trauma in the form of mental and physical health conditions such as PTSD and a higher likelihood of developing chronic illnesses (Chang et al., 2019). However, unlike adults, children may have a diminished capacity to understand why they are experiencing trauma. They process these experiences through a different lens (King et al., 2015). A child may have a harder time than an adult understanding why someone could find the death of their family member justifiable for the attainment of geopolitical goals.

Armed conflict is not only a source of trauma through direct exposure to danger but also can indirectly produce many of the adverse childhood experiences (ACEs) known to be prerequisites to developing later mental and physical health problems, as well as increased susceptibility to being further traumatized through increasing other risk factors (Chang et al., 2019). These ACEs include, but are not limited to, witnessing, or experiencing violence or neglect, parental mental health problems or substance usage, and separation from parents or other family members. Risk factors include poverty, stress, social disorder, limited resources and educational/economic opportunities, food insecurity, housing instability, and a lack of community activities for youth. The threat and destabilization that are produced by armed conflict both produce and facilitate trauma.

Resistance to Armed Conflict and Trauma

Resistance to armed conflict and the trauma it produces has taken many forms throughout history. This resistance may be in the form of protests that can range anywhere from boycotts and marches to riots or even self-immolation, such as the famous example of Thích Quảng Đức in 1963 whose act protested the prosecution of Buddhists in South Vietnam, or the more recent example of Aaron Bushnell protesting in favor of Palestinian liberation. However, this kind of direct action as resistance is not the only form of resistance. This chapter will focus on creative outlets as resistance, namely, art and poetry. More specifically, the art and poetry of children and youth; people for whom direct action such as marching may not always be practical or ethical.

RESISTANCE IN THE FORM OF ART AND POETRY

Functions of Art

The origins and purposes of art in human history come from many perspectives. Some consider art as an extension of skills that can be seen in other non-human animals. Others consider art to be specific to humanity, much like reason. Prehistoric art has been recorded dating back to 50,000 BC. The influence of art and culture is bidirectional and has been for as long as people have been making art. Art is shaped by existing cultural practices, while also shaping those practices in response. Evolutionary psychologists propose that humans developed the capacity to create art for mate selection or social and cognitive development, thus making art an adaptation. However, this approach is not without its pitfalls and criticism – primarily, that many evolutionary psychological claims in this area are not supported by empirical evidence (Seghers, 2015).

For many, the debate over the origins and purposes of art is solved by accepting art simply as a means of entertainment. The value of art as entertainment versus something more, and to the degree that those forms are distinguishable, is a topic of debate (Chaudhry, 2022; Hamilton, 2023). This chapter takes the perspective of art as a tool for resistance and well-being. We talk about the usefulness of art in many ways throughout this chapter; these illustrate how art can be much more than a means of entertainment. Below are some important functions of art that are especially relevant to conflict zones, which will be referenced throughout this chapter.

- Responding to a situation of helplessness.
- Giving voice to the voiceless.

- A site of resistance.
- Bringing comfort to the suffering.
- A meaningful form of engagement for passing the time and overcoming despondence.
- Uniting people for a common cause.
- Achieving solidarity with the outside world.
- Dealing with trauma.
- Promoting healing, and improved physical and psychological well-being.
- Providing ways to imagine and build a new world.
- Regenerative power to transcend limitations of perspectives.
- Shaping reality.
- Recording life and society in ways that other forms of history cannot.

The relevance of art becomes especially important in the context of war and conflict. War and conflict create a backdrop of predominantly negative experiences (chaos, fear, and uncertainty). Art can provide powerful ways to respond to such situations. Art serves as a vehicle for resistance that can both unite and empower those resisting. Indeed, even under the most disheartening circumstances, art can be an avenue for freely expressing one's thoughts and imagination.

Regenerative Power of Art

It is worth noting that, in many cases, the techniques and processes of art go beyond mere depiction of reality or ideas and become a wellspring of (re)generating ideas and perspectives. One of the ways in which the regenerative power of art can be seen is through transmediation. Transmediation involves transforming creative expression from one medium to another. To be precise, "The process of transmediation involves taking the meaning that is symbolically expressed in one sign system and moving it to some other sign system" (Leland & Bangert, 2019). For example, reading a poem and expressing it as a painting or dance afterward, or reading prose and acting it out as a drama. Transmediation does not only have the capacity to generate ideas, but it also enables one to see multiplicity of views, voices, and perspectives. This facilitates going beyond any one right or wrong answer to a problem or situation.

Transmediation has been said to be useful in reflective thinking as the person engaged in transmediation is compelled to make connections between two different sign systems (Siegel, 1995). This may provide a sense of regeneration and expand the horizon of meaning. This applies to art in every form. In language, for example, poetry may expand meaning beyond the more creatively limited forms of non-fiction text or more strictly prosaic writing. Poetry is a dense, concise, and creative means of communicating ideas.

Prose tells, poetry shows – often leaving interpretation up to the reader. It has many forms, styles, and conventions which demand both critical and creative thinking, as well as a firm grasp of language. The same emotion communicated through a paragraph in a novel might be captured through a clever line break to imply a double meaning in a poem. In this sense, poetry parallels visual art in that much of what it depicts is often steeped in metaphor and intention that is implied by its form, often providing few easy answers to the questions it evokes. This is true for other forms of creative expression such as dance or music, which may also evoke multiple interpretations.

In addition, artwork being subject to different interpretations can also lead to the use of old artworks in new contexts and with new meanings. This is why ancient artworks and narrative themes seem to resurface time and again. For example, Shakespeare's Macbeth recontextualized in the Bollywood movie *Maqbool* (Bhardwaj, 2004), the image of Icarus from Greek mythology invoked in the Hollywood movie *Birdman* (Iñárritu, 2014), or the story of Proteus and Prometheus in the A24 film *The Lighthouse* (Eggers, 2019). These timeless and perpetually relevant stories have been captured on film, in prose, and in art. In this way, creative expression can serve symbolic ends across generations and societies, including as a means of resistance.

Leland and Bangert (2019) used transmediation to investigate prospective teachers' responses to reading censorship-related articles. Some of the main observations in their study were (1) expression of art entailed a sociopolitical stance and, therefore, may be a conduit to subtle transition from thought to action. (2) The artistic responses revealed certain aspects of the person's identity and/or their thought process. For example, when a participant's response expressed fear and/or confusion, this was coded as a teacher dilemma. Depicting communities standing against censorship reflected a prospective teacher as a "community person." (3) Artistic responses can shed light on the evolving identities of the participants. Engaging in art can be helpful in bringing clarity to one's views and thereby help overcome a state of ambivalence. This is exemplified by how two of the prospective teachers began with defending book censorship but ultimately ended up taking a critical stance. (4) Artistic responses are not neutral and, in the case of this study, reflect that teaching is not neutral either. Rather, they are indicative of and champion-specific beliefs and actions. Artistic expressions that challenged censorship were coded as reflective of resistance. Such examples are clear examples of art being a means of resistance. To critically evaluate a situation may itself be an act of resistance.

As an example, one prospective teacher created a painting titled *Keep an Open Mind* in response to reading articles on censorship of children's books after being asked to express their views using transmediation (Leland & Bangert, 2019). The artist represented their perspective by depicting ideas flowing in and out of a person's head. One interpretation of this painting suggests a state of flux in the human mind. Alternatively, one could reasonably perceive their transmediation exercise to represent the free flow of ideas, rather than an explicit rebuke of censorship. Thus, for an artwork to be critical and act as a site of resistance, it does not have to be (very) explicit in its social or political insinuations. The mere depiction may be a site of resistance.

Art and Poetry as Resistance

Art is not a mirror held up to reality but a hammer with which to shape it. (Bertolt Brecht, 1964)[1]

People often picture resistance in the form of direct action through efforts such as protests; however, direct action is not the only way through which people resist. Just as Naji al-Ali created Handala (Shahad, 2008), many others have used creative expression in the form of art or poetry to signal their resistance (see Fig. 4.1). Some of our most beloved art, both classic and contemporary, was created for this purpose.

According to many thinkers, art has an inherent quality of being critical, transformative, and non-conforming, along with possessing the capacity to make people identify with emotional content. In being critical, non-conforming, and transformative art itself acts as a form of resistance (Singh, 2021). Likewise, because of these features, art is considered by many to be inherently political in nature. For example, when the American filmmaker Francis Ford Coppola introduced his film *Apocalypse Now* at the Cannes Film Festival, he said, "My film is not about Vietnam. It is Vietnam." (Bahr et al., 1991; Coppola, 1979) Like the film, this quote exemplifies a critical perspective of the American intervention in Vietnam. Consider German filmmaker Wim Wenders' statement, "Every film is political. Most political of all are those that pretend not to be: 'entertainment' movies. They are the most political films there are because they dismiss the possibility of change. In every frame, they tell you everything's fine the way it is. They are a continual advertisement for things as they are" (Wenders, 1992).

Thus, it is not difficult to understand why art featuring political content often challenges existing power structures and the status quo. This in turn can mobilize people, change perceptions, and shift popular opinion. Because of this, time and again, history has witnessed authoritarian regimes ban art, imprison artists, and sometimes even deport or execute them. For instance, many Iranian artists like Shirin Neshat and Mohsen Makhmalbaf are living in exile. Award-winning filmmakers like Jafar Panahi have been imprisoned due to their critical views of the government ("Jafar Panahi," 2023).

The work of UK street artist Banksy is a contemporary example of art as resistance. Despite engaging in political protest through street art since the 1990s, Banksy's identity remains unconfirmed. His poignant images often feature role reversals that satirize those whom he is criticizing or are more deliberate displays of resistance as seen in his piece *No Trespassing* which depicts a Native American man holding a sign displaying the words "no trespassing" (Banksy, 2010). Despite the illegal nature of his work, it has grown a large following and has been showcased in museums. In one especially notable display, a print of *Girl with Balloon*, one of his most famous pieces, began unexpectedly shredding itself the moment after selling at auction for 1.4 million dollars (Pruitt-Young, 2021).

Similarly, the long history of art as resistance can be seen in classical works such as Eugène Delacroix's (1830) masterpiece *Liberty Leading the People*. This painting depicts the French figure Marianne as the personification of liberty, carrying a bayonetted rifle in one hand and the French flag in the other, leading men to victory during the July Revolution of 1830. In a letter to his brother, while working on the piece, Delacroix wrote, "[...] if I haven't fought for my country at least I'll paint for her."

Poets as well have long written about war and conflict. Two famous examples are John McCrae's In Flanders Fields and Wilfred Owen's Dulce et Decorum Est (McCrae, 1995; Owen, 1920). The former is a memoir of the dead, a reminder of the fleeting nature of life and to carry on for those who made the ultimate sacrifice, "Take up our quarrel with the foe:/To you from failing hands we throw/The torch; be yours to hold it high." The latter, a scathing criticism of war's glorification, "Come gargling from the froth-corrupted lungs,/Obscene as cancer, bitter as the cud/Of vile, incurable sores on innocent tongues, —/My friend, you would not tell with such high zest/To children ardent for some desperate glory,/The old Lie: *Dulce et decorum est/Pro patria mori.*"

The Age of Internet and Social Media

With technological advancement and the proliferation of internet access, art in many forms has been made accessible by and for general society. Instruction for learning technical skills, as well as the capacity for rapid dissemination of work, has been made affordable and accessible in ways previously available to only those with considerable resources. In other words, a democratization of the discipline of art has taken place. Given the more democratic atmosphere of the world in general, today's children and youth may be quick to artistically register their voices when they feel or experience something wrong in society. They may not be practicing high art, but they are often able to strike a chord with and capture the imagination of the people (Scheibe, 2020). Be it Greta Thunberg's call for climate justice or young peoples' responses to the circumstances of George Floyd's passing, pleas for social justice through social media posts, blogs, YouTube, TikTok videos, and similar means have increasingly become a means to protest, rally support, and call for action (Scheibe, 2020).

Furthermore, broad access to the internet has allowed global insight into the experiences of children and youth in armed conflict zones that previously would have only been accessible through news reports. This can be evidenced by the abundance of footage coming out of places like Gaza, even after attempts to cut off electricity and communication have been made (Al-Shalchi, 2024). People, including children and youth, can share their experiences and creative activities quickly and broadly in ways not previously seen. Often, mere recording of incidents can be immensely useful. During the anti-CAA (Citizenship Amendment Act) protest in India in 2019, there were many incidents of police brutality (Voice of America, 2019). Many pictures and videos recorded on cell phones erupted on social media (*Indian Police Beating Up Students*, 2019). Such videos revealed the situation to Indian society as well as to the outer world.

Unfortunately, violence often goes unrecorded. Even when recorded, it may sometimes lead to potential negative consequences. For example, there have been many instances where social media posts have led to the arrest and imprisonment of youth; among numerous such arrests throughout India, many Kashmiri youths, including some journalists, were arrested under a draconian Indian law called UAPA which gives sweeping powers to the state authority to arrest individuals on suspicion of terrorist activities ("Kashmir Journalist Arrested," 2022; Kuchay, 2020; Patel, n.d.; Zargar, 2020). Similarly, a young couple in Iran was arrested and sentenced to prison for posting a video of them dancing on social media (Reals & Wassef, 2023). In another case, a couple was arrested for posting romantic and parkour stunt images and videos on social media (Malekian, 2020). As recently as March 11, 2024, two women have been arrested for playing fictional folk characters and dancing in the streets which was deemed as defiance of social norms according to authorities (Tayebi, 2024).

CHILDREN'S ART AND POETRY AS A FORM OF RESISTANCE

"In all forms of art, part of you is in the trauma, and part of you is a step away from it".
—Maya Angelou (Moran & Shoop, 2002)

ART AS A SITE OF RESISTANCE FOR CHILDREN

Ordinary acts or expressions can become extraordinary tools to protest, cope with suffering, and come to terms with reality. As an example, during the Syrian revolution of 2011, children would create and share political cartoons on social media (al-Natour, 2012). One image of this nature portrayed Syrian children as an opposing force to Bashar al-Assad using the game *Angry Birds* as a motif (Iisalo, 2009). In the image, Syrian children were paralleled with Palestinian children who are sometimes referred to as "the children of the stones" for resisting occupation by throwing stones at Israeli soldiers (al-Natour, 2012).

Importantly, for an act to be an act of resistance, it does not necessarily have to be confrontational. According to Walker (2015) in a study on Sri Lankan women who lost loved ones in ethnic conflict, claiming normality through simple acts like tree planting ceremonies becomes an act of resistance. Sometimes, articulating simple narratives of things happening in the present or the past helps in making meaning of fears and loss (Kohli & Mather, 2003). These embraces of normality can also act as sites of resistance for children, as will be showcased later in this chapter.

ART AND CHILDREN AS HUMANIZING FORCES

Providing a Voice to the Voiceless

Art has long been a method of capturing what is difficult to put into words. A striking image can be rapidly disseminated to thousands of people, capturing emotional responses in a much more immediate, automatic way than other forms of communication. Kevin Carter's 1993 photograph *The Vulture and the Little Girl* is one such example. It depicts a young child who collapsed on the half-mile journey to a UN feeding center in Sudan while a vulture waited a few feet behind. The publication of this image led to a frenzy of donations to organizations fighting hunger in Sudan. While the child is reported to have survived, Carter took his own life four months after being awarded a Pulitzer Prize for the photograph. This example illustrates the powerful impact of both art and the suffering of children as a means of evoking empathy and action.

As some of the most vulnerable members of society, children's suffering often becomes the measure of suffering in society. Those outside of conflict zones can connect with their suffering and empathize with them to a degree that may come less easily for adults in conflict zones because there is an understanding that children are inherently defenseless and innocent. Indeed, conflicts are often characterized by the number of children (along with women, who are not traditionally combatants in many societies) who have perished. By sharing their perspectives and stories, children help the world to understand and empathize with the suffering of their people. Then, in turn, the world may take necessary actions toward ending the conflict.

This is especially impactful for audiences in the global West, who have historically embraced the "romantic model" of childhood. That is, an idealized version of childhood where children do not have to engage in things like child labor (Antic, 2022). In response, children and their experiences are often highly politicized. While highly motivational in fostering action, this manner of thinking can lead to an underestimation of the complexity of children's thoughts and experiences.

Children's creative expression may lack the sophistication of high art, but the simplicity, honesty, and sincerity of their work highlight the experience of living in armed conflict zones in a unique way that cannot be captured elsewhere. The Ukrainian artist Nataliia Pavliuk put it succinctly when commenting on children's artwork in war-affected Ukraine, "To some, it's just 'scribble'. But to us, these are the most sincere and finest works of art" (Jacobs, 2023). Furthermore, while children can and do lie, they struggle with the necessary skills to maintain convincing and complex deception, particularly if they are very young (Lee, 2013).

People likely empathize with the confusion and fear that children must feel, which may be especially apparent in their artwork that possesses an inherent genuineness. This is why their creative works can elicit empathy and solidarity from the global community. Moreover, by expressing their views and stories through art, they invoke the concept of "the moral third"; that they are not different from other human beings, they wish for a normal life just as other people in other places do; and like all humans, they deserve the same dignity (Clacherty, 2021; Haker, 2023).

HOW TRAUMA INFLUENCES CHILDREN'S ART

When children experience trauma, this can make it difficult to communicate with others verbally or emotionally (Desmond et al., 2015). Creative expression is one method of communication that may help children process their feelings and engage with others regarding those feelings. Research has shown that having children engage in drawing is an effective means of understanding their perspectives and experiences, particularly when it comes to topics that are difficult or taboo (Søndergaard & Reventlow, 2019).

Children's fears and concerns often influence their artwork. For example, several children studied during the COVID-19 pandemic were shown to express their fears by drawing images that included pictures of large COVID-19 cells surrounding the air outside of their homes. These images were coupled with statements about believing they would become ill if they went outside, as well as sentiments of loneliness and isolation (Abdulah et al., 2021). In another study, children's drawings predicted migraine (vs nonmigraine) headache diagnoses 90% of the time, with similar predictive value when assessing migraine improvement through serial drawings (Stafstrom et al., 2005). Along similar if more extreme lines, drawings made by Jewish children at the Terezín concentration camp during the holocaust reflect themes such as claustrophobia, food, fragility, and dehumanization (Grossman, 1989).

HOW CREATIVE EXERCISES INFLUENCE RESPONSES TO TRAUMA IN CHILDREN

The Power of Expression

Sites of armed conflict impede the normal functioning of human life, even more so for children and youth who have less control over their circumstances. In the backdrop of chaos, violence, and destruction, the usual opportunities that are afforded to children for entertainment, comfort, safety, or education may be rendered unavailable. For example, schools may be closed or destroyed, playgrounds can become inaccessible, and children may be subject to displacement. All of these are classified as risk factors for later trauma-associated mental and physical health problems (Chang et al., 2019). Children thrive in environments of security, stability, and routine. The loss of normalcy that arises from armed conflict can overwhelm them emotionally and physically (Fasfous et al., 2013).

Critically, in such dire circumstances, any living being may face learned helplessness which can strip them of motivation, hope, and aspiration. Learned helplessness occurs when those who experience repeated stressors begin to believe that there is nothing they can do, and thus stop trying, even when opportunities for change arise (Seligman, 1972). Nevertheless, despite these harrowing circumstances, art can act as a powerful tool to save them from helplessness. Through the power of expression, people can process and communicate their emotions, pain, and suffering, as well as their hopes, dreams, and aspirations. Indeed, engaging with others through art may foster a phenomenon referred to as "learned helpfulness" – where undertaking altruistic acts fosters a sense of control and purpose (Bosqui & Marshoud, 2018). Learned helpfulness is at least moderately effective in promoting well-being in youth exposed to war and armed conflict. Thus, in some ways, artistic expressions may become a home for the homeless, a voice of the voiceless, and a hope for the hopeless.

Transmediation and Overcoming the Barriers of Language

As mentioned earlier, transmediation is the process of taking meaning and ideas from one domain of symbols and signs (e.g., literary source) and expressing them into another domain or sign system (e.g., a painting) (Leland & Bangert, 2019). In this process, one can use any of the various forms of expression such as painting, drama, music, and poetry.

It is sometimes the case that children or youth who have experienced trauma and who suffer from PTSD develop disabilities or impairments in their communication (Armsworth & Holaday, 1993). In such situations, transmediation may especially be helpful in overcoming the language barrier and allowing children to communicate emotions and ideas in a way that is safe and comfortable for them; art has been shown as an effective means of fostering children's communication on emotionally challenging topics (Søndergaard & Reventlow, 2019).

I Never Saw Another Butterfly

Even when art is created to reflect pain and suffering, it may still be restorative of an individual's well-being. By venting emotional experiences through art, one may bring forth calmness and clarity. In many ways, art provides a means to confront the future. In addition, art may record aspects of reality that otherwise may go unheard. One example of art helping to confront the present can be seen in art created by Jewish children at Terezín concentration camp during World War II. *I Never Saw Another Butterfly* is a collection of art by Jewish children and youth while they were detained in concentration camps during the Second World War (Volavkova, 1993). It is a record of great importance. Consider the ending stanza from the poem *Homesick* by an unknown author from this collection, "Yet we all hope the time will come/ When we'll go home again./Now I know how dear it is/And often I remember it."

In this poem, we can see the same longing for home that Naji al-Ali expressed through the character of Handala. When people see that the suffering, dreams, and aspirations of displaced people are similar across cultures, times, and locations, they may better experience sympathy and empathy for those people. Thus, telling stories and expressing perspectives can lead people to overcome their tendency toward tribalism and begin to soften the divides between in-groups and out-groups. They may be better able to see that the so-called others are not really others but are instead part of the same human family.

Healing and Well-being: Reconciliation with the Past

While the importance of art as a form of resistance cannot be overstated, it is worth noting that artistic activities can act as a therapeutic means to deal with stress and trauma and thereby may result in healing. It is a generally accepted idea supported by psychological research that engaging in artistic activities can provide an emotional outlet and help mitigate the emotional damage of trauma (Zhang et al., 2023). It is a safe and constructive outlet for the release of pain and anger that may enable people to find solace and hope amid adversity. This is exemplified by the discipline of art therapy, which began in the early 1940s and has steadily grown in popularity (Junge, 2016).

Moreover, art is a means of fostering a sense of purpose that may empower children to regain a degree of control over their lives and emotions. In one study, children in Nigeria who had experienced kidnapping and later developed PTSD showed improvement in their symptoms after engaging in creative expression for therapy, whether that be art, music, or poetry. However, art was the most effective (Zhang et al., 2023). Creative activities may also enable children to connect with their cultural heritage and to the wider community of people who aspire to make a safe and peaceful world to live in.

It also must be noted that engagement in art does not always occur in clinical or therapeutic settings. Armed conflict zones do not always have the resources to provide therapy. However, limited resources available can be used for things like art and have proven to be helpful. For example, engaging in art projects in Syria helped children heal from their suffering (al-Natour, 2012). Engaging in ritualistic tree-planting ceremonies and grieving through these rituals and expressions was used by a non-profit group in Sri Lanka (Walker, 2015).

Handala

Handala, a simple cartoon of a child facing away from the viewer, is a foundational symbol of Palestine. The man who illustrated Handala, Naji al-Ali, first drew him in 1969 and it was in 1973 that Handala turned his back (Shahad, 2008). Handala was a way of representing his own experiences; his family was driven from their home in the Palestinian village of Al-Shajara to Lebanon when he was 10 years old. Naji was later assassinated on July 22, 1987. However, the character of Handala has lived on as a symbol of resistance for the Palestinian people, having been denied their right to return, for decades since.

As exemplified by Handala, art can be a way to reconcile with the past as well as provide a means of resistance. In addition to allowing Naji al-Ali to communicate his own experiences, Handala became a long-standing Palestinian symbol. By expressing his story and creating the character of Handala, he may have been making sense of his own suffering and trauma. Simultaneously, he also created a means through which countless others were able to do so.

Handala represents justice and its possible realization. From this perspective, justice will only be realized, and Handala will only grow old when the displaced people of Palestine are granted their right to return and a full restoration of their rights. His character provides a universal narrative to identify with for those who have been displaced due to conflicts and violence. Handala is a symbol of Palestine, but his story is one that may provide the solidarity of shared experiences to displaced people all over the world.

THEMES OF CHILDREN'S ART FROM ARMED CONFLICT ZONES

Promoting Resilience and Empowerment: Hope for the Future

Art and poetry may empower children to envision a better future for themselves and others. This is often reflected in art works of children and youth that depict ideas of dignity, strength, peace, and unity. Furthermore, engagement in artistic activities facilitates learning and developing skills that may help children to efficiently deal with their practical environment, as well as to become better citizens down the line and improve circumstances for future generations.

Art may become a canvas for the expression of an imagined future. That imagined future may exemplify what kind of nation, what kind of political system, or what kind of society people want to create. Children and youth can be the agents of such necessary change. For instance, the role of children and youth was crucial in a series of revolutionary movements in the Middle East, in general, and in Syria, in particular. It is claimed that schoolchildren were the first to protest the regime of Bashar al-Assad by writing slogans and making graffiti on the school walls (Yazbek, 2012, as cited in al-Natour, 2012). Therefore, the Syrian revolution in 2011 began with children's protests. During this time children's art reflected their imagined world of equal rights and opportunities which was in sharp contrast with the imagined nation of the establishment. This was seen in the conflict as a struggle due to differently imagined nations by the two opposing forces: city dwellers (especially Damascus) who are close to the Assad regime and the Syrian security forces, and rural people who speak a different accent than the *Shami* accent used in Damascus (al-Natour, 2012).

Reimagining of a Better World: Raising the Level of Consciousness

War and conflict put human beings in a state of anxiety, fear, and survival. When it comes to children, survivors of trauma may often fall victim to various maladaptive coping strategies such as avoidance and substance abuse, which can have long-lasting influences on their lives (Choi et al., 2015; Wadsworth, 2015). States of anxiety and fear limit thinking to the immediate necessity of survival. In such situations, fear reinforces the thoughts and behaviors that have been helpful to that end (i.e., survival) and inhibits new ways of thinking. In other words, people may get imprisoned by a narrow, parochial mindset of survival and may be entrapped by vicious dichotomies like living versus dying, us versus them, flourishing or perishing, and so on.

The process of expression through art has inherent delays, in comparison with the instantaneous nature of speech. This allows the mind to engage in a deeper level of processing, which permits greater reflection on the content of one's expressions. This reflective quality, coupled with the feeling of safety that art may provide, may allow a person to think outside of the box and, thus, find improved solutions to life like greater peace, greater harmony, or greater human dignity.

This is one reason children and youth affected by conflicts sometimes create artworks reflective of peace, happiness, friendship, or similar positive themes. An example of this is Iranian filmmaker Mohsen Makhmalbaf's (1996) *A Moment of Innocence*. Makhmalbaf was influenced in his youth by the Islamist revolution and due to that influence he ended up stabbing a policeman. Many years later, in this semi-autobiographical film, he reimagined the same event with a message of peace. Breaking the vicious cycle of survival instincts and fear may take years, but art can facilitate the process.

Here, in some limited sense, art may function like a religion by contributing to the elements of transcendence and universalism. Religion is often considered to be a path to self-transcendence as it deals with higher realities. This may help in resolution of conflicts at tribal or sectional levels by bringing people together. One study found that making people think about God increased their pro-sociality toward outgroup (followers of other religions) members (Pasek et al., 2023).

Is it possible that art can have a similar effect of self-transcendence and pro-sociality that religion has? The German philosopher Friedrich Nietzsche talked about the possibility of art in a world without God and as a replacement of God (Pothen, 2000). Whether one believes in God or not, it is generally supported that art moves our emotions and can inspire us to experience transcendence of some sort. For example, in one study, exposure to photographic art induced self-transcendent emotions in the participants (Al-Kire et al., 2023).

The idea of self-transcendence is important here because it frees us from the limitedness of our vision. This idea is captured by the phrase, "The world that we have made as a result of the level of thinking we have done thus far creates problems that we cannot solve at the same level as the level we created them at," which has been attributed to Albert Einstein, one of the humanities most famous modern thinkers. Should this not imply that being at a higher level of consciousness may promote a greater possibility of resolution of lower-level conflicts, even if such resolution is only conceptual? At a minimum, art – with its sociological value – may contain the possibility of going beyond one's immediate self and, therefore, may result in the transcendence of our mundane and parochial existence leading to a greater likelihood of peace and conflict resolution (Writes, 2019).

When people become capable of reimagining a better world, they may also raise their awareness of the notion that a better world might require the resolution of lower-level conflicts. For example, raising one's level of consciousness from identification with a family, to identification with one's nation, to identification as a global citizen. These heightened levels of consciousness and belonging may foster a sense wherein antagonistic elements can be reimagined as part of the experience of community and be addressed through those new roles. As mentioned about the studies above, art is capable of inducing transcendence (Al-Kire et al., 2023), and transcendent ideas like God can result in pro-social behaviors (Pasek et al., 2023).

In the transmediation study discussed earlier, one subject drew an image that depicted community members standing together and smiling in support of the free flow of ideas without censorship (*Community Members Resisting Censorship*, Leland & Bangert, 2019). While many subjects rightly drew images expressing the conflict between people supporting and people opposing censorship, this image went a step further by reassigning the role of community members to emphasize the hope for convergence over divergence. This can be considered an example for the idea of a higher level of consciousness, one in which harmony has been emphasized instead of hostility.

APPLICATIONS IN THE REAL WORLD

Given the benefits and usefulness of art, it is important to teach art from an early age. Many thinkers have advocated and continue to advocate for art education to be an essential component of general education. To substantiate this point, in a systematic review, the authors have highlighted the importance of arts in education (Vazquez-Marin et al., 2023). According to the authors, the ultimate end of both positive psychology and sustainable human development is the well-being of the individual. In this endeavor, arts in positive education can help to build character strength, improve socioemotional competencies, and facilitate critical thinking – an important connector between character strength and competencies (Vazquez-Marin et al., 2023). Art and creative activity help develop critical thinking and generate fresh perspectives on the world. Intertwining creative expression with other forms of education helps one absorb knowledge in many domains.

Arrested Development

Conflicts and wars lead to trauma and suffering in children and youth. For example, PTSD is very common among refugee children (Dimitry, 2012; "Mental Health," n.d.; "The Healing Power," n.d.); such trauma may hinder the normal development of children and youth. While Handala is a symbol of resistance, given the interpretive and regenerative power of art, it is also symbolic of arrested development. A child (one among many Handalas) may fixate on the idea of returning home, a possibility that may never become available in their lifetime. This may hinder children's normal development.

Therefore, it is not just adequate to restore the physical security and well-being of children and youth affected by conflicts and wars, but it is equally important to restore their mental well-being. Art is very useful for this purpose from being a means to express pain and suffering to being a means of protesting for a better future, to ultimately coming to terms with life by integrating the past, present, and future elements of life.

Some Art Projects Around the World

When the multifaceted usefulness of art becomes apparent, its utilization as a powerful toolbox for change becomes obvious in turn. Accordingly, many art projects around the world have come into existence in the context of conflicts, wars, displacement, and other harsh conditions.

THE USA

One example is the Borgen Project (UK, 2019). Refugee children are at increased risk of PTSD, which in many cases is chronic in nature ("Mental Health," n.d.). While recognizing other needs of refugee children such as food, shelter, and vaccination, the Borgen Project (a non-profit organization working against global poverty) also focuses on the psychological healing of displaced children utilizing the power of art (UK, 2019). According to Joel Bergner, co-founder of

ARTOLUTION, the healing power of art should be used to save a whole generation of refugee children.

UKRAINE

The New York Times article *Tanks and Teddy Bears: Ukrainian Children Paint the War* depicts Ukrainian children's art in the backdrop of an ongoing conflict (Jacobs, 2023). These children's artworks were brought by the artist Nataliia Pavliuk from Ukraine to be exhibited in the Ukrainian Institute of Modern Art, located in the Ukrainian enclave in Chicago, IL, USA. These works were created by art students as well as children who were offered to engage in art therapy at social service centers. Interestingly, Pavliuk observed that many children painted images about war (tanks, soldiers, planes, etc.). However, the children who were most traumatized often made lighter images (flowers, sun, smiley faces, animals, etc.).

Many of these artworks were done in hospitals, orphanages, and art studios. To accomplish this, Pavliuk and her daughter took the basic requirements (paints, pastels, etc.) to these places and urged children to paint. As an example, one Ukrainian child who had been affected by the war painted a soldier carrying a child who was holding a teddy bear in front of an orange and black background which resembled fire and smoke. Many of these images were for sale under the title *Children of War* to continue this work (Jacobs, 2023).

SOUTH AFRICA

Many psychosocial support programs have used picture-story books for displaced and migrant children. One such instance where art has functioned as a form of resistance is an artbook project by the community counseling center Sophiatown Community Psychological Services' *Families on the Move Program* in Johannesburg, South Africa (Clacherty, 2021). A clinical psychologist directs this program, which is led by social workers and trained lay counselors. They provide individual and family-level counseling to adult clients. For children, they provide psychosocial support through holiday projects of which artbook-making has been a part since 2008.

Artbooks are mixed media forms of art that incorporate both visual and textual expression. Through artbooks, this project has collected stories of children affected by war and displacement. It aims to integrate the psychological well-being aspect of art with the general idea of empowering children who have been displaced and affected by war and conflicts. Through this, children express the internal and external aspects of their lives using simple narratives and imagery, which helps them engage in meaning-making during their otherwise chaotic lives.

As observed by the author (Clacherty, 2021), artbooks have helped these affected children to:

- process difficult or traumatic memories
- cope with the past

- face present injustices
- express feelings in a safe way
- foster and develop agency

Some of these books have been included in the African Storybook project which is a non-profit literacy initiative that facilitates educators and children to publish picture storybooks in various African languages (*African Storybook*, n.d.). Thus, not only have these artbooks helped children in coping, meaning-making, resisting, etc., but they have also served as an advocacy tool.

Cultural Differences

Culture and art are related. Some emphasize that the relationship is bidirectional, whereas others give more weight to culture as a prominent influence on art (Niu & Sternberg, 2001; Restoy et al., 2022; Shao et al., 2019). Religious-ideological frameworks, political systems, and the existing language of art often determine the boundaries of artwork that is being produced or will be produced. Consider, for instance, Islamic art in medieval times. Since depiction of human and animal figures was arguably prohibited in Islam, much of the religious art focused on calligraphy, ideas of symmetry, architecture, etc. It must be noted though that there are variations in Islamic art due to local cultures (e.g., Indonesia) as well (Firmanto & Yunani, 2022).

Similarly, in Western liberal societies, there is more freedom available to artists in terms of censorship regarding the form and content of their artwork. Accordingly, their forms of expression may differ significantly (e.g., distortions of religious or national symbols like burning the national flag). In armed conflict sites too, these influences are at play. For example, in a more liberal society, transformation of religious symbols and ideas may be more tolerable in art. Sometimes, even the burning religious texts have been used as a form of expression. In India, it is a frequent form of resistance by the Dalit community (the lower level in the Hindu caste hierarchy) to burn the Hindu religious text *Manu Smriti* or *The Laws of Manu* because this religious text allegedly sanctioned their exploitation ("Manusmriti Set on Fire," 2023). In comparison, the burning of a religious text may be unthinkable in more conservative societies as in some parts of the Islamic world ("Protests against Quran Burning," 2023).

Cultural Similarities

Yet, beneath the surface-level differences, there are deeper-level commonalities. This is likely to be so because the psychophysical makeup of humans is very similar across the world, and so is their environment. All humans are similar physically in that all humans share similar anatomy, and the Human Genome Project has revealed that they share about 99.9% of their genetic makeup (Collins & Mansoura, 2001). Moreover, the underlying cognitive processes are also the same (Nisbett & Norenzayan, 2002). This should not be surprising given common ancestry and shared forms of life in terms of practices that are not available to non-human animals such as rationality, intellectual pursuits, civilizational structures, and artifacts. This could be the reason why there are common elements and themes found in artworks everywhere. For example, the depiction of animals, dancing, and hunting is a common theme in primitive cave paintings whether in the Chauvet Cave in France or at the Bhimbetka rock shelters in India.

Not only are culture and human cognition related (Nisbett & Norenzayan, 2002), but all humans share similar facial expressions of emotions (Ekman, 1993). Moreover, some themes and values appear to be universal in human societies, e.g., love, compassion, jealousy, and so on. This may lead to commonalities of themes across cultures. American author Joseph Campbell analyzed storytelling across space, time, and culture where he identified universal themes and elements in hero stories.

Typical features of these hero stories are the seven common elements/themes found in the master narrative *The Hero's Journey*: protagonist, shift, quest, allies, challenge, transformation, and legacy (Campbell, 1949, as cited in Rogers et al., 2023). Such commonalities not only are a basis of cultural similarities but may be utilized as a potential intervention to make people's lives more meaningful. Rogers and colleagues used the storytelling process for narrative intervention in which people reframed their life stories as a hero's journey. The results of their study suggested that perception of a hero's journey in one's life can predict as well as cause an individual to experience an increased/enhanced sense of meaning in life (Rogers et al., 2023).

Likewise, art produced by children and youth in sites of armed conflict tends to portray some common elements like the depiction of horror, loved ones, and better times. Sometimes, it may be a literal depiction of things that are present at the sites of conflict. For example, whether from war-affected Ukraine or Gaza, children have drawn paintings of tanks, fighter planes, and soldiers (Damluji, 2011; Jacobs, 2023). In other places, children may draw houses, flowers, sunshine, or similar objects reminiscent of happy memories. Inanimate objects can be powerful and emotional expressions of children's feelings.

For example, like the Ukrainian child from before who included a teddy bear in their painting, one child from Gaza painted an image of trees weeping (Damluji, 2011; Jacobs, 2023). These paintings depict mundane objects through the perspectives of traumatized children, which may not have the same impact if created by an adult. Moreover, there are protagonists and antagonists relevant to conflict sites. For example, the Syrian President was depicted as an antagonistic character in the Syrian children's political cartoon mentioned earlier, whereas a Ukrainian soldier served as a protagonist in the Ukrainian child's painting described above. Numerous common themes are a testimony to the universality of human emotions and expressions.

"Art is Useless."

We have deliberately kept this subheading antithetical to the main idea of this chapter, as we intend to caution against exaggerated claims about the efficacy of art. There is no doubt that art has many positive functions apropos resistance, expression, communication, and mental well-being. Nevertheless, it is not a panacea to large-scale social–political and structural problems. At best, it can only supplement rather than supplant other necessary measures.

It is not just war or experiences of violence and displacement that affect individual well-being but post-conflict living conditions as well. For example, people who are displaced due to war may lack legal documents, leading to harassment from bureaucratic authorities and other disadvantages. For example, displacement due to war has made it difficult for migrants in South Africa to access health and education services (Clacherty, 2021). These later experiences compound with past trauma or may at least become significant stressors (Walker & Vearey, 2019).

In one study, researchers investigated post-traumatic stress and depression among youth in post-war Sierra Leone (Newnham et al., 2015). They found that daily stressors mediated the relationship between war exposure and psychological distress. Furthermore, daily stressors mediate the relationship between war exposure and post-traumatic symptoms (Miller & Rasmussen, 2010). Therefore, in addition to trauma-focused clinical approaches, this highlights the importance of psychosocial approaches to well-being. This implies improving the material conditions of life. Moreover, individualized trauma-focused clinical approaches may be costly, and human resources may not always be available. Psychosocial approaches may work more effectively at the community level.

Thus, art can never be a substitute for basic needs like food, shelter, security, etc. You cannot paint your way out of starvation. Abraham Maslow (1943) talked about the hierarchy of human needs in which physiological and safety needs come before anything else. Creative expression can serve many roles in Maslow's hierarchy, from connecting with others to self-actualization. However, it is difficult and, in some contexts, may be irrational to prioritize those needs over basic survival. It is within these cautionary boundaries we propose that art should be zealously supported, articulated, and advocated.

CONCLUSION

To conclude, the scope of children's art goes beyond mere artistic expression or entertainment. It serves as a form of resistance, provides a voice for the voiceless, empowers them to effectively deal with stress and trauma, and promotes healing. Through various social media platforms, technology has facilitated the democratization of art that can be used to express protest and mobilize opinions. And in conflict zones which generally have a lack of resources to afford clinical therapy, psychosocial support has proved to be a useful substitute. Therefore, it is important to recognize the importance of children's art and promote it within the overall framework of resistance, resilience, relief, and rehabilitation.

NOTE

1. This quote captures the semantic meaning intended by the authors and is commonly attributed to Bertolt Brecht, however this attribution is sometimes disputed. We have provided a reference to one of his works which expands upon the theme of the quote, as cited in Henry and Verica (2015).

ACKNOWLEDGMENTS

We would like to note that this chapter was a work of equal contribution between authors. Additionally, we would like to thank Dr. Tamanna Shah for her invaluable guidance through the writing process as well as our colleague Dr. Cameron Mackey for providing valuable insight. Finally, Raghu would like to dedicate his work on this chapter to Aparna.

REFERENCES

Abdulah, D. M., Abdulla, B. M. O., & Liamputtong, P. (2021). Psychological response of children to home confinement during COVID-19: A qualitative arts-based research. *International Journal of Social Psychiatry*, *67*(6), 761–769. https://doi.org/10.1177/0020764020972439

African Storybook. (n.d.). https://www.africanstorybook.org/

al-Ali, N. (n.d.). *Handala*. https://upload.wikimedia.org/wikipedia/en/f/f5/Handala.gif, CC BY-SA 4.0. https://commons.wikimedia.org/w/index.php?curid=139337731

Al-Kire, R. L., Callaway, K., Rowatt, W. C., & Schnitker, S. A. (2023). Original photographic art induces self-transcendent emotions. *Psychology of Aesthetics, Creativity, and the Arts*. Advanced online publication. https://doi.org/10.1037/aca0000610

al-Natour, M. (2012). Nation, gender, and identity: Children in the Syrian revolution 2011. *Journal of International Women's Studies*, *14*, 28–49.

Al-Shalchi, H. (2024, March 3). *Destruction from the war with Israel has cut Gaza off from the outside world*. NPR. https://www.npr.org/2024/03/03/1229402063/gaza-communications-cell-phone-internet-service-blackouts-paltel

Antic, A. (2022). Introduction: Politicizing children: Transcultural constructions of childhood and psychological trauma in the modern world. *Culture, Medicine, and Psychiatry*, *46*(3), 603–614. https://doi.org/10.1007/s11013-022-09805-1

Armsworth, M. W., & Holaday, M. (1993). The effects of psychological trauma on children and adolescents. *Journal of Counseling & Development*, *72*(1), 49–56. https://doi.org/10.1002/j.1556-6676.1993.tb02276.x

Bahr, F., Hickenlooper, G., & Coppolla, E. (Directors). (1991). *Hearts of darkness: A filmmaker's apocalypse* [Documentary]. Zoetrope Studios.

Banksy. (2010). *No trespassing* [Spray paint]. The Banksy Museum. https://museobanksy.es/wp-content/uploads/2023/02/prohibido-el-paso-museo-banksy-espana.jpg

Bhardwaj, V. (Director). (2004). *Maqbool* [Film]. Kaleidoscope Entertainment.

Bosqui, T. J., & Marshoud, B. (2018). Mechanisms of change for interventions aimed at improving the wellbeing, mental health and resilience of children and adolescents affected by war and armed conflict: A systematic review of reviews. *Conflict and Health*, *12*(1), 15. https://doi.org/10.1186/s13031-018-0153-1

Brecht, B. (1964). A short organum for the theatre. In J. Willet (Ed.), *Brecht on theatre: The development of an aesthetic* (pp. 179–205). Methuen.

Chang, X., Jiang, X., Mkandarwire, T., & Shen, M. (2019). Associations between adverse childhood experiences and health outcomes in adults aged 18–59 years. *PLOS One*, *14*(2), e0211850. https://doi.org/10.1371/journal.pone.0211850

Chaudhry, R. (2022, September 16). *Arts vs. entertainment: Is there a difference?* The Queen's Journal. https://www.queensjournal.ca/arts-vs-entertainment-is-there-a-difference/

Chen, G., & Gueta, K. (2016). Childhood abuse and mental health problems: Does gender matter? *Psychiatric Quarterly*, *87*(1), 189–202. https://doi.org/10.1007/s11126-015-9371-5

Choi, K. W., Sikkema, K. J., Velloza, J., Marais, A., Jose, C., Stein, D. J., Watt, M. H., & Joska, J. A. (2015). Maladaptive coping mediates the influence of childhood trauma on depression and PTSD among pregnant women in South Africa. *Archives of Women's Mental Health*, *18*(5), 731–738. https://doi.org/10.1007/s00737-015-0501-8

Clacherty, G. (2021). Artbooks as witness of everyday resistance: Using art with displaced children living in Johannesburg, South Africa. *Global Studies of Childhood, 11*(1), 7–20. https://doi.org/10.1177/2043610621995820

Collins, F. S., & Mansoura, M. K. (2001). The human genome project: Revealing the shared inheritance of all humankind. *Cancer, 91*(S1), 221–225. https://doi.org/10.1002/1097-0142(20010101)91:1+<221::AID-CNCR8>3.0.CO;2-9

Coppola, F. F. (Director). (1979). *Apocalypse now*. United Artists.

Damluji, M. (2011, September 26). *Witnessing the censored exhibit: "A child's view from Gaza."* Jadaliyya. https://www.jadaliyya.com/Details/24452

Delacroix, E. (1830). *Liberty leading the people* [Painting]. The Louvre. https://www.louvre.fr/en/whats-on/exhibitions/delacroix-1798-1863#selected-works

Desmond, K. J., Kindsvatter, A., Stahl, S., & Smith, H. (2015). Using creative techniques with children who have experienced trauma. *Journal of Creativity in Mental Health, 10*(4), 439–455. https://doi.org/10.1080/15401383.2015.1040938

Dimitry, L. (2012). A systematic review on the mental health of children and adolescents in areas of armed conflict in the Middle East. *Child: Care, Health and Development, 38*(2), 153–161. https://doi.org/10.1111/j.1365-2214.2011.01246.x

Eggers, R. (Director). (2019). *The lighthouse* [Film]. A24.

Ekman, P. (1993). Facial expression and emotion. *American Psychologist, 48*(4), 384–392. https://doi.org/10.1037/0003-066X.48.4.384

Fasfous, A. F., Peralta-Ramírez, I., & Pérez-García, M. (2013). Symptoms of PTSD among children living in war zones in same cultural context and different situations. *Journal of Muslim Mental Health, 7*(2), 47–61. https://doi.org/10.3998/jmmh.10381607.0007.203

Firmanto, A., & Yunani, A. (2022). *The Islamic iconoclasm in Indonesia: Dialectics of Islamic moderation with local culture* [International symposium on religious literature and heritage (ISLAGE 2021)]. Malang, Indonesia. https://doi.org/10.2991/assehr.k.220206.012

Grossman, F. G. (1989). The art of the children of Terezín. A psychological study. *Holocaust and Genocide Studies, 4*(2), 213–230.

Haidar, D. (2023, December 4). *'Wounded child, no surviving family': The pain of Gaza's orphans*. BBC. https://www.bbc.com/news/world-middle-east-67614139

Haker, H. (2023). Vulnerability in times of war: The necessity of the moral third. *De Ethica, 7*(3), 7–29. https://doi.org/10.3384/de-ethica.2001-8819.23737

Hamilton, A. (2023). Against modernism and postmodernism on art and entertainment: A Kristeller thesis of entertainment. *The British Journal of Aesthetics, 63*(1), 41–56. https://doi.org/10.1093/aesthj/ayac014

Henry, S. E., & Verica, J. M. (2015). (Re)visioning the self through art. *Educational Studies: Journal of the American Educational Studies Association, 51*(2), 153–167. https://doi.org/10.1080/00131946.2015.1015353

Iisala, J. (2009). *Angry birds* [Video game]. Chillingo.

Iñárritu, A. (Director). (2014). *Birdman or (the unexpected virtue of ignorance)* [Film]. Searchlight Pictures.

India: Deadly Force Used Against Protesters. (2019, December 23). *Human rights watch*. https://www.hrw.org/news/2019/12/23/india-deadly-force-used-against-protesters

Jacobs, J. (2023). Tanks and teddy bears: Ukrainian children paint the war. *The New York Times*. https://www.nytimes.com/2023/01/03/arts/design/ukraine-children-war-art.html

Jafar Panahi: Prominent Iranian film director leaves jail. (2023). *BBC News*. https://bbc.com/news/world-middle-east-64519948

Junge, M. B. (2016). History of art therapy. In D. E. Gussak & M. L. Rosal (Eds.), *The Wiley handbook of art therapy* (pp. 7–16). Wiley Blackwell.

Kashmir Journalist Arrested for "Anti-national" Content on Social Media. (2022, May 2). *Live mint*. https://www.livemint.com/news/india/kashmir-journalist-arrested-for-anti-national-content-on-social-media-11644027928240.html

King, L. S., Osofsky, J. D., Osofsky, H. J., Weems, C. F., Hansel, T. C., & Fassnacht, G. M. (2015). Perceptions of trauma and loss among children and adolescents exposed to disasters a mixed-methods study. *Current Psychology, 34*(3), 524–536. https://doi.org/10.1007/s12144-015-9348-4

Kohli, R., & Mather, R. (2003). Promoting psychosocial well-being in unaccompanied asylum seeking young people in the United Kingdom. *Child & Family Social Work*, *8*(3), 201–212. https://doi.org/10.1046/j.1365-2206.2003.00282.x

Kuchay, B. (2020, April 20). *Kashmir journalist charged for 'anti-national' social media posts*. https://aje.io/5f5um

Lee, K. (2013). Little liars: Development of verbal deception in children. *Child Development Perspectives*, *7*(2), 91–96. https://doi.org/10.1111/cdep.12023

Leland, C. H., & Bangert, S. E. (2019). Encouraging activism through art: Preservice teachers challenge censorship. *Literacy Research: Theory, Method, and Practice*, *68*(1), 162–182. https://doi.org/10.1177/2381336919870272

Makhmalbaf, M. (1996). *A moment of innocence* [Film]. MK2 Production.

Malekian, S. (2020, May 22). *Iranian couple practicing parkour arrested for romantic rooftop photos*. ABC News. https://abcnews.go.com/International/iranian-couple-practicing-parkour-arrested-romantic-rooftop-photos/story?id=70828138

Manusmriti Set on Fire to Commemorate Ambedkar's 1927 Resistance to Oppression and Exploitation of People. (2023). https://www.thehindu.com/news/national/karnataka/manusmriti-set-on-fire-to-commemorate-ambedkars-1927-resistance-to-oppression-and-exploitation-of-people/article67674486.ece

Maslow, A. H. (1943). A theory of human motivation. *Psychological Review*, *50*(4), 370–396. https://doi.org/10.1037/h0054346

McCrae, J. (1995). *In Flanders' fields*. Project Gutenberg.

Mental Health. (n.d.). *Refugee health technical assistance center*. https://refugeehealthta.org/physical-mental-health/mental-health/

Miller, K. E., & Rasmussen, A. (2010). War exposure, daily stressors, and mental health in conflict and post-conflict settings: Bridging the divide between trauma-focused and psychosocial frameworks. *Social Science & Medicine*, *70*(1), 7–16. https://doi.org/10.1016/j.socscimed.2009.09.029

Moran, W. R., & Shoop, S. A. (2002, February 18). Maya Angelou prescribes arts for trauma survivors. *USA Today*. http://usatoday30.usatoday.com/news/health/spotlight/2002/02/18-angelou-spotlight.htm

Newnham, E. A., Pearson, R. M., Stein, A., & Betancourt, T. S. (2015). Youth mental health after civil war: The importance of daily stressors. *British Journal of Psychiatry*, *206*(2), 116–121. https://doi.org/10.1192/bjp.bp.114.146324

Nisbett, R. E., & Norenzayan, A. (2002). Culture and cognition. In H. Pashler (Ed.), *Stevens' handbook of experimental psychology* (1st ed.). Wiley. https://doi.org/10.1002/0471214426.pas0213

Niu, W., & Sternberg, R. J. (2001). Cultural influences on artistic creativity and its evaluation. *International Journal of Psychology*, *36*(4), 225–241. https://doi.org/10.1080/00207590143000036

Owen, W. (1920). Dulce et decorum est. The British Library/The Wilfred Owen Literary Estate via First World War Poetry Digital Archive. Retrieved March 17, 2024, from http://ww1lit.nsms.ox.ac.uk/ww1lit/collections/document/5215

Pasek, M. H., Kelly, J. M., Shackleford, C., White, C. J. M., Vishkin, A., Smith, J. M., Norenzayan, A., Shariff, A., & Ginges, J. (2023). Thinking about god encourages prosociality toward religious outgroups: A cross-cultural investigation. *Psychological Science*, *34*(6), 657–669. https://doi.org/10.1177/09567976231158576

Patel, D. (n.d.). *UAPA: A draconian law, dire need to revisit the legislation*. Legal Service India. https://www.legalserviceindia.com/legal/article-7517-uapa-a-draconian-law-dire-need-to-revisit-the-legislation.html

Pothen, P. (2000). Art and atheism: Nietzsche, Zarathustra, and the "godless" work. *Journal of Nietzsche Studies*, *19*, 56–70.

Protests Against Quran Burning Held Across the Middle East. (2023). AP News. https://apnews.com/article/protests-and-demonstrations-denmark-pakistan-islamabad-islam-eeb9b836645a9967c08c2c9fa39c89d0?utm_source=copy&utm_medium=share

Pruitt-Young, S. (2021, September 7). *A Banksy piece was shredded at auction in 2018. Now, it may sell for millions more*. NPR. https://www.npr.org/2021/09/07/1034962331/banksy-shredder-girl-with-balloon-love-is-in-the-bin-auction-sothebys

Reals, T., & Wassef, K. (2023, January 2). *Iran couple reportedly sentenced to decade in prison after posting dance video on Instagram*. CBS News. https://www.cbsnews.com/news/iran-couple-dancing-reportedly-sentenced-prison-instagram-video/

Restoy, S., Martinet, L., Sueur, C., & Pelé, M. (2022). Draw yourself: How culture influences drawings by children between the ages of two and fifteen. *Frontiers in Psychology*, *13*, 940617. https://doi.org/10.3389/fpsyg.2022.940617

Rogers, B. A., Chicas, H., Kelly, J. M., Kubin, E., Christian, M. S., Kachanoff, F. J., Berger, J., Puryear, C., McAdams, D. P., & Gray, K. (2023). Seeing your life story as a Hero's journey increases meaning in life. *Journal of Personality and Social Psychology*, *125*(4), 752–778. https://doi.org/10.1037/pspa0000341

Scheibe, C. (2020, July 18). *Striking a chord: Using media to protest the critical issues of our time*. LinkedIn. https://www.linkedin.com/pulse/striking-chord-using-media-protest-critical-issues-our-cyndy-scheibe

Seghers, E. (2015). The artful mind: A critical review of the evolutionary psychological study of art. *The British Journal of Aesthetics*, *55*(2), 225–248. https://doi.org/10.1093/aesthj/ayu073

Seligman, M. E. P. (1972). Learned helplessness. *Annual Review of Medicine*, *23*(1), 407–412. https://doi.org/10.1146/annurev.me.23.020172.002203

Shadad, N. (2008, September 1). The journey of Naji al-Ali and his Handala character. *Yemen Times*. https://yementimes.com/the-journey-of-naji-al-ali-and-his-handala-character-archives2008-1186-culture/

Shao, Y., Zhang, C., Zhou, J., Gu, T., & Yuan, Y. (2019). How does culture shape creativity? A mini-review. *Frontiers in Psychology*, *10*, 1219. https://doi.org/10.3389/fpsyg.2019.01219

Shirin Neshat. (2011). *Transcript of 'Art in exile'*. TED. https://www.ted.com/talks/shirin_neshat_art_in_exile/transcript

Siegel, M. (1995). More than dords: The generative power of transmediation for learning. *Canadian Journal of Education/Revue Canadienne de l'éducation*, *20*(4), 455.

Singh, P. (2021, July 28). *The power of art: An instrument for activism & resistance*. Feminism in India. https://feminisminindia.com/2021/07/08/the-power-of-art-an-instrument-for-activism-resistance/

Søndergaard, E., & Reventlow, S. (2019). Drawing as a facilitating approach when conducting research among children. *International Journal of Qualitative Methods*, *18*, 160940691882255. https://doi.org/10.1177/1609406918822558

Sowder, K. L., Knight, L. A., & Fishalow, J. (2018). Trauma exposure and health: A review of outcomes and pathways. *Journal of Aggression, Maltreatment & Trauma*, *27*(10), 1041–1059. https://doi.org/10.1080/10926771.2017.1422841

Stafstrom, C. E., Goldenholz, S. R., & Dulli, D. A. (2005). Serial headache drawings by children with migraine: Correlation with clinical headache status. *Journal of Child Neurology*, *20*(10), 809–813. https://doi.org/10.1177/08830738050200100501

Tayebi, A. (2024, November 3). *Two women arrested in Tehran for dancing dressed as fictional folk character*. RFE/RL's Radio Farda. https://www.rferl.org/a/iran-women-arrested-dancing-character/32857358.html

UK, E. (2019, July 20). *The healing power of art after war*. The Borgen Project. https://borgenproject.org/the-healing-power-of-art-after-war/

Vazquez-Marin, P., Cuadrado, F., & Lopez-Cobo, I. (2023). Connecting sustainable human development and positive psychology through the arts in education: A systematic review. *Sustainability*, *15*(3), 2076. https://doi.org/10.3390/su15032076

Voice of America. (2019, December 17). *Video shows Indian police beating up students in New Delhi*. [Video]. YouTube. https://youtu.be/Hx2WBRTVjw0?si=TtdMFCflunptfoLJ

Volavkova, H. (Ed.). (1993). *I never saw another butterfly: Children's drawings and poems from Terezin concentration camp, 1942–1944*. Schocken Books.

Wadsworth, M. E. (2015). Development of maladaptive coping: A functional adaptation to chronic, uncontrollable stress. *Child Development Perspectives*, *9*(2), 96–100. https://doi.org/10.1111/cdep.12112

Walker, R. (2015). Absent bodies and present memories: Marking out the everyday and the future in Eastern Sri Lanka. *Identities*, *22*(1), 109–123. https://doi.org/10.1080/1070289X.2014.935383

Walker, R., & Vearey, J. (2019). *Gender, migration and health in SADC: A focus on women and girls*. Sonke Gender Justice. https://genderjustice.org.za/publication/gender-migration-and-health-in-sadc/

Wenders, W. (1992). The logic of images: Essays and conversations. In M. Hoffman (Trans.) Faber & Faber. (Original work published 1988).

Writes, S. (2019, August 27). *Promoting peace through art*. Global Campaign for Peace Education. https://www.peace-ed-campaign.org/promoting-peace-through-art/

Zargar, S. (2020, January 3). *In Kashmir, a spree of arrests for alleged 'misuse' of social media and masking apps*. https://scroll.in/article/954711/in-kashmir-a-spree-of-arrests-for-alleged-misuse-of-social-media-and-vpns

Zhang, L., Wan, R., Iyendo, T. O., Apuke, O. D., & Tunca, E. A. (2023). A randomized control trial establishing the effectiveness of using interactive television-based art, music, and poetry therapies for treating the post-traumatic stress disorder of children exposed to traumatic events. *Psychiatry Research, 330*, 115582. https://doi.org/10.1016/j.psychres.2023.115582

PART II

MEDIA PORTRAYAL OF NARRATIVES AND LIVED EXPERIENCES

CHAPTER 5

MEDIA INTERVENTION FOR YOUNG CHILDREN DURING MASS TRAUMA EXPERIENCES: PROMOTING THEORY OF MIND AND RESILIENCE

Erin L. Ryan

University of Tennessee at Chattanooga, USA

ABSTRACT

Young children are particularly vulnerable in times of war and conflict, but they often emerge as resilient agents of change, promoting social justice and community rebuilding post-conflict. The likelihood of this type of trauma response, however, is largely dependent upon the tactical interventions offered to them during the trauma experience. News media portrayals of war and conflict can serve to heighten negative effects for children living in conflict zones, but entertainment and curriculum-based media can be used strategically to mitigate or moderate those effects.

Keywords: Young children; war; trauma; resilience; media; theory of mind; peace communication

INTRODUCTION

> Children are both our reason to eliminate the worst aspects of armed conflict and our best hope of succeeding in that charge. – Dame Graça Machel, human rights activist & former first lady of Mozambique and South Africa (Bürgin et al., 2022, p. 846)

A quick Google search lists 10,000+ worldwide combat-related deaths in 2023 alone, and ongoing war/conflict in at least 10 areas of the globe, including civil wars in Myanmar and Syria, the ongoing deadly conflict between Israel and Hamas, drug cartel conflicts in Mexico, Islamist insurgency in the Maghreb region of North Africa, and the Russo-Ukraine war. Children in those regions are directly affected by these mass trauma events, and children around the world witness the fallout on their media screens. Bürgin and colleagues (2022) noted that roughly 400 million children have been exposed to war in the last three decades; there is an urgent need for support, political action, and collective engagement during and after mass trauma exposure to both prevent and reduce harm to children and to support their caregivers.

This chapter will focus on young children and their mediated experiences during mass trauma, using a "risk and resilience" framework. The Organization for Economic Co-Operation and Development defines *resilience* as

> the ability of households, communities, and nations to absorb and recover from shocks, whilst positively adapting and transforming their structures and means for living in the face of long-term stresses, change, and uncertainty. Resilience is about addressing the root causes of crises while strengthening the capacities and resources of a system in order to cope with risks, stresses, and shocks (OECD, 2024, np).

As Masten and colleagues (2015) noted, using a resilience framework is particularly appealing for scholars in the "effects of extreme adversities on children" space because it highlights shared goals of individuals, families, teachers, communities, societies, etc., to mitigate risk and support resilience among this group. Young children are particularly vulnerable in times of war and conflict, but they often emerge from their experiences as resilient agents of change, promoting social justice and community rebuilding post-conflict. The likelihood of this type of trauma response, however, is largely dependent upon the tactical interventions offered to them during the trauma experience. Media can offer one such intervention (e.g., Foulds et al., 2024).

Entertainment and news media are just one part of a child's environment but can take on a powerful role in the social–ecological framework. Bronfenbrenner and Morris (2006) situate human development as resulting from reciprocal interactions between people and their environment(s), whereby those interactions take place (1) on an individual level; (2) within a microsystem of family, school, and peers; (3) within an exosystem of community and neighborhood influences; and (4) within a macrosystem comprised of societal and cultural belief systems. Media are unique in that they factor into each of these nested levels and, thus, can assist in healing and resilience just like other cultural and community influences.

The chapter begins with an overview of young children and their understanding of war and conflict. The chapter then covers the ways in which young children's physical and mental health is affected by mass trauma experiences.

Next, the chapter will focus on media exposure and conclude with a focus on strategic media-based interventions.

YOUNG CHILDREN'S UNDERSTANDING OF WAR AND CONFLICT

Gathering data on preschoolers' understanding of war and conflict is tricky. There are clear ethical issues (e.g., exposing children to potentially harmful content, harming already-traumatized victims, and exposing researchers to trauma, to name a few), pre-trauma/disaster baseline data is rarely available, and very young children may not be able to verbalize their thoughts and feelings quite yet. However, some informative data exist around "peace communication" and peacebuilding that is relevant to the discussion. When asked to describe or define "peace," children as young as three often identify it as the "absence of war" (e.g., Coughlin et al., 2011; Hall, 1993; McLernon & Cairns, 2001; Myers-Bowman et al., 2005; Tephly, 1985).

In a classic study, Tephly (1985) interviewed four-year-olds in the United States and reported they defined "war" with the activities of war, whereas "peace" was associated with calmness, quietness, and privacy. Myers-Bowman and colleagues (2005) reported that war was generally described by young children in relation to its objects and activities like killing, arguing, weapons, and bombing. Coughlin et al. (2011) studied 5- to 10-year-olds in the United States and the United Arab Emirates and found that US children talked about people and countries at war and fighting, whereas children in the United Arab Emirates were much more graphic, discussing weapons, blood, destruction, fighting, and enemies. McLernon and Cairns (2001) noted in their comparison of young children from a low-political violence area of England versus a high-political violence area of Northern Ireland, the children in Northern Ireland were more likely to emphasize weapons, soldiers, and military activities. In general, then, the literature reports that young children understand war in terms of objects (weapons, bombs, etc.) and activities (killing, military operations, etc.), and peace as its opposite: the absence of war or violence (Sunal et al., 2012).

According to Lemish (2007), there is a dearth of media produced for children ages 2–6 that deal with conflict resolution, and this likely extends to this age group's understanding (or lack thereof) of war and conflict. Unfortunately, many young children are exposed to mass trauma events via television news; in fact, television is a child's main source of information about war (e.g., Götz, 2007). As Masten and Narayan (2012) noted, the public has been routinely exposed to traumatic, devastating, and highly publicized conflicts and disasters since the terrorist attacks in the United States on September 11, 2001. Not that these alarming events all began after 9/11 *per se* (see La Greca et al., 2002 and Norris et al., 2002 for pre-9/11 reviews), but there was a noticeable uptick in coverage after that infamous date.

Children tend to remember bad news better than good news; they can easily recall specific scenarios from televised war reports (Toivonen & Cullingford, 1997).

Qualitative research points to ways in which children construct their own meanings about war and conflict from news coverage, and there are some clear gender differences worth highlighting. For example, research after the first Gulf War noted that when children between ages two and six drew pictures of "what they thought war looked like," boys seemed more interested in the topic and could recall specific details, drawing human-less pictures focused on technical details, weapons, and machinery. Girls were less informed and tended to focus on the suffering of the people involved (Gillard et al., 1993).

Young children also tend to base their concepts of war on personal experience. When Miljević-Ridjički and Lugomerarmano (1994) interviewed preschool children (both from Zagreb and refugee children) about the war in Croatia in the early 1990s, their analysis revealed children used information from the media in addition to their own personal experience with things like air-raid sirens, bombardments, and shootings to make sense of their experience. The authors concluded that these children had a more mature comprehension of war than usually expected at the preschool age. This may speak to Gerbner's notion of *resonance* when looking through a Cultivation Theory lens: everyday reality plus television content provides a double dose of messages about real-world violence, making the world a "mean and scary" place (Gerbner, 1998).

One way young children express their understanding of war and conflict is through play. War, weaponry, and even superhero play can help young children make sense of mass trauma events. Rosen (2015) noted that this violently themed play can actually be a site for critical discussion; it can be a space for new social imaginations and a lens through which children and adults can talk about war, conflict, and the worlds they want to live in. "War play" is banned and/or discouraged in many preschools; however, research shows that banning can encourage children to hide areas of interest, confusion, or concern. Instead, Levin and Carlson-Paige (2006) recommend to parents and teachers that they work through these difficult themes by facilitating such play and fostering a sense of safety in its expression. Carter and Woodyer (2023) further argue that paying attention to, and engaging with, children's war play becomes a vehicle for thinking differently about young children's political agency and ability to enact resistance – which definitely speaks to resilience.

Parents and caregivers, of course, do their best to act as a buffer against both scary media content and frightening, real-world trauma. Many parents engage in protective silence surrounding war and conflict, particularly with very young children. Masten and colleagues (2015) noted that younger children have lower exposure to disasters due to immature cognition, limited mobility, and the direct efforts of their caregivers to act as gatekeepers; they are monitored more closely than older children. These "buffering effects" in the midst of mass trauma events related to a child's proximity to parents, caregivers, and teachers have been noted in the literature since World War II (e.g., Freud & Burlingham, 2011). However, war and conflict often result in massive disruptions to a child's everyday life, including missing school and peer groups, interruptions to communication systems, and economic issues and problematic international relations that might result in major changes to everything from diet to transportation (Masten & Narayan, 2012).

Masten et al. (2015) concluded that the restoration of these routines in family, schools, and communities is imperative to the resilience and recovery of children.

YOUNG CHILDREN'S HEALTH AND MASS TRAUMA EXPERIENCES

As Masten and Narayan (2012) noted, there is considerable interest in knowing "whether and how specific kinds of exposures cause more or specific kinds of problems in traumatized children, particularly because this could be helpful for intervention design and planning" (p. 237). Interestingly, the American Psychological Association (APA, 2010) reported that clinical data suggest that war-affected children demonstrate tremendous capacity for resilience. During mass trauma, children and their families are exposed to severe forms of stress through violence, displacement, inadequate healthcare, separation, loss, malnutrition, and resettlement; however, many of these children can overcome these adversities to lead healthy and productive lives (see Bouchane et al., 2018). The development of this type of resilience is a dynamic process that takes place within and through the multiple social–ecological contexts of children's lives. As noted above, entertainment and news media are typically a part of this ecosystem.

So, what are the effects of mass trauma experiences on a young child's health? Some of the most insightful scholarship in this area stems from the Buffalo Creek Dam disaster of 1972 and the Australian bushfire of 1983. After a poorly constructed dam in Buffalo Creek, West Virginia, USA, burst and killed 125 people, researchers gathered data about the child survivors from legal documents and completed a follow-up study 17 years later (Korol et al., 2002). Short-term findings indicated "dose" effects (i.e., greater exposure, or cumulative exposure, to trauma leading to more symptoms), with symptoms including posttraumatic stress disorder (PTSD), depression, anxiety, belligerence, somatic complaints like pain and fatigue, sleep problems, and behavioral problems. Older children displayed more symptoms, whereas younger children reported specific fears and age-related problems like potty training. The follow-up study showed substantial recovery (indicating that the dose effects had largely dissipated); however, participants showed a higher rate of PTSD than non-traumatized participants.

In the Australian study, over 800 children exposed to the bushfire were studied and compared to 725 children in a neighboring area. The fire-exposed children displayed more symptoms than their counterparts (MacFarlane & Van Hooff, 2009) and these symptoms were strongly related to separation from their mothers (as opposed to dose/direct exposure to the fire). A follow-up study in 2009 showed slight lingering anxiety and high rates of PTSD related to fire. The takeaway: the effects from mass trauma exposure were mostly short-term, loss and injury to loved ones had a more powerful effect than the event itself, and parental availability, function, and support all played significant roles in children's responses (Masten & Narayan, 2012).

As Shaw (2003) explained, children's "psychological responses to trauma are comparable to that of adults with one exception: the children's responses are mediated through a developing organism continuing to mature physically, cognitively, emotionally, and socially, and who is usually living within a family system" (p. 238). During the preschool years, most children are learning developmental tasks like emotion regulation, bodily function regulation, separation from caregivers (at daycare, preschool, etc.), and the fantasy-reality distinction. Punamäki (2002) noted that any violent or unpredictable environment will severely challenge young children's abilities to master these tasks.

We know from Chimienti et al.'s (1989) research, for example, that young children in war zones are at risk for severe separation anxiety, and loss of bladder control, and can engage in the physical destruction of objects. Stress reactions range from specific fears, dependent behavior, prolonged crying, lack of interest in their environment, psychosomatic symptoms, and aggression (Bürgin et al., 2022). As noted above, parents play a crucially supportive role during mass trauma experiences, and even temporary separation from parents or caregivers during this vital developmental period can be very stressful for preschool-aged children; they don't yet have the cognitive capability to understand that the parent or caregiver will return (Masten et al., 1990).

In addition to mental health concerns, research suggests that exposure to trauma in childhood may also alter biological responsiveness. Pratchett and Yehuda's (2011) work demonstrated that traumatic events may lead to hypothalamic–pituitary–adrenal hyperactivity, one of the most consistent biological findings in both anxiety and depression-related disorders. This may function to protect a young child's developing brain from excessive cortisol, the primary stress hormone. Taken a step further, this would indicate that the stress regulatory system could be permanently altered in children exposed to trauma (e.g., Gunnar & Quevedo, 2007); they might be more vulnerable to subsequent traumatic events and fail to develop an appropriate adaptive response to trauma, which increases the risk for PTSD.

Interesting research is also emerging related to genetic moderators that increase the effects of adversity and trauma on children, with studies linking variations in the serotonin transporter gene to susceptibility to post-traumatic anxiety and/or depression, and even aggressiveness. Disturbances in the serotonin system are known to contribute to the psychopathology of several mental health-related disorders (Houwing et al., 2017). And neuroimaging studies of young children exposed to trauma show both decreased brain volume and frontal cortex abnormalities, which could be related to genetic changes (Balters et al., 2021).

However, adaptive systems can mediate the severity of these negative effects. Contemporary developmental psychopathology focuses on human adaptation and how it arises from interactions between people and their environment, from the molecular level to the societal; this includes culture, media, and the wider ecology of life experiences (Cicchetti, 2013). Mass trauma situations highlight the interdependence of our adaptation/development on the function of many large-scale systems (that are largely out of our control) like national emergency response systems, weather patterns, and governmental systems, as well as the "social microsystems" in a child's life, such as family, friends, and school (Masten et al., 2015).

Additionally, we know that important factors for adaptation include promotive and protective factors such as intelligence, self-regulation skills, problem-solving skills, hope and belief that life has meaning, self-efficacy, close and supportive relationships with competent caregivers, religious beliefs and practices, good schools, safe neighborhoods, and community support (Cicchetti, 2010). Many of these adaptive elements are part of the social microsystem. Social safety theory explains that cognitive schemas of "social safety" develop during early childhood in relation to a child's appraisal of themselves, their social world, and their projected future. These schemas will be negatively affected by mass trauma experiences *and* by the meanings/narratives people in their social circle – their parents in particular – attribute to those experiences (Slavich, 2020). Taken together, adaptation systems and social safety theory point to a real opportunity to create and use media tools to mitigate extremely negative responses to mass trauma events.

Foulds et al.'s (2024) review of the intersection of coping strategies and educational media for young children is informative here. They note that the ability to deploy coping strategies is dependent upon biological, cognitive, social, and emotional development and that young children need assistance to use coping strategies effectively. Coping strategies can include task-oriented coping (i.e., finding solutions/taking action to reduce the stressors), emotion-oriented coping (i.e., using emotions to manage stress and seek support), and avoidant coping (i.e., distancing or removing yourself from the stressors) (Delvecchio et al., 2022). Media crafted for young children can support these coping strategies and moderate and mediate the development of psychopathologies such as anxiety and depression. In fact, there is evidence to suggest that the very act of engaging with media is itself a coping strategy that supports mood management and emotion regulation (Wolfers & Schneider, 2021).

MEDIA EXPOSURE TO DISASTER AND CONFLICT

Though older children likely have greater access to traditional, online, and social media and, thus, perceive a greater threat from war/conflict coverage (e.g., Comer et al., 2008), and the potential for media access will vary depending on its availability in a child's geographic area, media exposure to mass trauma events is also important to take into consideration. Generally, young children exhibit acute symptoms of distress when they are exposed to intense media reports.

As noted above, scholarship emerged after 9/11 (e.g., Otto et al., 2007) that confirmed findings reported after the Challenger explosion (Terr et al., 1999) and the Oklahoma City bombing (Pfefferbaum et al., 2003): dose effects (i.e., children showing more distress in response to more severe events or events that closely affect the caregiver relationship) were present, but effects were also moderated by age of the viewer, media access and use, developmental understanding of the content, and parental mediation. Some children displayed PTSD symptoms, and many younger children experienced distress because they didn't comprehend the trauma being televised, they did not know that news coverage was replaying the same incident on a loop (and thought it was happening again and again), and they were negatively affected by their parents' emotional reactions. Clinical experts recommended that parents carefully monitor media exposure for very young and/or very sensitive children in order to mitigate this distress (Bonanno et al., 2010).

The ways in which young children make sense of their media experiences can be difficult to capture, particularly when we take a more humanistic approach in which children are viewed as agentic, socially competent people who act in meaningful ways based upon their interpretations, perspectives, world views, and self-image. This viewpoint diverges from the traditional "media effects" research tradition which searches for quantifiable data. However, one intriguing route explored by Götz et al. (2005) was an examination of media exposure and the resulting make-believe worlds created by children. These researchers noted that

> media are part of children's everyday life experiences and provide both a wide range of content as well as diverse forms of relationships that are integrated into their realities in a way that extends far beyond the moment of consumption (p. 16).

This approach is grounded in the concept of *objectivation* – originally attributed to Berger and Luckmann (1966) – wherein human expressivity "manifests itself in products of human activity that are available both to their producers and to other[s] as elements of a common world" (p. 49). The researchers looked for what they termed "media traces" or media appropriations in children's responses to their prompts to attempt a reconstruction of children's meanings or interpretations of their world. This fascinating approach resulted in nine categories of make-believe worlds, two of which inform the current topic: the world of harmony and peace and the world of conflict and threat.

The most popular world was dubbed the "world of harmony and peace" (Götz et al., 2005). This world was drawn and described by children as lush, tranquil, peaceful, and beautiful and was a space where children were free to explore and enjoy themselves. Children described a "complete absence of danger," a "safe haven," a "safe, sunny preserve for animals," and a sense of personal security and tranquility (pp. 46–47). Drawings included vegetation, wild animals, and a cloud-like esthetic, with an overall feeling of harmonious well-being. The second most popular world was quite the opposite: the "world of conflict and threat." Here, researchers saw drawings and explanations of strife and conflict, fighting, and violent struggles; kingdoms had to be protected, and children used weapons (swords, spears, bows, and arrows), magic, personal cunning, and special abilities to rescue their loved ones. In this world, children incorporated fear and adrenaline to provide their make-believe world with emotional realism (Götz et al., 2005).

When discussing explicit and implicit media traces, the authors argue that everything in a child's make-believe world is either taken from direct experience or is somehow related to the media, and they make sophisticated use of their mediated worlds. Children are often running from unfriendly Pokémon or escaped dinosaurs from Jurassic Park, and they tend to reference all forms of media (i.e., television, movies, videos, computer games, and books). The media traces appear to be used to help these children symbolize their personal experiences and as a language to help articulate their personal narratives of a world in which they have a space for exploring who they desire to be. And the fact that children tend to follow content interests across media forms (i.e., they watch *Bluey* on television, play *Bluey* videogames, and read *Bluey* books) provides a media environment ripe for helping children process conflict and threat.

The results of this research demonstrated that children want to experience feelings of well-being and thrill, bond with others, protect and be protected, and demonstrate their own specialness and independence (Götz et al., 2005). The worlds of "harmony and peace" and "conflict and threat" were the major contexts for their make-believe; they could expand on positive real-life experiences and correct negative experiences. The authors concluded that the role media play for children should be taken very seriously. Children *do* want to be engaged with real-world issues and, thus, have a need for "diverse media offerings in a variety of genres that go beyond the common fiction narratives of 'perfect worlds and happy endings'" (p. 199).

Götz and colleagues (2005) stressed that producers have a responsibility to offer children media texts and characters that offer new possibilities for experimentation with a diverse range of roles and plots. In order for children to benefit from these texts, one key developmental milestone to focus on with very young, preschool-aged children is their theory of mind (TOM) capability. TOM refers to the ability to understand the mental state of someone else and to virtually "engage in a form of mind reading" (Durand, 2005, p. 92). Some researchers label this ability as perspective-taking and/or empathy, and it typically emerges by age four (Astington et al., 1988). Feshbach and Feshbach (1997) noted that a key element in realizing media's educational potential is the role played by a child's capacity for empathy, which facilitates social understanding and communication; empathy is a cognitive and emotional process that can be influenced or enhanced by media texts. Curriculum-based media can augment TOM; studies have shown a relationship between media exposure and TOM development (e.g., Adrian et al., 2005).

Interestingly, the concept of "war" is likely related to a child's development of TOM skills like perspective-taking. Selman (1980) noted that an awareness of others' perspectives using role-taking/perspective-taking is important to interpersonal relations, and a necessary milestone in accurately perceiving the world. Selman offered a five-level sequence of gradual acquisition of perspective-taking, culminating at stage five in late adolescence. Preschoolers, by contrast, are at stage zero; they're not able to understand the difference between their own point of view and the point of view of other people; they confuse their own thoughts with those of others (Sunal et al., 2012). Without perspective-taking ability, children cannot understand how their actions will affect the attitudes and perceptions of others toward them (and, by extension, how the actions of a nation or nation-state will affect the attitudes of other nations). Although preschoolers can label others' overt feelings, they struggle with understanding the oftentimes scaffolded, cause-and-effect reasoning behind social actions like war and conflict. This is where educational media can assist.

MEDIA INTERVENTION STRATEGIES

As Ungar and Theron (2020) so succinctly noted, resilience is linked to a child's ability to harness resources, but the resources must be provided in order to be harnessed. Multisystemic and multilevel approaches are required. One approach can involve media; there is a real opportunity to use media strategically as an intervention and resilience-building tool during and after mass trauma events. Indeed, Global TIES for Children (2023) reported a causal link between engaging with educational media content and children's ability to apply emotion-regulation coping strategies. Sesame Workshop has taken this to heart and has invested heavily in developing coping-related content as part of their outreach programs in several parts of the world, such as *Rechov Sumsum/Shara'a Simsim* and *Ahlan Simsim* in Israel, Gaza, Lebanon, Jordan, Syria, and Iraq, as well as hybrid and direct distribution of Sesame content to Venezuelan migrant children and children stuck in the border crisis in the United States. [They also launched a "Welcome Sesame" initiative across Ukraine in 2023 to help Ukrainian children cope with the devastating effects of conflict and displacement (see Rigby, 2023), but no data are publicly available about those efforts at this time.]

Sesame Workshop's (2023) approach to socio-emotional learning (SEL) is based on exploring the intersection of executive functioning (a key indicator of TOM skills) and emotional, cognitive, and social development in order to support young children's coping and self-regulation (Foulds et al., 2024). They also borrow from the "nurturing care framework," which identifies five necessary components of a nurturing care environment: good health, adequate nutrition, responsive caregiving, safety and security, and *opportunities for early learning* (Nurturing Care for Early Childhood Development, 2020, italics mine). McCoy et al. (2022) found that nurturing care interventions that support children's resilience and responsive parent–child relationships can both buffer children from the effects of stress and help children and adults strengthen their resiliency skills. This is important because we know that prolonged and severe stress can negatively influence physiological responses to stress and even affect brain architecture (Bouchane et al., 2018).

SESAME WORKSHOP'S INTERVENTIONS

Rechov Sumsum/Shara'a Simsim, a production of Israeli and Palestinian children's media producers in the late 1990s, presented bilingual *Sesame Street*-like episodes focusing on teaching understanding and mutual respect (Brenick et al., 2007). Characters crossed from the Palestinian street *Shara'a Simsim* to the Israeli street *Rechov Sumsum* and vice versa, while the narratives focused on acceptance, friendship, and the appreciation of differences and similarities between the two communities. Sesame updated this approach in 2003 with *Sesame Stories*, a co-production of Israeli, Palestinian, and Jordanian children's media producers, which aimed to positively influence children's social and moral judgments, including stereotype reduction.

Studies revealed several positive outcomes from *Rechov Sumsum/Shara'a Simsim* and the program was deemed a success. After exposure to *Sesame Stories*, most children in Brenick et al.'s (2007) study responded with positive or inclusive moral explanations for moral reasoning problems; it was deemed developmentally relevant and appropriate, gave children a strong positive social and intergroup foundation, and encouraged mutual understanding and respect. Additionally, the authors noted: "In war-torn areas of the world, adults are often under extreme stress and/or living in difficult circumstances. A positive show for children provides a different world, one in which the stress and trauma of daily life are absent, and children can be exposed to a range of positive cultural and social messages" (p. 304).

Ahlan Simsim (Welcome Sesame), which premiered in 2020, is an Arabic-language co-production of *Sesame Street* targeted to children in Syria, Lebanon, Jordan, and Iraq, as well as children displaced from various areas of the Middle East and North Africa. Foulds (2023) found that families who co-viewed *Ahlan Simsim* programming reported several positive outcomes: improved emotional vocabulary and increased emotion regulation among both children and parents, and family conversations about their new emotional vocabulary, expressions of feelings, and practicing of coping techniques. Global TIES for Children (2023) also reported positive outcomes in Jordanian kindergarten classes, with children displaying greater emotion identification and application of breathing strategies that helped them manage their strong emotions post-viewing.

After using a hybrid distribution method of Sesame content to help Venezuelan migrant children, Foulds and colleagues (2024) reported several positive outcomes. They curated 300 videos, activity sheets, infographics, and other text- and image-based resources for children displaced from their homes in Venezuela focused on four themes: emotion regulation and management/SEL, "learning everywhere" activities, health-focused activities, and community-focused activities to support a positive sense of self and belonging. They loaded these resources on microcomputers, programmed them into a WhatsApp chatbot for parents, trained local partners to aid caregivers in downloading content for use at home, helped shelters, community kitchens, children's hospitals, and libraries adapt their spaces to integrate Sesame resources, and trained service providers of in-person programming. They found that the SEL content was the most viewed, downloaded, and requested in all of their target countries. Ever mindful of the living conditions of these families, they then created lesson plans packed with "joyful, play-based activities that could be implemented on the move" to continue to support Sesame's content and utility (p. 9).

Foulds and colleagues (2024) also reported on their work with children at the Southern US border, where more of a direct distribution model was necessary (rather than relying on traditional media hardware like over-the-air television). After the border closures in 2020, the *Sesame Street in Communities* initiative worked to assist the displaced migrant children by partnering with teams on-site to curate a set of family-facing resources to help them "cope with the trauma of forced displacement, process and communicate their experiences, and develop a sense of belonging in a new place" (p. 10). Using *Sesame Street* characters and storylines, they created videos such as "Give Yourself a Hug" to show how a self-hug can help when you have big feelings, and another where characters put the finishing touches on a "welcome bag" for a new family moving into the neighborhood to encourage hospitality and optimism in host communities. Findings revealed that the content helped children and families "identify their strengths, acknowledge the changes brought upon by resettlement and displacement, find opportunities for learning, and celebrate who they are and who they could become in their new or 'for now' home" (p. 10). Foulds et al. (2024) noted that the biggest takeaway from the experience was that content for children and family's needs to be designed in a way that is useful in a variety of settings, both resourced and under-resourced.

CONCLUSIONS ABOUT MEDIA INTERVENTIONS

Warshel (2021) noted that efforts like those of Sesame Workshop are an excellent effort at *peace communication* (i.e., any communication intervention that tries to mediate between people in conflict) and a great alternative to the news for observing mediated relations between Palestinians and Israelis. As explained above, if we construct young childhood as though it was merely comprised of ignorance, irrationality, anxiety, and panic – and children as passive victims of political violence – we cannot create effective policy decisions about how best to use media strategically to respond to children's needs during and after mass trauma events. In other words, perhaps preschool-aged children don't need us to completely shelter them from the constructs of conflict. As Cairns (1983) observed of children in Northern Ireland, "children are not always passive victims... there is evidence that they can be politically active" (p. 135). Warshel (2007) cautioned both policymakers and media producers to treat children as active members of the public and noted that children have engaged in both nonviolent and violent political protests, playing an active role in armed conflicts around the world. In fact, 92% of the 6- to 10-year-olds in her study of the Israeli–Palestinian conflict knew they were in the midst of armed political conflict, and 92% of those children understood with whom they were in conflict.

However, in her recommendations for media producers and practitioners, Warshel (2021) does caution content creators not to "outstretch" the boundaries between programming and reality. The child participants in her 2007 study of *Rechov Sumsum/Shara'a Simsim* had an appreciation for the peacebuilding efforts in the program, but also saw the content as "utopian" and either unrealistic or only occasionally plausible. They understood that the show did not portray their lived experience accurately, but rather that it served as a model for how things *should* be. They saw the programming as escapist and cathartic, and some children enjoyed the program precisely for that reason; it was perhaps the only "artifact in their environment that embodied them with their partners in conflict through nonviolent relations" (Warshel, 2007, p. 324). Rather than the overt peacebuilding of *Rechov Sumsum/Shara'a Simsim*, Warshel (2021) recommends the *Sesame Stories* approach of pulling back and humanizing/demystifying the identity of the "other" through separate, but analogous, stories.

Lemish (2007) concurs that young children are likely more aware of current social conflicts than we think, and they crave media that addresses their questions, needs, and concerns. They are future citizens, participants in the public sphere, and political activists. Children growing up in conflict zones in the midst of trauma understand that experience as concrete and personal. News programs may be eliciting fear responses; rather than buffer or shield them from learning more, it is important to enable them to articulate their emotions surrounding the trauma, provide them with outlets to express them, and create programming that can help them see options for conflict resolution. Lemish and Götz (2007) summarize this recommendation here:

> What children are exposed to and the opportunities they have to challenge, elaborate, develop, and make sense of these images play a significant role in the way they grow to understand situations of conflict and war… there is a need and desire to involve media directed at children in a much more pro-active way in facilitating peace building, mutual understanding, prejudice reduction, and conflict resolution efforts as a means for developing and sustaining a culture of peace (pp. 334–335).

Teaching the cycle of conflict resolution, rather than the more nebulous term "peace," in children's media allows child viewers to map common conflicts in their lives to more general conflicts. Educating children in this way, and then engaging them in conversation, allows them to ask questions and raise dilemmas, encourages critical reflection, informs them of possible actions, provides them with other sources of information or comfort, and fosters a more positive, optimistic, empathetic outlook (Lemish & Götz, 2007).

Positive adaptation, protective effects, empathy, conflict resolution expertise, and resilience have the potential to cascade – protecting individuals and communities in the short and long term – so it is crucial to offer young children strategies via media intervention to augment their ability to grow as change agents (Patterson et al., 2010). In addition to using traditional media like television programming, multimedia approaches to teaching empathy, conflict resolution, and trauma response have been quite successful. Creative art and expressive treatments are often utilized with traumatized refugee children (e.g., Rousseau et al., 2003). Visual art and drawing exercises are well suited for young children with limited language skills and children who may not tolerate a direct discussion of traumatic events. Symbolic expression techniques, such as digital storytelling or drama activities, help children share and process their traumatic experiences (Porterfield & Akinsulure-Smith, 2007). Rousseau et al. (2003) implemented several school-based programs utilizing creative expression for refugee and immigrant children across different developmental stages and successfully used sand-tray play with preschoolers, storytelling and drawing with school-age children, and drama therapy with adolescents. Media-based activities using interactive technology such as tablets can assist with these artistic expressions.

Empathy is a learnable skill, and we can use media to teach it. Everhart and colleagues (2016) define empathy as "an ability or set of abilities *that can be developed, taught, practiced, and cultivated*" (emphasis mine, p. 3), and through media production, parents, caregivers, and educators can cultivate skills like empathy and perspective-taking. Honing these skills can aid in conflict resolution and peacebuilding. Media production can be useful for opening up dialog after mass trauma, even for the smallest voices. For example, participatory photography can be used to help children heal after experiencing violence (Baú, 2015), and narrative reconstruction of trauma has been a successful part of trauma and grief component therapy (e.g., Layne et al., 2008). Guiding children through these activities helps to build resilience. As Sunal and colleagues (2012) highlighted, an understanding of peace is fundamental to the peacemaking process and to pro-social behaviors in young children, and this includes "helping them learn to respect themselves and others, negotiate differing views, and work together in pairs and small groups" (p. 1). So, let's teach them peace and conflict management through their media, help them develop TOM skills, and give them outlets to express their trauma reactions. These interventions can play a significant role when they (1) are developmentally appropriate and (2) balance the informational and emotional needs of young children.

REFERENCES

Adrian, J. E., Clemente, R. A., Villanueva, L., & Rieffe, C. (2005). Parent-child picture-book reading, mothers' mental state language, and children's theory-of-mind. *Journal of Child Language, 32*, 673–686.

American Psychological Association. (2010). *Resilience and recovery after war: Refugee children and families in the United States.* APA.

Astington, J. W., Harris, P. L., & Olson, D. R. (1988). *Developing theories of mind.* Cambridge University Press.

Balters, S., Li, R., Espil, F. M., Piccirilli, A., Liu, N., Gundran, A., Carrion, V. G., Weems, C. F., Cohen, J. A., & Reiss, A. L. (2021). Functional near-infrared spectroscopy brain imaging predicts symptom severity in youth exposed to traumatic stress. *Journal of Psychiatric Research, 144*, 494–502.

Baú, V. (2015). Participatory photography for peace: Using images to open up dialogue after violence. *Journal of Peacebuilding and Development, 10*(3), 74–88.

Berger, P. L., & Luckmann, T. (1966). *The social construction of reality: A treatise in the sociology of knowledge.* Doubleday & Company.

Bonanno, G. A., Brewin, C. R., Kaniasty, K., & La Greca, A. M. (2010). Weighing the costs of disaster: Consequences, risks, and resilience in individuals, families, and communities. *Psychological Science in the Public Interest, 11*(1), 1–49.

Bouchane, K. Y., Yoshikawa, H., Murphy, K. M., & Lombardi, J. (2018). *Early childhood development and early learning for children in crisis and conflict.* UNESCO. https://inee.org/resources/early-childhood-development-and-early-learning-children-crisis-and-conflict

Brenick, A., Lee-Kim, J., Killen, M., Fox, N. A., Raviv, A., & Leavitt, L. (2007). Social judgments in Israeli and Arab children: Findings from media-based intervention projects. In D. Lemish & M. Götz (Eds.), *Children and media in times of war and conflict* (pp. 287–308). Hampton Press, Inc.

Bronfenbrenner, U., & Morris, P. A. (2006). The bioecological model of human development. In R. M. Lerner & W. Damon (Eds.), *Handbook of child psychology: Vol. 1. Theoretical models of human development* (6th ed., pp. 793–828). Wiley.

Bürgin, D., Anagnostopoulos, D., Vitello, B., Sukale, T., Schmid, M., & Fegert, J. M. (2022). Impact of war and forced displacement on children's mental health – Multilevel, needs-oriented, and trauma-informed approaches. *European Child & Adolescent Psychiatry, 31*, 845–853.

Cairns, E. (1983). The political socialization of tomorrow's parents: Violence, politics, and the media. In J. Harbison (Ed.), *Children of the troubles: Children in Northern Ireland* (pp. 120–126). Stranmillis College.

Carter, S., & Woodyer, T., (2023). Childhood, playing war, and militarism: Beyond discourses of domination/resistance and towards and ethics of encounter. In J. M. Beier & H. Berents (Eds.), *Children, childhoods, and global politics* (pp. 155–166). Bristol University Press.

Chimienti, G., Nasr, J., & Khalifeh, I. (1989). Children's reactions to war-related stress: Affective symptoms and behavior problems. *Social Psychiatry and Psychiatric Epidemiology, 24*, 282–287.

Cicchetti, D. (2010). Resilience under conditions of extreme stress: A multilevel perspective. *World Psychiatry, 9*(3), 145–154.

Cicchetti, D. (2013). An overview of developmental psychology. In P. D. Zelazo (Ed.), *The Oxford handbook of developmental psychology: Vol. 2. Self and other* (pp. 455–480). Oxford University Press.

Comer, J. S., Furr, J. M., Beidas, R. S., Weiner, C. L., & Kendall, P. C. (2008). Children and terrorism-related news: Training parents in coping and media literacy. *Journal of Consulting and Clinical Psychology, 76*(4), 568–578.

Coughlin, C., Mayers, G., Dizard, J., & Bordin, J. (2011). Cultural context and children's perceptions of conflict and peace. *Nurture, 5*, 18–28.

Delvecchio, E., Orgilés, M., Morales, A., Espada, J., Francisco, R., Pedro, M., & Mazzeschi, C. (2022). COVID-19: Psychological symptoms and coping strategies in preschoolers, schoolchildren, and adolescents. *Journal of Applied Developmental Psychology, 79*(101390), 1–12.

Durand, V. M. (2005). Past, present, and emerging directions in education. In D. Zager (Ed.), *Autism spectrum disorders: Identification, education, and treatment* (3rd ed., pp. 89–109). Lawrence Erlbaum Associates.

Everhart, R., Elliot, K., & Pelco, L. E. (2016). *Empathy activators: Teaching tools for enhancing empathy development in service learning classes*. Virginia Commonwealth University VCU Scholars Compass. https://scholarscompass.vcu.edu/community_resources/42/?utm_source=scholarscompass.vcu.edu%2Fcommunity_resources%2F42&utm_medium=PDF&utm_campaign=PDFCoverPages

Feshbach, N. D., & Feshbach, S. (1997). Children's empathy and the media: Realizing the potential of television. In S. Kirschner & D. A. Kirschner (Eds.), *Perspectives on psychology and the media* (pp. 3–27). American Psychological Association.

Foulds, K. (2023). Co-viewing mass media to support children and parents' emotional ABCs: An evaluation of Ahlan Simsim. *Early Childhood Education Journal, 51*(8), 1478–1488.

Foulds, K., Solomon, S., Cameron, S., Casas, C., Cohen, D., Wright, T., Kohn, S., & Tomchinsky, J. (2024). Using diverse distribution platforms to support young children's coping strategies in the midst of crisis and conflict. *Communication Studies, 75*(5), 613–628. https://doi.org/10.1080/10510974.2024.2339565

Freud, A., & Burlingham, D. T. (2011). *War and children* [reprint from 1943]. In P. R. Lehrmen (Ed.). Literary Licensing, LLC.

Gerbner, G. (1998). Cultivation analysis: An overview. *Mass Communication & Society, 1*(3/4), 175–194.

Gillard, O., Haire, R., Huender, S., & Meneghel, M. (1993). Children's recollections of television coverage of the Gulf War. *Media Information Australia, 67*, 100–106.

Global TIES for Children. (2023). *Lessons and impacts of Ahlan Simsim TV program in pre-primary classrooms in Jordan on children's emotional development: A randomized controlled trial*. New York University.

Götz, M. (2007). "I know that it is Bush's fault": How children in Germany perceived the War in Iraq. In D. Lemish & M. Götz (Eds.), *Children and media in times of war and conflict* (pp. 287–308). Hampton Press, Inc.

Götz, M., Lemish, D., Aidman, A., & Moon, H. (2005). *Media and the make-believe worlds of children: When Harry Potter meets Pokémon in Disneyland*. Lawrence Erlbaum Associates.

Gunnar, M., & Quevedo, K. (2007). The neurobiology of stress and development. *Annual Review of Psychology, 58*, 145–173.

Hall, R. (1993). How children think of and feel about war and peace: An Australian study. *Peace and Conflict: Journal of Peace Research, 30*(2), 181–196.

Houwing, D. J., Buwalda, B., van der Zee, E. A., Boer, S. F., & Olivier, J. D. A. (2017). The serotonin transporter and early life stress: Translational perspectives. *Frontiers in Cellular Neuroscience, 11*, 117. https://www.frontiersin.org/articles/10.3389/fncel.2017.00117

Korol, M., Kramer, T. L., Grace, M. C., & Green, B. L. (2002). Dam break: Long-term follow-up of children exposed to the Buffalo Creek disaster. In A. M. LaGreca, W. K. Silverman, E. M. Vernberg, & M. C. Roberts (Eds.), *Helping children cope with disasters and terrorism*. American Psychological Association.

La Greca, A. M., Silverman, W. K., Vernberg, E. M., & Roberts, M. C. (2002). *Helping children cope with disasters and terrorism*. American Psychological Association.

Layne, C. M., Saltzman, W. R., Poppleton, L., Burlingame, G. M., Pasalic, A., Durakovic, E., Music, M., Campara, N., Dapo, N., Arslanagic, B., Steinberg, A. M., & Pynoos, R. S. (2008). Effectiveness of a school-based psychotherapy program for war-exposed adolescents: A randomized controlled trial. *Journal of the American Academy of Child & Adolescent Psychiatry*, *47*(9), 1048–1062.

Lemish, D., & Götz, M. (2007). *Children and media in times of war and conflict*. Hampton Press, Inc.

Lemish, P. (2007). Developing children's understanding of conflict resolution through quality television. In D. Lemish & M. Götz (Eds.), *Children and media in times of war and conflict* (pp. 287–308). Hampton Press, Inc.

Levin, D. E., & Carlson-Paige, N. (2006). *The war-play dilemma* (2nd ed.). Teachers College Press.

MacFarlane, A. C., & Van Hooff, M. (2009). Impact of child exposure to disaster on adult mental health: 20-year longitudinal follow-up study. *British Journal of Psychiatry*, *195*, 142–148.

Masten, A. S., Best, K. M., & Garmezy, N. (1990). Resilience and development: Contributions from the study of children who overcome adversity. *Development and Psychopathology*, *2*, 425–444.

Masten, A. S., & Narayan, A. J. (2012). Child development in the context of disaster, war, and terrorism: Pathways of risk and resilience. *Annual Review of Psychology*, *63*, 227–257.

Masten, A. S., Narayan, A. J., Silverman, W. K., & Osofsky, J. D. (2015). Children in war and disaster. In M. H. Bornstein, T. Leventhal, & R. M. Lerner (Eds.), *Handbook of child psychology and developmental science: Ecological settings and processes* (7th ed., pp. 704–745). John Wiley & Sons, Inc.

McCoy, D., Seiden, J., Cuartas, J., Pisani, L., & Waldman, M. (2022). Estimates of a multidimensional index of nurturing care in the next 1000 days of life for children in low-income and middle-income countries: A modelling study. *The Lancet Child & Adolescent Health*, *6*(5), 324–334.

McLernon, F., & Cairns, B. (2001). Impact of political violence on images of war and peace in the drawings of primary school children. *Peace and Conflict: Journal of Peace Psychology*, *7*(1), 45–59.

Miljević-Ridjički, R., & Lugomerarmano, G. (1994). Children's comprehension of war. *Child Abuse Review*, *3*(2), 134–144.

Myers-Bowman, K. S., Walker, K., & Myers-Walls, J. A. (2005). "Differences between war and peace are big": Children from Yugoslavia and the United States describe peace and war. *Peace and Conflict: Journal of Peace Psychology*, *11*(2), 177–198.

Norris, F. H., Friedman, M. J., Watson, P. J., Byrne, C. M., Diaz, E., & Kaniasty, K. (2002). 60,000 disaster victims speak: Part I. An empirical review of the literature, 1981–2001. *Psychiatry*, *65*(3), 207–239.

Nurturing Care for Early Childhood Development. (2020). *A closer look at the nurturing care components*. https://nurturing-care.org/wp-content/uploads/2020/12/closer_look_nov.pdf

OECD. (2024). *Risk and resilience*. https://www.oecd.org/dac/conflict-fragility-resilience/risk-resilience/

Otto, M. W., Henin, A., Hirshfeld-Beker, D. R., Pollack, M. H., Biederman, J., & Rosenbaum, J. (2007). Posttraumatic stress disorder symptoms following media exposure to tragic events: Impact of 9/11 on children at risk for anxiety disorders. *Journal of Anxiety Disorders*, *21*(7), 888–902.

Patterson, G. R., Forgatch, M. S., & DeGarmo, D. S. (2010). Cascading effects following intervention. *Developmental Psychopathology*, *22*(4), 941–970.

Pfefferbaum, B., Seale, T. W., Brandt, E. N., Pfefferbaum, R. L., Doughty, D. E., & Rainwater, R. M. (2003). Media exposure in children one hundred miles from a terrorist bombing. *Annals of Clinical Psychiatry*, *15*(1), 1–8.

Porterfield, K., & Akinsulure-Smith, A. (2007). Therapeutic work with children and families. In H. Smith & A. Keller (Eds.), *Like a refugee camp on First Avenue: Insights and experiences from the Bellevue/NYU Program for survivors of torture* (pp. 299–335). Jacob and Valeria Langeloth Foundation. https://www.survivorsoftorture.org/publications

Pratchett, L. C., & Yehuda, R. (2011). Foundations of post-traumatic stress disorder: Does early life stress lead to adult post-traumatic stress disorder? *Development and Psychology, 23*(2), 477–491.

Punamäki, R. (2002). The uninvited guest of war enters childhood: Developmental and personality aspects of war and military violence. *Traumatology, 8*(3), 45–63.

Rigby, L. (2023). *Sesame workshop expands efforts to support Ukrainian children affected by ongoing conflict through new broadcast.* https://sesameworkshop.org/about-us/press-room/sesame-workshop-expands-efforts-to-support-ukrainian-children-affected-by-ongoing-conflict-through-new-broadcast/

Rosen, R. (2015). Children's violently themed play and adult imaginaries of childhood: A Bakthinian analysis. *International Journal of Early Childhood, 47*(2), 235–250.

Rousseau, C., Lacroix, L., Bagilishya, D., & Heusch, N. (2003). Working with myths: Creative expression workshops for immigrant and refugee children in a school setting. *American Journal of Art Therapy, 20*, 3–10.

Selman, R. L. (1980). *The growth of interpersonal understanding: Developmental and clinical analyses.* Academic Press.

Shaw, J. A. (2003). Children exposed to war/terrorism. *Clinical Child and Family Psychology Review, 6*, 237–246.

Slavich, G. M. (2020). Social safety theory: A biologically based evolutionary perspective on life stress, health, and behavior. *Annual Review of Clinical Psychology, 16*(1), 265–295.

Sunal, C. S., Kelley, L. A., & Sunal, D. W. (2012). What does peace mean? Kindergarteners share ideas. *Social Studies Research and Practice, 7*(2), 1–14.

Tephly, J. (1985). Young children's understanding of war and peace. *Early Child Development and Care, 20*(4), 271–285.

Terr, L. C., Bloch, D. A., Michel, B. A., Shi, H., Reinhardt, J. A., & Metayer, S. (1999). Children's symptoms in the wake of Challenger: A field study of distant-traumatic effects and an outline of related conditions. *American Journal of Psychiatry, 156*(10), 1536–1544.

Toivonen, K., & Cullingford, C. (1997). The media and information: Children's responses to the Gulf War. *Journal of Educational Media, 23*(1), 51–64.

Ungar, M., & Theron, L. (2020). Resilience and mental health: How multisystemic processes contribute to positive outcomes. *Lancet Psychiatry, 7*(5), 441–448.

Warshel, Y. (2007). "As though there is peace:" Opinions of Jewish-Israeli children about watching Rechov Sumsum/Shara'a Simsim amidst armed political conflict. In D. Lemish & M. Götz (Eds.), *Children and media in times of war and conflict* (pp. 287–308). Hampton Press, Inc.

Warshel, Y. (2021). *Experiencing the Israeli-Palestinian conflict: Children, peace communication and socialization.* Cambridge University Press.

Wolfers, L., & Schneider, H. (2021). Using media for coping: A scoping review. *Communication Research, 48*(8), 1210–1234.

CHAPTER 6

CHILDREN THROWING STONES AS A METAPHOR OF COUNTER-HEGEMONY

Kazım Tolga Gürel

Independent Researcher, Turkey

ABSTRACT

Since capital is not evenly distributed across the world geography, each geography has different ways of life. Likewise, capitalism prevails within nation-states, which are the governorships of capital, and this is the main cause of inequalities. These inequalities lead to the consumption of a different industry in areas where industry or consumer culture cannot spread: The arms industry. For this, the conflict of elements with the necessary ethnic or sectarian distinctions is triggered and encouraged by the nation-state's and corporations' policies. The state, as the governorship of capitalism and the companies behind it, supports the consumption of the products of the arms industry, one of the most important economic factors of capitalism, precisely in these areas. Conflicts between armies and so-called "terrorist" groups are very convenient and functional points for the arms industry to find new markets. In this study, the reality of "stone-throwing children," which is a part of the Kurdish people's struggle for existence, has been going on in various grammars for nearly a hundred years, and the representation of this reality in mainstream newspapers in Turkey will be shown. The Diyarbakır branch of the Human Rights Association of Turkey and 11 non-governmental organizations have reported that between 2006 and 2010, 4,000 children between the ages of 12 and 18 were detained or imprisoned for periods ranging from 2 months to 4 years. The findings of academic articles on the representation of stone-throwing children in the media will be summarized.

Keywords: State; news; hegemony; nationalism; stone-throwing children; conflict

INTRODUCTION

Although the idea of human rights has come to the fore throughout history with conventions such as the Medina Document (622 A.D.), the Magna Carta (1215), the French Declaration of the Rights of Man and the Citizen (1789), and the U.N. Universal Declaration of Human Rights (1948), these rights have been distorted and put into practice in many places in the interests of capitalist rulers. The state, the apparatus of the ruling classes, takes on different faces every period and takes on different types of political forms in line with the interests of the economy. Nation-states, which can provide a "legal framework" for de facto dictatorship and even massacres, justify the famous anarchist philosopher Bakunin's statement that law is the whore of politics.

The state, an apparatus established to provide profit and rent to the ruling classes, can even legitimize dictatorships, as Bonaparte's example of "being elected president through elections and then declaring himself emperor through coup d'état policies while in office." The people must remain indifferent to the lawlessness or are so blinded that they can support it. Nationalism and religious arguments precisely produce this populism and blindness.

In the 18th Brumaire, Marx's primary aim was to show how even social groups that should support revolutionary communism due to their position in the structural relations of production could rely on a despot. The working class and the oppressed supported Bonaparte's dictatorship. Underneath the desire for political stability, manifested in the belief in the regime of a despotic dictator like Bonaparte, Marx discovered the need for economic stability in a capitalist society. The bourgeoisie and the peasants, small business people, medium-sized producers, artisans, and the unemployed hailed Bonaparte as a model in their interests. In other words, 18 Brumaire examines the mutual establishment of a political and economic regime, each conditioning the other (Marx, 2016).

Karl Marx's work on 18 Brumaire is still essential today. Because Bonaparte-like dictatorships continue in many countries today, the world has still not overcome the paradigm dominated by Bonaparte-like dictators and oligarchies. To maintain their policies in various geographies, these capitalist oligarchies continue their policies, sometimes through their states and organizations. The wars produced by these policies are called "terror" in a way that varies according to the parties involved.

"It was only in the time of the second Bonaparte that the State seemed to have made itself completely independent. The wheel of the State had thoroughly consolidated itself in opposition to civil society (Marx, 2016, p. 92)" is still valid for a state that is now integrated with many ideological apparatuses from which civil society can draw support. Most societies support the nation-state and are manipulated and sanctified by its ideological apparatus. From the moment a group is called a "terrorist," the vast masses, who are much more emotional and suffer from an eclipse of reason, reflexively support the policy of the State (Shah, 2024). This situation often leads to the commercial press following events with the logic of the nation-state to sell more and reach the masses. Populist political rhetoric gets a lot of press coverage, and those who support anti-state policies are labeled "terrorists," even if they are children. The opposition and participation in the war caused by policies are the subject of a "brainwashing" operation when it comes to children.

Considering the difference between the care given to the child of an Israeli citizen and the Palestinian child in Gaza, it can be seen that the idea of human rights has never really been put into practice. Although there are relative differences, inequality of property and capital is the basis of rights inequalities. Economic inequalities bring with them inequalities in cultural and social capital. Inequality of property brings with it unequal organization of life and unequal positioning in life. This is the reason why there are children throwing stones at the police or soldiers on the streets.

In 2013, during the Gezi Park protests in Turkey, a banner unfurled by anarchists with black flags on the street summarizes the whole event: "No Justice, No Peace!" In a world where the inequalities produced by capitalism are perceived as "normal," many phenomena that are called "peaceful" or "normal" are a series of practices that involve highly symbolic violence and, even if they are not armed, spread a severe war to every aspect of life (Shah, 2019). Beyond material deprivations, spiritual deficiencies and meaninglessness have brought all life to a scale of violence. Since people cannot read the pain, they feel in their own lives as "political," they call this pain "normal." However, "normal," as Deleuze (2023) has shown, involves intense violence.

Human subjectification is directly realized through many forms of violence. However, if we look at anthropology, ancient knowledge, and the characteristics of past societies, this normalized violence is certainly not natural (Taylor, 2005; Tomasello, 2009). The conditions that enable a child to throw stones cannot be separated from the regional deprivations produced by capitalism. Regional deprivations are related to the policies of marginalization imposed on specific geographies by nation-states, the apparatus of capitalism. Although its borders vary according to groups and individuals and its existence is debated, the fact that some activist children in the geography called "Northern Kurdistan" throw stones at the state forces of the Republic of Turkey can be read within the framework of these policies. Kurds living in this region, which was included within the borders of the Republic of Turkey under various agreements after the First World War, were assimilated or forced to migrate through various strategies. These people, who initially tried to be dissolved within the Turkish identity, started to make politics with their own identity as a result of the struggles for many years, even though they were not yet officially recognized as Kurds by the Turkish Constitution. During these struggles, stone-throwing children have often appeared in street clashes with state forces and have been represented in the media in various ways (Shah, 2020).

A SHORT HISTORY OF THE KURDS OF TURKEY

Like almost every empire, the Ottoman Empire was a collection of people. After the 1699 Treaty of Karlofça, the empire began to lose territory intensively, and as it retreated to its lands in Anatolia, many of its inhabitants migrated to Anatolia and became trapped in this geography. Many geographies of colonies of the empire broke away from the Ottoman Empire during the decline, and Anatolia was left behind. Anatolia became a miniature of the empire's diversity of peoples and was home to various peoples, most of whom were Muslims. The Republic of Turkey was founded on October 29, 1923, after the so-called "War of Independence." The first constitution during the war was in 1921, which recognized the existence of two majority peoples, the Kurds and the Turks, but the subsequent constitution of 1924 did not mention the word, Kurd. It was claimed that all people living in the Republic of Turkey were Turks.

The Kurdish movement entered a period of silence after various debates during the founding years of the Republic of Turkey and some debates and uprisings during the Single Party Period of Mustafa Kemal and his friends. The 20-year period following the Dersim massacre of 1937–1938 was a period of silence for Kurds in Turkish Kurdistan (Şur & Çakmak, 2018, p. 248). The 1960s are considered the formative years of the contemporary Kurdish national movement, which would become more active and massive from the mid-seventies. After the military suppression of the Kurdish uprisings of the 1920s and 1930s, the 1940s and 1950s were relatively quiet as the state established its authority in the Kurdish provinces. However, this quiet period began to change in the early 1960s, and the Kurdish question and the protracted Trial of Kurdish political activists, later known as the 49'lar Trial, reappeared on Turkey's political agenda (Güneş, 1960).

In 1971, mass arrests and trials were conducted in the East. The Revolutionary Eastern Culture Ocakları and the Kurdistan Democratic Party of Turkey were the most critical organizations representing the masses. ... The military prosecutors in charge of the Diyarbakır and Siirt Provinces Martial Law Command insisted on stereotypical claims about Kurds and the Kurdish language formulated by the official ideology. They said that even people who spoke Kurdish and did not know a word of Turkish were Turks. Even though there was an interpreter between the prosecutors or the court and the defendants, it was claimed that there was no such language as Kurdish and that the language known by this name was a dialect of Turkish. Professors and universities enthusiastically defended these views expressed by prosecutors. The 1971 Eastern Trials opened a critical period in the history of the Kurds. During the hearings, Kurdish people began thinking about their identity and categories, such as Kurdish people, Kurdish society, Kurdish history, Kurdish language, Kurdish culture, Kurdish literature, and Kurdistan (Beşikçi, 1990).

The foundations of the thesis that "Kurdistan is a colony," which began to be discussed within leftist groups in the 1970s, brought along the decision to "organize separately from the Turkish left" for some groups. The process of organizing and developing collective action of the multi-part Kurdish movement also coincides with these years. Moreover, this thesis was decisive not only in the 70s but also in the following two decades and brought with it the idea of "national struggle." However, the 1970s were the period of organization and collective action of the multi-part Kurdish movement, which emerged with the decision to "organize separately from the Turkish left" based on the thesis that "Kurdistan is a colony." Moreover, this thesis and the approach to the National Liberation Struggle determined not only the 70s but also the next two decades. The thesis "Kurdistan is a colony" in the 1970s formed the framework of the Kurdish movement's line of organization and action in the 80s and 90s. It evolved into a structure that created a hegemonic power around the actions and claims of the PKK, the movement's armed wing. One of the most apparent reasons for this evolution was the prolonged exclusion of the Kurds from Turkish politics and the closure of their legal political avenues.

Arguments for Kurdish existence and politics begin with the leftist movement in Turkey. At the First Congress of the Communist Party of Turkey, which convened in Baku in the early days, the word "Kurdistan" was used to denote the geographical space of the Kurds in a document called "Report of the Communist Organizations of Turkey." In a meeting held in 1920, party founder Mustafa Suphi is known to have used the term "Kurdish Communists" (Karadeniz, 2018). Dr. Hikmet Kıvılcımlı, who left the TKP and stood at a unique point in the Turkish left, also made determinations in the 1930s that Kurds were a separate people (Küçükaydın, 2009, p. 302).

In 1961, Kurdish intellectuals were sentenced to various penalties in a lawsuit filed by the state for publishing poetry in Kurdish. In this case, known as the "49'lar case," Kurdish intellectuals selected for writing Kurdish articles were put on trial for gathering around the newspaper they published. These intellectuals, including Kurdish intellectual Musa Anter, were sentenced to death, but the "crime" of publishing poetry in Kurdish was punished with imprisonment (Ateş, 2019). The policies of denial of Kurdish identity, language, and culture became the state policy of the Republic of Turkey, and it can be argued that this anti-Kurdish reflex still exists in large segments of the population, even though it has relatively faded.

The Partiya Karkeren Kurdistan (PKK) organization, which has been carrying out violent attacks since 1984, has been turned into an apparatus for suspending discussions on the political solution to the Kurdish question. Various circles leaning on the static can consolidate their political engagements and continue to feed the profit centers underlying these engagements due to the lack of a solution to the Kurdish issue. Demands for balanced and politically fair participation and the establishment of legal, political parties can be shut down under the heading of "terrorism" by highlighting the PKK, and discourses of fear and terror strengthen Turkey's right-wing conservative politics. The demands of Kurdish journalists, politicians, and intellectuals are not covered in the media, and almost every time they appear in the media, they are conflated with terrorism. Any demands related to Kurdish politics are interpreted as reinforcing the PKK and terrorism.

The PKK was founded in 1978 as a move against the Turkish state's repression and military interventions in Eastern Anatolia (Northern Kurdistan). The PKK guerrillas carried out their first armed actions against the military bases of the Turkish army in 1984 and continued until the kidnapping of Abdullah Öcalan in Kenya in 1999. The disastrous consequences of the war include 30,000 casualties on both sides, 4,000 villages burned, 3 million displaced people, and thousands of political prisoners. Although the war appears to have officially ended, PKK guerrillas still maintain military positions in Southern Kurdistan (Northern Iraq) due to Turkey's ongoing military operations against the Kurdish regions (Westrheim, 2010). The Turkish authorities, on the other hand, justify these operations on the grounds of ending the PKK and the country's border security.

Recognizing that the PKK is an integral part of the Kurdish Question, and its solution is a necessary, but not sufficient, start toward a solution. Suppose the PKK is to be treated as a "terrorist organization" and PKK members are to continue to be labeled as "terrorists." In that case, there is no other way than to approach the issue in the context of "security" policies and to take enforcement measures against PKK members. From this point of view, the PKK's "descent from the mountain" would involve the surrender of the organization's cadres to Turkey's legal authorities or waiting for them to be handed over by "third parties" (the US, Iraq, or Iraqi Kurdish authorities), or the liquidation of the organization by Öcalan. These different options have been tried and exhausted and have lost their reality and viability (Çandar, 2011).

The repression of legal Kurdish politics under the label of "terrorism" continues to this day. Many people who enter the Kurdish political movement are subjected to various strategies of intimidation. People who are in prison and whose freedoms are restricted simply because of their rhetoric are labeled as "criminals." The PKK armed movement is used by right-wing conservative politicians who benefit from the continuation of the status quo of the Republic of Turkey as an apparatus to prevent Kurdish political demands and to perpetuate nationalist propaganda to the masses.

HEGEMONY OF MAINSTREAM NEWSPAPERS IN TURKEY

In Turkey, mainstream newspapers have been the bosses' property since their inception, and these bosses are in many ways in contact with the dominant political classes. To think differently about national unity and solidarity outside the laws that apply in society is a cause for great shame and marginalization. Dissenting on national issues or going outside the state discourse is enough to be considered a "terrorist." Thinking or commenting outside the discourse produced within the framework of the principle of "One state, one nation, one homeland," as seen in the fascist regimes of the 1940s, brings with it being labeled as separatist, traitor, or terrorist. To produce this hegemony, state apparatuses constantly manipulate the masses through schools, religious institutions, and the media. This hegemony is a class hegemony that has been in place since the founding, and those who think differently, especially about nationalism, are silenced through various strategies, from prosecution to murder. The conflict between the police and the press in antidemocratic countries disappears under fascism. The press and the police speak the same language. In Turkey, when it comes to the Kurdish issue, the discourse of the state and mainstream newspapers converges as in fascist regimes.

Journalism in Turkey, which Duran refers to as "vertical journalism," functions based on the state at the top of society disseminating information, opinions, and thus ideology to the masses. Vertical journalism is the pumping of the ideology necessary to rule society without rebellion and the support of the press to the state for the production of consent. In this type of journalism, journalists are ambassadors of the state before the public (Duran, 2000, p. 19).

The origins of Gramsci's phenomenon of hegemony are related to the fact that when a social class seizes government power, it becomes the dominant group and struggles to remain as the ruling group (Fiori, 2014, p. 281). For the ruling classes to remain the dominant power, they must constantly reproduce hegemony. Hegemony is a concept used in Marxist literature before Gramsci. The idea of hegemony was first mentioned in Plekhanov's writings of 1883–1884. With the concept of hegemony, Plekhanov emphasized that the Russian working class should not be content with the economic struggle against employers but should wage a political struggle (Laclau & Mouff, 2015, p. 31). With Gramsci, ideology is placed in the hegemony-centered concept. The ability of political power to secure the consent of the governed without resorting to open force and violence constitutes the problem of the theory of dominant ideology (İyigüngör, 2009, p. 5).

Hegemony is based not on violence but on the production of consent. It is a cognitive phenomenon that controls minds and directs ways of thinking. It is the shaping of thoughts and ideas that are thought to be personal with the help of social instruments based on consent. It is an intellectual atmosphere that normalizes all kinds of power relations and exploitation practices in life and is reproduced through relationalities about attitudes, opinions, beliefs, and attitudes.

The hegemony, which has been in place since its founding, has been reintegrated with much more precise lines in Turkey, especially after the 1980 military coup. The coup dismantled and suppressed the production of counter-hegemony, especially the forces that created cracks in the hegemony of the capitalist state, such as the civil society organizations, associations, parties, and unions of the working class. In order to understand the transformation of the press into an ideological apparatus of the state, it is necessary to trace the political economy transformation process of Turkey's mainstream newspapers before and after the coup. According to Gramsci, an ideology that does not correspond to the needs of a historical period cannot exist (Gramsci, 1999, p. 341). Following the political economy process in newspapers will reveal the needs that led these newspapers to speak the same language and reproduce the same discourses as the state.

The press in Turkey has always been under state control. The state's touch on the press has sometimes been covert and sometimes overt. Since Turkey has no unionization process, as seen in the press in England and France, there can be no talk of a free press. According to Akalın, the coups contributed to the struggle for supremacy of the industrial bourgeoisie against the agrarian bourgeoisie.

Mainly, the 1971 coup d'état was carried out to ensure the superiority of the comprador bourgeoisie over the agrarian bourgeoisie, which held the power of capital (Akalın, 2002, p. 48). The 1980 coup d'état in Turkey aimed to protect the comprador bourgeoisie against the increasing working-class movements in the 1970s and the fear of communism brought by these movements.

The military-bureaucrat rule, masked by bourgeois democracy, protected the industrial bourgeoisie for a long time. In the early 2000s, when it had developed sufficiently, it felt the need to break the rules of the old system with Recep Tayyip Erdoğan. The bourgeoisie broke the political-economic shackles of the old Republic that had hindered it. The AKP rule and the subsequent Erdogan despotism, which can be characterized as a hidden dictatorship, happened because the Turkish ruling classes needed to break the old chains and overcome various economic crises. However, the dominant hegemony in Turkey perceived these transformations for the needs of the bourgeoisie as bipolar wars. Massive privatizations took place behind a political atmosphere dominated by polarizations such as secularist-religious, Kemalist-liberal, etc., and the Turkish bourgeoisie broke the last shackles of the welfare state and evolved toward a complex capitalist model. Within this capitalist evolution, there have also been changes in the political economy of the press.

Due to a lack of capital, the state played a role in Turkey's first emergence of the press. The press in Turkey started to industrialize in the 1960s, and the influence of economic factors increased after the 1980s (Sözeri & Güney, 2011, p. 15). Later, especially after the 1990s, private capital became active in the country, and investments in the media sector increased as this capital took over it. Özgentürk emphasizes that newspaper ownership in Turkey had a structure that passed from father to son within the family until the 1950s, 60s, 70s, and even 80s. However, in the 1990s, a change in the structure is noticeable. Since the 90s, large capital owners in Turkey have started to enter the media sector and become the dominant power in the sector day by day. Since these years, almost no media companies have passed down from father to son (Özgentürk, 2008, p. 51).

REPRESENTATION AND MEDIA

When hegemony, which ensures that the power of the masses is used in production, is eroded, or not sufficiently controlled, this power has the potential to turn into rebellion. The state apparatus must, therefore, constantly reproduce hegemony. When the nationalism used for this purpose is based on a single ethnicity, counter-subjectivization begins in the masses who do not feel that they belong to this ethnicity. The counter-hegemony produced by the organizations formed by these subjects with various strategies confronts oppression as an element of resistance. As a result, the repression of the state apparatus is always associated with capital accumulation. However, resistance is associated with acts of exclusion and marginalization that can be counted within the practices of counter-subjectivation. All kinds of relations that make the sovereign dominant may be hurtful for those outside the meaning blocks of belonging. These relations and even the language used can be a reminder of historical exclusion and the political processes and outcomes related to these exclusions.

Being called with a wounding language subconsciously reflects the master's effort to consolidate his place. However, Butler also refers to the duality of the process here. Being called with a wounding language and naming can paralyze the person but also cause resistance (Butler, 2019). Injurability can cause clustering, anger, grouping, and resistance. It seems illogical to pick and choose vulnerability from the clusters of resistance. Indeed, vulnerability changes and conditions social relations. According to Butler, vulnerability is not just a passive attitude. It is a set of shaped social relations, including practices of resistance. Seeing vulnerability as shaped social relations and actions can help to understand why forms of resistance emerge in the forms they do. While domination is not always followed by resistance, these spaces of resistance opened up by vulnerability may need to be defined appropriately if ways of framing power fail to grasp the cooperation of vulnerability and resistance (Butler, 2020).

Althusser (2001) mentions that ideology represents the imaginary relations between individuals and their actual conditions of existence (p. 109). According to Althusser's definition, the fact that the actual conditions of existence of the people in the events are constructed in the news through the representation of a "stone-throwing child" without making them question their actual conditions of existence sufficiently reveals the ideological aspect of representation. According to Jacques Lacan, the impossibility of direct contact between reality and the "real" and the necessity of the symbolic fabric in the construction of consciousness can be mentioned. The news becomes an ideological apparatus that settles in the space between the real and the "real" in the Lacanian sense and functions within this space. The misconstruction of reality, an integral part of the human condition, is woven into a symbolic fabric, a curtain, by closing within the framework established by the official ideology thanks to the news. In this sense, the news subjectivizes and reconstructs a child in an act of resistance. It calls the children "stone-throwing children." Althusser's (2001) statement that "ideology calls individuals as subjects (p. 115)" emerges in news reports on stone-throwing children.

News construction is a process of actualizing a reality and subjectivizing the perpetrators of reality. In a sense, this is the problem of representation. According to Metzger, the subject of representation can be a public person in general, various groups and organizations, politics, and ideologies; however, representation is the activity of the representer rather than the represented. In this sense, it always carries an intention (Metzger, 2006, p. 59). This intention is sometimes determined by the journalist who creates the representation and sometimes by the gatekeepers of the newspaper. The ideological perspectives of the constructors can consciously or unconsciously determine the intention in the selection or construction of news. News presents a manipulated, limited, doctored, or distorted image of the phenomenon it represents.

News is one of the primary constituents of social thought that forms the fabric of our daily lives. Chomsky (1993), who is interested in the control of thought in democratic societies, states that rather than exerting an overt and coercive influence, the media exerts a standardizing influence by disseminating selected information and social codes to the receptive audience. He argued that due to the secrecy of the influence, the recipients do not censor it, thus ensuring their voluntary participation. However, the reason for this acceptance in the news about Kurds in Turkey goes beyond the secrecy of the effect; it is the fact that the blocks of meaning that produce the discourse of "we" pervade the intellectual environment. Any crack that may occur in the hegemony of "we" based on the discourse of "one homeland, one nation, one state" is directly prevented by the legal repression apparatus. The majority that the news reaches are forced to construct the messages within the discourses of the official ideology since they cannot question the content of the messages that reach them and cannot access other intellectual perspectives.

REPRESENTATION OF "STONE THROWING CHILD" IN THE MEDIA

If one stone is thrown, it is a punishable act. If a thousand stones are thrown, it is a political act.

Ulrike Meinhof (1981, p. 87)

The archaic act of "throwing stones" is one of the most prominent primate reflexes in the face of danger (Kühl et al., 2016). In many wild populations, stone-throwing tools are known from the literature of anthropology and archaeology (Schick et al., 1999). In this sense, "throwing stones" is one of the oldest acts of turning toward a threat in order to protect one's space and oneself.

The stone-throwing of children and women in protests in Kurdish cities and neighborhoods can be seen in many of the Kurdish people's struggles for their rights in the 20th century. However, it is possible that the increase in the number of children among the insurgent masses since the 2006 Nevroz, when protests against the killing of 14 PKK militants with chemical weapons intensified, was due to the touch of the armed wing of the Kurdish movement. Although the allegations on this issue mostly revolve around state rhetoric, there may be a grain of truth in them. In the early 2000s, during the "intifada" (uprising, awakening) declared by Palestinian organizations between 2000 and 2005 against the actions and oppression of the State of Israel, the number of children throwing stones against Israeli soldiers and police officers rose symbolically. In the same years, the famous social scientist Edward W. Said's much-discussed photograph of children throwing stones became popular. It is possible that the PKK also supported the efforts to elevate stone-throwing children as a symbol of resistance in protests in Kurdish provinces during this period and organized it as a strategy. However, without socio-political reasons and the violent oppression experienced by Kurds, such a policy and strategy would not have been organized.

The reasons for children's participation in the protests are controversial. While sources close to security units state that children are used and directed by the terrorist organization (Ördek, 2014), some others state that they participate entirely of their own volition (Yağcıoğlu, 2010, p. 110). In the media, there are news reports that children are manipulated, and rather than recognizing children as terrorists, it is noteworthy that there are discourses that children are used as pawns with expressions such as "being driven to the front lines," "using children as shields for themselves" and "children and women are used on the streets" (Durna & Kubilay, 2010, pp. 75–77).

Durna and Kubilay (2010), in their study "Violence of the Press: The Case of 'Stone-Throwing Children' in Political Demonstrations," the stereotype of "children throwing stones at the police," which became widespread in the media when children threw stones at the police during the demonstrations in Cizre on February 15, 2006, on the anniversary of Abdullah Öcalan's capture, was analyzed based on three themes and six case studies. For the analysis, themes titled "child victim of violence," "child involved in violence in protests," and "child as the addressee of the state's preventive measures" were created. To analyze the presentation of the themes and the sample events selected for these themes, Akşam, Cumhuriyet, Hürriyet, Ortadoğu, Taraf, and Yeni Şafak newspapers were selected from the national press. As a result of this study, Durma and Kubilay found that children who participated in resistance protests were more likely to be subjected to symbolic violence and discrimination due to their ethnic identity. In the details of the news articles, references to the ethnic identity of the delinquent child are given in a way that catches the reader's eye. Thus, the ethnic and cultural identity of the "delinquent child" is implied to the reader, and children and the ethnic group to which children belong are presented as "monsters" to be feared. In addition, it is emphasized that Kurds give birth to many children, and precisely for this reason, children are left on the streets because they cannot be taken care of by their families and thus become prone to commit crimes.

Narin's 2011 article analyzed the representation of children involved in crime on the websites of popular newspapers. It was found that children involved in crime were described with narratives legitimizing violence, cliché judgments, and expressions; it was observed that they were the subject of news in an ethically problematic and secondary context. The media, representing and constructing social reality, does not present children involved in crime as subjects in the news but uses them as figures to attract attention (Narin, 2011).

In a study conducted in the Kurdish neighborhoods of Mersin province in Turkey, Gürbüz interviewed more than 90 women and children. The families of the children participating in the protests work in shanty houses, usually in informal jobs and without insurance. The average number of children is around 5–6. Children attend school for half of the day and work in various jobs such as apprenticeships in industry and shoe shining for the other half of the day, and after a while, most of them stop their education. The majority of these children are child laborers either permanently or periodically. A significant number of children are registered in juvenile courts, ranging from substance abuse to extortion (Gürbüz, 2013). These findings pointed out by Gürbüz show the impact of the reflections of the lack of a social state on children.

In Çetin's research conducted in Batman, a Kurdish province, the families and relatives of 103 of the children in question were interviewed. An important finding regarding the children who participated in the protests is that there are many individuals in the families and relatives of these children who were arrested, convicted, joined illegal organizations, and subjected to unsolved murders, especially for political reasons. This issue can be said to effectively politicize children and their participation in these events (Çetin, 2013).

In Ekmen's study on the representation of children in the media, the media news was analyzed. As a result of the study in which content analysis, discourse analysis, and interviews were conducted, it was seen that the ideologically structured news media reproduced social inequality with the news on "stone-throwing children." The news reports of Hürriyet, Cumhuriyet, and Zaman newspapers in 2009–2010 were analyzed, and it was observed that the discourses of state officials came to the forefront in this analysis. State officials are the ones who speak in the news reports, and therefore, the discourses of the state on the issue are reflected in the press (Ekmen, 2014).

It is interesting to note that this mobilization of Kurdish children in the late 2000s, which was on Turkey's agenda, started after the end of the "low-intensity war." Kurdish children were mobilized in the context of the 2000s when negotiations between the EU and Turkey increased, new reform packages were prepared in the name of democratization and minority rights, and a hopeful atmosphere began to emerge, especially in an environment where the feeling that "the solution of the Kurdish issue had never been this close" prevailed and the "Kurdish Initiative" created hope in everyone (Darıcı, 2009). Interestingly, when the winds of peace are blowing on the Kurdish issue in Turkey or when there are major socio-political crises, the war flares up again.

CONCLUSION

Political issues are subject to distortion through the propaganda of states and organizations and disinformation through constructed representations. As of the end of the 2000s, many comments have been made on the "stone-throwing child" representation. These comments were not presented in their full dimensions by the mainstream media channels of the people of Turkey. The news and messages on the subject that flowed through these channels and the various opinions clustered around state discourses perpetuated the delusion of a democratic media. Due to the legal pressure on the country's civil society organizations and the Kurdish media, which continues to this day, comments and opinions on the issue cannot be discussed openly.

The Kurdish issue in the Republic of Turkey is a problem that has persisted since its inception and has resulted in the loss of many lives on both sides. The basis of this problem is the creation of institutions based on the definition of a nation-state based on a single ethnicity in Anatolia after the collapse of the empire with a multi-ethnic population.

The state and advertising budgets have controlled the Turkish press since the country's foundation. Any class opposition that could have created a free press was harshly suppressed, and the working-class newspapers had limited influence. Therefore, we can speak of a press controlled or directly owned by the ruling classes. The mainstream media censored or completely blacked out coverage of the Kurdish issue.

Since 2006, the representation of "stone-throwing children" has been brought to the forefront and has been covered by mainstream newspapers in Turkey for a while by limiting the perspectives of discussion. State discourses were repeated on the various deprivations experienced by these children living in social inequalities, as shown in academic studies conducted in Mersin and Batman, the historical evolution of the Kurdish issue, and the details of their participation in the resistance. Different perspectives on this issue, and especially the opinions of those close to the Kurdish movement, were heard in the marginalized Kurdish media.

REFERENCES

Akalın, U. S. (2002). *Türkiye'de Devlet-Sermaye İşbirliğinin Ekonomi Politiği: Devletin Ekonomideki Yeri ve Rolü*. Set Yayınları.
Ateş, E. (2019). *Türkiye Sosyalist Solunun Kürt Meselesine Bakışı: 1960-1971*. Marmara Üniversitesi, Ortadoğu SosyolojisIi ve Antropolojisi AnabiliM Dalı. Yüksek Lisans Tezi.
Beşikçi, İ. (1990). *Devletlerarasi Sömürge Kürdistan*. Weşanên Rewşen.
Çandar, C. (2011). Dağdan İniş-PKK Nasıl Silah Bırakır. *Kürt Sorununun Şiddetten Arındırılması, Türkiye Ekonomik ve Sosyal Etüdler Vakfı Yayınları, Temmuz, 40*.
Çetin, E. (2013). *Kitlesel eylemlere katılarak kanunla ihtilafa düşen çocuklar: Batman örneği* [Master's thesis, Sosyal Bilimler Enstitüsü].
Chomsky, N. (1993). *Medya Gerçeği*. Çev:Abdullah Yılmaz. Tüm Zamanlar Yayıncılık.
Darıcı, H. (2009). Şiddet ve özgürlük: Kürt çocuklarının siyaseti. *Toplum ve Kuram, 2*, 17–41.
Deleuze, G. (2023). *İktidar: Foucault Üzerine Dersler. Çev: Münevver Çelik, Sinem Özer*. Otonom Yayıncılık.
Duran, R. (2000). *Medyamorfoz*. Avesta Yayınları.
Durna, T., & Kubilay, Ç. (2010). Basinin Şiddeti: Siyasal Gösterilerde "Polise Taş Atan Çocuklar" Örneği. *Ankara Üniversitesi SBF Dergisi, 65*(03), 5.
Ekmen, Ö. (2016). *Türkiye Medyasında Taş Atan Çocukların Temsili*, (Yayınlanmamış Yüksek Lisans Tezi). Ankara Üniversitesi.
Fiori, G. (2014). *Antonio Gramsci: Bir Devrimcinin Yaşamı, Çev: Kudret Emiroğlu*. İletişim Yayınları.
Gramsci, A. (1999). *Selections from the prison notebooks*. Elecbook.
Güneş, C. (1960). *Altmışlı Yıllarda Kürt Siyasal Aktivizmi. Edt: Mete Kaan Kaynar* (pp. 701–725). İletişim Yayınları.
Gürbüz, H. (2013). Taş Atan Çocuklar "Mersin Örneği". *VII. Ulusal Sosyoloji Kongresi, 101*.
İyigüngör, V. (2009). *Medyada Tanıklık: Türkiye'de Askeri Darbeler*. İstanbul Beta Basım.
Karadeniz, F. (2018). *Türkiye Komünist Partisi Yayınlarında Kürtler*. Belge Yayınları.
Küçükaydın, D. (2009). *Bir Devrimcinin Teorik ve Politik Otobiyografisi*. Köksüz Yayınları.
Kühl, H. S., Kalan, A. K., Arandjelovic, M., Aubert, F., D'Auvergne, L., Goedmakers, A., Jones, S., Kehoe, L., Regnaut, S., Tickle, A., Ton, E., van Schijndel, J., Abwe, E. E., Angedakin, S., Agbor, A., Ayimisin, E. A., Bailey, E., Bessone, M., ... Boesch, C. (2016). Chimpanzee accumulative stone throwing. *Scientific Reports, 6*(1), 22519.
Laclau, E., & Mouff, C. (2015). *Hegemonya ve Sosyalist Strateji- Radikal Bir Politikaya Doğru. Çev: Ahmet Kardam*. İletişim Yayınları.
Marx, K. (2016). *Louis Bonaparte'in 18 Brumaire'i (Der achtzehnte Brumaire des Louis Bonaparte) Çev: Erkin Özalp*. Yordam Kitap.
Meinhof, U. M. (1981). *Die Würde des Menschen ist antastbar*.
Metzger, J. P. (2006). L'information-Documentation. In B. Vacher & S. Olivesi (Eds.), *Sciences de l'Information et de la Communication. Stéphane Olivesi (der) içinde* (pp. 43–62). PUG.
Narin, B. (2011). Suça karışmış çocuklara yönelik temsil çalışması:'Taş atan çocuklar'a taş atan medya. *I. Türkiye Çocuk Hakları Kongresi Yetişkin Bildirileri Kitabı*.
Ördek, M. Y. H., and Çakmakçı, Ö. A. C. (2014). *PKK terör örgütünün çocukları kullanma usul ve yöntemlerinin analizi*. https://www.icisleri.gov.tr/kurumlar/icisleri.gov.tr/IcSite/strateji/deneme/YAYINLAR/%C4%B0%C3%87ER%C4%B0K/PKK_COCUK_almanca.pdf

Özgentürk, N. (2008). *Cumhuriyetten Günümüze Basının Kısa Tarihi*. [Edt: Melda Davran, Ali Sekmeci]. Alfa Yayınları.

Schick, K. D., Toth, N., Garufi, G., Savage-Rumbaugh, E. S., Rumbaugh, D., & Sevcik, R. (1999). Continuing investigations into the stone tool-making and tool-using capabilities of a bonobo (Pan paniscus). *Journal of Archaeological Science*, *26*(7), 821–832.

Shah, T. M. (2019). Social justice and change. In S. Romaniuk, M. Thapa, & P. Marton (Eds.), *The Palgrave Encyclopedia of global security studies* (pp. 1–4). Palgrave Macmillan.

Shah, T. M. (2020). Children of Kashmir and the meaning of family in armed conflict. In S. Frankel, S. McNamee, & L. E. Bass (Eds.), *Bringing children back into the family: Relationality, connectedness and home* (pp. 213–216). Emerald Publishing Limited.

Shah, T. M. (2024). Emotions in politics: A review of contemporary perspectives and trends. *International Political Science Abstracts*, *74*(1), 1–14.

Sözeri, C., & Güney, Z. (2011). *Türkiye'de Medyanın Ekonomi Politiği: Sektör Analizi*. Tesev Yayınları.

Şur, Y. Ç. T., & Çakmak, Y. (2018). *Kürt Tarihi ve Siyasetinden Portreler*. İletişim Yayınları.

Taylor, S. (2005). *The fall*. Iff Books.

Tomasello, M. (2009). *Why we cooperate*. The MIT Press.

Westrheim, K. (2010). *Dağları Seçmek: Alternatif Bir Kimlik Projesi olarak PKK*. Toplum ve Kuram Yayınları.

CHAPTER 7

BEGINNING OF LIFE, END OF LIFE: EXAMINING ONLINE MEMORIALS OF CHILDREN IN SITES OF ARMED CONFLICT

Aya Diab and Danielle L. Johnson

University of South Florida, Tampa, FL, USA

ABSTRACT

Children in armed conflict sites exist as a representative of the beginning of life in a space that serves as a constant reminder of the end of life. When children die in these spaces, they become representatives of the pervasive death that looms in and around armed conflict sites. Narrating children through online memorials is one way in which to breathe life back into these children and highlight the atrocities in armed conflict spaces. Looking specifically at the Syrian Civil War, this piece examined English language memorials for children who have died in the Syrian Civil War to understand narrative similarities and differences. The authors first hypothesized that regardless of the post, children were regarded with positive language, as established by previous child memorial research. Second, we hypothesized that there could be some noticeable differences in who's to blame for the children's death in two main ways: blaming the regime of Bashar Al-Assad or the Armed Syrian Opposition. Despite focusing on memorials about children, children were missing from the memorials (Theme A: Where Are the Children?). Ever present in the memorials was the conflict between Bashar Al-Assad and the Armed Syrian Opposition (Theme B: Blame Game: Bashar Al-Assad and the Armed Syrian Opposition).

This chapter expanded the research areas of online narratives, children in armed conflict sites, and the end-of-life topic area.

Keywords: Online narratives; war narratives; memorialization; memorials; online memorials; End-of-life (EOL); Children in War; Syrian Civil War; Syria; thematic analysis

INTRODUCTION

Armed conflict and war impact families tremendously where they shatter the fabric of communities in society and force individuals to dislocate in which they are left with no choice but to flee their homes to protect their livelihoods. While civilian experience may differ from conflict to conflict depending on factors like intensity, duration, and proximity, among others, as Merrilees and Lee (2018) note, families who experience armed conflicts in general are prone to stressors and hardships that could persist with them long after the conflict is formally over (p. 248).

Furthermore, contemporary war and armed conflict are both proven to primarily put children and families at great risk because they create distress and uncertainty about safety in one's home, schools, places of worship, playgrounds, and hospitals, among others (Merrilees & Lee, 2018, p. 249). These spaces are mainly where children live and grow, and where family support is nurtured and relied upon (Merrilees & Lee, 2018, p. 249). Additionally, these spaces that were once safe havens simultaneously turn into places of war, in which schools are used as "military bases and interrogation centers," and increased violence alters the stability that these spaces gave to their communities (Jacob, 2018, p. 46). For instance, Jacob (2018) notes that children during the civil Syrian war were catalysts in the protests that marked the beginning of the conflict in which they were regarded in multiple forms – fighters and direct targets of violence. Consequently, children were caught in the "crossfire" in which they were displaced and forcibly thrust into unforeseen circumstances, ultimately acting as tools in political rhetoric, material for global media, and sometimes justification for interventions (p. 46). Therefore, children unwillingly turn into an important part of the broader socio-political landscape where the conflict is unfolding, rather than just acting as a topic or a category for humanitarian organizations and countries to factor into their agendas (Jacob, 2018, p. 47).

Since the war in Syria began in 2011, around 30,000 children have been killed and 5,000 are still detained or forcibly disappeared, according to a report released by The Syrian Network for Human Rights (SNHR, 2023). One of the resulting factors of the war is online memorials to commemorate those who passed away. To examine how families, friends, and loved ones remember children, specifically, in online memorials such as the subreddit r/syriancivilwar, this chapter aims to analyze Reddit posts using LDA and topic modeling to extract themes (thematic analysis) evident in individuals' posts. For instance, we expect to see themes emerge regarding how these children are remembered and who users are blaming for the deaths.

Beginning of Life, End of Life

In this chapter, we will be using the terms armed conflict and war interchangeably, where they both refer to the civilian experiences ranging from "hearing about attacks in the news to separation from family due to death or abduction. Separation may also be the result of being internally or internationally displaced" (Merrilees & Lee, 2018, p. 249).

Inspired by Braun et al.'s (2022) commitment to reflexive thematic analysis and our personal commitment to reflexivity, the authors want to foreground their positionalities at the beginning of this piece. The lead author is a trilingual (Arabic, Turkish, and English) Muslim woman from Jordan who understands armed conflict sites and grew up in the capital Amman where neighboring countries were in an active state of war, like Syria and Iraq. The supporting author is a monolingual agnostic woman from the United States who has not been directly involved in armed conflict sites. With these positionalities in place, we acknowledge that our work is a means by which to uplift the Syrian people and the online memorials they have created for their lost children. We hope this chapter can bring greater attention to children in armed conflict sites and highlight how they are memorialized in online spaces.

CHILDREN AND ARMED CONFLICT NARRATIVES

Children have been affected by armed conflict to varying degrees, including their gender, race, ethnicity, age, and locality of the armed conflict (Wessells, 2016). According to Jacob (2018), "the profile of children affected by conflict has increased significantly since the mid-1990s" (p. 36). The impact of armed conflict on children has become present in narratives related to, among other things, resilience, vulnerability, spirituality, child soldiering, and emotional expression (Boyden & de Berry, 2004; Kar, 2020; Merrilees & Lee, 2018; Noguera, 2013; Ray, 2017). One narrative route often overlooked is the memorialization of children who have died in and during armed conflict. Written by family members and friends, these memorials provide a space for children to be remembered and honored.

NARRATIVES IN ONLINE SPACES

The way in which social media users discuss, narrate, and experience wars, armed conflicts, and memorializations online is constantly shifting. McDowell and Braniff (2014) state that "remembrance is a crucial element of the healing process" for conflict resolution. For example, online sites can serve as "open spaces where members of the mourning community, as well as the public, can also participate in reading, open discussion, writing texts or posting thoughts," where these virtual sites now act as an extension or continuation to physical memorials (Kizel, 2014, pp. 423–424; Walter, 2015). These spaces are where both collective memory and individual memory are shaped and enabled by the Internet, consequently creating possibilities for the construction of memorials "devoted to tragic or catastrophic events and the exercise of collective memory (Recuber, 2012, as cited in Kizel, 2014). Consequently, online memorials became spaces that offer families and individuals the capacity to express their grief, remembrance, and solidarity in the context of armed conflict (Walter, 2015).

One of the primary functions of online memorials is to signal safety and provide information about the well-being of individuals in conflict zones. Seen in Van Ommering and el Soussi (2017) work, the digital memorialization of individuals under forced disappearance in armed conflict sites allowed survivors to signal their safety and to highlight fellow Lebanese community members who were still missing. The launching of Fushat Amal (Space of Hope) gave survivors and families the means to build solidarity within digital communities while remembering their loved ones (Van Ommering & el Soussi, 2017). We believe remembrance is also relevant for healing during active armed conflicts and is often present in the narratives crafted around the death of children. Examples of online remembrance techniques (hereinafter referred to as online memorials) include obituaries (Fowler, 2007; Hume & Bressers, 2010), eulogies (Davis et al., 2016), memorial posts (Carroll & Landry, 2010; Danilova, 2014; Hess, 2007; Roberts, 2012), and virtual cemeteries (de Vries & Rutherford, 2004; Roberts, 2004, 2006).

ONLINE MEMORIALS

Memorials serve as a space for remembering individuals after their passing. These spaces are increasingly regarded as sites in which members can express and come to terms with circumstances in post-conflict societies (Selimovic, 2013, p. 335). As the internet has evolved, so have online memorials. These memorials are a way to access information about and remember loved ones, friends, family members, and other figures in one's life who have died. Furthermore, as Bell (2006) notes, virtual memorials support "the ethical impulse to commemorate the dead, most often those killed in wars" (p. 20). In addition, the qualities of online memorials consequently make the space for mourners to interact with memorials which can lead to a therapeutic environment by allowing for "action, narrative work, meaning-making, expressions and negotiations of continuing bonds with the deceased, and virtual support networks" (Maddrell, 2012, p. 46). The second author has spent several years examining online memorials in her research and personal life, as she has lived through the death of close family members and the memorialization that comes with them. These online memorializations have allowed community members to engage with death and loss in a controlled environment since the loss was not attributed to war. In addition, these examinations have focused on memorials of older people with expansive familial and social networks in non-armed conflict sites.

When thinking about memorials, one major question pops up for the researchers: What does it mean to memorialize a child online? In the context of armed conflicts, memorializing a child online can be used to: signal the safety and security of some family members who were directly caught in the conflict; highlight the innocence of a child's life; resist oppression regimes that lead to the child's death; and bring attention to the conflict's impact to a wider audience (Chaudhry, 2017; Viejo-Rose et al., 2015). Both authors, despite differences in direct experience with armed conflict sites, understand the necessity and gravity of online memorials, especially those about children. Thinking of these online memorials, we hypothesize the following:

> *H1*. Children will be discussed with positive language (e.g., affirmative of their strengths [kindness, resilience, etc.]).
>
> *H2*. There will be differences in who is blamed for the children's deaths in memorial posts.

METHOD

Syria is one of many countries experiencing heavy, long-term armed conflict (Wessells, 2016). In fact, "[t]he deadly nature of contemporary armed conflicts is most visible in the Syrian war, which has featured chemical attacks on civilians, caused nearly 200,000 deaths, and left a multitude of unexploded remnants of war" (Wessells, 2016). Selecting r/syriancivilwar provided a clear opportunity to understand how children impacted by armed conflict are memorialized. While online forums are great resources, it is important to acknowledge the potential barriers and biases of online forums. Barriers include access to technology and social networking sites. Meanwhile, posts that have passed through moderation may indicate specific ideologies, misinformation, disinformation, or biased perspectives may have been favored due to the moderation team's beliefs, the rules of the subreddit, and/or Reddit's Terms of Service. In addition to the barriers and biases of forums, there are ethical considerations related to online research (van Dijck, 2013). Users posting in online spaces may not be informed about how public or private their posts are and may not have the opportunity to provide informed consent for their memorials to be utilized in scholarly work. By providing anonymity and using a reflexive inductive thematic analysis, this research highlights the knowledge provided by posts on the r/syriancivilwar subreddit while giving users the privacy they deserve.

While the beginning of the Syrian Civil War officially began on March 15, 2011, r/syriancivilwar did not come to fruition until over two years later, on May 6, 2013 (reddit.com/r/syriancivilwar). This piece looked at memorial posts from March 15, 2014, to March 15, 2019. These dates were selected to ensure memorial posts existed on the forum and the memorials were directly related to the Syrian Civil War rather than co-occurring under other events, like COVID-19. Additionally, these dates represent the heart of the Syrian Civil War, with three intense phases of armed conflict and attempts at international intervention (Yacoubian, 2021). We conducted a thematic analysis of English posts on r/syriancivilwar examining memorial posts about children to understand how narrative is constructed.

Generally, thematic analysis refers to the process(es) of coding and generating themes from qualitative data sets (Braun & Clarke, 2006, 2019). In an inductive thematic analysis, these themes are ultimately used to understand patterns that have emerged within the data set of interest (Braun & Clarke, 2012; Braun et al., 2022; see Trinh & Faulkner, 2023 for an example of inductive thematic analysis). In utilizing the reflexive inductive thematic analysis approach, we acknowledge that we are only painting by numbers that were already present in the data, rather than making broad strokes over a blank canvas. Letting the data guide the themes allows the research to begin surpassing the rigidity of imposing author biases, but the rigor of the thematic analysis procedures (including the reviewing of themes and determining significance) ultimately required author bias.

Why thematic analysis? In using this method, we want to meaningfully engage with the data and give agency to the posters of these memorials and ultimately the children and adolescents that were lost in the Syrian Civil War. Parsing out themes from the original posters' words allows us to situate ourselves as stewards of the knowledge they have presented us rather than detritivores feasting on the death and destruction caused by armed conflict. In conducting this piece, we wanted to highlight the importance of analyzing the languages of Arabic and English. Communication scholarship is focused on Western perspectives and positions the English language and English translations as the standard scholars must adhere to. There is a need to emphasize and highlight non-English, non-Western perspectives, especially those that are increasingly marginalized due to age (children) and life experience (armed conflict). However, collecting a wide body of posts in Arabic was difficult, as many posters utilized English as the message language.

We posit that English was the primary language used to increase the visibility of memorials to a global audience. With this in mind, we chose to exclusively focus on English-language posts. The exclusion of non-English language posts was a difficult decision, and we acknowledge several limitations of focusing on a singular language. For users who know English in varying degrees (fluent, professional, elementary, limited, or no understanding), the breadth and depth to which they can articulate their memorials will differ greatly. Furthermore, users with no knowledge of English may choose to post their memorials in Arabic (or other languages), which we did not capture in our project. The exclusion of non-English perspectives also means that we may be losing out on other themes and meaning making from posters in r/syriancivilwar. As discussed in our conclusions, we hope to see scholastic engagement with the Arabic language posts in a comparative analysis.

After extracting and cleaning relevant memorial posts from r/syriancivilwar, these posts underwent LDA and topic modeling scripts in R to bring relevant topics to the surface. These topics were organized in a word cloud (see Fig. A7.1) and the prevalence of each of these topics was measured (see Fig. A7.2). In the word cloud, the larger a word is, the more prevalent it is in the data. From the word cloud, themes were parsed out and explored below.

RESULTS

After analyzing the data, the following themes emerged: (A) Where are the Children? and (B) Blame Game: Bashar Al-Assad and the Armed Syrian Opposition. How these themes were parsed from the word cloud and their connection to the Syrian Civil War and depictions of war online will be discussed.

Where Are the Children?

Despite examining online memorials focused on children in armed conflict sites, children seemed to be all but absent except in the word *children*. Humanity was present, as referenced in the strong presence of the word *people* (see Fig. A7.1 for size). When comparing the size of *people* versus the size of *children* (Fig. A7.2) the focus on humanity generally (prevalence scaling = 0.06) superseded the focus on specific types of people, such as children (0.02). Similarly, nationality was recognized in the words *Syrian, Iranian, Iraqi, Iraq,* and *American*. This supports the ideas by Billig (1995) that nationhood cannot be written off in memorialization. The specific types of murders were a major focus of the posts. Larger conversations around who (in the moment) was the cause of death included descriptions like *inspectors, rebels, rebel, agent, police,* and *protestors*. The memorials highlighted those who were responsible for murdering *people*, whether that be the Syrian people or the members of Bashar Al-Assad. In summary, people dying and the groups of people responsible for killing were the focus of the memorials on r/SyrianCivilWar, rather than the children who had died.

In *H1*, we suggested that children would be discussed with positive language (e.g., affirmative of their strengths [kindness, resilience, etc.]). However, despite focusing on online memorials about children, children were noticeably absent and not discussed in any language type (positive, neutral, or negative). It is hard not to ask: Where are the children?

Blame Game: Bashar Al-Assad and the Armed Syrian Opposition

Turning our attention to larger organizational blame, *Assad* (see Fig. A7.1 for size), *government, regime,* and *police* were prominent topics. Furthermore, *propaganda* was a major topic, supporting the idea that propaganda was spread about which group should be trusted. Within the blame game, the methods being used to harm and murder people in the Syrian Civil War were also major topics. *Sarin* (toxic gas), *attack, launch missile, forces, saa (Syrian Arab Army), shooting,* and *concentration/camps* were present in varying degrees (prevalence range of 0.01 to 0.08). The focus of memorials was not on the children, but on who was causing death (as seen in theme one) and destruction by what means.

In *H2*, we believed that there would be differences in who is blamed for the children's deaths in memorial posts. With children largely absent from the memorial posts, *H2* is not fully supported. However, differences in who is blamed for death in the Syrian Civil War are supported, with Bashar Al-Assad and the Armed Syrian Opposition being the two organizations referenced throughout the memorial posts.

DISCUSSION

The themes presented above highlight major concerns for children and youth in armed conflict sites. First, children are largely absent from war narratives, including narratives that are supposed to center around their existence. This is an inadvertently dehumanizing practice with which the innocence of youth and the beginning of life are erased in favor of highlighting the atrocities of war. Furthermore, young people (children and youth) are adultified in these written accounts to undercut the vulnerability and strife that come with losing youth in war. Interestingly, these accounts are not reflective of all armed conflict spaces, as seen most recently with the ongoing Palestinian genocide. Children in Palestine are being interviewed, photographed, videoed, and martyred daily, which stands in stark contrast to the findings here.

The more generalizable theme would have to be the second, Blame Game. Regardless of the type of armed conflict that exists (i.e., civil war, genocide, international war), there are often multiple sides in which someone can position themselves. In the case of the Syrian Civil War, the main sides that were taken were Bashar Al-Assad and the Armed Syrian Opposition.

Taking Sides

Taking sides can be a way to promote unity among people in armed conflicts. For instance, in the context of the Syrian Civil War, online memorials on r/syriancivilwar show a clear division between individuals supporting Bashar Al-Assad and individuals backing the Armed Syrian Opposition. This stark polarization can be seen as a way for individuals to find solidarity and unity amidst the chaos and devastation of war. By aligning themselves with a particular group/side, individuals may, in turn, feel a sense of belonging and a shared purpose, which can be vital in the process of coping with hardships and losses that may be experienced during the conflict.

As proven by Tajfel and Turner (2004) and the Social Identity Theory (SIT), individuals derive a sense of self-esteem and identity from their membership in groups. In the context of armed conflicts, individuals may align themselves with a specific side to maintain a positive social identity and boost their self-esteem. SIT can help explain how and why individuals' sides where it could possibly promote unity among group members. Furthermore, taking sides can also serve as a way of asserting one's identity and values in a situation where there is constant uncertainty. Through publicly taking a specific position, individuals may feel that they are contributing and fighting for their beliefs. Consequently, this sense of purpose and shared meaning could be crucial in situations like armed conflicts where violence and destruction occur repeatedly.

Blame Game

After taking sides, blaming the opposing group likely follows. For instance, blaming one side for the destruction or death can also be a coping mechanism that individuals use to deal with the losses of war, life, and family. The blame game theme that was identified in the memorials on r/syriancivilwar can be interpreted as a coping mechanism for those who suffered losses during the conflict. Through blaming and attributing responsibility for the destruction and death to a specific side, individuals may find solace or a way to make sense of their experiences and new realities. Individuals may also find it as a way to channel their grief and anger. In situations where loss of life occurs, specifically of children, assigning blame can provide a sense of justice or order – even symbolically. Through holding one group accountable, individuals may feel that they are honoring the memory of their children and demanding justice. As proven by Heider (2013) and the Attribution Theory, people may assign causes to events and behaviors where in the context of coping with the losses of war, they attribute blame to one side which ultimately serves as a way of making sense of the situation and explaining the suffering they are experiencing. Attribution Theory can also help in explaining how individuals assign responsibility to a specific faction to provide a sense of order and justice.

Both emerging themes provide valuable insights into how individuals may cope with trauma and losses of armed conflict where they highlight the complex psychological and social processes at play in the context of war and memorializing passed children online. The "Where are the children" theme, which highlights the absence of children from online memorials despite the clear focus on child victims, resonates with current research on the invisibility and marginalization of children in armed conflicts. For instance, past research has shown that children's experiences and perspectives can be overlooked by adult narratives of war (Carpenter, 2006) and how child soldiers in the context of the "war on terror" and their experiences can be framed through adult-centric narratives (Hyndman, 2010). Consequently, this theme highlights the need for greater attention and representation of children's narratives in the discourses surrounding armed conflicts. The "Blame game" theme, which revolves around attributing the responsibility for the destruction and death to one group, can be explained through various theoretical lenses like the attribution theory (Heider, 1958), or the SIT (Tajfel & Turner, 1979). These theories explain how individuals assign blame and maintain positive group identity in the face of conflict and trauma. Simultaneously, the blaming game and taking sides between the two main groups in the conflict can serve as a means of creating meaning and order amidst chaos and promoting a sense of unity and shared purpose among those who suffered.

While the findings of the study are drawn from the specific case of the Syrian Civil War and the online memorials of children on r/syriancivilwar, they can potentially inform our general understanding of children's experiences in other conflicts and other contexts. Furthermore, while both themes shed light on the social processes that unfolded amidst the Syrian Civil War and have their place and relevance in research, it is important to recognize the limitations of generalizing from a single case study that had its own unique historical, political, and cultural context that could shape the way children are remembered and memorialized online. Nonetheless, this study and emerging themes provide valuable starting points for further exploration. While the contexts can differ, we believe the "Blame game" theme in specific can be generalized to other armed conflicts where it can manifest in different ways and different contexts.

CONCLUSION

Memorialization of children in posts on r/syriancivilwar shows us that children, even when they are supposed to be the focus of discussion, are still largely excluded from armed conflict narratives. By removing children from armed conflict narratives, victims of all ages will continue to be dehumanized. As their narratives are erased, advocacy efforts for children can be severely impacted as the record of their suffering is (un)intentionally wiped from the collective consciousness that is the internet. Furthermore, advocacy groups intending to assist child victims and families of armed conflict may find it difficult to obtain and allocate resources, as the children being impacted are absent from the constructed narratives.

Limitations

In crafting and executing this project, several limitations presented themselves. First, this chapter highlighted a specific subreddit (r/syriancivilwar), but memorials could have popped up on other, broader subreddits (e.g., r/syria). Similarly, Syria was the country of choice for this book chapter because of the impact of the Syrian Civil War on the Middle East. This did not consider online memorials for children and adolescents in other countries experiencing armed conflict.

This book's focus is on both children and adolescents in spaces of armed conflict. However, this chapter focused on children by coding the words child, children, kid, and kids. Adultification bias (Koch & Kozhumam, 2022) could have influenced the language used to describe adolescents and children (e.g., "young person," "little man"), which may have filtered outposts.

Additionally, constraints on the coding program limited filtering capabilities, so capturing a robust and succinct data set may have been hindered. When analyzing posts in r/syriancivilwar, we were unable to analyze posts written in Arabic, due to constraints of the coding program. Future scholarship could explore Arabic posts, specifically those written in both Arabic and Arabizi (Arabic words written with English letters and Arabic numerals).

Future Directions

As stated above, language and coding program development were limiting. Future research could find (memorial) posts in Arabic and English and develop word clouds in both languages to see if, despite differences in language, the same themes emerge. For researching developing their own work or adapting the work displayed here, think about culturally relevant terms for children and adolescents to cast a wider, but focused and culturally, net in the sea of internet information. This could be as simple as focusing on and coding for adolescents exclusively (e.g., tween/tweens, pre-teen/pre-teens, teen/teens, teenager/teenagers, and adolescent/adolescents), coding for additional terms (e.g., little man/woman/person; young man/woman/person), or coding for both children and adolescents.

As previously mentioned, this chapter focused on memorials for Syrian children, but war is unfortunately prevalent across the world. Future iterations of this work could examine memorials based in other areas where armed conflict is present. Furthermore, comparisons could be made between memorials for children versus adolescents within the same country or memorials for the same age groups across countries and continents. Big data research could sift through the comprehensive results of memorials for children and adolescents across countries and continents.

While not the focus of this chapter nor the book at large, further insights into online memorials could be a fascinating avenue of discovery. Examining a memorial poster's relationship to the deceased, such as a parent posting about their child, is one such area. While also outside the scope of this book, changing the age groups and the time frame (times of peace versus times of war) being examined could be interesting.

Concluding Thoughts

Online memorials for children in armed conflict spaces, specifically in the Syrian Civil War, are a unique place to uncover what it means to have been a child in an armed conflict site. Through LDA, topic modeling, and thematic analysis, the topics (A) Where are the children? and (B) Blame Game: Bashar Al-Assad and the Armed Syrian Opposition were uncovered. *H1* is not supported, as children are barely regarded in the memorials dedicated to them. Instead, there is a focus on victims (*people*) generally and the types of murderers in the armed conflict site. *H2* is partially supported, as the conflict from the Syrian Civil War was ever-present in the memorial posts. Although children were absent, methods of war and the large organizational bodies in conflict were present. This chapter has brought significant insights into how children in spaces of armed conflict are memorialized online, with particular attention to the lack of attention children receive (even in their own memorials) and how physical conflict translates online.

REFERENCES

Bell, D. (Ed.). (2006). *Memory, trauma and world politics: Reflections on the relationship between past and present.* Springer.

Billig, M. (1995). *Banal nationalism.* SAGE.

Boyden, J., & de Berry, J. (2004). *Children and youth on the front line: Ethnography, armed conflict and displacement.* Berghahn Books. https://www.jstor.org/stable/j.ctt9qddzv

Braun, V., & Clarke, V. (2006). Using thematic analysis in psychology. *Qualitative Research in Psychology, 3*(2), 77–101. https://doi.org/10.1191/1478088706qp063oa

Braun, V., & Clarke, V. (2012). Thematic analysis. In H. Cooper, P. M. Camic, D. L. Long, A. T. Panter, D. Rindskopf, & K. J. Sher (Eds.), *APA handbook of research methods in psychology, Vol. 2 Research designs: Quantitative, qualitative, neuropsychological, and biological* (pp. 57–71). American Psychological Associations. https://doi.org/10.1037/13620-004

Braun, V., & Clarke, V. (2019). Reflecting on reflexive thematic analysis. *Qualitative Research in Sport, Exercise and Health, 11*(4), 589–597. https://doi.org/10.1080/2159676X.2019.1628806

Braun, V., Clarke, V., Hayfield, N., Davey, L., & Jenkinson, E. (2022). Doing reflexive thematic analysis. In S. Badger-Charleson & A. McBeath's (Eds.), *Supporting research in counselling and psychotherapy: Qualitative, quantitative, and mixed methods research* (pp. 19–38). Palgrave Macmillan.

Carpenter, R. C. (2006). *'Innocent Women and Children': Gender, norms and the protection of civilians.* Routledge.

Carroll, B., & Landry, K. (2010). Logging on and letting out: Using online social networks to grieve and to mourn. *Bulletin of Science, Technology, & Society, 30*(5), 341–349. https://doi.org/10.1177/0270467610380006

Chaudhry, L. (2017). 'Raising the Dead' and cultivating resilience: Postcolonial theory and children's narratives from Swat, Pakistan. In M. Denov & B. Akesson (Eds.), *Children affected by armed conflict*. Columbia University Press. https://doi.org/10.7312/deno17472-003

Danilova, N. (2014). The politics of mourning: The virtual memorialisation of British fatalities in Iraq and Afghanistan. *Memory Studies, 8*(3). https://doi.org/10.1177/1750698014563874

Davis, C. S., Quinlan, M. M., & Baker, D. K. (2016). Constructing the dead: Retrospective sensemaking in eulogies. *Death Studies, 40*(5), 316–328. https://doi.org/10.1080/07481187.2016.1141261

de Vries, B., & Rutherford, J. (2004). Memorializing loved ones on the World Wide Web. *OMEGA, 49*(1), 5–26. https://doi.org/10.2190/DR46-RU57-UY6P-NEWM

Fowler, B. (2007). Collective memory and forgetting: Components for a study of obituaries. *Theory, Culture, & Society, 22*(6), 53–72. https://doi.org/10.1177/0263276405059414

Heider, F. (2013). *The psychology of interpersonal relations*. Psychology Press.

Hess, A. (2007). In digital remembrance: Vernacular memory and the rhetorical construction of web memorials. *Media Culture & Society, 29*(5), 812–830. https://doi.org/10.1177/01634437070805

Hume, J., & Bressers, B. (2010). Obituaries online: New connections with the living - and the dead. *OMEGA, 60*(3), 255–271. https://doi.org/10.2190/OM.60.3.d

Hyndman, J. (2010). The question of 'the political in critical geopolitics: Querying the 'child soldier' in the 'war on terror'. *Political Geography, 29*(5), 247–255.

Jacob, C. (2018). 'Children and armed conflict' and the field of security studies. In J. M. Beier (Ed.), *Childhood and the production of security* (pp. 24–38). Routledge.

Kar, S. (2020). An obituary for innocence: Revisiting the trauma during the Khmer Rouge Years in Cambodia through children's narratives. *Rupkatha Journal on Interdisciplinary Studies in Humanities, 12*(1), 1–9. https://dx.doi.org/10.21659/rupkathaa.v12n2.12

Kizel, A. (2014). "Life goes on even if there's a gravestone": Philosophy with children and adolescents on virtual memorial sites. *Childhood & Philosophy, 10*(20), 421–443.

Koch A., & Kozhumam, A. (2022). Addressing adultification of Black pediatric patients in the emergency department: A framework to decrease disparities. *Health Promotion Practice, 23*(4), 555–559. https://doi.org/10.1177/15248399211049207

Maddrell, A. (2012). Online memorials: The virtual as the new vernacular. *Bereavement Care, 31*(2), 46–54.

McDowell, S., & Braniff, M. (2014). Introduction. In *Commemoration as conflict: Rethinking peace and conflict studies*. Palgrave Macmillan. https://doi.org/10.1057/978137314857_1

Merrilees, C. E., & Lee, Y. (2018). The role of emotional security, narrative, and resilience for youth and families in contexts of armed conflict. *Family Court Review, 56*(2), 248–257. https://doi.org/10.1111/fcre.12338

Noguera, R. T. (2013). The narratives of children in armed conflict: An inference to spirituality and implication to psychological intervention. *International Journal of Children's Spirituality, 18*(2), 162–172. https://doi.org/10.1080/1364436X.2012.755954

Ray, A. (2017). Everyday violence during armed conflict: Narratives from Afghanistan. *Peace and Conflict: Journal of Peace Psychology, 23*(4), 363–371. https://doi.org/10.1037/pac0000281

Roberts, P. (2004). The living and the dead: Community in the virtual cemetery. *Omega, 49*(1), 57–76.

Roberts, P. (2006). From MySpace to our space: The functions of web memorials in bereavement. *The Forum: Association for Death Education and Counseling, 32*(4), 1–4.

Recuber, T. (2012). The prosumption of commemoration: Disasters, digital memory banks, and online collective memory. *American Behavioral Scientist, 56*(4), 531–549. https://doi.org/10.1177/0002764211429364

Roberts, P. (2012). '2 people *like* this': Mourning according to format. *Bereavement Care, 31*(2), 55–61. https://doi.org/10.1080/02682621.2012.710492

Selimovic, J. M. (2013). Making peace, making memory: Peacebuilding and politics of remembrance at memorials of mass atrocities. *Peacebuilding, 1*(3), 334–348.

SNHR. (2023). *On World Children's Day: SNHR's 12th Annual Report on violations against children in Syria [en/ar] - Syrian Arab Republic*. ReliefWeb. https://reliefweb.int/report/syrian-arab-republic/world-childrens-day-snhrs-12th-annual-report-violations-against-children-syria-enar#:~:text=The%20report%20documents%20the%20killing,were%20killed%20by%20Russian%20forces

Tajfel, H., & Turner, J. C. (1979). An integrative theory of inter-group conflict. In W. G. Austin & S. Worchel (Eds.), *The social psychology of inter-group relations* (pp. 33–47). Brooks/Cole.

Tajfel, H., & Turner, J. C. (2004). The social identity theory of intergroup behavior. In J. T. Jost & J. Sidanius (Eds.), *Political psychology* (pp. 276–293). Psychology Press.

Trinh, V. D., & Faulkner, S. L. (2023). Using the communication theory of identity to examine identity negotiation among LGBTQ+ college students with multiple conflicting salient identities. *Communication Quarterly*, *71*(2), 154–174. https://doi.org/10.1080/01463373.2022.2136009

van Dijck, J. (2013). Disassembling platforms, reassembling sociality. In J. van Dijck (au.), *The culture of connectivity: A critical history of social media* (pp. 24–44). https://doi.org/10.1093/acprof:oso/9780199970773.003.0002

Van Ommering, E., & el Soussi, R. (2017). Space of hope for Lebanon's missing: Promoting transnational justice through a digital memorial. *Conflict and Society*, *3*(1), 168–188. https://doi.org/10.3167/arcs.2017.030113

Viejo-Rose, D., & Stig Sørensen, M. L. (2015). Cultural heritage and armed conflict: New questions for an old relationship. In E. Waterton & S. Watson (Eds.), *The Palgrave handbook of contemporary heritage research* (pp. 281–296). Palgrave Macmillan.

Walter, T. (2015). New mourners, old mourners: Online memorial culture as a chapter in the history of mourning. *New Review of Hypermedia and Multimedia*, *21*(1–2), 10–24. https://doi.org/10.1080/13614568.2014.983555

Wessells, M. G. (2016). Children and armed conflict: Introduction and overview. *Peace and Conflict: Journal of Peace Psychology*, *22*(3), 198–207. https://doi.org/10.1037/pac0000176

Yacoubian, M. (2021, January 1). *Syria timeline: Since the uprising against Assad*. The United States Institute of Peace. https://www.usip.org/syria-timeline-uprising-against-assad

APPENDIX

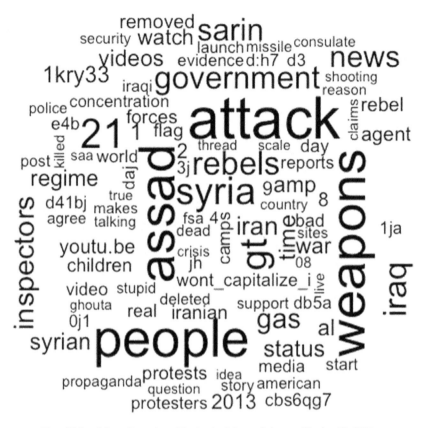

Fig. A7.1. Most Prevalent Topics in Memorials on r/SyrianCivilWar.

Beginning of Life, End of Life 129

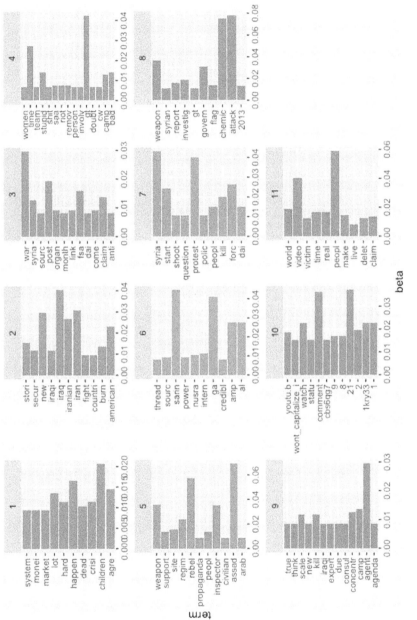

Fig. A7.2. Prevalence Scaling of Individual Words.

CHAPTER 8

CAPTURING RESISTANCE: UNVEILING VISUAL NARRATIVES OF YOUTH ACTIVISM IN THE ISRAEL–PALESTINE 2023 CONFLICT THROUGH MEDIA POSTED ON INSTAGRAM

Sonali Jha[a] and Mary-Magdalene N. Chumbow[b]

[a]*Colorado Department of Corrections, USA*
[b]*Clinical Trust Solutions, USA*

ABSTRACT

Amid the Israel-Hamas conflict in October 2023, social media platforms such as Instagram, have emerged as crucial platforms for millions seeking real-time insights, as well as those disseminating information about the conflict. Trending search terms on Instagram, such as "graphic Israel footage", "live stream in Israel right now," or #FreePalestine and #SaveSheikhJarrah, revealed a collective thirst for unfiltered frontline perspectives by users. Interestingly, individuals actively posting about the conflict experienced shifts in follower engagement, exemplified by the suspension of activist, Shaun King, whose 6-million followership Instagram account was disabled in December 2023.[1] Digital platforms play critical roles in escalating tensions, exposing governmental cruelty, and rallying international support (Burum, 2016; David, 2014). The case of Palestine and Israel underscores online media's role in constructing narratives and mobilizing resistance. This study seeks to illuminate the connection between visual storytelling, youth activism, and social media dynamics during conflict (Abushbak et al., 2020; Burum, 2016; David, 2014; Pruchnic, & Ceraso, 2020). This chapter examines textual and visual content by applying Textual-Visual Thematic Analysis to content posted on Instagram. This is done to understand Instagram users' discourse in October 2023 on Instagram. It analyzes how content shapes narratives and seeks to identify any patterns in the narratives shared by selected Instagram users. As such, this study aims to offer insights into the role that social media, particularly Instagram, plays in influencing narratives, fostering youth activism, and shaping public discourse during conflict.

Keywords: Israel; Palestine; Gaza; Instagram; social media platforms; war; youth activism

INTRODUCTION

Narrative is present in myth, legend, fable, tale, novella, epic, history, tragedy, drama, comedy, mime, painting, stained-glass, windows, cinema, comics, news items, conversation.

Barthes (1977)

Social media is a vital element of people's everyday routines. Social media and the internet can be used for various objectives, including advertising, disseminating political and financial trends, gathering user feedback on items, spreading spam, and sharing news. Social media allows users to share thoughts and build relationships through posts, comments, messages, and likes. Social media enables individuals to express their thoughts, feelings, and opinions quickly and easily (Alarifi et al., 2016; Öztürk & Ayvaz, 2018). Parallelly, social media platforms are commonly used for communication, information sharing, and advertising. Social media platforms are commonly used for purposes such as communication, information, and marketing. However, one major aspect of social media is the fact that it is used for political purposes, since many people online are interested in sharing their political opinions and reading about political news. Many others use it to design their campaigns, and many try to create awareness through the social media platforms to reach the target audience in the most effective way possible (Öztürk & Ayvaz, 2018).

It is the consumers who have access to new digital platforms, who also become the producers by creating their profiles and projecting their lives. Additionally, they have the option to now share any kind of information about themselves or the society near or on the other end of the world. This feature of social media creates a platform for collecting people's opinions that could be effective in making any policy change. This is mostly done through collecting data and analyzing their comments, likes, types of posts shared, and interactions, taking the themes, patterns, and emotions to build or generalize a theme prevalent given the issue (Pang & Lee, 2008; Park et al., 2016).

There are an estimated 3.4 billion active social media users spending more than 2 hours and 23 minutes every day. Additionally, social media users are found to be on four social media sites per day, with the top social media platforms being Facebook (95%), Twitter (84%), Instagram (74%), LinkedIn (62%), and YouTube (61%) (Kemp, 2023). According to research by Alwan et al. (2020) when people face conflicting advice, individuals often seek guidance from influential individuals, including supply chain members (e.g., merchants or manufacturers) and value-added influencers (e.g., industry analysts or professional consultants). Influencers, news broadcasters, and journalists on social media platforms are individuals who have a broad impact digitally, especially on Instagram. This, therefore, presents the opportunity to examine Instagram users' pages on an issue that has created an impact and plays a significant role in the success of the political and viral posts era where people tend to either gratify their thoughts or seek entertainment. The conflict between Palestine and Israel is not something new. However, how people talk about it, where they talk about it, and what kind of news they share about the conflict, is an interesting aspect to look at. In this chapter, we analyze young Instagram users' content on Instagram, a photo and video-sharing social media platform, as shared during the first week of the Israel–Palestine war in 2023. According to Kemp (2023), Instagram has more than a billion monthly active users and 500 million daily users. It is the second most downloaded free software on the Apple Software Store. Additionally, Instagram is reportedly the second most popular platform among teens behind Snapchat, with more than half of its users aged 18 to 34. People use Instagram to see images, 51% to watch videos, 45% to share material, 23% to network, and 11% to find/shop for products. Video content is popular on Instagram. In 2019, the amount of time spent watching Instagram videos increased by 80%. How-to instructions are the most popular videos on Instagram (80%) (Alwan et al., 2020; Kemp, 2023). Given the vast number of professionals on Instagram, as well as the different relationships that exist among them, giving an effective approach to identify journalists has increasingly been regarded as an essential aspect.

BACKGROUND

During October 2023, as tensions between Israel and Hamas in Gaza rose, the whole world watched in horror as brutal violence erupted, killing numerous people and forcing thousands of residents to become homeless. Some Instagram users, started to work relentlessly to record the everyday atrocities happening around them.

Users 1 for instance, the chosen users used their Instagram accounts to share real-time information, images, and firsthand stories of the effects of airstrikes and explosions on the civilian population. The photos incorporated the tagging people, background music, photos, and hashtags like #Gazaunderattack and #freePalestine, #israel #gaza #bombing, and more that swiftly acquired steam, catching the attention of international journalists, activists, and officials and most importantly the sufferings of the general public. However, many who had no clue of the complex and multifaceted situation of Israel and Palestine were struggling to understand the situation, and parallelly the news was overflowing with lots of narration. Few looked for alternative social media posts and channels for alternate perspectives after becoming frustrated with the conflicting narratives given in conventional media (Gonen et al., 2020; Huda et al., 2022; Zahoor & Sadiq, 2021). Ultimately, it was noted that a few posts of some influencers and journalists on platforms such as Facebook provide a genuine and uncensored view of life in Gaza but much-integrated propaganda (Seo & Ebrahim, 2016). However, many were intrigued by a few posts that carried a negative connotation and contacted the journalists and influencers who shared posts of daily catastrophes in Israel and Palestine through direct messages, resulting in an unusual interaction between two people on opposite sides of the debate. The conversations would have gradually grown into a genuine relationship marked by mutual respect and a desire for peace, which is what we anticipate.

Palestinian resistance to Israeli occupation is a long-standing, unsolved, and brutal battle of repression and struggle that has received significant international attention. Since the establishment of the State of Israel in 1948 and the subsequent displacement of Palestinians from their land (the Nakba), as well as the military occupation of the remaining Palestinian territories since 1967, there has been ongoing resistance to a settler-colonial regime attempting to erase them, a framework widely acknowledged in previous research (Confino, 2019; Fischer, 2022; Gelvin, 2014; Shah, 2012, 2024b). Hayes (2023) states in the research that the struggle for representation is the central resistance of Palestinian resistance against Israeli oppression. Hayes (2023) quotes Edward Said and states that research underlined the sense of impotence caused by a lack of control over how Palestinians are portrayed, connecting this to Western bias and the broader problem of othering Arabs and Muslims.

The image of Palestine and Palestinians in Western mainstream media supports this denial of self-representation by frequently matching with Zionist narratives depicting Palestinians as a threat and their land as vacant. However, the idea suggests that the media can also be used as a fight for regaining self-representation. As Ashcroft (2004) as cited in Hayes (2023), transformation can occur by presenting realistic images showing the reality of Palestinian experiences, moving away from the conventional presentation of despair, violence, and victimization and toward a portrayal that portrays Palestinians *"valid cultural reality."* Intractable conflicts, like the Israeli–Palestinian conflict, have a significant impact on the societies involved, influencing their ethos and perspectives. Intergroup talks are often utilized as techniques to reduce prejudice and improve relations between Israeli Jews and Palestinians. There has been little study on using online discussions for Israeli–Palestinian peacebuilding and reconciliation.

Social media is the current most viewed platform fulfilling many purposes from getting informed in real time to being entertained and voicing out for personal or others' rights. However, it revolves around user-generated content to facilitate all the communication offering activism and resistance. Social media access holds the power to change the mainstream media narratives, and foster communities and individuals for action. For example, with the Arab uprisings in the early 2010s and the Black Lives Matter (BLM) movement, we can examine the social media capabilities for creating an impact. In these movements, imagery has proven critical for communicating information to both national and international audiences, drawing on a long tradition of utilizing images to elicit empathy and sympathy with people impacted.

Recognizing that visual images are never neutral but are shaped by diverse practices, technologies, and understandings, we aimed to explore how Instagram users utilized images and videos to convey their narratives regarding the social and political dynamics informing their existence, as well as their portrayal to the global audience. No research has focused on the image analysis with the text. Hence, in this chapter, we have demonstrated the pivotal role of visibility for Instagram users who acted as activists, as they strived to advance their cause through their social media handles. By raising awareness and attracting attention to their issues, Instagram users can garner support and mobilize individuals to instigate change. We examine the images, videos, and captions that interact with the posts they share.

DATA SELECTION

The study looks at the Instagram accounts of 5 Instagram users who have between 100,000 and 18 million followers, and whose posts had constant engagement with an average of 100 likes and 50 or more comments in the month of October 2024. The study analyzed posts made by these users in the week right after the most recent bout of the Israel–Palestine war began in October 2023. These Instagram users were purposely chosen due to their high engagement, the number of followers, and the fact that they consistently shared their journey with raw content from Gaza. The study involved content posted by the five individuals. Additionally, only one week of content was analyzed – content that was posted between October 7th and 14th October 2023 on the selected Instagram accounts.

LITERATURE REVIEW

Overview of the Israel–Palestine Conflict and Its Impact

The Israel–Palestine conflict has a strong historical origin. It goes back to the early nineteenth century, being marked by several aspects including complicated issues of politics, demographics, and religion (Gelvin, 2014). The historic conflict has been reported to be shaped by events such as Israel's declaration of Jerusalem as its capital and the relocation of the US Embassy, which drew attention from the Organization of Islamic Cooperation, historical suffering, such as the Holocaust and the Nakba, shaping collective understandings of historical truth and existence (Confino, 2019; Fischer, 2022). The Israel–Palestine conflict is one of the longest and most impactful inter-state conflicts globally, which has resulted in four major wars and has left Israel as the occupying power over a large swathe of territory not allocated to it by the United Nations in 1947 (Pratiwi et al., 2022).

This conflict has also been described as an instance of colonization by fundamentally alien white Europeans (the Jewish–Israelis) of the non-white, colonized, indigenous Arab people of Palestine (Gelvin, 2014; Rowley & Taylor, 2006).

The conflict has also led to the development of theoretical frameworks to understand the sociopolitical realities of Palestine and Israel, such as settler colonialism as a suitable theoretical and methodological framework for comprehending these realities. The conflict has been described as a specific case of the ethnic regime, which enables, assists, and promotes the central Zionist project of Judaizing Israel/Palestine (Yiftachel & Yacobi, 2003). Additionally, the conflict has been associated with the logistics of occupation, where Israel's targeted military destruction of Palestine's key logistical nodes and immobilization programs systematically disrupt and undermine the flow of Palestinian goods (Alimahomed-Wilson & Potiker, 2017; Yiftachel & Yacobi, 2003). This war has been the topic of analysis not just in newspapers, but also for several debates on international platforms, which has influenced public opinion and news framing (Dajani Daoudi & Barakat, 2013; Imtiaz et al., 2022). The conflict has also been seen through the lens of settler colonialism, highlighting the intricacies of the issue and the necessity for decolonization (Shah, 2023). Additionally, the conflict is said to have major geopolitical relevance and worldwide impact, with consequences ranging from polarization to hostilities escalating, humanitarian crises emerging, and peace processes being initiated (Gelvin, 2014; Tessler, 2009), even the fight against COVID-19. Hence, with years of complexities, it is just not a conflict that is limited to its inter-region/state, but its impact extends beyond the region, influencing global politics, demography, religion, and other aspects, making it challenging to resolve (Shah, 2013). It has also been subject to extensive media coverage, including the use of social media platforms by traditional news organizations, influencing the perception, and understanding of the conflict globally.

EMERGENCE OF YOUTH ACTIVISM IN CONFLICT ZONES

Activism in general is a term with multiple meanings or interpretations – it can be described as the act of an individual or a group of individuals, engaging in activities that seek to foster an action, to create awareness of an issue, or to cause social change. This could be concerning social issues, social injustice, education, etc. The connotation of a term changes from place to place and grows when it is spread globally via media outlets. Similarly, the diversity of activism varies from country to country, and even within states, reflecting different views and approaches inspired by media stories. Furthermore, the context around language and activity is affected by media discourse's socio-cultural, political, and historical effects (Hussein, 2012). Across the world, throughout history, a lot of atrocities have taken place, and activism has taken place either as a community or as an individual has initiated, attracting others to speak against them (Murthy, 2018; Teruelle, 2012). However, over time when numerous young people came together in the forefront to create a social change, it earned the connotation of youth activism. Youth activists in the 21st century are still working to create a better, more equitable future for themselves (Bañales, 2012; Cortés-Ramos et al., 2021; Fullam, 2017). Parallelly, research in the field of youth activism happening on social movements has analyzed real-world examples, such as the Occupy movement, the Arab Spring, protests against the Dakota Access Pipeline, and the Black Lives Matter movement, to illustrate the role of social media. Scholars have accounted for instances of social media activism that have accelerated the growth of online movements, often spilling over into offline activities (Cox, 2017; Harlow, 2012; Raheja, 2017).

While it could mean a lot of good things, there has been a lot of conflict when it comes to defining the word "youth." The word "Youth" is not static. Youth's behavior, perspective, and characteristics are not constant. It, hence, emphasizes the dynamic and ever-evolving nature of the youth, be it from any corner of the world. Youth cross the path of growth, development, and change in their beliefs, values, and actions. This is when youth activism becomes problematic. It is a category that is hard to define. In the United States, youth activism emerged during the 19th century. Early research highlights the crucial role of young, often university-educated individuals in the Civil Rights movement, notably their involvement in sit-ins across the southern United States in the early 1960s and the 1964 Freedom Summer campaign for African American voter registration in Mississippi. Students also played pivotal roles in various movements, including the Free Speech Movement, the anti-Vietnam War movement, and the women's rights movement (Earl et al., 2017; Fullam, 2017; Yilmaz, 2017). Recent movements such as the #MeToo, and #BlackLivesMatter movements continue to rely on the recruitment and mobilization of young people in high school and college settings (Anderson, 2012; Stone, 2021; Wiltfang & McAdam, 1991).

Research on political socialization challenges the "deficit model" which views youth as less engaged and incomplete members of society needing instruction in political involvement. This model creates barriers by assuming youth disinterest in politics, neglecting their agency in political socialization. Unlike past campus activism research, an interdisciplinary approach now examines how youth develop political engagement (Earl et al., 2017). Instead of being taught how to engage correctly, youth autonomously shape their political views through experiences like discussions, activities, and participation in events, with families, schools, and institutions providing raw material and feedback (Anderson, 2012; Osler & Starkey, 2003; Youniss et al., 2002).

The prevailing media portrayal of youth activism primarily focuses on protests and demonstrations, reminiscent of historical coverage during the student protests of the 1960s and early 1970s (Murthy, 2018). This narrow representation has led many to associate youth activism solely with visible actions. Despite recent reports on student uprisings in Europe, overall, youth activism tends to receive minimal media coverage, resulting in limited awareness among the general public (Houston, 2015; Teruelle, 2012). It is argued that young people and their engagement in activism should not automatically be equated with adults or treated as a unique subset of adult activism. Research spans various fields, including sociology, political science, communication, and education, addressing youth agency, challenges they face in interactions with organizations, and the impact of adults on youth activism. Contextual factors, such as institutionalized politics, the emergence of movement societies and fan activism, and the widespread use of Internet technologies, also significantly influence youth activism (Anderson, 2012; Shah, 2021; Stone, 2021; Wiltfang & McAdam, 1991).

Considering the variation of activism and news reporting and grasping has changed, few critics argue that young people seem uninterested and disconnected from social issues and politics. Some media outlets complain about the younger generation being self-centered, lazy, ignorant, and narcissistic. The reasons suggested for this perceived disengagement include a lack of trust in those in power, a feeling of entitlement, and arrogance. For some, these attitudes in young people are seen as a warning sign for the decline of society. For instance, the rise of teenage activism in conflict zones is a vital and complex topic that has sparked interest from a variety of academic areas. Understanding what motivates young people to engage in activism in conflict zones is critical for understanding its evolution and potential role in effecting social and political change (Fullam, 2017; Murthy, 2018). Urdal (2006) conducted an important study on the association between youth bulges and political violence, underlining the heightened likelihood of armed conflict that comes with youth bulges. This study sheds insight into the demographic factors that influence the formation of youth activism in conflict zones. It reports that when we evaluate the function of democracy, two perspectives – opportunity and motive – produce opposing predictions. According to the opportunity perspective, political violence is more likely in less autocratic nations, but the motive-oriented perspective contends that more political oppression increases the motivation for violence. Empirical research, such as an inverted U-shaped link between democracy and conflict, indicates that highly autocratic and very democratic cultures are more peaceful.

According to the motivation perspective, the exclusion of big youth groups from political processes may result in violent behavior to press for democratic reforms. Moreover, when educated youth confront limited social mobility as a result of authoritarian administration, there is a higher risk of radicalization toward terrorism, especially under autocratic regimes. In essence, the motivational literature predicts that young. In short, the motive-oriented literature predicts that youth bulges have a greater influence on political violence in more autocratic governments. Other factors that influence or affect youth activism are demographic dividend, rapid growth in higher education, or the size of youth itself.

The rise of youth engagement in conflict zones, particularly during the Israel–Palestine conflict, is a major and multifaceted issue. Young people's participation in conflict zones has been related to a variety of issues, including demographic trends, intergenerational views, and the effects of systemic injustice (Shah, 2019). The experiences of young individuals in Israeli, Palestinian, and Palestinian–Israeli conflict zones emphasize the necessity for youth-led conflict transformation (Aubert et al., 2018; Sherrod et al., 2006). In this approach, young people are empowered to observe, identify, question, and challenge societal forces, actively contributing to conflict resolution (Gottesman, 2016).

This highlights the crucial role that youth play in addressing and altering the dynamics of prolonged conflicts.

Research also indicates that in conflict zones like Israel/Palestine, the younger generations express lower levels of hope for peace and harbor less reconciliatory attitudes compared to older generations (Hasler et al., 2023). The difference in outlooks between generations underscores the significance of comprehending intergenerational dynamics within conflict areas and recognizes the potential for youth activism to shape the future trajectory of conflict resolution. The impact of conflict-supporting narratives and media representation significantly influences youth activism. Sociopsychological analysis reveals that these narratives serve to perpetuate dominance within societies and globally (Schori-Eyal et al., 2014). Media portrayal of conflicts, like the Israel-Palestine conflict, has implications for intercultural communication and may affect the participation of young people in activism (Muzammal & Ghuman, 2021; Roy, 2012). Furthermore, the role of social media and digital platforms in shaping youth activism in conflict zones is noteworthy. The analysis of social media coverage of the Israel–Palestine conflict indicates the importance of these platforms for news gathering and dissemination, suggesting their potential influence on youth engagement with conflict-related issues.

Role of Social Media: Instagram as a Platform for Visual Narratives

Over time, the way people access information has changed significantly. In the past, sources like newspapers, radio, and television were prominent. People would gather around these devices to stay informed about local and global news. However, with the advancements in technology, especially the rise of the internet and social media, individuals can now connect globally at any time through computers or mobile devices. This shift from traditional sources to modern technology has transformed how information is communicated, making it faster and more accessible. With the arrival and access to social media, it has evolved a participatory culture for youth expression, empowerment, activism, and advocacy for any social issue, national or international (Bratchford, 2016; Miah & Omar, 2012).

Participatory media involves alternative media where individuals and communities share personal stories to raise awareness or challenge mainstream narratives. Media representations, according to Bleiker and Kay (2007), can be naturalist, humanist, or pluralist. Naturalists view the media as objective, humanists aim to evoke compassion but may lead to unintended pity, while pluralist approaches involve individuals sharing their stories, disrupting mainstream hierarchies. Participatory media allows for active social meaning construction, diverse voices, and nuanced understandings of conflicts. Youth media amplifies young voices, combining creativity and activism to initiate dialogue and action on various issues (as cited in Norman, 2009).

Past studies have looked at the cross-platform strategy of organizations and their advocacy for the conflict between Palestine and Israel on Facebook, Twitter, and Instagram accounts that post in English to an international audience. Past studies have looked into how social media is used to promote intergroup conversation and reconciliation and few have researched visual activism integrated with new media technologies (Bratchford, 2016; Hayes, 2023). However, the current study examines how Instagram users utilize their accounts for visual activism and as a means of protest, enhancing and defining visual outcomes (especially looking at the kind of pictures and videos shared right after the aftermath of the most recent bout of the conflict).

RESEARCH QUESTION

To investigate the visual narratives of young people during the Israel–Palestine 2023 conflict as portrayed by Instagram users, this study seeks to answer the following questions:

1. What are the thematic patterns and trends evident in the content shared by actively engaged young Instagram users regarding the Israel–Palestine conflict?
2. What are the emotional and psychological responses of young Instagram users toward the Israel–Palestine conflict?

METHODOLOGY

With the existence of social media platforms such as Instagram, the intensity at which visual research methods are now becoming a more welcome methodological approach to understanding society and culture. According to Cox et al. (2015), digital visual data such as videos and photographs, are now used more frequently in research. As a result, several scholars have proposed ways to study visual data through content and thematic analysis (Trombeta & Cox, 2022). For this study, Textual-Visual Thematic Analysis (TVTA), as proposed by Trombeta and Cox (2022), is applied to a week's worth of data. These data include photographs and short videos, also known as Instagram reels, that were posted by five Instagram users between October 7th and October 14th, 2023, when the most recent bout of the Israeli–Palestine war, began in Gaza. For purposes of this study, as well as to protect the identity of the Instagram users (IG Users) whose content was analyzed, they are assigned numbers 1 through 5. As such, content by the first user would be referred to as content by IG User 1.

Although originally designed in the context of photo-elicitation, TVTA is a comprehensive research method that comprehensively includes already-established thematic analysis steps, while not overlooking the analysis and interpretation of visual data (Trombeta & Cox, 2022). Thematic analysis is a non-linear process of studying data that is most often broken into six steps after data has been collected: data reviewing and familiarization, generation of initial codes, searching of themes, reviewing of themes, defining, and naming of themes, and reporting (Braun & Clarke, 2006). According to Trombeta and Cox (2022), TVTA builds on this method, by breaking a visual analysis into three phases: Phase 1 – analysis of textual data (if conducting interviews or collecting textual data of any other form); Phase 2 – Analysis of images integrated with interviews; and Phase 3 – Reporting of images and interviews' relationships.

DATA COLLECTION

In this study, TVTA is used to analyze both the captions that accompanied posted visuals, as well as the visuals themselves. First, the data were collected by purposively selecting the five Instagram users' pages and sifting through them to identify content only posted within the given time frame. All this data were entered into an Excel workbook, with each user having a dedicated sheet that had about eight columns. These columns included: the user's Instagram bio (the short description found at the top of the Instagram user's page), the date that the content was posted, the caption accompanying said post, the link to the post, the media type, the number of media put up on that post, a column identifying whether human beings were visible in any of the visuals that had been posted, and a column that described the content. A snapshot of the working workbook is shown in Table 8.1.

After data were collected and described using the workbook as discussed above, the first phase of the thematic analysis process began.

THEMATIC ANALYSIS

The present research aims to systematically analyze images and text found in the hashtags #FreePalestine and #SaveSheikhJarrah posts on Instagram. To do this, the authors collected one week's worth of audio-visual content that was posted by five Instagram users, who were identified by the authors to be leaders in the Israel-Palestine conflict social media discourse. This identification was made by reviewing the users' pages, and focus was put on their followership, as well as the number of comments made on each post. Secondly, an exploration of the captions accompanying each post was done. This was done with the aim of presenting a more composite understanding of the #FreePalestine and #SaveSheikhJarrah phenomena presented by users on Instagram, as the chosen social media platform.

Trombeta and Cox (2022) argue that, for visual data to be thoroughly studied and analyzed, there needs to be an integration of both textual data and visual data. In this study, therefore, studying how Instagram users created awareness and carried out activism during the onset of the most recent bout of the Israeli–Palestine war, started with the captions that accompanied each post. Seeing as each of the five users had their own Instagram accounts which they used to post in their own ways, thematic analysis of their posted content was conducted separately. Data familiarization meant that the data collected from each user's page was read actively, and at times, comparisons of each user's caption and posts were done just to give the authors a better understanding of the Instagram users' style of writing, differences/similarities of opinions, etc. The comparison was

Table 8.1. Workbook Showing Data Collection and Analysis.

Date of Post	Caption	Link	Media Type	No. of Media	Contains Human Beings: Y/N	Content Description
Oct 7th	Multiple Israeli air strikes on different places in Gaza city. #photography #israel #gazaunderattack #gaza	https://www.instagram.com/p/CyGq80kMPe9/?utm_source=ig_embed&ig_rid=7b1dde6f-f3d2-40da-a96e-5fc099cf0fbc&img_index=1	Images	6	Y	Images show human beings in distress; one has two people hugging, with one seemingly in pain/crying; another shows someone with blood on his face; another one has two young people sitting amidst torn-down building structures; two show firefighters and first responders trying to fight a fire (fire not visible – just smoke)
Oct 7th	Israeli Warplanes destroyed a residential building in the middle of Gaza city. #israel #gaza #gazaunderattack #palestine	https://www.instagram.com/p/CyG1nJzrnue/	Video	1	N	This video shows at least three buildings being blown up in a matter of seconds; a third building is blown up after the smoke from the first three buildings has gone down; voices can be heard yelling in the background amidst the sounds of the explosion
Oct 7th	It's come to look like Ghost Street... One of the most famous streets in Gaza (Al Shuhada) became a ghost's street after the Israeli warplanes destroyed a residential building in the middle of the city. #photo #gaza #gazaunderattack #palestine	https://www.instagram.com/p/CyHFzgwrnnC/?img_index=1	Images	3	Y	These three images show people out in the rumbles in the evening; they are carrying flashlights and seem to be searching for something/someone; they show torn-down buildings and vehicles
Oct 7th	Israeli warplanes bombed residential building (Palestine building) in the middle of Gaza city. #gaza #bombing #israel #gazaunderattack	https://www.instagram.com/p/CyHJ2berCZu/?img_index=1	Images	3	Y	These are still images from the video earlier posted showing the blowing up of several buildings.

important, as it allowed the authors to not only familiarize themselves with the different aspects of the data but also to search for and discover patterns in the way the discussion of the war was going on Instagram (Braun & Clarke, 2006). A separate worksheet was created on the same workbook, to code the captions. The codes were broken down into seven categories, based on the words used, as well as the tones. Color coding was a preferred method, as the analysis was being conducted manually, and colors helped to break down the data in a more visually appealing, yet easy-to-understand way (see Table 8.2).

During analysis and coding, a review of the arising themes was done, to ensure that each caption was coded in an appropriate manner, without missing out on anything, or miscoding. After this, a third review of the codes was done to determine whether certain captions could have more than one code in them, based on the codes that had already been identified. During this review, several captions were indeed carrying more than one code, which led to secondary, and even tertiary colors to be added alongside the primary colors. For instance, Table 8.3 shows a caption by one of the Instagram users that reads: "Please do something to stop these brutality attacks ... Israel just wiped the whole of Gaza's most beautiful neighborhoods." This caption carries three codes in it. The primary code, right from the opening sentence, is the code showing the author asking/request for assistance – through this caption, the author is asking that somebody somewhere, does something to end the calamity. Reading on further, the reader is introduced to two different themes in the second sentence. In this sentence, the author shares: (1) the actions of Israel and (2) a reminiscent/sentimental thought on neighborhoods considered as "most beautiful." Looking at this caption, it is evident that it carries three different themes – the author is asking for help while reporting an alleged attack by Israel on Gaza, and finally, sharing a thought on the section of Gaza that the Israeli government allegedly attacked, claiming that those were the most beautiful neighborhoods.

After coding and creation of themes was done, and reviewing of these codes and themes was done severally, a definition of the themes was done, as follows:

Theme One: War, Brutality, and Violence – this refers to words and/or phrases used to talk about the state of battle/war that either Israel or Palestine was in. Through these phrases, the authors sought to enlighten their readers/followers, on the attacks suffered by one side against the other side.

Table 8.2. Color Coding Scheme Used to Analyze Captions.

Colors	Codes/Themes
Light Berry Red	Mention of Israel Attack on Palestine/Palestinians
Light Orange	Reminisces of famous/beautiful structures, streets, etc.
Light Green	Self-Reflective post
Light Magenta	Displacement, Migration, Aid, Support, Community
Yellow	No Captions
Cyan	Request for assistance, calling on God
Brown	Giving Up/Losing Hope/Demoralized

Table 8.3. Scheme of Coded Captions.

Captions & Primary Colors	Secondary Colors	Tertiary Colors
(Light green) From early morning I turned my camera on to cover the ongoing craziness and massive attacks that Israel launched towards Gaza and Gazans I am here and there trying to cover what I could without thinking about my back or that I even slept for the last two days. As the other journalists too. (I'm available for assignments)	(Light berry red)	
(Light magenta) I tried to reduce the #trauma they got after leaving their houses and escapes to UNRWA schools by letting them make fun in front of the camera. Dozens of Palestinians flee from their homes east of Gaza to the middle of the city, using UNRWA schools as a shelter to protect them from the ongoing violence and bombing. #unrwa #war #gaza #kids		
(Light berry red) Israeli warplanes targeted a residential apartment and murders more than 5 people while they were sleeping in the early morning 8 October 2023. #photo #photography #war #israel #gaza		
(Light magenta) We didn't even sleep.. We waited the dusk light so we could go out and see what Israel bombed. Multiple residential buildings and towers got destroyed and dozens of Gazans had to flee to the streets, schools and hospital. To survive their lives. #photo #gaza #israel	(Light berry red)	

Theme Two: Aid, Support, Community, and Displacement – the captions that were categorized under this theme, were captions that showed how those affected by the war were receiving support, supporting each other, and/or were being displaced. These would include captions that spoke of how people were fleeing from their homes, as well as those that asked for assistance or shared how humanitarian groups were supporting displaced individuals.

Theme Three: Family, God, and Hope – Under this theme, the captions expressed reverence for a higher and supernatural being, explicitly calling on this being to rescue them, save those who were being attacked, and stop the war. On the other hand, some of the captions shared a semblance of the authors hoping for a better future for their countries/regions or losing hope of their being a better future. Other captions also spoke about the authors' own families and how they were being affected by the war.

Theme Four: Mental Health – Here, captions that had phrases of self-reflection, which at times sounded like the author feeling guilty and mentally turmoiled, were grouped together. Although not that many, the captions spoke to much more than a sense of lost hope – they shared the effect that the war was having on these individuals as they lost people close to them, were being forced to leave their homes, and were visiting sites of destruction day in, day out.

ANALYZING THE VISUAL CONTENT

After a thematic analysis of the captions was conducted, a thorough review of the images and videos that accompanied each caption was done. During this review, the main questions asked were:

- What is in the visual content that supports or reinforces what was learned from the textual data (captions)?
- What is in the visual content that contradicts what was learned from the textual data/captions?
- What is in the visual content that is not in the captions?
- What is in the captions that is not in the visual content?

The above "guidance" questions were adapted from the work of Trombeta and Cox (2022) and played a huge role in enabling the visual content to be integrated with the textual data, which in this case, were the captions. To answer these questions, both the visual and textual data were revisited, as comparisons were made to get the needful answers for each question. The process of answering these questions went beyond comparing the visual and textual data. It also involved coding each visual content, an act that allowed the organization of the visual content according to arising themes. Using the already existing color codes, each visual content was coded as shown in Table 8.4.

The color codes for the visual content slightly differed from the ones identified in the textual content. This is because text gives readers/viewers more in terms of feelings and thoughts. However, by watching the videos posted, looking at the pictures, and reading the captions accompanying each visual content, one could begin to tell the tone of the post, as well as what the posters were thinking when putting the posts up.

Table 8.4. Color Coding Scheme Used to Analyze Visual Content.

Colors	Codes/Themes
Light Berry Red	Depicts Acts of Violence/violence in motion
Light Orange	Shows displacement/migration, pain
Light Green	Shows destroyed buildings
Light Magenta	Shows Aid, Support, Community

After coding was done, the answers to each of the "guidance" questions were sought, as reported in the discussion section below.

RESULTS AND DISCUSSION

The analyzed visual content was used by the five Instagram users to create and communicate information, awareness, and narratives about the Israel–Palestine war from the perspective of Palestinian Instagram users. This study emphasizes the role of social media in information diffusion, particularly during times of calamity. To understand the thematic patterns and trends that were evident in the content shared by Instagram users regarding the Israel–Palestine conflict, as well as what the emotional and psychological responses of these users were toward the conflict, thematic analysis of visual content as well as captions (textual content), was conducted. This section discusses the results in detail, using the four "guidance" questions mentioned previously, to expound further.

What Is in the Visual Content That Supports or Reinforces What Was Learned from the Textual Data (Captions)?

A very common pattern in the visual content shared by all five Instagram users was the theme of war, brutality, and violence. This was evident not only in many of the photos and videos that were shared but also in the captions that accompanied many posts. Through images and videos of flames, air strikes, demolished buildings, burnt cars, and the solemn procession of dead bodies being carried, along with the captions that were made with these posts, readers and viewers are introduced to the violence existing in the region during the war.

Many images and videos powerfully captured the tragic reality of the violence, a good example being the pictures of air strikes. For instance, IG User 1 shared a picture of an air strike occurring in Gaza at the time. The image showed a golden/bright orange sky that coincided with sunset, along with buildings being blown up in the near distance. The image was captioned "*Gaza – Oct 2023*," nothing more.

A video shared by IG User 2 included a caption along with said video. The caption used said, "*Israeli Warplanes destroyed a residential building in the middle of Gaza city.#israel #gaza #gazaunderattack #palestine*." The video showed a residential area with three tall buildings under a clear sky, being struck down slowly with warplane strikes and the dark gray flames covering up the space and slowly covering every demolition under it. Within a few seconds, the three buildings along with other small residential buildings struck by warplanes, gradually vanished as dark gray flames engulfed them. Initially marked by the pristine blue of the sky, the scene transitioned into one dominated by dark gray smoke, with airstrike sparks intermittently lighting up the frame.

These two are examples of the visual contents shared by the five users and analyzed for this study. The visual content showed several occurrences including multiple air strikes in the sky and flames spreading across the clear sky and residences being diminished into the flames of the warplane and air strikes. Systematically, of all the posts where airstrikes were captured, none of them had background music accompanying the visual content. Instead, the IG users who posted them used the natural sound of the air strike, and sounds of people's fear and shock were heard, which spoke to a more solemn tone, compared to other posts that had some background music in them.

Another common type of visual content that showcased violence, war, and brutality, was the type of content that showed demolished buildings and burnt cars. Additionally, the theme of aid, support, and displacement is seen in some of the visual content. For instance, apart from depicting violence and portraying the raw realities of armed combat including scenes of damage and destruction, some of the images and videos showing airstrikes conveyed the need of urgent international measures to protect civilians in crisis zones and seek peaceful settlements to disputes. Images showing humanitarian personnel, or individuals carrying bodies of those who had succumbed to injuries and other life-threatening incidents as a result of the war, sustain the depiction of this theme. IG User 2 shared pictures on Oct 9th that showed large, demolished buildings covered with dust and roads also in gray color, difficult to understand where the boundary for the road was. Additionally, the images showcased a few civilians trying to rescue bodies from the demolished buildings and taking people out from the buildings including women and children. Lastly, some images also included children and adults looking at the damaged buildings, while others rummaged through the destruction. Through these stunning visual narratives, the critical need for peace, humanitarian intervention, and collective action by international organizations to intervene.

Images and videos that showed the theme of aid, support, community, and displacement were not that different from the theme of war, brutality, and violence – they offered a glimpse of the effects of the violence's aftermath. The visual content portrayed scenes of grief and emotional distress, such as crying individuals, people mourning over dead bodies, and children in shock or fear. To showcase the gravity of the situation, a lot of images and videos posted by the IG users whose content was analyzed for this study, included women and children, while a few had men crying and rushing with injured humans and dead people into healthcare centers.

Other pictures and videos that showed how the people of Gaza were receiving aid and support, while showcasing aspects of community and displacement were those of women crying and children injured and in fear or of children seemingly lost and in despair. This visual content evoked empathy and underlined the human misery that exists in conflict zones.

Concurrently, scenes of human suffering and anguish played out in some of the visual content that was analyzed – these showed the raw emotional upheaval that people in Gaza faced amid catastrophes. Individuals crying, mourners weeping for lost loved ones, and children overcome with shock and anxiety highlight the events' devastating psychological impact (Shah, 2020). For example, in one video, an injured child is shown crying over his injuries and shouting *"BABA,"* to mean father. Amidst this tragic backdrop, the sight of children in distress suggests a looming humanitarian crisis, as people struggle with scarcity and the desperate chase of basic commodities such as water. Despite the damage, hints of resilience appear as individuals continue with their regular activities, exhibiting tremendous courage in the face of adversity.

Acts of caregiving and solace, amidst the chaos, serve as poignant reminders of human fortitude. Meanwhile, journalists tirelessly bear witness to these harrowing scenes, their emotional reactions underscoring the gravity of the events unfolding before them. The scenes of destruction and displacement further underscore the magnitude of the crisis, with burnt buildings and fleeing refugees bearing testament to the upheaval wrought by conflict. Throughout these narratives, flames emerge as a potent symbol, representing the destructive force and pervasive danger inherent in the tumultuous environments captured by the media. The Instagram users shared pictures and videos of hospitals and treatment centers where people are being treated.

Despite facing terrible conditions, these Instagram users also shared content that fell under the themes of God, Family, and Hope. For example, people gathering to collect water to drink or play in the middle of devastation. Acts of caring, such as a lady soothing a toddler or a man kissing a dead body, exhibit perseverance and emotional strength in the face of hardship. On the other hand, children playing around a burnt car is another example of how children are too innocent to understand the misery and problems the area is facing. Another image showed a young boy carrying two bags of bread and walking through a destroyed zone while pushing a bicycle. All this visual content specifies that no matter what misery one goes through in one's daily life, there will always be the need to keep on living.

What Is in the Visual Content That Contradicts What Was Learned from the Textual Data/Captions?

The majority of the visual content collected for analysis was more focused on using visuals compared to adding perspective or focus via captions or engaging audiences with comments. The majority of the posts included tagging of others and the use of background music in the case of video content, to evoke emotion, leaving everything to the audience's interpretation (Shah, 2024a).

However, when captions were included, they were used to emphasize the emotions that the visual content emoted. For example, User 1 shared the same video on October 7th and October 8th with different captions. The video shared on October 7th was captioned, *'The street is not suitable for photography, and the Tower of Palestine is completely destroyed* ♥☹☹.*'* The video was posted once more on October 8th and was captioned, *'The street that I used to like to photograph daily* ♥☹*'*, (translated from Arabic via Google). The caption directs the viewers toward the idea of displacement and loss felt by the residents of Gaza.

Interestingly, as days passed, several posts were captioned with words showcasing God being above all and God will suffice and will do justice. Videos with such captions had videos of either hospital or destruction videos. This reflected the hope in the community. Many of the posts were captioned with words seeking blessings and mercy from God. However, the visual content accompanying these captions showed violence and brutality – air strikes, and demolition of buildings and residential areas. This shows some contradiction in captions used, versus the visual content accompanying them.

Capturing Resistance 149

Such posts that had captions such as *"God help us"* accompanying pictures of injured children, air bombings, and videos of the demolished buildings and hospitals are restrictive of sharing the emotions and words spoken or, as in the case of a video shared by IG User 3 while he was on the scene of chaos in Gaza, the breath of the heavy breathing and panicky voice of the recorder as he walked through the damage. Additionally, the panic and chaos shown at hospitals with children crying, can be felt through the videos, but the captions accompanying the posts did not always speak to the same themes.

What Is in the Visual Content That Is Not in the Captions?

Since the analyzed Instagram accounts did not have long captions, it was easy to see that a lot of what was captured in the visual content was left to the imagination of the audience. For example, an image shared by IG User 3, did not include a caption. Instead, the post was a video of a man sitting amidst rumbles, with fire blazing in the surroundings, amidst destroyed buildings. Little is said by the poster, about what is going on, but by watching the video of this man seated there, one can depict a lot – destruction has happened, the man is concerned about what is going on, and destruction is still happening even as people are still dealing with the destruction that just happened.

Captions go a long way in explaining what is happening in posted visual content, especially on platforms such as Instagram. However, the captions can never truly depict the emotions of the content as much as the visual content itself would. For instance, in the video mentioned, even without a caption, the viewer is able to understand the gravity of the situation, simply by watching the video and listening to the background sound of people talking frantically, while fire blazes in the background. In another video, a man whose facial expression is blank, is seen sitting amidst demolished building pieces with a big dirty teddy bear and few other medium-sized stuffed animals. In the video, the destruction and people walking by him do not seem to be at the top of his mind, as he seems lost in thoughts. Because the video included sound but no caption, one is left to wonder if he was deep in thought because he had lost his children, or why the stuffed animals were of much significance to him.

Another aspect of the content that cannot be captured by any form of text is sound – in most of the videos, viewers are introduced to the gravity of the situation in the area, not only by seeing the images or videos but also by listening to what is happening in the captured videos. For instance, in the videos posted by IG User 3 showing air strikes on some buildings in Gaza, one can not only watch what is happening, but can also hear how the missiles are headed toward the buildings, and how they land on the buildings. The sound does not only end there – in the aftermath of the strikes, one can hear how the buildings are falling, even as one watches everything in the video. In some ways, these sounds play a huge role in magnifying the gravity of the situation.

What Is in the Captions That Is Not in the Visual Content?

The visual content shared by all five Instagram users shares a lot more similarities than the captions they each used in their content. Out of five Instagram users, only two Instagram users used highly descriptive captions frequently. For instance, on October 6th, the day the first attack took place, the caption that accompanied a post shared by IG User 4 read, "*Palestinian youth carry the body of a martyr from the Erez crossing on a motorcycle during the confrontation with the Israeli army on the northern border of the Gaza Strip.*" An image shared by IG User 2 on October 8th with the caption, "*A Palestinian man sits in the rubble of a building after it was struck by an Israeli airstrike, in Gaza City, Sunday, Oct. 8, 2023...*"

Hence, some of the Instagram users whose work was analyzed shared visual content that showcased and described the pictures as they were, with words that evoked emotion in their audience. The captions carried little emotion and were laid out professionally (as media personnel/journalists would) while accompanying visual content that was tragic/highly emotive.

Interestingly, the other three Instagram users took a different approach when captioning the visual content that they shared, as well as when selecting the type of visual content they shared. They used background music and voice overs on the videos they shared, apart from using captions that evoked emotion in their audiences. Some of the voiceovers and captions included words and phrases seeking hope and justice from God, describing their lives, and adding narratives on how they were working to get the news and how they were suffering.

For example, IG User 1's caption on a post read, "*We didn't even sleep... We waited for the dusk light so we could go out and see what Israel bombed. Multiple residential buildings and towers got destroyed and dozens of Gazans had to flee to the streets, schools and hospitals. To survive their lives. #photo #gaza #israel.*"

Some of the identified Instagram users used emojis that expressed heartbreak and a lot of the captions used were in Arabic. Thus, even without translating what they were saying in the captions, the captions alone spoke volumes about their feelings, and told the audience what to expect when swiping left to view more content, or when clicking on the videos to watch them. As such, the captions showcased the reality of what people were going through, and their audiences could relate just by looking at these captions.

ADDITIONAL SENTIMENTS EXPRESSED IN THE VISUAL AND TEXTUAL CONTENT SHARED

Throughout the images and videos shared an inclusion of the Instagram users' misery is noted. For example, one user shares a video of meeting her children after a month of separation due to the war. Another IG user shared a video of himself walking and smiling, and in the background music with a caption asking for forgiveness should he leave (the caption does not detail where he is going or when). It just depicts a sense of lost hope, and that this IG user had given up.

The presence of journalists collecting and documenting events during this war, emphasizes the importance of media in being present to tell the stories during conflicts and humanitarian catastrophes. The data collected and analyzed showed the depiction of journalists sobbing or being emotionally impacted while reporting, thus emphasizing the personal impact that experiencing and reporting tragic occurrences, has even on journalists. The users, some of whom also double as journalists according to their Instagram page description, share a glimpse of people immigrating – in one video, the viewers see a video which has one of the Instagram users showing herself in the process of migrating, with eyes full of tears.

Additionally, even though the chaos was at its peak, people who could, whenever they could, tried their best to capture everything and share it on social media. From chaos in the hospital to the prayers being offered to the dead bodies, and air strikes and bombing happening, viewers see these Instagram users trying to capture every little detail.

THE SYMBOLISM OF FLAMES

Images and videos showcasing flames of fire are very commonly shared by these five Instagram users. In this study, the analysis revealed that flames represented the destruction force of conflict and violence, parallelly also capturing and denoting chaos, upheaval, and transformation of the residents into immigrants. Fire, therefore, serves as a symbol of the devastation of war. For example, an image where there are flames in the background during sunrise in wide-angle, depicts the demolition of the cities and the Palestinian people regardless of the time of day.

Furthermore, the great heat and brightness of the flames shown in some of the content, create an atmosphere of urgency and danger, exacerbating the sense of peril and vulnerability felt by those caught up in the struggle.

However, flames also carry the symbolic connotation of renewal, as well as resistance and defiance in the face of adversity and persecution. The images of fire burning amidst the ruins of conflict-ravaged landscapes capture the spirit of resilience and resistance, expressing individuals' and communities' desire to stand firm in the face of brutality and injustice. In this way, flames become a symbol of hope and defiance, signifying the human spirit's resilience in the face of adversity.

CONCLUSION AND LIMITATION

This analysis emphasized the use of written captions to provide context for photos within the broader context of the Israel–Palestine war of 2023. The Instagram users whose accounts were analyzed consistently reiterated this narrative across a continuous flow of images and videos throughout the week of October 7th to October 14th. From analyzing the content shared, it was clear that the users introduced a new angle of news from the war-impacted region, different from what was shared in mainstream media. This new angle contested mainstream narratives found in popular media, which often depicted the conflict as a mutual cycle of violence between equal parties, with Palestinians portrayed as threats to Israel's national security. From the analysis of content shared by the five Instagram users, it was clear that the violence occurring in Palestine affected the Palestinians in ways that were not covered in popular media. It was also clear that, while the content shared might have been biased, as all the Instagram users seemed to share content from the Palestinian perspective, it was raw enough for audiences' miles across the world, to see exactly what the conflict was doing to the common man in the war-torn area. Each of the four themes that arose in the shared content through the captions used and/or the visual content that was posted, showed the human side of the people on the ground. From videos of people mourning to captions full of emotive emojis and words that evoke high emotions in their audiences, the five Instagram users proactively used Instagram as a news-sharing platform to tell untold stories of what was happening in Gaza. In the captions, we see them mention God, and the need for the world to help Palestinians, as well as plain out telling their audiences what was happening on the ground. Some showcase pure vulnerability when the conflict directly affects them, crying on camera after the loss of family members, and using captions that indicate their mental state of loss of hope that things will ever get better.

Looking at these accounts, it is clear that Instagram was a powerful sharing platform for sharing news about the war in Gaza and asking for humanitarian aid. Even amidst stories of Meta, Instagram's parent company, shutting down certain Instagram accounts during this period, these five Instagram users showed courage as they continued to post several times daily, and drew attention to the side of the conflict that was not being aired on mainstream media at the time.

This study was not without its share of limitations. Due to limited resources, the study only included an analysis of content shared within one week alone. Additionally, the study only looked at content shared by only five Instagram users, who all happened to be Palestinian. Furthermore, the inability to get approval from the IG users on time, for their visual content to be used in this chapter, meant that the reader here is unable to be visually introduced to some of the content analyzed in this study. The authors had to, instead, textually describe some of the visual content.

For further studies, analysis of content posted for a longer duration of time, as well as by more social media users of diverse origins, would be advisable. Also, comparison studies looking at the difference in conflict news coverage between private/individual citizens on social media, versus international/mainstream media houses, would shed more light on the impact conflict has on local communities as opposed to the international community.

NOTE

1. https://www.nbcnews.com/news/us-news/activist-shaun-king-says-meta-banned-instagram-palestinian-stance-rcna131244

REFERENCES

Abushbak, A. M., & Majeed, T. (2020). *The role of social media in mobilizing crowd protest – A case study of Palestinian anger against Israel's Military measures at Al-Aqsa compound on Instagram.* Studies in Indian Place Names.

Alarifi, A., Alsaleh, M., & Al-Salman, A. (2016). Twitter Turing test: Identifying social machines. *Information Sciences, 372,* 332–346.

Alimahomed-Wilson, J., & Potiker, S. L. (2017). The logistics of occupation: Israel's colonial suppression of Palestine's goods movement infrastructure. *Journal of Labor and Society*, *20*(4), 427–447.

Alwan, W. H., Fazl-Ersi, E., & Vahedian, A. (2020). Identifying influential users on Instagram through visual content analysis. *IEEE Access*, *8*, 169594–169603.

Anderson, N. S. (2012). Youth activism. In N. Lesko & S. Talburt (Eds.), *Keywords in youth studies: Tracing affects, movements, knowledges* (pp. 314–318). Routledge. https://doi.org/10.4324/9780203805909

Ashcroft, B. (2004). Representation and its discontents: Orientalism, Islam and the Palestinian crisis. *Religion*, *34*(2), 113–121. https://doi.org/10.1016/j.religion.2003.12.003

Aubert, S., Barnes, J. D., Abdeta, C., Nader, P. A., Adeniyi, A. F., Aguilar-Farías, N., … Tremblay, M. S. (2018). Global matrix 3.0 physical activity report card grades for children and youth: Results and analysis from 49 countries. *Journal of Physical Activity and Health*, *15*(s2), S251–S273. https://doi.org/10.1123/jpah.2018-0472

Bañales, S. (2012). *Decolonizing being, knowledge, and power: Youth activism in California at the turn of the 21st century* [Doctoral dissertation, UC Berkeley].

Barthes, R. (1977). Introduction to the structural analysis of narratives. In S. Sontag (Ed.), *Image-Music-Text*. Fontana.

Bleiker, R., & Kay, A. (2007). Representing HIV/AIDS in Africa: Pluralist photography and local empowerment. *International Studies Quarterly*, *51*(1), 139–163.

Bratchford, G. (2016). *Visual activism in Israel, the occupied Palestinian territories and Gaza* [Doctoral dissertation, Manchester Metropolitan University].

Braun, V., & Clarke, V. (2006). Using thematic analysis in psychology. *Qualitative Research in Psychology*, *3*(2), 77–101.

Burum, I. (2016). *Democratizing journalism through mobile media: The Mojo revolution*. Routledge.

Confino, A. (2019). The holocaust and the Nakba: Memory, national identity and Jewish-Arab Partnership. *Palestine-Israel Journal of Politics, Economics, and Culture*, *24*(3/4), 20–28.

Cortés-Ramos, A., Torrecilla García, J. A., Landa-Blanco, M., Poleo Gutiérrez, F. J., & Castilla Mesa, M. T. (2021). Activism and social media: Youth participation and communication. *Sustainability*, *13*(18), 10485.

Cox, S. M., Guillemin, M., Waycott, J., & Warr, D. (2015). Visual methods and ethics: Stories from the field. *Visual Methodologies*, *3*(2), 1–3.

Dajani Daoudi, M. S., & Barakat, Z. M. (2013). Israelis and Palestinians: Contested narratives. *Israel Studies*, *18*(2), 53–69.

David, A. B. (2014). Israeli-Palestinian conflict and social media. In *Encyclopedia of social media and politics* (pp. 741–744). Sage Publications.

Earl, J., Maher, T. V., & Elliott, T. (2017). Youth, activism, and social movements. *Sociology Compass*, *11*(4), e12465.

Fischer, N. (2022). Entangled suffering and disruptive empathy: The Holocaust, the Nakba and the Israeli–Palestinian conflict in Susan Abulhawa's Mornings in Jenin. *Memory Studies*, *15*(4), 695–712.

Fullam, J. (2017). Becoming a youth activist in the internet age: A case study on social media activism and identity development. *International Journal of Qualitative Studies in Education*, *30*(4), 406–422.

Gelvin, J. L. (2014). *The Israel-Palestine conflict: One hundred years of war*. Cambridge University Press.

Gonen, Y., Tenenboim-Weinblatt, K., & Kampf, Z. (2020). Mediating the opponent's news: A study of inter-media citations in the Israeli–Palestinian conflict. *Media, War & Conflict*, *15*(3), 334–352. https://doi.org/10.1177/1750635220953656

Gottesman, S. (2016). Hear and be heard: Learning with and through music as a dialogical space for co-creating youth led conflict transformation. *Voices: A World Forum for Music Therapy*, *17*(1). https://doi.org/10.15845/voices.v17i1.857

Harlow, S. (2012). Social media and social movements: Facebook and an online Guatemalan justice movement that moved offline. *New Media & Society*, *14*(2), 225–243.

Hasler, B. S., Leshem, O. A., Hasson, Y., & others. (2023). Young generations' hopelessness perpetuates long-term conflicts. *Scientific Reports*, *13*, 4926. https://doi.org/10.1038/s41598-023-31667-9

Hayes, J. (2023). Palestinian solidarity on social media: The distribution of images of occupation on Twitter, Facebook, and Instagram by advocacy organisations (Doctoral dissertation, University of Sheffield).

Houston, C. (2015). How globalization really happens: Remembering activism in the transformation of Istanbul. *International Journal of Urban and Regional Research*, 39(1), 46–61.

Huda, M. N., Nurmandi, A., Qodir, Z., Sutan, A. J., Misran, M., Utaminingsih, N., ... Suswanta, S. (2022). Social media role to support Palestinian on Palestine – Israel conflict *Proceedings of the International Conference on Sustainable Innovation on Humanities, Education, and Social Sciences (ICOSI-HESS)*, pp. 901–913. https://doi.org/10.2991/978-2-494069-65-7_71

Hussein, B. A. S. (2012). The Sapir-Whorf hypothesis today. *Theory and Practice in Language Studies*, 2(3), 642–646.

Imtiaz, A., Khan, D., Lyu, H., & Luo, J. (2022). Taking sides: Public opinion over the Israel-Palestine Conflict in 2021. *arXiv preprint arXiv:2201.05961*.

Kemp, S. (2023, February 4). *Digital 2023: Global Overview Report - DataReportal – Global Digital Insights*. DataReportal. https://datareportal.com/reports/digital-2023-global-overview-report

Miah, M., & Omar, A. (2012). Technology advancement in developing countries during digital age. *International Journal*, 1(1), 30–38.

Murthy, D. (2018). Introduction to social media, activism, and organizations. *Social Media+ Society*, 4(1), 2056305117750716.

Muzammal, M. I. R. D. T., & Ghuman, K. (2021). Digitalization of conflicts: An analysis of social media coverage of Palestine-Israel Conflict by traditional news organizations.

Norman, J. M. (2009). Creative activism: Youth media in Palestine. *Middle East Journal of Culture and Communication*, 2, 252–274

Osler, A., & Starkey, H. (2003). Learning for cosmopolitan citizenship: Theoretical debates and young people's experiences. *Educational Review*, 55, 243–254.

Öztürk, N., & Ayvaz, S. (2018). Sentiment analysis on Twitter: A text mining approach to the Syrian refugee crisis. *Telematics and Informatics*, 35(1), 136–147.

Pang, B., & Lee, L. (2008). Opinion mining and sentiment analysis. *Foundations and Trends® in information retrieval*, 2(1–2), 1–135.

Park, S. J., Park, J. Y., Lim, Y. S., & Park, H. W. (2016). Expanding the presidential debate by tweeting: The 2012 presidential election debate in South Korea. *Telematics and Informatics*, 33(2), 557–569.

Pratiwi, F. I., Syarafi, M. A. R., & Nauvarian, D. (2022). Israeli-Palestinian conflict beyond resolution: A critical assessment. *Jurnal Ilmu Sosial dan Ilmu Politik*, 26(2), 168–182.

Pruchnic, J., & Ceraso, A. (2020). Platform utopianism after democracy. In *Platforms, protests, and the challenge of networked democracy* (pp. 17–37). Springer International Publishing.

Raheja, M. (2017). Imagining indigenous digital futures: An afterword. *Studies in American Indian Literatures*, 29(1), 172–175.

Rowley, C. K., & Taylor, J. (2006). The Israel and Palestine land settlement problem, 1948–2005: An analytical history. *Public Choice*, 128(1–2), 77–90. https://doi.org/10.1007/s11127-006-9045-9

Schori-Eyal, N., Halperin, E., & Bar-Tal, D. (2014). Three layers of collective victimhood: effects of multileveled victimhood on intergroup conflicts in the Israeli–Arab context. *Journal of Applied Social Psychology*, 44(12), 778–794.

Seo, H., & Ebrahim, H. (2016). Visual propaganda on Facebook: A comparative analysis of Syrian conflicts. *Media, War & Conflict*, 9(3), 227–251. https://doi.org/10.1177/1750635216661648

Shah, T. M. (2012). *Collective memory and narrative: Ethnography of social trauma in Jammu and Kashmir* [Doctoral dissertation, Kansas State University].

Shah, T. M. (2013). *Chaos and fear: Creativity and hope in an uncertain world*.

Shah, T. M. (2019). Social justice and change. In S. Romaniuk, M. Thapa, & P. Marton (Eds.), *The Palgrave Encyclopedia of global security studies*. Springer Verlag.

Shah, T. M. (2020). Children of Kashmir and the meaning of family in armed conflict. In S. Frankel, S. McNamee, & L. E. Bass (Eds.), *Bringing children back into the family: Relationality, connectedness and home* (Vol. 27, pp. 213–216). Emerald Publishing Limited. https://doi.org/10.1108/S1537-46612020000027015

Shah, T. M. (2021). *Women as "Sites of Gendered Politics"*. Misogyny Across Global Media.

Shah, T. M. (2023). *Global patterns of decolonization and the right to self-determination: A comparative-historical analysis of East Timor and Kashmir* [Doctoral dissertation, The University of Utah].

Shah, T. M. (2024a). Emotions in politics: A review of contemporary perspectives and trends. *International Political Science Abstracts, 74*(1), 1–14.

Shah, T. M. (2024b). Decolonization and peacebuilding: The case of Timor Leste and Kashmir. In P. Pietrzak (Ed.), *Dealing with regional conflicts of global importance* (pp. 262–278). IGI Global. https://doi.org/10.4018/978-1-6684-9467-7.ch013

Sherrod, L. R., Flanagan, C. A., Kassimir, R., & Syvertsen, A. K. (2006). Youth activism: An international encyclopedia. *Choice Reviews Online, 43*(10), 43-5671-43-5671. https://doi.org/10.5860/choice.43-5671

Stone, L. (2021). Youth power – youth movements: Myth, activism, and democracy. *Ethics and Education, 16*(2), 249–261.

Teruelle, R. (2012). Social media and youth activism. In H. S. Noor Al-Deen & J. A. Hendricks (Eds.), *Social media usage and impact* (pp. 201–217). Lexington Books.

Tessler, M. (2009). *A history of the Israeli-Palestinian conflict*. Indiana University Press.

Trombeta, G., & Cox, S. M. (2022). The textual-visual thematic analysis: A framework to analyze the conjunction and interaction of visual and textual data. *The Qualitative Report, 27*(6), 1557–1574. https://doi.org/10.46743/2160-3715/2022.5456

Urdal, H. (2006) A clash of generations? Youth bulges and political violence. *International Studies Quarterly, 50*(3), 607–629.

Wiltfang, G. L., & McAdam, D. (1991). The costs and risks of social activism: A study of sanctuary movement activism. *Social Forces, 69,* 987–1010.

Yiftachel, O., & Yacobi, H. (2003). Urban ethnocracy: Ethnicization and the production of space in an Israeli 'mixed city'. *Environment and Planning D: Society and Space, 21*(6), 673–693.

Youniss, J., Bales, S., Christmas-Best, V., Diversi, M., Mclaughlin, M., & Silbereisen, R. (2002). Youth civic engagement in the twenty-first century. *Journal of Research on Adolescence, 12,* 121–148.

Yilmaz, S. R. (2017). The role of social media activism in new social movements: Opportunities and limitations. *International Journal of Social Inquiry, 10*(1), 141–164.

Zahoor, M., & Sadiq, N. (2021). Digital public sphere and Palestine-Israel conflict: A conceptual analysis of news coverage. *Liberal Arts and Social Sciences International Journal (LASSIJ), 5*(1), 168–181. https://doi.org/10.47264/idea.lassij/5.1.12

CHAPTER 9

THE EVOLVING FAMILY AND THE LYRICAL CHILD

Haoyue Zhang

China Children's Film Studio, China

ABSTRACT

In this chapter, the author compares two representations of the child from two famous films by the Fifth Generation's top director in China, Chen Kaige, Yellow Earth (1984) and Together (2002). The girl's story in the former and the boy's story in the latter show respectively the dissolution of the Party/state as an extended family home, and it being replaced by the atomized, fluid, and flexible family home in the new state-led neo-liberal order. Compared with the girl, the boy in the new century tries to convey an equally lyrical articulation of the family/home, but differently, with a strong sense of his subjectivity. Thus, the boy's voice in Together, self-reflective, artistically innovative, and affective, becomes a voice of resistance against authoritarian neoliberalism in post-socialist China.

Keywords: The child; cinematic representation; evolving family home; lyricism; neo-liberal order

INTRODUCTION

In his "The disintegration of the collective body of me: Changes of individualism in Modern China" (2009), Xu Jilin traced the evolution of individualism in Chinese history within the framework of ego versus society, or "one body of me" versus "a collective body of me." The "collective body of me" descends from the transcendental natural order described in ancient China to the scientific rules and rationality of the 19th century, which then split between the nation-state, society, and humankind, each with its own different theoretical trends. However, Xu forgot that the societal and the individual mediates the family home, which relates to the individual no less than the society but serves the society no more than the individual.

In her "All Chinese Families Are Alike" (2007), Rey Chow analyzed the power relationships in Chinese families living in the United States through reading them as ethical apparatus, functioning for the sake of sexual recreation and procreation, and material obsession. If this apparatus feels closed off somewhat, then it has to open up to wider social relationships for the sake of the child in the long and uncertain process of procreation and nurturing. In this sense, it is very meaningful to look into the representations of the family home and the individual child as the symbolic miniatures of the connections of society versus ego.

Xu believes that the connection between the individual self and the societal in the 1980s China was organic and cohesive as such, but it has become broken since the rising marketization in the 1990s. Agreeing with Xu's observation, I will position my analysis of the relationships between the family home and the child in China's post-Maoist social transition of three decades, which Xu roughly divides into the 1980s (from the Reform and Open-up policy in 1978 to Tian'anmen crackdown in 1989), and the 1990s onwards. I will look into two representative films from these two stages, *Yellow Earth* (1987) and *Together* (2002), directed by Chen Kaige, a very well-established filmmaker spanning the post-Maoist social transition. In both films, the central character is a child tightly woven into the different domains of the family home: the dysfunctional patriarchal family, the disillusioned big family of the party-state, and the fluid global capitalist family. I will examine the shifting meanings and forms that surround the relationships between the family home and the child.

However, my concern is to analyze the child's transcendental desire for a "bigger me," who appears profoundly lyrical. In this way, the family acquires another layer of connotation: a hotbed to nurture a universal organic life. This organic life, spontaneous, artistic, affective, and infectious, is characterized by a strong lyrical penchant, as both spiritual pursuits and esthetic articulations are sought. Although lyricism has long roots in Chinese history, I will be discussing its presence in the post-socialist period that forms the background to the films analyzed in this chapter. Using as a point of departure, comments from Chinese literature writer Shen Congwen and scholars such as David Der-wei Wang and Rey Chow, I will conclude by addressing questions about the representation of the family home and the child: Is the family home effective in bringing the child to a wider "collective body of me?" How can we evaluate the holistic and abstract affective life that the film's protagonist tries to obtain? Furthermore, how can we understand the dialogue that the film attempts to have with the authoritarian neo-liberal Chinese society since the 1990s?

THE GIRL'S STORY IN *YELLOW EARTH*

Yellow Earth (Film), at one level, is a simple story set in 1939, two years after Japanese armies invaded the northeast provinces of China. A propagandist from the Communist Liberation Army, Gu Qing, comes to collect folk songs in a small, isolated northwestern village in Shaan'xi Province. In his host family is a widowed father, his 13-year-old daughter, Cui Qiao, and his 10-year-old son, Hanhan. Gu Qing learns that the local peasants customarily marry off their teenage daughters for dowries. It seems this will be the fate of the daughter, Cui Qiao. Gu Qing's attempt to change her fate gets no response from her father. On his way back to the army, Gu Qing finds out that Cui Qiao has been waiting to follow him to "the liberated area." Gu Qing refuses to bring the girl without getting permission from the army. He agrees to come back for her before her forced wedding. However, by the time he returns, Cui Qiao has long disappeared on a boat in the turbulent Yellow River to run away from her husband. Only throngs of farmers play a rain dance in thick dust with a bursting energy of survival.

Ambiguous Big Family: Disillusions Against the People's Savior

As a seminal film piece that seems familiar with its patriotic content, but visually strangely alienating, *Yellow Earth* announces the sprouting of China's new wave film movement in post-Maoist China. Deviating from the sentimentalism and straightforwardness of the revolutionary realist art of Mao's period, *Yellow Earth* subtly deconstructs the Communist Party's stereotypical image as the omnipresent and omnipotent savior that holds together the nation as one big harmonious family. While employing the subject matter and characters in revolutionary realistic films, typified by a story of a poor and exploited peasant who encounters a Party member, usually a male, and is guided into a new life free from trouble, *Yellow Earth* instead inverts this formula, showing what revolutionary realism wouldn't show. In this way, the ambiguous or uncertain side of the big revolutionary family is explored. The consequence is, no matter the size of the family for the child, it is obsolete, dysfunctional and incomplete. I will exemplify and explain this argument through my textual analysis of the "gaze" in socialist realistic films and its deviations in *Yellow Earth*.

The "gaze" in socialist realistic films serves as the most powerful apparatus to invoke viewers' identification with and confidence in the Party. This gaze is usually a low-angled close-up of a male Party member, whose line of sight is directed out of the frame with no specific object. The sense is of both contemplation of the past, but more, determination for the future. The viewer is not supposed to identify what the gaze is really falling upon or what the man is thinking but needs only to imagine and believe it must be something profound and powerful. In this way, the gaze testifies to the Party's "ownership of the present and the future, as well as a version of the past" (Donald, 2000, p. 125). Gu Qing, as the Party's messenger and advocate, uses this kind of unfathomable gaze several times when he sympathizes with, or meditates on, the peasants' bitter life.

However, in the climactic scene when Cui Qiao asks Gu Qing to take her away, Gu Qing looks down and mumbles that he has to ask the Army's leader first, after an embarrassing silence. Two variations of socialist realistic "gaze" happen here: first, Teshome Gabriel noticed that "the proletarian heroes in socialist realistic films are usually positioned on the left in relation to the characters classified as belonging to the exploitive classes of old China, who are usually on the right" (Browne, 1994, p. 42), because in traditional Chinese culture, the left space symbolizes superiority and significance in relation to the right. This spatial order is reversed: Cui Qiao is on the left, while she keeps walking in the foreground, so our gaze is mainly led by her. Second, after Gu Qing has promised to come back later, and a relieved Cui Qiao says that she believes in him, his close-up reaction shot follows, as expected, but he has a stony, unidentifiable expression. In the place of what should be a low-angle close-up of a determined visage looking out of the frame is an eye-level medium shot of them both. With no suggestion of their thoughts, the two stand like statues in the blowing wind for 10 seconds and eventually do not break free. As individuals, they can only go so far and no further.

In socialist realist films,

> generalizing personal into collective, and romanticizing political groups as big families, constituted the primary narrative strategy, which conjured up an illusion of the revolutionary family as such. A whole series of films helped build up the signified meaning that the revolutionary team is a sweet home in the first place. (Pan, 2000, p. 55)

In children's films from that category, such as *Little Solder Zhang Ga* (Film, 1963) and *Shining Red Star* (Film, 1974), audiences can seldom remember that the two boys are orphans since they don't seem lonely, miserable, or sad. On the contrary, losing their parents and the family home only makes them tougher and more determined to devote themselves to the revolution. Dai Jinhua also talked about the imagined integration of small families and big revolutionary families in socialist realism discourse, which aims at requiring the loyalty of individuals in a new and warm "big family" after breaking up with their old and cold "small families" (Dai, 2005, p. 146).

The irony is after Cui Qiao abandons her "small family," she is no longer accepted by the "big family." Gu Qing doesn't come to get her before her arranged wedding as he had promised. She runs away from her husband's home, and before she jumps onto a boat headed for the liberation area, she complains to Hanhan that "your sis is suffering." This is not only the accusation of the "human-eating" patriarchal Confucian society, but also the challenge to the Party and socialist ideals.

One of the most dominant themes in the 1980s for intellectuals was the disarticulation of the Party/state from the people/nation. By exposing the traumatic experiences of people during the Cultural Revolution, diverse cultural trends had belied the representations of the Party/state as a warm and communal "big socialist family" (Dai, 2005). If *Yellow Earth* is not against the socialist premises per se, which Cui Qiao anticipates and dies for, it casts doubts on their utopian nature and the Party's ability to realize them. For example, Cui Qiao never sees the liberated area and the people there. What she imagines is based completely on Gu Qing's description. After he returns to the army, there is only one scene showing the "liberated life:" a big array of drummers dancing in flying dust, energetic and happy, but primitive and vague as well. Staring at the men in the same dusty and ragged black coats worn in Cui Qiao's village, Gu Qing is lost in thought: his "unfathomable gaze" again. What can he do about this substantial spilling out of natural and human energy? We are not told. To this point, both the small family and the big family are deconstructed as sterile land, with dysfunctional institutions and a lost utopia, from all of which the individual child, especially the girl, tries to break away.

Dysfunctional Patriarchal Confucian Family

The film reveals the "Otherness," or being objectified, of girls in the patriarchal Confucian system, which not only alienates them socially but also hollows them economically and paralyzes them mentally. In the scenes where Gu Qing criticizes forced marriage, the father always occupies half of the frame in the foreground, whereas Cui Qiao is placed in the other half, but far behind her father and out of focus. The stove's jumping fire projects on her face, suggesting her nervous attention to the talk that influences her life. Illiterate and isolated, Cui Qiao can't imagine any solution to escape her fate as a piece of property in a loveless marriage.

A woman's life path is usually arranged in accordance with patriarchal Confucian social orders, such as obeying her father's commands before her marriage, obeying her husband's directives during marriage, and obeying her son's arrangements without her husband. Judith Stacey employs the term patriarchy, "to indicate a family and social system in which male power over women and children derives from the social role of fatherhood and is supported by a political economy in which the family unit retains a significant productive role" (1983, p. 12). The father's decision to sacrifice Cui Qiao, instead of her brother, to pay for the family debt, is both cultural and economic.

In the film, we see the family farming, but never harvesting. The land is limitless but also fruitless. One scene especially symbolizes the close and fragile nature of such production: the family sits on the plowed soil for lunch. The father stands up from the bottom of the frame to look up at the enormous gray sky, which occupies two-thirds of the screen, murmuring, "The sky is cloudy all the time, but doesn't rain. A drought might come. Guess this is divine punishment," to which Gu Qing responds with soft mocking giggles outside the frame, deriding the old man's superstition. Then Cui Qiao, holding a big bowl of porridge at head level, comes into the frame from the bottom but stops at her father's chest. While the father seems crushed by the sky, Cui Qiao is even worse: only her head floats on the bottom line. Employing such extreme composition, the two shots reveal not only the marginalized and subaltern position of the girl but also the sense of deep powerlessness seizing all the peasants, passive supplicants instead of active creators, who are dwarfed and crushed by an intimidating and all-powerful nature.

Yellow Earth suggests the connection between the backward mode of production and the peasants' mental stagnation, which is worsened in the patriarchal Confucian social order. The domestic work Cui Qiao does is very repetitive and time-consuming: besides carrying buckets of water 10 miles every day, which the film shows three times, she also sews, cooks, cleans, and spins yarn. The film employs many still shots and stable long takes to convey such associations visually and emotionally. Worse than Cui Qiao's brief and shy conversations with Gu Qing, Hanhan barely speaks at all. Like a silent statue in motion, his principal activity is merely to shepherd the farm animals.

Singing, contrasted by the scarcity and difficulty of dialogues, becomes significantly meaningful and poetic, in terms of not only storytelling, but also mood creation. While Gu Qing's speech is words-based, therefore ephemeral, precise, and logical, Cui Qiao's singing is perpetual, metaphoric, and emotional. Hanhan's bed-wetting song is no more than nonsense. The father's only song, about a girl's tragic life, is unconsciously self-reflective, repetitive, and brief.

However, since

> the subject has no experience of temporality, has no link with the past or the future, then it is without language – that is, it lacks the means of representing "I." This creates a schizophrenic condition in which the subject fails to assert its subjectivity and fails also to enter the Symbolic Order. (Hayward, 2000, p. 282)

The symbolic order here is the language that the child lives in and with, whose perpetuity and motionlessness mirror her lack of subjectivities.

Representing "the hope of the whole Chinese nation" according to the director (Chen, 1984), Cui Qiao has passed on this archetype of the victimized child since the New Culture movement in the 1920s. In Lu Xun's seminal short story *Madman's Diary* (1918, pp. 14–24), which is believed to have initiated "the literary renaissance," the madman cries "perhaps there are children who have not eaten human flesh. Save, save the children." Mary Ann Farquhar explained, "save them from what? From the savage superstition of Confucian beliefs? From the madness and immorality of Chinese tradition? From retrogression, and ultimately, extinction?" (1999, p. 29). While Lu Xun's analysis of childhood is based on a sense of linear progressive development, it is also "charged with emotional symbolism that was rampant in the Maoist era and is still used today" (p. 29).

Chen Kaige, together with other Chinese intellectuals in the 1980s, revealed crashing anxiety through the victimized child. After 30 years of segregation during the Mao era, Deng's market reform and opening-up policy allowed in a flood of foreign art and theories, which expanded Chinese intellectuals' horizons, but also threw them into an anxious self-consciousness: they realized how monolithic people's thinking still was, how primitive the production mode was compared with the Western countries, how low the people's living standards were, and how marginalized and isolated they, themselves were from the Communist Party's control. In alignment with the Party's open-up and market policy, *Yellow Earth* is a film "pro Deng's reform" (Yao, 1989). However, at the same time, the film also throws doubt on it because of disillusionment in both the patriarchal family and the Party-state as a big family.

THE BOY'S STORY IN *TOGETHER*

The film *Together* was made 20 years later after *Yellow Earth* when the open-up policy and marketization of the 1980s merged into global neoliberal orders since the new century. In *Together*, accompanied by his father, Xiaochun, a 13-year-old violin prodigy, comes to Beijing to improve his skills from a small southern city. While the father struggles to support the son in the big city as a floating laborer, the boy gets to know versatile people in his pursuit of love, art, and a profession.

Reassembling the Family Home

The Party/state as a big family falls apart in *Together*. As its authoritarian representative, Beijing Children's Palace, where Xiaochun strives for his first significant violin contest, appears corrupt and cold-hearted to migrant children without social connections or money, no matter how talented they are. Like a wooden statue full of wormholes, the Party/state in *Together* even loses its charming illusion that promises salvation and liberation for the poor, like in *Yellow Earth*. However, living in the shabby dormitory of this institution is secluded Jiang, a teacher who despises the cronyism and vulgar tastes that are common everywhere. With teacher Jiang, Xiaochun receives his first and best real music education in Beijing. The collective Party/state shatters into individuals with whom the child may find guidance and salvation. Out of loneliness and the love of music that they share, the boy slowly softens the sour teacher and befriends him. Jiang inspires him to play the instrument with emotions and affect. To the boy, Jiang's room is not only where his tutor is found, but also his shelter from the competitive and mechanical life of the city.

On the debris of collective family homes, there are two types of Individual family homes in *Together*. As the film starts, father Cheng is shouting to Xiaochun to help for a neighbor's sake, while the boy is having his hair cut on the other side of a river. Following the boy's fast footsteps through winding alleys and across a bridge, with soft music playing in the background, we understand that this is an idyllic, provincial southern town. As the camera glances through a scroll of hectic preparations for the childbirth celebration and labor process, the boy stands still and plays the violin. As soon as a piece of brisk and energetic music rises up, credits start to roll across on stills of a violin, and we are forced to concentrate on the music itself, which ends with the addition of the angry cries of a newborn. As the boy has helped to lead a woman through her troubled childbirth, the father is forced to accept money in gratitude. This flowing, idealistic, but also realistic sequence immediately tells us that the boy is the father's pride and joy in this single-parent family.

In a medium shot of father Cheng, we see that he gets a letter in the mail and smiles happily. The letter bridges the transition smoothly to the next shot, in which Xiaochun bikes Cheng home, with the town's radio announcing that Xiaochun is being enrolled in Beijing Children's Palace, a top art institution for children in China. That same night the father and the son start to pack, without hesitation or nostalgia, to pursue the boy's violin path in the metropolis. This incomplete but intimate family functions like a highly efficient instrument in spite of their extremely tight budget and zero social connections in Beijing. In a fast montage sequence showing Cheng's hustling and bustling as a floating laborer in the big city, the father's efforts to support the boy are dramatized. He tirelessly bargains between two vendors over a one-cent difference. After he loses the money he hides in his hat, he has to scramble for whatever jobs he can get to pay for their shabby room and the costs of Xiaochun's tutor.

After teacher Jiang, Cheng forces the boy to switch to a more successful and influential professor for tutoring, no matter how heartbroken both Xiaochun and Jiang feel. Here in Professor Yu's pseudo-family home, unfolds an individualized hub for the reassembly of resources and talents to compete in the neoliberal global age. Impressed by Xiaochun's talent and potential, Professor Yu invites him to move in for intense training for an international contest. Only during training sessions, Xiaochun get to see Yu and another girl student in residency, who regards the country boy as her biggest threat in the international competition. To make Xiaochun concentrate harder, Professor Yu maneuvers deliberately to deprive the boy of the chance to see his father or his violin, which has become a symbol of the mother he has never met. Yu's home is modern and sophisticated, with modern amenities, but it is cold, with blue light and the interior space separated by walls or furniture.

The Fluid Family and the Knowing Child

Throughout the Fordist stage from 1945 to the early 1970s in the industrial West, when mass production and mass consumption were dominant features, the nuclear family was regarded as the typical pattern of the family home. It functioned more like a "cocoon" that not only nurtures and protects children, but also "conceals the labor of consumption, childcare, and sexuality" from the outside world (Lee, 2001, p. 73). By the end of the 20th century, childhood studies generally presented adults as complete human beings – rational, stable, independent, capable, responsible, and therefore, powerful, whereas children were still human "becomings" in development, opposite in many aspects to the adults.

However, the economic recession of the 1970s sweeping through the West forced the gradual adoption of this "flexible accumulation," a term coined by David Harvey to describe the new economic strategy since then.

> All a flexible manufacturing business needed in order to thrive was a core of managerial staff, access to part-time and short-time contract workers and a group of other businesses – subcontractors – from which to buy services and parts, as and when they were needed. (Harvey, 1991, p. 141)

This fundamental change reshaped general perceptions about adults, especially the family man. He has to be flexible, adaptable, and dependent on extensions and supplements to learn, to communicate, and to improve. In other words, he cannot be as complete, stable, and independent as he once was. At the same time, children are losing their innocence early because of the "total disclosure medium" (Postman, 1982) of television exposing them to sexuality and "the availability of goods and the possibility of making choices between goods" (Lee, 2001, p. 75).

Childhood studies have seen stronger and stronger voices that adults and children are both human "becomings" in "the age of uncertainty" since the late 1990s (Lee, 2001; Prout, 2005). Barbo Johansson (2010) traced the seesaw theorizations between human beings and "becomings" since the 1980s and proposed to position adults and children in specific situations to define the concepts. Through her survey of Nordic children's consumption behaviors, she found that parents and children constantly switch between the status of being and becoming according to various expectations of the consumer society (Johansson, 2010).

Johansson's analysis applied to the Chinese family home in the late capitalist global paradigm is interesting. Compared with the West, it seems Chinese "flexible accumulation" relies on and consolidates the regional uneven distribution of capital, from financial, industrial, and cultural to human resources, since the 1990s in the wake of fast industrialization and urbanization. To pursue job opportunities, rural or suburban families (or single parents) must migrate to metropolis or more developed areas. Long-distance and pervasive migrations in China inevitably generate complicated new relationships in family homes. Expected to know or not know certain "secrets" of their families by adults, children fluctuate between the status of human beings and becomings. For example, Cheng does not want Xiaochun to know about sexuality at his age and to get distracted from violin learning, so he forbids the 13-year-old from hanging out with Lily, a sugar baby socializing with rich men. Yet he never hides the family's economic problems from the boy. The father tells the son every detail of how he has hidden the saved-up labor money in his hat, how it was perched on his head safely until someone snatched it away, how they no longer have much money for basic living, and how frustrated and regretful he is. These anxieties would be too heavy and worrisome for a teenage boy to bear. Many parents might not share the story with their children, yet Cheng does.

Another example of this fluid parent–child relationship that alternates between becoming and being lies in the secret of the boy's background. Cheng tells Xiaochun that his mother died after the boy was born, so the boy can practice hard to realize his mother's dream, as presumed through the violin left to the boy. The perpetual lack of "the mother" becomes such an efficacious card to play, conjuring up deep sympathy, that each time Cheng plays the card he manages to get the boy a good tutor. However, the terminal truth is, the boy is an orphan that Cheng has picked up in a railway station. In other words, the family home is totally comprised of would-be strangers. The reason Cheng wants the boy to succeed is that he believes the violin accompanying the abandoned infant suggests the mother's wish for the boy. Pseudo father Yu tells the boy this ultimate secret right before the international competition so that the boy can play with all his gratitude and emotions for Cheng. No matter how heavy and cruel the process of becoming to being turns out to be for the child, the family home cannot be taken for granted as a natural cocoon anymore.

"When people in general are perceived as becomings instead of beings, the focus is transformed from individuals and entities to the flows and connections of events" (Johansson, 2010, p. 90). Indeed, as the family home intends to become, with each temporal pool reassembling resources, and talents in a constant migration, the family home appears more like an event, an occasion, and a journey, whose focus is boiled down to the relationships and connections between each other in the process. In this way, neither the adult nor the child can completely dominate, dictate to, or validate the family home by him/herself. The fluid family home can only be constructed and maintained with fluid adults and children, who have to imagine and perform their subjectivities through constant adjusting of themselves in upcoming events and new assemblages.

Subjectivity as One Kind of Lyrical Expression

Children in *Yellow Earth* do not present distinct subjectivities because they symbolize the nation/people, whose subjectivity is suppressed and deprived. Yet the child in *Together* appears to be the opposite of this. Robyn McCallum claims that subjectivity, "an individual's sense of a personal identity as a subject" (1999, p. 4), can be divided into individual, subject, and agent. Throughout the film, Xiaochun makes decisions by and for himself. He is sensitive to challenges to his self-respect, so he runs away when his dad implores Mister Jiang to tutor him for the reason that he never gets to see his mother. Xiaochun chooses the people he wants to befriend, such as Lily, to whom he somehow feels ambiguously attached. He has a strong will and clearly articulated opinions.

Father Cheng also possesses strong agency, but his subjectivity is ambiguous because his agency does not serve himself as the obvious motivating purpose. Indeed, he devotes himself completely to the boy, not only economically, but also mentally and emotionally. Even his name in their hometown is "Xiaochun's dad," and this defines his identity. His subjectivity is paradoxically built on his willingness to give up his existence as a subject. In this sense, the family home is the outcome of his complete sacrifice, not only because of what he has done for the boy but because of what he knows will come: someday, he has to disown Xiaochun for the boy's future and best interest. Sadly, this is the situation for many parents in the neoliberal era, since the flow of resources and labor will unavoidably sweep their children away to areas all over the world. For lower-class parents without social connections and resources to keep their children nearby, such relinquishment for the good of the children is not only common but also supposed to be lucky for the children, which is exactly what Cheng tells Xiaochun about Professor Yu's offer of residency in his home.

For Cheng, the family home means an instrument that can be given up at any time for the boy's success. Yet it does not take long for us to realize that Cheng, who appears simple-minded and stubborn, actually follows both pragmatic and affective values. On the one hand, he holds a totally altruistic value with Xiaochun, an orphan he has found during a trip. On the other hand, the values motivating his actions for the boy's success are actually very pragmatic and selfish. Struggling between these two conflicting value systems, he sacrifices his interests and suppresses his feelings to make himself, willingly, a tool, for the boy.

Contrary to Cheng, what Xiaochun wants is to be the object of affection, a goal that his artistic expression can address and help him attain. The film first builds up Xiaochun's emotional attachment to his violin. As a keepsake from a mother he had never known, the violin represents a void in his life that can never be redeemed. In a sense, this void stimulates him to fill it with certain articulations. The violin helps him not only to build up a close relationship with Lily and teacher Jiang, but also reveals his deeper self to them. Therefore, when Cheng and Yu strip him of these connections to concentrate on skills and competition, his art becomes meaningless without the object of his affection, and that causes devastation of his world. Xiaochun's resistance is fierce and ferocious. He sells his mother's violin to buy Lily a fur coat.

Suppose late capitalist society has produced "a shifting, mobile, fluid subjectivity" (Kapur, 2005, p. 134), generated from multiple identities and constant switching between being and becoming status. In that case, this struggle of subjectivity confronts an essential question in neoliberal China: what is the significance of constructing a child's subjectivity? if fame and money become the goal and meaning of life, then what is most important for the child to pursue, emotional happiness, physical health, or career development? These choices that are not necessarily contradictory to each other, however, become an essential and unavoidable question that each parent has to face in a schizophrenic and uncertain world.

Shen Congwen (沈从文), a contemporary Chinese writer who went from fame in the 1930s to oblivion in the 1950s, painfully searched for the answer to pragmatic utilitarianism and affective attachment in socialist construction at the threshold of the new communist regime. At the time he was criticized for being conservative and indulging in old feudal times, when the Party's proletarian art was becoming the exclusive directive. Bearing deep attachments to local traditional culture, customs, and spiritual obsessions, Shen felt an unbridgeable rupture between what he liked and what the new state required of him: a lyrical poetic writer from an outdated old society. In a family letter written in 1952, at a time of what now must be considered a naïve but passionate modernization that quickly slid into bureaucratic formality, a cult of power and leaders, and admiration of instrumentality, he bitterly compared his affective value system with the new pragmatic one. He claimed,

> pursuit of both pragmatism and affections sometimes can combine, but most of the time they contradict each other. To be affectionate and affective in life often collides with striving for utilities and skills. In such a hard balancing act, affections are usually regarded as useless and even stupid. (2002, p. 17)

If everyone advocated to realize his or her instrumentality, like "a screw in the machine of the new epoch," then, such a collective and national goal has been replaced by the pragmatic values of individuals competing in the marketplace since the 1990s. In either situation, such words as "affect" and "affections" seem lachrymose, weak, and outdated. In Shen's dictionary, affect(ion) means "(writers') profound understandings and sincere love of people that develops from personal affiliations and goes beyond skills" (1952). He described one night when he could not sleep because of the continuous coughing from the other side of a thin wall, realizing that "life's joy and sorrow are all rooted in common people," and that "these joys and sorrows indeed live in me." Because of his understanding of these various life forms, interests, rules, evaluations, constraints, and challenges, he believed that he needed to do lots of work "with a more passionate and altruistic attitude. Everyone says, 'love our country, love our people,' but how to love and what to do are very different" (2002, pp. 20–21).

Buried in Shen's words is a profound paradox about the individual subject: one must optimize one's subjectivity by relating to or immersing oneself in others, a concept that Xu describes early about "one body of me" versus "a collective body of me." The family home in *Together* becomes such a medium through which both the adult and the child help each other search for deeply believed values to construct subjectivity.

If Cheng's choice is to live with two contradictory value systems and therefore, with a ruptured subjectivity, Xiaochun makes an opposite decision. Xiaochun yields his candidacy for the international contest to the girl who realizes her love of music after her failure, then he rushes to the railway station to play his competition song for his father, who is ready to return to their hometown alone. By choosing to play for the one he loves, Xiaochun shatters the pragmatic instrumentality that seized him and the girl, and validates affective and affectionate values, with which Cheng identifies. In this way, the family home is invested with another dimension's meaning: it becomes an arena for the adult and the child to develop and interact with separate values, while acknowledging each other's subjectivities.

When these emotions and affections are so strong and excessive that they need to be released, they will naturally lead to some narration or expression, which, according to David Der-wei Wang, is characterized by pensive and meditative lyricism. Pursued through such continuous dialogue between the subject's experiences and sentiments, the child's subjectivity cannot get away with certain kinds of lyrical presentation. This presentation is not necessarily a performance per se, since the latter does not need to relate to truth or forgery. Through reading lyrical writer Shen Congwen's works, art pieces in daily life as well as other forms of esthetic experiences in his far-reaching affiliations, David Der-wei Wang claimed,

> Lyricism can be defined to be a literary category, especially the special title for poetry that takes exerting individual subjectivity as the first priority in the west; but it can also be regarded as a discourse, a representation of aesthetic perspective, one type of daily life practice, and most importantly and most arguably, one kind of possibility for political imagination or dialogue. (2010, p. 72)

Based on this definition, lyrical presentation of one's subjectivity has to be self-reflective as a discourse, artistic in display, understandable in daily praxis, and invariably political in antagonistic society. The last sequence depicting Xiaochun playing his contest violin piece for his father, to bid goodbye, best exemplifies these characteristics. Three parallel storylines briskly intercut together: Xiaochun searches for Cheng in the railway station and finally plays the score passionately in the lobby; (in washed-out blue and gray) Cheng runs around with an abandoned infant and a violin in another railway station; the girl in residency plays the same violin piece in an international contest under the accompaniment of an advanced orchestra. Intercuts converge into the final climax, where a flowing panoramic shot of Xiaochun looks down into the lobby of the railway station, while Cheng walks in with the company of Lily and teacher Jiang. As soon as the boy spots his father, he runs down the stairs. Instantly Tchaikovsky's upbeat and fast third movement from the Violin Concerto in D Major bursts out, together with the boy's shout, "Dad!"

The shot cuts to Cheng, holding a baby, jostled by crowds, answering "hi!" Then the eruption of music and emotions are tuned down softly when the boy finally stands face to face with his father. In a meditative and convoluted variation, the shot cuts to Cheng finding a baby lying on a bench, but his inquiry is muffled by the railway station's announcements and the baby's cries. The symphony whirls deeply in the background when the two scenes intercut back and forth several times, then the exuberant and energetic main musical score soars up seemingly to celebrate the triumph of affections, or to express enormous gratitude. The close-up of Xiaochun's fingers pressing precisely on strings pulls out to the girl in the music hall, who is playing as perfectly and with feeling as the boy surrounded by common travelers in the railway station. Heavy and bleached colors, present and past, history and imagination, elegant classical music, mundane daily life noise, profession, and affects all weave together, ignited by the family and home on the edge of separation.

When the music piece stops resonating, all the images blackout. After three seconds of relaxation in darkness and silence, the lights in the bright railway station dreamingly come back, still, without sound. Slowly, Xiaochun claps a high-five with Cheng and hugs him deeply, and passengers around them start to applaud. In different venues, presented to and celebrated by disparate audiences, the music on stage and the music in real life are welded together into one piece.

> In this film music presents its nobility, for it never separates itself from daily life. Blooming out of poor but not base low-class life, the music grows in stress and eventually wins over people's hearts with feelings, just as the protagonist Xiaochun. (Fan, 2006)

While the two children invest feelings and words in their lyrical expression communicating with their audiences, their expression is also political in the sense that it breaks through the boundary of high and low class, locations noble and ordinary, and the single binary separation between profession and affection.

Xiaochun's lyrical tribute to his father, but more profoundly to an affectionate and affective way of life is infectious, so the characters who have decided to give up their apathy and escapism (such as teacher Jiang) and their hollow professionalism (such as a female student of Professor Yu) all join the tableau in the final scene, sharing Xiaochun's joy and tears.

CONCLUSION

While the neo-liberal authoritarian society has embraced pragmatic, rational, and industrious individualistic values, the family home, no matter how fluid and adaptable it has to be, is presented as the last fort, where the child is imagined as some kind of adhesive binding a universally affective and affectionate life. With all its connections and occasions, the family home is embodied as the spiritual community that connects each temporal and fluid family together. In *Together*, Chen Kaige breaks through the boundaries of class, education, occupation, and even personality to present the family home and the affective value system it represents as our hope.

However, revolutionary and thought-provoking in challenging neo-liberal values, as the family home is in the film, it is self-contradictory due to the segregation of the teenage boy from the bigger social context, practical problems, and the time itself. For example, Xiaochun never has any teenage friends; neither has he any connections with his rural hometown or any official institution (such as school). Although the film tries to conjure sympathy and sentiments by playing with the lower class social status of Xiaochun and Cheng, the film never bothers to "trivialize" money issues. From Lily and Cheng to Professor Yu, no one cares about money at all. Even Xiaochun's background, the biggest secret in the film, seems very ambiguous and suspicious. Because we can't identify the location of the scene where Cheng picks up the abandoned baby – it is Cheng's memory or Xiaochun's imagination, or both or neither – the boy seems to live outside of the real past.

Xiaochun's segregation from time is also reflected in the rupture between adulthood and childhood in the film. Although adults desire future outcomes for the child, we are not given any premonition about how the child is going to maintain his artistic spontaneity and affection in the future. Mister Jiang might be the only one with whom Xiaochun can share his love of music and feelings, but Jiang is inept at self-development, not only facing capitalist competition but also in his personal life.

Consequently, *Together* casts the family home as a utopia that is suspended in the realm of the spiritual, instead of a connecting point between both the secular/practical and the spiritual/moral. Philosopher, historian, and activist Zhang Taiyan said a century ago about his research and praxis, "It starts with spiritualizing the secular, then ends with going back to the secular based on spiritual truth" (自揣平生学术，始则转俗成真，终乃回真向俗。) (1982, p. 47). If the family home does not provide a path for the child to connect with the real secular world, no matter what spiritual truth the family home has inspired the child to seek out, then the family home has to be terminated in the end, like a sentimental and melancholy eulogy.

Avoidance of touching upon the dimension of bringing the spiritual/affective back to the secular/pragmatic reveals not only the difficulty of bigger and functional communities in existence, but also the limitations of an emerging middle class in the 1990s. Challenged by

> its political commitments in the socialist revolution, modernist values of social development, and its actual choices of certain beneficial policies, the Party is hard pressed to choose a constant stand on whether to restore its historical appeal/legitimacy or to admit/comply with the socialist voice from the bottom up. (Yu, 2008, p. 78)

However, it seems that the burgeoning middle class since the late 1990s does not believe any of the paradigms: capitalism, authoritarian Party/state with monopolizing power, or socialism.

Starting to grow in the 1990s after the crackdown of the Tiananmen democratic movement, in a system without sufficient and systematic social securities for individuals, the middle class felt more unsecured in the authoritarian system because of its greater capital (not only financial) compared with the lower class, and less political power compared with the privileged Party officials. On the one hand, they enjoy and support the free competition of neoliberalism; on the other, they suffer from and worry about how capital alienates as well as about the Party/state's abuse of its power. That is why *Together* can only go as far as the boy's own lyrical confirmation of the affective value, among the contradictory values that the family home has been relying on; and that also explains why the family home has to separate in the face of more intense international competition. In this sense, *Together* is still the imagination of a middle-class elite about the best resistance a young neoliberal individual can accomplish in the face of a deepening post-socialist transition.

REFERENCES

Browne, N. (1994). Political economy of Chinese melodramas. In N. Browne, P. G. Pickowicz, V. Sobchack, & E. Yau (Eds.), *New Chinese cinema: Forms, identities, and politics* (pp. 40–56). Cambridge University Press.

Chen, K. (1984, April 6). *Director's Words on Yellow Earth*. Zhihu(知乎) https://zhuanlan.zhihu.com/p/445210725

Chow, R. (2007). All Chinese families are alike: Biopolitics in *Eat a Bowl of Tea* and *The Wedding Banquet*. In R. Chow (Ed.), *Sentimental fabulations, contemporary Chinese films: Attachment in the age of globalization* (pp. 123–144). Columbia University Press.

Dai, J. (2005). *Mapping the mirror city*. Yuan Liu Publishing House, Tai Wan.

Donald, S. H. (2000). *Public secrets, public spaces: Cinema and civility in China*. Rowman and Littlefield.

Fan, D. (2006, November 28). *Bullets, guns, affects and string: Re-watch together*. Douban (豆瓣). http://movie.douban.com/review/1094736/

Farquhar, M. A. (1999). *Children's literature in China: From Lu Xun to Mao Zedong*. East Gate.

Harvey, D. (1991). *The condition of postmodernity: An enquiry into the origins of cultural change*. Blackwell.

Hayward, S. (2000). *Cinema studies*. Routledge.

Johansson, B. (2010). Subjectivities of the child consumer: Beings and becomings. In Buckingham & Tingstad (Eds.), *Childhood and consumer culture* (pp. 80–93). Palgrave.

Kapur, J. (2005). *Coining for capital: Movies, marketing, and the transformation of childhood*. Rutgers.

Lee, N. (2001). *Childhood and society: Growing up in an Age of Uncertainty*. Open University Press.

Lu, X. (1918, May). Mad Man's Diary. *La Jeunesse*新青年, *4–5*, 14–24.

McCallum, R. (1999). *Ideologies of identity in adolescent fiction: The dialogic construction of subjectivity*. Routledge.

Pan, R. (2000). *Prosperity and fatigue of new China's films in 17 Years* (Vol. 6, pp. 40–56). Film Art.

Postman, N. (1982). *The disappearance of childhood* (pp. 67–154). Delacorte Press.

Prout, A. (2005). *Future of childhood*. Routledge.

Shen, C. (2002). Pragmatism and affects. In H. Nan (Ed.), *Abstract lyricism* (pp. 19–28). Yue Lu Book House.

Stacey, J. (1983). *Patriarchy and socialist revolution in China*. University of California.

Wang, D. D. (2010). *The tradition of lyricism and China's modernity: Eight lectures in Pecking University*. San Lian Press.

Wu, G. (2002, June). End of the reform and continuity of history. In *The 21st Century*. Online version. Hong Kong. cuhk.edu.hk/ics/21c/media/online/0205014.pdf

Xu, J. (2009, Spring). The disintegration of the collective body of me: Changes of individualism in Modern China. In Deng (Ed.), *China social science compilation* (Vol. 26, pp. 75–93). Fudan University Press.

Yao, X. (1989, January). *China's new films: from the viewpoint of ideology*. Film Art, China Film Art Publishing House.

Yu, J. (2008, July 29). *China's grassroots: My research and standpoint: A public speech*. China People's University.

Zhang, T. (1982). Compilations of Master Zhang (章氏丛书). Shanghai People's Publishing House (Original work published in 1919).

CHAPTER 10

LOSS OF NAIVETY AND INNOCENCE: WAR CHILDHOOD IN THE NINETIES BALKANS

Julija Ovsec

Faculty of Arts, Charles University Prague, Czech Republic

ABSTRACT

The nineties of the 20th century were marked by wars at the breakup of Yugoslavia, by a generation of children whose lives turned overnight. Many had to leave their homes and become refugees. What was a reality for many children is also reflected in literature whose protagonists are coming-of-age children. The novels Ukulele Jam *by Alen Mešković and* Hotel Zagorje *by Ivana Simić Bodrožić as a primary motive take European tragedy whose consequences still resonate today. There are two ways in which youth literature represents war – as the scenery or as the central theme of a story. War is a political and social event whose effects are transmitted to everyone regardless of gender, age, or social status. As the portrayal of literary heroes strives to be as believable and authentic as possible, the lives of literary characters trapped in the vortex of war reflect the same characteristics. Life routines change; there is often a school dropout, lack of food, children's play changes, and children, in addition to the general poverty and chaos, also face the loss of friends, family members, violence, and home. The environment often begins to reject them. In the formerly known world, they appear as aliens who need to be removed or adapted to the new society. The transition from the socialist to the capitalist socio-economic system was based on repeated repatriarchalization, in particular in strengthening the old public and private dichotomies and reviving conservative ideologies on the family and gender.*

Keywords: Coming of age; war novel; children in literature; war childhood; European literature; South-Slavic literature

INTRODUCTION

This chapter is a discussion on the comparison of two coming-of-age novels: the novel *Hotel Zagorje* (2010) by Croatian writer Ivana Simić Bodrožić and the novel *Ukulele Jam* (2011) by Alen Mešković, who was born in Bosnia and Herzegovina but moved to Denmark as a refugee during the nineties. Both novels are set in time and space in the early 1990s in Croatia. In addition to temporal and spatial coherence, they also share some standard features, including a similar narrative arc, the theme of the novel, and the choice of the adolescent as the main narrator, which differ in essential components: a novel *Hotel Zagorje* tells us the story of a growing up girl, and in the novel *Ukulele Jam* the narrator of a story is a growing-up boy. Given the many similarities between the novels, I decided to compare the depiction of a girl's and a boy's character and analyze if there were any differences in their depiction. I was particularly interested in whether the characters are active and critical toward society, how they accept the given situation, their main characteristics, and their position toward war and refugee status. I wonder how war and growing up in wartime are depicted if there is a gender-based difference in telling the story, and how the coming-of-age novels correspond with the ideology present in the war followed by the formation of new countries on the territory of the former Yugoslavia state. Is the gender or the narrator important?

One of the central themes in literature that chooses children as narrators is that of growing up, which is mainly the subject of the problem novel in contemporary literature. Books for young people coming of age became a phenomenon in the second half of the 20th century. J.D. Salinger pioneered the phenomenon with his novel *The Catcher in the Rye*, which deals with this in-between state when childhood is over, and adulthood begins. The characters realize that there is no going back (Nikolajeva, 2004). The *Catcher in the Rye* is often seen as a seminal work of American literature, capturing the disillusionment and alienation felt by many teenagers. The protagonist, Holden Caulfield, resonates with readers due to his honesty and complexity. Additionally, the novel explores themes such as identity, innocence, and the transition to adulthood, making it relevant across generations. The protagonists of the books selected for this discussion confront issues of identity and coming of age, with an additional dimension added by the war, in which ideological beliefs and national identities are particularly pronounced and growing up is put on the fast track.

One can use stories to accomplish and display a sense of one's self (Shah, 2023; Stahl, 1989). In the case of coming of age, readers can help with identity formation, recognizing oneself in characters, and taking on the characteristics of how to deal with given situations and what social roles to take on. Therefore, it is necessary to critically analyze presentations of different genders in coming-of-age novels and the ideologies their portrayal is inscribing. The individual does not choose the ideology but is simply in it before they are conscious. Innocence is an ideologically important space in which we can successfully communicate ideology. That is why a naive, innocent child protagonist is a blank space on which we can project ideology. For literature analysis, ideology is instrumental because literature and culture are the fields in which ideology is produced and reproduced. Literature inevitably collides with ideology, which inscribes itself in literary forms, styles, conventions, genres, and the institution of scholarly production. Literature exposes, criticizes, and reproduces ideology (Todd, 2007).

Althusser's ideas have significantly impacted literary theory and continue to be influential today. Louis Althusser introduced the concept of interpellation in his influential essay "Ideology and Ideological State Apparatuses." Interpellation refers to the process by which individuals are hailed or addressed by ideological forces and, in turn, recognize themselves as subjects of a particular ideology. In other words, interpellation is the process by which individuals are called upon by institutions and practices within society to identify with and internalize particular ideological values and beliefs. Althusser (2014) argued that this process is central to functioning ideological state apparatuses such as the family, the church, the media, and the educational system.

WAR IN COMING-OF-AGE LITERATURE

There are two ways in which coming-of-age literature represents war: war as the scenery and as the central theme of a story. War is among the »taboo topics« that began to appear relatively late in the literature with growing-up characters, by surviving the romantic conception of child and childhood, and by reducing the didactic role of literature for younger readers. War is a political and social event whose effects are transmitted to everyone regardless of gender, age, or social status. The Happening of War completely changes the experience of reality and the way of life. In real life, war changes, or it is meant to change the experiential world of young people, destroying security and illusions and undermining ethical-moral conventions. Life circumstances are entirely different (Gričar, 2010).

As the portrayal of literary heroes strives to be as believable and accurate as possible, books reflect the same characteristics in the lives of literary characters trapped in the vortex of war. Life routines change. There is often a school drop-out, lack of food, children's play changes, and children, in addition to the general poverty and chaos, also face the loss of friends and family members, violence, and refugees. The environment often begins to reject them in the formerly known world. This time, they appear as aliens who need to be removed or adapted to the new society.

There are many ways to write the war. It can be extraordinarily traumatic, scenery, adventure, or exciting. Although we can present war as exciting, dangerous, and interesting, it is never good (Fox, 1999). War is always portrayed as an adverse emergency, and its end is eagerly anticipated so that life can return to the old rails. The end of the war always brings a turning point in society, bringing the onset of peace and the rebuilding of society and the lives of individuals (Shah, 2012).

Literature expresses war through the motives on which it forms the stories of the heroes. A war-themed novel has a particular relation to reality, as it reflects critical consciousness by projecting a critical attitude toward existing society through the individual as well as the collective psychology of the hero. A war-themed novel is a type of action novel, but it is also a character novel or a group of characters novel. The vast majority is also a documentary insofar as we understand work as a fixed-term document. The dominant process is retrospective but can contain many autobiographical events and elements. A war-themed novel is thematically and motivationally rich, as there is hardly any topic that it would not address (Ivanović, 1963).

War often appears as a backdrop or catalyst for the protagonist's growth and development in coming-of-age novels. War can profoundly affect characters' lives, shaping their values, beliefs, and perspectives (Shah, 2013, 2024b). It can force them to confront the topics of death, loss, and trauma, which are central themes in their fast-track journey to adulthood. Exposing characters to the harsh realities of the world strips away the innocence of the youth. Loss of innocence is a common theme in coming-of-age narratives as characters grapple with the complexities of violence, war conflict, loss of home, and loss of body autonomy.

Common motive also faces moral dilemmas related to war, such as questions of loyalty, duty, and the justifiability of violence. These dilemmas can manipulate their values and integrity, change their perspective, and even lead to a change of heart. Young characters are facing a tough fight to keep parts of their old identity, often connected to nationality and culture from which they are coming. They face a hard choice of what cultural predispositions they should keep as they struggle to define themselves amidst the chaos and destruction of conflict. War experiences shape characters, ultimately forging their identities in the process. They must stay resilient and adapt to the challenges of living in a world torn apart by violence, often fighting for their survival.

NARRATIVES OF A WAR EXPERIENCE

Characterization of the heroes of the two selected novels is a warlike experience that they convey to their vision of the world. They experience both the war and its aftermath directly, and their lives are fully affected as they leave their home and become refugees or expatriates. In the novel *Ukulele Jam*, storytelling is interwoven with the reminiscence of the bombing and shooting in Miki's hometown. In contrast, the portrayal of direct war action in the novel *Hotel Zagorje* is limited to showing violence through the media (primarily television and newspapers) as the heroine leaves the city before the siege.

Boštjan Gričar, in the text *Narrative Representations of War in Youth Prose,* divides war youth narrative prose according to narrative perspective: (1) into prose narrated by a (perspective) adult narrator who wants to pass on his vision and understanding of war to the reader; (2) to prose that is narrated from the perspective of a child and offers limited understanding and interpretation, which can be misleading. However, individual texts are not characterized by a unity of perspective since sometimes these two perspectives are intertwined in the texts, at some part dominating one and in the other dominating the other one (Gričar, 2010). Contemporary literary theory uses the term unreliable narrator to name the second type of narrator.

Harlamov (2010) refers to Wayne C. Booth's (1983) *The Rhetorics of Fiction*, summarizing that when a reader finds a narrator's story "plausible," his opinion "wise," and his judgments »just« - the narrator (for the reader) is reliable. We can call him a reliable narrator. However, when the narrator seems to the reader to be »unbelievable,« his opinion "unwise," and his judgments "unjust," such a narrator (for the reader) is unreliable and is called an unreliable narrator. Bruno Zerweck (2001) introduces frame theory, which is when the reader connects with real-life frames. Frames are part of the reader's knowledge of the world, deciding what is real and what is not. Whether the narrator is reliable depends on the production's cultural and historical background and reception.

The type of unreliable narrator, however, may also include a children's perspective that shapes the narratives in both novels. Personally involved or hurt unreliable narrator shows emotions and affection toward the elements of the fictional world, which causes his view of them to be strongly subjectively defined and distorted, which makes his reporting on the aspects of the fictional world unreliable, different from how the reader concretizes these elements or how their context or the text as a whole gives them (Harlamov, 2010).

In both novels, the characters respond emotionally to events and talk about them from their limited space, time, age, and experience. Nevertheless, the writing and storytelling of selected storytellers show significant differences that we can interpret through the prism of gender stereotypes.

In the novel *Hotel Zagorje*, the heroine is naive and childish, conveying her influences from the environment reflected in her storytelling and positions. She is not critical of her environment and society; she only reproduces the chosen ideology, does not develop an ideological-critical perspective, and does not resist practices and stereotypes, even though she soundly judges the environment. While we can read certain parts of the narrative ironically (gender stereotypes) or critically (critique of the state's attitude toward refugees), writing is clumsy, prone to misinterpretation if the readers do not have adequate critical leadership that teaches them to resist, to read critically. It reflects the unreliability of the narrator, her opinion, and the society's opinion, which she accepts. The heroine is characterized by girls' gender stereotypes, including naivety, disinterest in social problems, caring for the family (she constantly cares for her mother, father, and brother), and pleasing the crowd.

In the novel *Ukulele Jam*, the main narrator for his age is a highly mature young boy who is critical of his environment and what is happening in it. Through his experiences, he forms an opinion and does not take over the general thinking of the environment but identifies himself as an alien. Although possessing stereotypical boyish characteristics, which include active participation in society, desire for recognition, individuality, adopting adult behavioral patterns, and heroic staging, the narrative also denies them, as the protagonist is a highly emotional boy who clearly expresses his emotions (many times a motif of crying appears), he sees girls as the same thinking beings, not only as sexual objects, his activities include comforting his mother, and others. He rejects the ideology of nationalism, which is the complete opposite of the novel *Hotel Zagorje*, which reproduces nationalist ideas.

The girl's narrator seems unreliable and naive, while the boy's narration is clear and believable, giving us a more wholesome picture of the experience. Both narrators are children under the strong influence of emotions. However, the girl's narration is more prone to disconnect from what the reader and narrator make of it, which leads to another stereotype that females are less reliable at telling history and big stories.

GROWING UP AS THE MAIN MOTIVE OF NOVELS

One of the central broad themes of the coming-of-age novel is growing up, which is realized through the development and maturation of protagonists as they navigate various challenges and experiences. They undergo significant growth and transformation throughout the novel, often starting as naive and inexperienced and gradually maturing and learning the challenges they face while coming of age. They undergo identity formation, navigate relationships, encounter challenges that require resilience, courage, and determination, lose their innocence, and achieve independence. They must accept their past, embrace their identity, and set their path toward the future.

Growing up is a central motive of both of the chosen novels. Both protagonists face the acceptance of responsibility and the transition to adulthood, and the transition time is significantly shorter as the war circumstances require them to grow up and assume responsibility faster. As can be seen from the excerpt about the relationship with a father from the *Ukulele Jam* novel below:

> *In the war, when grenades were flying around our ears, he did not want to decide what I needed and what I needed to do. If I asked him for advice, he would always answer:*
>
> *- Do whatever you want. In just a little while, you will not be a child anymore.*
>
> */.../*
>
> *- It was different in the war – he pleaded. – If I would say 'stay here' and a grenade would fall on this place, it would be my fault. If I sent you somewhere else and a grenade would fall there, I would be guilty again. It was ridiculous. Now things are different.* (Mešković, 2015)

Growing up during a war requires changing patterns. War is also a period in which children and adolescents are expected to be more mature and grow up quickly into appropriate social roles. Childhood is interrupted, and responsibility shifts for life to a young hero who decides for himself. As a result, this also leads to an awareness of one's mortality and the mortality of loved ones, as well as the transience of life, which is a sign of maturation and the gradual abandonment of infantile childhood.

War as a growing up is a form of storytelling that highlights the chaos and instability that war creates in the lives of children and adolescents. It pulls the child out of daily routine and creates the inability and powerlessness to reconstruct the peace of pre-war life (Shah, 2024a). War circumstances are crucial in the growth of adolescent characters. Still, they can be reflected in the struggle with depression and suffering, food shortages, and death. Changed life circumstances force the teenage hero to take care of others and take responsibility for themselves (Zima, 2001). The main characteristic of emergent social circumstances is rapid variability and instability, which is reflected in the growing up of children and adolescents who quickly jump from one period to another, and their maturity is often not comparable to the maturity of their peers growing up in peace and prosperity. Children and adolescents growing up in war contexts are even more marked, as teenage years are when the main identity characteristics of an individual have formed and have a decisive influence on the development of personality traits.

Fast maturing is well-written in the novel *Ukulele Jam*, where the main character, Emir (his nickname is Miki), takes responsibility for his actions and cares for the family at the end of primary school. Not only is he perceived as an adult by the surroundings, but he also sees himself as a kind of grown-up, which is well presented in the following descriptions of the military occupation of his hometown and the army mobilization of men when soldiers order all men to leave the bus:

> *I got up at the same time as Neno and my dad, but the old man pushed me back into the seat and said:*
>
> *- Watch your mom!*
>
> *- But ... I am a ...*
>
> *I am a man too, I wanted to say, but he did not let me:*
>
> *- Stay here and watch over her!* (Mešković, 2015)

The quote shows that a young, not yet 15-year-old boy has been placed to care for his mother and her safety, which is a huge responsibility. From this, we can also recognize the classic patriarchal pattern that a man must take care of women's safety, in which case, since the father and the elder son are absent, this concern falls on the shoulders of the youngest son. The mother's role is blurred and minimal. The mother is not recognized as a role model who can make decisions and bear responsibility. The role is defined solely based on her gender.

Miki bears much responsibility for himself, and his life can be seen in other places, whereas as a 15-year-old, he acts highly mature and responsible. Namely, he arranges himself for high school enrollment, validates refugee certificates for the whole family, and quickly starts working and earning money to help his family and take care of himself – he buys shoes that are urgently needed, and he also spends some money for fun with friends, food and music cassettes.

The heroine from *Hotel Zagorje* is the complete opposite, dealing solely with her growing-up issues and developing her identity. Through childhood and early teens, the narrator builds her identity on a national identity. Only later, at puberty, does she upgrade her identity by belonging to the grunge subculture, with patriotism to her high school and the other components of her life. Throughout the book, nationalism is intertwined with the narrative, with which the young storyteller strikes everywhere. Her visibility is crucial to her, and she gains popularity among her peers, especially among boys. She writes about herself as a popular girl whom the other girls envy. She wants the attention of older boys, whose affection represents almost a social status – success and popularity are constantly associated with male affection and recognition, thus clearly reproducing the gender stereotype that women's success is directly linked to partnership and family (Shah, 2020, 2021).

As a girl, she is successful in school, again representing the stereotype of a virtuous girl who respects authority and follows social norms. As she enters high school, her attitude toward the school changes. She often misses classes, has poor grades, stops trying at school, and does not attach too much importance to education. When the problems at school get too big, the class teacher advises her to enroll in a less demanding school, which her mother prevents. She believes in her daughter more than the heroine herself. Here, a slightly more active role for the mother is acceptable, as the mother oversees her adolescent daughter's life. Both are assigned to the female gender, so the mother's activity does not exceed stereotypical gender frames. The heroine is insecure, confused, and undecided, and others always make significant decisions. Skipping school and resisting school authority are expressed as characteristics of teenage behavior; they do not carry the function of social resistance or rejection of the school as a state ideological apparatus (Althusser, 2014).

She is passive and always makes decisions in the hands of her mother and brother, thus embodying the stereotype that women need to be protected and cared for. Her mother, too, is a passive character who rarely actively intervenes to resolve a family situation. The big savior of the family is the absent father, and the elder brother temporarily assumes his role. Accordingly, the heroine does not take responsibility or make decisions about her life.

By expressing such passivity, the author minimizes the girl's role in society and portrays her as a faithful follower of her parents. Although there is rebellion in the novel, it is only related to the general teenage rebellion, which is related to absenteeism, late coming home, and drinking alcohol. Rebellion has no social function and is nowhere labeled anti-war but merely an element of typical teenage behavior. On the contrary, the heroine expresses herself as extremely nationalistic and patriotic, constantly emphasizing her nationality. Nationalist expression is the only time she shows her active role and voices her opinion. However, nationalism is chosen for her; it is not her discourse. It is soaked up from the environment and forced on her. After each nation decided to exit, the new Croatian identity was given to her, and she repeated it throughout her life. When she is on vacation with an Italian family and is referred to by her family's father as "bambina Yugoslava," she reacts violently and angrily and impolitely bumps him:

Croazia, no Jugoslavija, bambina Croazia. (Simić Bodrožić, 2011)

The novel reflects nationalism at many points, including an incident on a holiday with an Italian family, where she meets a girl named Maja from Belgrade at a children's party. She does not want to talk to Maja, as she is convinced that they speak different languages, escalating her to reject the girl's friendship. She moves to the other end of the room, sits on her chair, and, while shivering, thinks about returning home (which she had to leave behind due to the war). While we can understand the girl's aggression as a reflection of her emotional instability and ignorance, this is precisely the pattern that reproduces the conception of nationalism and violence through a naive, childlike perspective.

Schooling in a *Ukulele Jam* novel carries a different function. As a primary schooler, Miki is looking forward to entering high school as he wants to follow in the footsteps of his older brother, Neno. Although he is not eligible for education as a Bosnian refugee in Croatia, he still does his best to be admitted to high school, and he gets a donor from abroad to cover the costs of his education. Although not admitted to the desired high school but to a technical high school, Miki fought for schooling and his successes in the school, which we can understand as resistance to a system that rejected him. Miki makes his own decisions concerning education; he is an independent and active hero who consciously decides his actions. Moving from high school to artisan school is also Miki's conscious act, which is a response to the financial distress and famine that the family is experiencing. Miki decides to help financially and relieve the family in this way.

Miki also identifies with the subculture. In his case, these are the hard rock and metal subcultures he expresses through his appearance and the music he listens to. Miki goes to a rock club called Ukulele and wants to make a good impression on the girls by playing guitar and singing famous rock songs. He exchanges cassettes with his friends, and some better-off friends also give him trendy clothes they no longer wear. Although Miki successfully builds and nurtures friendships, which through letters are kept alive even after his friends leave abroad, he still has problems integrating into society, not due to his character trait but to the fact that he is a Bosnian Muslim, a refugee. He is dating several girls in the novel. His greatest love is the refugee girl Jelena, who later moves to America with her parents. He thinks of Jelena holistically and, above all, finds her mental and emotional elements attractive. It is challenging for him when he and Jelena have to say goodbye. The author writes:

I wanted to cry, but I could not. Sadness has hardened in me. (Mešković, 2015)

The main character in the novel is a very emotional boy who also expresses his emotions in front of friends. Despite the fierce fate of a teenage refugee, he strives to maintain a positive attitude toward life and looks for ways to live life to the fullest despite the circumstances. The hero's storytelling is thoughtful and often more mature than one would expect from a teenager. On the contrary, the portrayal of the heroine at *Hotel Zagorje* is very infantile and naive, and her narration is very childish and unreliable. At the novel's beginning, the author uses a nine-year-old, first-person narrator who is overly infantile and has naive discourse. The heroine is ignorant and gullible, and at the start of the war, she is not even aware of or understands anything going on around her. We can also interpret ignorance as a signal from an unreliable narrator. The discourse in which the protagonist expresses herself improves through the novel and becomes better adapted to the heroine's age, but her naivety and passivity do not disappear.

REFUGEE OR EMIGRATION – YUGOSLAVIA OR CROATIA?

During and after wars fought on the basis of nationality, old national identities are seen as nostalgic or often refused. Rejecting old national identities can symbolize defiance against the previous regime and its symbols of power and authority. People may reject this identity as a means of distancing themselves from the injustices and atrocities committed by the former government (Shah, 2019). Refusing old national identities can be part of nation-building as newly independent countries seek a unified national identity. Comparable processes also took place in the 1990s, when, with the break-up of Yugoslavia, new states began to emerge on its territory, with identities shaped based on nationalism. To establish a social framework, new states always need a new past (Kuljić, 2006) written through individuals' stories.

In the novel *Hotel Zagorje*, everything related to the socialist republic of Yugoslavia is rejected and stigmatized. The heroine builds her identity on a new national identity, with which she strongly identifies herself (in the novel, she repeats herself as a Croat) and deliberately separates herself from people of other nationalities. She characterizes Serbs and Slovenes as bad. The same confirmation comes from other characters in the novel, who also emphasize the grandeur of the newly emerged Croatia.

The heroine in the novel evens out with everyone who does not fit her national ideas. She distinguishes between refugees and exiles who, by her definition, differ in that they are Croats and Bosnians – again basing her definition on nationality:

> *A beautifully dressed lady in our wagon told her companion that the refugees were doing the drain because they were traveling here and there all God's days. I looked at her and smiled, knowing that we were exiles and the refugees were those from Bosnia.* (Simić Bodrožić, 2011)

The whole narrative is imbued with nationalism, and it is no stranger to glorifying Croatia and fighting in the war. National identity is a historical construct, so continuity of difference is the basis of differentiation from others. Identity testifies to far-reaching racial, blood, cultural, mental, and religious differences. Among the ideological images of the past, the most active are those that seek to differentiate between different groups by emphasizing their more or less inventive peculiarities: identity myths divide related peoples according to religion, script, and diet. Mythical and constructed identities in crises do not emphasize fertile cultural diversity but form inequality in the past and advocate for demarcation (extermination, displacement, segregation, subjugation, distrust) (Kuljić, 2006). Nationalist writing is especially problematic since children's naivety, which is not necessarily understood by the reader, at least from the perspective of an unreliable narrator, can be exploited for the unreflected and ideologically contentious writing and reproduction of hatred. In the case of the novel *Hotel Zagorje*, this is especially problematic since the book is included in reading for school-age children in Croatia. Despite winning literary prizes and being included in the school curriculum, the novel has received mixed reactions from the public. On one side, the author received support from established Croatian authors and critics, but there was also much written about the stigma of nationalism and the uncritical approach to it.

> That the definitions of refugees and exiles are the product of right-wing nationalist politics is also evident from the novel Ukulele Jam, where Miki writes that *"Bosnians were fleeing Bosnia, and Croats were persecuted from Croatia. And they kept reminding us of that."* (Mešković, 2015)

It also records:

> *Croats from Bosnia were much better talked about than us and Serbs, but they also did not have the same benefits as Croats from Croatia. Although they were Croats, they were also called refugees.* (Mešković, 2015)

Miki does not practice religious practices, but he is one of the Bosnian Muslims. It is evident that, above all, Miki's father favored socialist ideology and politics, which did not change even during the war. Miki is critical of the new emergence of nationalism and repeatedly brings him to the brink of despair. As he says:

> *In the city, you could get lost in the crowd. It was not written on my forehead that I was a Bosniak, a refugee, or a Muslim. At the Center, the story was different. There, everyone knew who I was and what I was.* (Mešković, 2015)

Unlike the novel *Ukulele Jam*, the novel *Hotel Zagorje* diverges from the socialist ideology and incorporates ideas of nationalism and Catholicism into the narrative, as "any positive memory of socialism narrows the space to nationalism since it is not effective until socialist internationalism is demonized" (Kuljić, 2006). Nevertheless, both novels problematize the degrading and socially disordered relationship between the state and society toward refugees, who are particularly obviously economically helpless and underprivileged: after the collapse of socialism, the Croatian state, the reference social environment of the novel, relied on a capitalist, market economy, in which war refugees are significantly less likely to raise capital and thus optimize social conditions. In the novel *Hotel Zagorje*, the girl's mother provides for her family's capital through black work. The *Ukulele Jam* novel also critiques the refugees' deprived status and life circumstances. Miki's father also goes to "Muscle Square," where he struggles daily for any physical work that could earn him at least a little money. Miki's mother is also used to making wool products sold as Croatian national products. In both novels, the characters receive clothing from the Red Cross, and both families live in dire social conditions.

Despite severe social conditions and constant discrimination, Miki strives to maintain the best possible relationship with most of the people living in the center, with classmates and other people he meets. However, because of his Bosniak roots, he has trouble making friends and is even more affected by the fact that friendships are volatile, as his peers are constantly leaving and moving with the hope of a better life and future.

Unlike Miki, the heroine of the novel *Hotel Zagorje* rejects most people around her despite being Croats. She describes her male classmates with adjectives like thick, stupid, retarded, and she describes her female classmates as stinky, with greasy hair, and ridiculous. The connection between people is reflected mainly at the national level and in the hatred of the adversary represented by all other former Yugoslav nations. The girl identifies with the Croatian nation and identifies Croats as the only good ones. When on vacation with an Italian family, as she said, she presents herself as the *"bambina Croazia,"* and among the slogans are also *"Tudjman buono, Tito no"* (Simić Bodoržić, 2011).

Such definitions highlight the nationalistic undertone of the novel, which conveys ideas to the young reader about the only true nation, the good nation, and its enemies. The demonization of Yugoslav internationalist socialism (with the concept of brotherhood between countries) and the construction of a new national history and collective identity are evident in the novel *Hotel Zagorje*. Anything that in any way associates with the former socialist republic is demonized and negative. The narrative contains direct descriptions of the destruction of Yugoslav symbols and monuments, with the heroine herself involved:

> *I assumed that they had probably again stolen something in the Etno village of Marshal Tito, something bigger perhaps because the small things had already been robbed. Nothing new. Even us girls liked to take revenge on the Serbs and the communists by writing all kinds of things in the book of impressions, and they even showed it on a television show as an example of the impoverishment of the Croatian cultural heritage. I wrote: Comrade Tito, thank you for the beautiful little room you provided for my mother, brother, and me, burn in hell./.../Only Tito's real house could no longer be reached because they had put a security guard in front. They probably feared that we would take away even that great statue in front of it.* (Simić Bodrožić, 2011)

Ukulele Jam has a different attitude toward the Yugoslav symbols. Miki is pleasantly surprised to see a painting of Josip Broz Tito on the wall of Master Boro's workshop and the cassette of the Bijelo Dugme band, considered one of the most famous rock bands of the former Yugoslavia. Amid the euphoria, Miki decides to buy all six tapes exhibited in the showcase, as they are a symbol of a happy past:

> *The unique riffs, tunes, and solos all electrified my body. I almost experienced a strong ex-yugo-retro-trip, though I didn't know the concept then. I sang unique refrains on the way to the market/.../ Good old Bijelo Dugme plates! My old turntable! My room!* (Mešković, 2015)

Due to Miki's national and religious affiliation, he suffers verbal and physical violence from strangers at a refugee center. Discrimination is especially apparent when Miki wants to enroll in high school, which is impossible without Croatian citizenship. Through a particular program, Miki obtains donors from abroad, who then pay him for a program so that he can continue his education. As a Bosniak in Croatia, he is also prevented from enrolling in college, destroying Miki's dream of studying and achieving his ideal of being educated. Miki tolerates discrimination and contempt valiantly but occasionally ends up in tears. He wants to leave Croatia and move to Sweden, where his friends and his brother are, and whereas a Bosniak, he will not be as stigmatized as in Croatia.

The religious affiliation with the creation of the new countries began to regain its validity, which is also evident from the novel *Hotel Zagorje*, where Christianity, or better Catholicism, occupies a special ideological place. In Croatia, in the

1990s, a re-Catholicization of society took place, introducing many conservative practices and views into every day and social life. In the novel, sayings such as, "*He who loves Croatia loves God*" appear, and religious practices become part of everyday life (introducing religion at school and daily prayer).

The motif that marks the transition from socialist atheist to anti-socialist Catholic society is also the conversion of a classroom in a political school to a church. New order removed books about the Socialist Party and Tito's paintings from the school, locked them up, and redecorated the room:

> *Room number five was converted into a church. They used to read mass there every Sunday. The big desk was redecorated into an altar and covered with a white tablecloth, under which were hundreds of books about the party and some framed Tito paintings. Behind the lecture hall were three confessionals, made of three pairs of chairs, facing each other. We prayed there to God on Sundays and went for a religion class.* (Simić Bodrožić, 2011)

With the re-Catholicization of Croatian society, there has been a shift from a socialist to a capitalist socio-economic order based on the processes of "re-repatriarchalisation." Reinforcement of the old dichotomies of public and private and the revival of conservative ideologies about family and gender, which exclude women from the public economic and political space and push them back into the artificially isolated private sphere of home and childcare, reflect "re-repatriarchalisation" (Burcar, 2009), which we see in the depiction of girl characters in the novel *Hotel Zagorje*. As a life goal, a girl sets an orderly family life, affirms and fulfills herself through the approval of boys and men, and yearns for a solution inevitably linked to a male figure (father, brother, partner). The heroine also pays great attention to her appearance, which helps her achieve her desired goals (boys' affection and establishing a position in society). In the foreground, it is no longer the heroine's intellectual and spiritual development but her physical appearance, which brings us back to the surviving conservative socio-sexual institutions of femininity. This return, however, negatively influences young readers because, through the literary socialization thus offered, it closes and shrinks the ways of their self-understanding and limits the possibilities of their self-realization (Burcar, 2007).

CONCLUSION

Coming-of-age novels are all about growing up. Characters undergo development and maturation as they navigate various challenges and experiences. They undergo significant growth and transformation throughout the story, often starting as naive and inexperienced and gradually maturing and learning the challenges they face while coming of age.

An important part is identity formation, followed by navigating relationships, encountering challenges that require resilience, courage, determination, losing innocence, and achieving independence. Protagonists should accept their past, embrace their identity, and set their path toward the future. Those processes are sped up in case of war since the environment is unstable, chaotic, and dangerous. Growing up during a war requires changing patterns. It is a period in which children and adolescents are expected to grow up quickly and approach life more maturely. Childhood is interrupted, and responsibility for life often shifts into the hands of a young protagonist, which leads to an awareness of one's mortality and the mortality of loved ones, as well as the transience of life, which is a sign of maturation and the gradual abandonment of infantile childhood. All these characteristics are inscribed into fictional characters.

The analysis showed a difference between the writing of the girl's and boy's characters. The girl is passive, naive, and ignorant. She depends on her surroundings, relying too heavily on her parents and older brother. Her situation assessment is valid but unreliable and problematic from a reader's perspective. It reflects the nationalistic influences of the environment in an unreflected way, and the only thing that pays attention is its growing up and establishment among peers. For the most part, the heroine is at the forefront of her physical appearance and development, and her intellectual and spiritual growth is pushed into the background, which brings us back to conservative institutions of femininity. There are many critically unaddressed gender stereotypes in the novel, but there is only their reproduction. With the collapse of 20th-century systems, a slide into conservatism is typical, which is also evident in the writing of girl characters in coming-of-age novels. While male characters have more rounded experiences and are written as active individuals, female characters can often fall into gender stereotypes.

In contrast to the heroine of *Hotel Zagorje*, Miki, the hero of the novel *Ukulele Jam*, is a well-regarded, active, and considerate character. He expresses his situation and takes responsibility for his life and decisions. Despite the stigmatization, he remains cheerful, with much vitality and will to live. He rejects the notions of nationalism and points to their separation of society, but above all, points to the futility of hatred and division into »ours« and "others." Despite his young age, Miki is mature and trustworthy but remains emotionally sensitive to social events and social atmosphere. In a war that belongs to men according to traditional sexual divisions, he finds himself better than the heroine of the second novel studied. His attitude toward the world is reflected and individualized. In contrast, the *Hotel Zagorje* heroine's attitude is solely based on the unreflected reproduction of nationalist policies, which the author tries to mask with the innocently unreliable perspective of a child narrator.

Through the chapter, I showed that there are gender differences between the narrators, which were mainly based on a reproduction of sexist, patriarchal stereotypes about women and girls. Those stereotypes still hold women as the second sex (Beauvoir, 2011) as being less reliable in telling history and participating in it actively. All this translates to girls, whose perspectives and stories of war should be considered as important as those of any other gender. To avoid gender stereotypes, we should strive for well-rounded, diverse, and authentic portrayals that reflect the complexity of real-life individuals. Girl characters should be developed with depth and complexity, giving them a range of motivations, desires, and flaws. Protagonists should engage in various activities and pursuits and display courage and resilience in adversity. They should have agency so that in case of the problematic reproduction of nationalism, the reader may oppose the protagonist and not accept their views. If the protagonist is passive, the reproduction of nationalism associated with the war ideology can reproduced surreptitiously.

REFERENCES

Althusser, L. (2014). *On the reproduction of capitalism: Ideology and ideological state apparatuses*. Verso Books.
Beauvoir, S. de (2011). *The second sex*. Vintage Books.
Booth, W. C. (1983). *The rhetorics of fiction*. The University of Chicago Press.
Burcar, L. (2007). *Novi val nedolžnosti v otroški literaturi: Kaj sporočata Harry Potter in Lyra Srebrnousta?* Sophia.
Burcar, L. (2009). Od socialistične k (neoliberalni) kapitalistični družbenoekonomski ureditvi: Redefinicija državljanstva žensk. *Borec: revija za zgodovino, literaturo in antropologijo, 61*(657–66), 296–331.
Fox, C. (1999). What the children's literature of war is telling the children. *Literacy, 33*(3), 126–131.
Gričar, B. (2010). Pripovedne predstavitve vojne v mladinski prozi. *Otrok in knjiga, 37*(78–79), 18–27.
Harlamov, A. (2010). Nezanesljivi pripovedovalec v sodobnem slovenskem romanu. *Jezik in slovstvo, 55*(1–2), 33–46.
Ivanović, R. (1963). Značilnosti romana z vojno tematiko. *Sodobnost, 26*(10), 975–982.
Kuljić, T. (2006). *Kultura sjećanja*. Čigoja štampa.
Mešković, A. (2015). *Ukulele Jam*. Booka.
Nikolajeva, M. (2004). Odraščanje: Dilema otroške književnosti. *Otrok in knjiga, 31*(59), 5–27.
Shah, T. M. (2012). *Collective memory and narrative: Ethnography of social trauma in Jammu and Kashmir* [Doctoral dissertation, Kansas State University].
Shah, T. M. (2013). *Chaos and fear: Creativity and hope in an uncertain world*.
Shah, T. M. (2019). Social justice and change. In S. Romaniuk, M. Thapa, & P. Marton (Eds.), *The Palgrave encyclopedia of global security studies* (pp. 1–4). Palgrave Macmillan.
Shah, T. M. (2020). Children of Kashmir and the meaning of family in armed conflict. In S. Frankel & S. McNamee (Eds.), *Bringing children back into the family: Relationality, connectedness and home* (pp. 213–216). Emerald Publishing Limited.
Shah, T. M. (2021). *Women as "Sites of Gendered Politics"*. Misogyny Across Global Media.
Shah, T. M. (2023). *Global patterns of decolonization and the right to self-determination: A comparative-historical analysis of East Timor and Kashmir* [Doctoral dissertation, The University of Utah].
Shah, T. M. (2024a). Decolonization and peacebuilding: The case of Timor Leste and Kashmir. In P. Pietrzak (Ed.), *Dealing with regional conflicts of global importance* (pp. 262–278). IGI Global.
Shah, T. M. (2024b). Emotions in politics: A review of contemporary perspectives and trends. *International Political Science Abstracts, 74*(1), 1–14.
Simić Bodrožić, I. (2011). *Hotel Zagorje*. (Prev. Maja Novak). Modrijan.
Stahl, S. D. (1989). *Literary folkloristics and the personal narrative*. Indiana University.
Todd, J. (2007). *Feminist literary history*. Polity Press.
Zerweck, B. (2001). Historicizing unreliable narration: Unreliability and cultural discourse in narrative fiction. *Style, 1*, 151–178.
Zima, D. (2001). Hrvatska dječja književnost o ratu. *Polemos, 4*(2), 81–122.

CHAPTER 11

CHILDREN AS PARTICIPANTS IN TERRORISM: UCHE AGUH'S *SAMBISA* (2016) AS A PARADIGM

Stephen Ogheneruro Okpadah[a] and
Damilare Ogunmekan[b]

[a]*University of Warwick, Coventry, UK*
[b]*University of Lagos, Nigeria*

ABSTRACT

In 2002, the organization, Jamat Al Asunnah Lid-Da'wa'l-Jihad popularly known as Boko Haram was created in North Eastern Nigeria. This organization which was founded by Mohammed Yusuf was to later adopt the ideology that Western Education was Forbidden. The decolonial stance of Boko Haram later degenerated into its campaign of violence, leading to the killing of its founder by the Nigerian state. Interestingly, the role of children in the advancement of the Boko Haram insurgency and how this impacts their psychological lives seems to have been overlooked in scholarship on terrorism. There remains a dearth of critical underpinning on how all of the above is represented in Nigerian film. To this end, this study examines child participation in terrorism in Nigeria and its effect on the psychological well-being of the child. Using the Boko Haram terrorist group as a paradigm, the authors argue that children, especially the girl child play a major role in the advancement of terrorism in Nigeria. The study engages in a content analysis of Uche Aguh's film, Sambisa (2016) to interrogate the challenges the child encounters in the face of terrorism in Nigeria and examines children as major actors in the enterprise of terrorism in Nigeria.

Keywords: Terrorism; film; Nigeria; Sambisa; child; conflict

INTRODUCTION

The scholarship on terrorism and how Nigerian filmmakers represent it has been exhaustive. This is against the backdrop of the rise in activities of terrorism in the most populous nation on the continent, for almost two decades. Prominent among activities of terror, is the Boko Haram insurgency in the North Eastern region of Nigeria. The Northeast region of Nigeria is comprised of Gombe, Adamawa, Yobe, Taraba, Borno, and Bauchi states. Although the activities of the group have been majorly restricted to the North Eastern part of the country, there have been cases of attacks in the nation's capital territory, Abuja, and Niger state. According to Ike et al. (2022, p. 2), "the Boko Haram group is deemed one of the deadliest terrorist groups in the world." Since the transition of the organization into an armed group in 2009, its activities have led to the death of more than 20,000 inhabitants in the region, the disruption of economic, educational, and agricultural activities, as well as the destruction of properties worth billions of naira. The activities of the terrorist group include suicide bombings, kidnappings, the massive displacement of people, and other terror-related atrocities. There have been various permutations that the upsurge and success of this terrorist group is a result of the high rate of illiteracy, religious extremism – the Sharianization of the region, and the political schema where opposition political parties promote armed insurgency to truncate the efforts of the government in power. According to Imam Rauf (2015), "the word Shariah in Arabic is a verbal noun stemming from the root sh.r.', meaning to initiate, introduce, or ordain. It refers to the total of God's shar" (p. 17). By Sharianization, we refer to governance rooted in the tenets and doctrine of Islam.

The role of children in the advancement of the Boko Haram insurgency and how this impacts their psychological lives seems to have been overlooked in the scholarship on terrorism (Shah, 2021). There remains a dearth of critical underpinning on how all of the above is represented in Nigerian film. To this end, this study examines child participation in terrorism in Nigeria and its effect on the psychological well-being of the child. Using the Boko Haram terrorist group as a paradigm, we argue that children, especially the girl child play a major role in the advancement of terrorism in Nigeria. The study engages in a content analysis of Uche Aguh's film, *Sambisa* (2016) to interrogate the challenges the child encounters in the face of terrorism in Nigeria and examines children as major actors in the enterprise of terrorism in Nigeria. In what follows, the study explores historically the concept of child terrorism in Nigeria with reference to Boko Haram.

CHILD TERRORISTS IN NIGERIA: THE BOKO HARAM CONTEXT

Before we proceed to explore the context of child terrorism and its practice in Nigeria, it is imperative to know who a child is. The term child is a social and cultural construct. For example, among the indigenous people of Mandinka in the Gambia and Kouroussa in Guinea, one remains a child until the traditional rite of transition into adulthood is completed (Cissoko, 2022). This practice is fully captured in Alex Haley's Novel *Roots* (1976) with the principal character, Kunta Kinte's initiation into adulthood, and in Camara Laye's *The African Child* (1953), where Laye is initiated into manhood. Among the Urhobo people in the Niger Delta region of Nigeria, there is the *Opha* ritual in which young maidens transit into adulthood, and are ripe enough for marriage (Agberia, 2006). According to Lansdon and Vaghri (2022), "Article 1 of International Law defines the child as a human being who is below the age of 18 years. [S]he is a human being from birth to the age of 18 years" (p. 407). The study employs Gerison Lansdon and Ziba Vaghri's definition of a child as we proceed in our discussion.

Children have witnessed and participated actively in different violent operations in Nigeria. Amongst such violent engagements was the Nigerian civil war that took place 1967–1970. Evidence abound of the impact of this war on children, and how some children of Biafra extract were either enlisted as soldiers or taught how to use arms. The film *Tears of the Sun* (2003) by Antoine Faqua fully captures the role of the child in this war. In this film, young boys kill helpless men, women, and their parents. The gory sight of some of the child soldiers shooting sporadically and cutting off the breasts of a nursing mother reveals the transformation of the child from an innocent creature who should be nurtured into a social normal, into a misnomer. The major drivers of this transformation are their introduction to hard drugs and assimilation of ideologies that are different from what society stipulates. This picture of radicalized children is also fully captured in Edward Zwick's *Blood Diamond* (2006), a narrative on the long-term Sierra Leone war, in Angelina Jolie's *First They Killed My Father* (2017), and Jean-Stephane Sauvaire's *Johnny Mad Dog* (2008).

One of the earliest cases of participation of a young Nigerian in terrorism-related affair was on December 25th, 2009 when 23-year-old Nigerian-born Umar Farouk AbdulMutalab attempted to detonate a bomb hidden in his underwear onboard a flight from Amsterdam to Michigan, USA. Although the bomb attempt was foiled, the name of a young Nigerian adult had been written on the marble of global terrorism. Not long after the AbdulMutalab's incident, the Nigerian child became a major participant in terrorism within Nigeria. This was with the growth of the Boko Haram insurgency in the North Eastern region of the country. On 14th April 2014, 279 girls aged between 16 and 18 were kidnapped at Government Girls Secondary School, Chibok, Borno State, by the Boko Haram insurgents (Okpadah, 2024). This kidnap of young girls created a shift in the war strategy of the terrorist group, it made visible, the effect of the insurgency on young people and most importantly, the integration of kidnapped children into the fold of terrorism. The success of child soldiers in the execution of tasks given to them culminated in more recruitment. This was possible with their being kidnapped. Hence, after the mass abduction of 279 schoolgirls in Chibok, other mass abductions followed suit.

In 2019, a report by UNICEF indicates that more than 3,500 young people were recruited by the terrorist group in Nigeria. According to Kenechukwu Mbajiorgu (2023, p. 3), "from 2017 to 2019, the UN verified that 1,385 children had been recruited and used by Boko Haram, although this number is likely to be far higher in reality." Mbajiorgu's statistics focus on only two years of the mitigation stage of the terrorist group. His 2019 report was recently replaced by a report made by the United Nations Secretary-General on children and armed conflict in Nigeria, since the inception of the armed group in 2009, up to 8,000 children have been recruited by the sect, including children as young as four years old. The recruitment of a large number of children by Boko Haram calls for us to question what capacity in which child soldiers function in the space of engagement, or for us to understand the role of the child in the advancement or sustenance of terrorism.

Children are recruited by Boko Haram insurgents for various reasons. It is pertinent to note that some of the reasons young people are introduced into the fold of terrorism are to get a boost in warfare strategy, recognition, and economic empowerment. The context of warfare strategy is multiple. First, children are machinery, used by terrorists to launch their attacks. Since they can be easily indoctrinated, it would be easier to convince them about the justification of the ideologies upon which the organization is built. Hence, they would easily key into the philosophy of the need to shun Western education and disrupt any activity that promotes the Western way of living. Children are also used as spies, to generate sensitive information for the organization. Beyond this, they also function as suicide bombers in public gatherings such as in churches, mosques markets, and other public places (Yenwong & Osagie, 2016). Here the life of the child becomes a weapon of mass destruction.

The weaponization of life is a practice that is prominent in the arsenal of Islamic terrorist groups and among Muslim extremist organizations. Children are naïve and are easier to cajole into committing suicide. According to Riaz (2011), a major rationale behind the interest in executing suicide practice is being made to "believe that one's life is less worthy than the group's honour, religion, or some other collective interests" (p. 1). We concur with Riaz's position because, in the context of the Boko Haram insurgency, participants are made to understand the imperative of the cause they fight for, and the honor they would achieve at death. Honor that accompanies suicide in this case (and in the case of Boko Haram), may include what Emile Durkheim (1951) refers to as "a desirable afterlife" (p. 43). In some cases, children are made to know that there is a massive reward for them in the afterlife when they are able to carry out the act of suicide. The desire for Suicide in this context, is altruistic, an obligatory suicide which Veronica Ward (2018) argues is "a sense of duty" (p. 89). Hence, other terminologies ascribed to suicide terrorism include human bomb, self-sacrifice, and martyrdom (Hasham, 2007), to validate the rationale for suicide action. Female children have been actors in this practice, perhaps because they are minimal suspects and bombing devices are well kept in their clothing. The clothing of the female child is influenced by the Islamic religion. It is one that covers the whole of her body.

When weapons of destruction are fixed on the bodies of female children, they are barely visible to the public as a result of the pattern of dressing. Boko Haram gained more recognition when it started to weaponize the lives of children. For example, Boko Haram became more prominent in the aftermath of the 2014 kidnap of the students of Government Girls Secondary School, Chibok. What followed this incident was the globally acclaimed Bring Back Our Girls campaign created to pressure the Nigerian government into driving the rescue of the abducted schoolchildren.

The kidnap of the schoolgirls affirmed the anti-western ideological standpoint of the Boko Haram terrorist group but also culminated in the interrogation of why children are a major target of terrorist groups all over the world and in North Eastern Nigeria. One position that cannot be contested is that it provides cheap warfare for terrorism. The availability of recruited children would reduce expenses accrued to recruiting adult soldiers. They could be paid less for their services compared to wages paid to adult members. The above pictures reveal how children are being compelled to become terrorists. Here, they are trained in the art of shooting the gun. Like terrorists, they wear a covering on their faces and heads to conceal their identities. At this juncture, we proceed to investigate the representation of the role children play in the Boko Haram insurgency and how this impacts them. The study uses Aguh's film, *Sambisa* as a case study.

UCHE AGUH'S *SAMBISA*

Numerous films have been used to capture the travails of the child in the landscape of terrorism. There is barely a film in the repertoire of the Boko Haram insurgency that does not represent the social and psychological transformation of children. Prominent among these films is Uche Aguh's film, *Sambisa*, a film that relays the aftermath of the capture of the secondary school girls in Chibok, in 2014. Uche Aguh's, *Sambisa* begins with three young girls running for their lives through the Sambisa Forest. One of the three girls is seen carrying her newborn son. They have escaped from the captivity of Boko Haram terrorists and have been running in the forest for three days, with neither food to eat nor water to quench their thirst. While in the forest, night falls and they lie down to sleep. Early the next morning, the cry of the baby jerks the mother off her sleep. The child's mother, Fatima, wakes the other two girls, Rukayyat and Aminata who are still fatigued. They proceed with the escape journey.

As they continue on the journey, they hear intermittent sounds of gunshots inside of the forest and they scamper for safety. Fatima who is tired and discouraged with the journey, part ways with the other two, leaving the baby with Rukayyat. Some days later, the two girls are rounded up by the terrorists. Surprisingly, the gang leader is Fatima's baby's father, Abubakar. Also, Fatima is the deputy of the gang. Fatima forcefully takes Abdul from Rukayyat. She later criticizes the terrorists that they do not fight for the cause of Islam, and that the Prophet Mohammed in the Quran did not stipulate their current actions of killing, maiming, and destroying places and people. Rukayyat slams them for their kidnap of 273 girls. Abubakar tells Abdul, another terrorist to shoot the former for her stubbornness. In tears, Abdul refuses, that Rukayyat is his sister. Abubakar hits Rukayyat to death with his gun. He tells Abdul that this world is not meant for girls, and that they can be treated anyhow. Abdul kills himself with his pistol. While Muhammad mourns him, Fatima pulls a gun at him. Surprisingly, Rukayyat who only got hurt by the gun by Muhammad, stands alongside Aminata, against Muhammad. The gun is still pointed at him when the film ends with the inscription, *Bring Back Our Girls*.

CHILD TRAUMA AND THE ROLE OF THE CHILD IN TERRORISM IN AGUH'S *SAMBISA*

Experiencing, witnessing, or being forced to commit acts of violence has long term debilitating effects on the mental and overall well-being and development of children. (O'Connor et al., 2021, p. 33)

The above submission captures the effect(s) of the weaponization of children by Boko Haram terrorists on the children's psychological and mental well-being in the North Eastern region of Nigeria. Using a child as a weapon impacts the development of the child. In the case of the girls in *Sambisa*, terrorism reconstructs their notion of life and existence. The three girls who flee from the den of the terrorists have experienced inhuman treatment at the hands of their adult male captors. In spite of their escape from the brutes, the girls remain disoriented. This could simply be because they doubt if they would be able to fit back into the society they are fleeing into.

In some cases, girls who are liberated from the camp of the terrorists by security operatives, are stigmatized whenever they return home. Stigmatization of these children especially of the girl children who are defiled, impregnated, and had sex slaves and wives by the terrorists is a major challenge. Sometimes, the girl child finds it difficult to be fully accepted into the family by parents and siblings. Some female escapees have rightly stated in interviews that they face the challenge of being accepted by family members and friends. Friends and the larger community refer to them as wives and former wives of terrorists (Maiangwa & Agbiboa, 2014; Oriola, 2023). Those who carry babies from marriage to the insurgents encounter more stigmatization. In the film, Fatima's conclusion that she is tired of proceeding with her colleagues on the journey for escape is partially premised on the disgrace she would encounter from people at home. She is torn between the decision to stay in the forest and die or get home and face the stigma of being raped and made a wife by the insurgents. For her, life in the forest is gradually becoming the norm. This becomes a new reality of which there is no option, thus, there is a forceful acceptance.

CHILD PARTICIPATION AND TERRORISM IN NORTH-EAST NIGERIA

While many children are forced to live in radicalized realities, children who are either active or passive participants in terrorism are exposed to violence and murder at a tender age. The child sees his parents and loved ones being slaughtered by the insurgents. The aftermath is the child's notion of violence and death as normative. This normalization of violence influences the well-being of the child. It constructs his or her notion of existence. He sees suicide bombing as an individual sacrifice toward advancing the kingdom of Allah. The children are being wrongly encultured by extremist Islamic scholars who claim that Western education is a sin. They are told to do all it takes to erase every iota of non-Islamic education, as this is the hallmark of Islam. This has led to suicide bombing of schools by children and in turn, disruption of academic activities.

In the past five or six years, more than 600 teachers have been killed, and up to 500 schools destroyed by Boko Haram terrorists (Ogunmekan, 2024). The sect detests Western education and operates on the basis of Sharia or Islamic laws. According to Jaarie Arvin (2021), for almost a decade, primary and secondary school activities have been shut down in some states as a result of the activities of Boko Haram. For years, Government Girls Secondary School was shut down as a result of the 2014 Boko Haram kidnap of almost 300 students. Numerous cases of closure of universities in the North Eastern region as a result of mass abduction of students and lecturers are a recurrent issue.

Aguh's *Sambisa* is an exposé of armed conflict in North Eastern Nigeria and the reasons the conflict festers. The film proves the participation of children in the insurgency and terrorism in the North Eastern Nigeria. It confirms children as vulnerable, as victims, and as brainwashed co-actors. Thus, they fall into the active and passive participant categories. The film gives an insight into the activities, tactics, and modus operandi of the armed non-state actors in the region. An important premise is the title, *Sambisa*. Sambisa has become popular as the hideout of the Boko Haram insurgents and the most dreaded place in Borno state, Nigeria. These insurgents find a "safe haven in the Sambisa Forest…" (Chika & Joseph, 2019, p. 32). From the movie, we can deduce that, it is within this vast forest that the Boko Haram terrorists live and keep their hostages. From this forest, they often attack villages and towns in the state and withdraw back into the forest afterwards.

Three young girls from among the Chibok school girls abducted on the 14th of April 2014, lost their way in the Sambisa forest while trying to escape. Unfortunately, the situation turns out to be that they actually not only get lost in the forest but are also being misled by Fatima, who is a good representation of the brainwashed child. When Aminatha asks her, "how much longer would we be walking like this?" (Aguh, 2016, 2:32), Fatima lies in her response, saying "we're almost there" (Aguh, 2016, 2:35). As she leads the two other girls, Rukayyat wonders how Fatima seems to know the forest so well. "Fatima, how do you know this forest very well like this? (Aguh, 2016, 2:56), Rukayyat asks. Again, Fatima deceives the girls in her evasive answer, "men, big gun, no brain. Girl, no gun, the big brain" (Aguh, 2016, 3:01). As is the case in this movie, children are deceived and made to believe that carrying out aggression against others or supporting it, is a noble act. While some cave in to the financial benefits promised to them by the terrorists, others are simply won over by religious indoctrination, while some others fall for a disguised show of kindness by the terrorists.

The escape journey is not very easy for Aminatha, Fatima, and Rukayyat because Rukayyat already has a baby after being forcefully married out to a terrorist – Abubakar. Again, this is an exemplification of gender-based crimes being committed by the Boko Haram terrorists, who against their young female captors' wills, marry them to men who are often far too older than them. Child marriage and the post-traumatic stress disorder (PTSD) that comes with it all count toward these crimes. Such unsolicited wedlock results in unwanted pregnancies and children with little or no parental care, who are made to grow and survive under extreme conditions. Unsurprisingly, such children develop delinquent tendencies, and the anomaly becomes a mainstream way of life for them. Hence, taking up arms to kill or aiding violence is their norm. In the movie, Rukayyat is bent against giving such kind of life to her child, which makes her resolve to escape with the child. However, Rukayyat's baby keeps crying, thereby making it difficult for the girls to have a quiet escape. In a way, it is a form of child endangerment, however, the girls are left with no other choice than to embark on the escape journey.

At a point in their journey, the girls decide to ease off the tension by having a moment of leisure to sing and play. However, this leisure break is short-lived by the sudden sounds of gunshots. The girls scamper for safety and are forced to continue their escape journey. By the events in this scene, it is laid bare how the child is robbed of his/her childhood benefits to play and have a good time. The child cannot enjoy the company of his peers, instead, he is toughened up and forced to grow into an adult. This denial of childhood rights and privileges is mutated into aggressive, violent, and anti-social behaviors such as stealing, substance abuse, chaos stirring, banditry, and armed conflict. Two examples from the movie are Fatima and Abdul.

Fatima is trained to be lacking in conscience and hard-hearted in spite of the fact that she is a girl and young too. She learns the art of treachery and gains the ability to be a traitor who deceives her friends and sells them out to the Boko Haram terrorists. She is grilled into losing her bowels of empathy and acting like a terrorist. When Aminatha complains she is tired after they have been walking in the forest for three days and running out of food and water, Fatima disregards Aminatha's show of tiredness by replying distastefully and yelling at her, "Aminatha! Aminatha! Keep walking! I don't have time for this now!" (Aguh, 2016, 5:29). Fatima undulates between a humane child and playing the role of an accomplice in crime against humanity as mandated her by the terrorists. At a time, she takes the baby from Aminatha and sings to it while the girls are sleeping. At this juncture, she is torn between two decisions, either to see her friends through the escape journey or deliver them to the Boko Haram terrorists. In the long run, she gives in to betraying her friends.

In the same way, Abdul is being nurtured to become a stone-hearted killer. In the usual fashion of the terrorists, Abubakar instructs Abdul to point his rifle at Rukayyat and "shoot her" (Aguh, 2016, 13:41). To Abubakar, that is the way for Abdul to become a real man like him. As Abdul hesitates, Abubakar challenges him, "Abdul, you are saying that you want to be becoming a man like.like me" (Aguh, 2016, 14:30). Abubakar tries to convince Abdul to believe that it is prestigious to become the kind of man that he (Abubakar) is, and the only pathway to achieving such kind of tough and prestigious manliness is by killing others even when it does not seem right to do so. Also, Abubakar uses religious brainwashing to push Abdul into committing murderous acts. Abubakar dares Abdul who has once shown interest in carrying out "the work of Allah..." (Aguh, 2016, 14:45), which he interprets as killing other people.

After Rukayyat challenges Abubakar and Abdul on behaving against the teachings of the prophet Muhammad, Abdul suddenly regains his consciousness of humanity. He refuses to shoot Rukayyat as instructed by his father. Abdul refers to Rukayyat as his sister. He proves the point that a fellow human belongs to one's family and it is wrong to take their lives. In this wise, Abdul sends a message to other children who are caught in the web of armed conflict participation that, psychological emancipation is possible, and it is a way to curb the menace of terrorism. Hence, the possibility of child resistance in violent participation.

Now, let us examine the inscription, *Bring Back Our Girls* as a slogan that comes to the fore at the end of the film and how the term goes beyond merely rescuing the girls that have been kidnapped by the insurgents. *Bring Back Our Girls* encapsulates bringing back the sanity and well-being of the psychologically displaced child. In the last scene of the film *Sambisa*, Fatima joins the terrorists. She defies the pleas of her friends to return to them. At this point, it is not just to bring Fatima from the forest to town. What is most important is how she can be re-integrated into the social system, to make her understand that violence does not pay. What is imperative is to make the girl children understand that not all men are rapists and killers. It is important these children become reoriented despite the disorientation given to them by the insurgents. Such orientation as the imperative of Western education and assurance of protection by society must be given.

The child terrorist sees himself as an independent human. He is made to understand that his survival and that of the cause that he advocates for is what is most relevant. The violence that he had been taught and witnessed affected his perception of life. The Swiss psychologist, Jean Piaget (1937) describes how child development is organized by environmental and biological factors. In his words:

> Child cognitive development is the progressive reorganization of mental process results from biological maturation and environmental experience on the way children construct an understanding of the world around them, experience discrepancies about what they already know and what they discover in their environment and adjust their ideas. (p. 17)

The reorientation of the child terrorist into this new culture of violence and destruction is fully articulated in the film. In the last scene, Abubakar teaches Abdul, a child terrorist, to shoot at Rukayyat despite his knowledge that the girl is his sister. Although Abdul refuses on the pretext that the girl is his sister, it is the norm for child terrorists to carry out orders even if it means inflicting harm on close relatives. This is a further establishment of the imperative of child protection and reorientation.

CONCLUSION

Nipping the menace of terrorism in the bud, particularly as it concerns Nigeria and the North Eastern states, cannot be possible without factoring in children and the roles they play in the advancement of terrorism. Jettisoning this fact would mean a continuous abuse of the child and continuity of terrorism particularly in North Eastern Nigeria. It is also a serious indictment on the state, as careless abandonment of children, which will spell continuous child endangerment.

On the one hand, it is important to secure the sanity of children and protect them from harm and abuse. The entrenchment of this may be fetched in the fundamental human right which entitles every human (children inclusive), with the right to life and liberty, education, freedom from slavery, and dignity of the human person, among others. The rights of children are however infringed upon with their continuous abuse and conscripting by terrorists. In *Sambisa*, Fatima, Aminata, and Rukayyat are dehumanized, enslaved, and stripped of their rights to education.

Also, child participation in terrorism is tantamount to the destruction of the social structure of the society thereby further establishing a ground for terrorism to fester. Some of the children who are caught in this web of violent participation or accomplices to terrorism, play out their roles based on filial and cognate responsibilities, and some others do so by religious dogma, indoctrination, or obligations. Abdul and Fatima are victims who fall within this bracket. Abdul is commandeered by Abubakar. He is instructed to carry out violence against other people. Abubakar makes Abdul feel indebted to the religious duties of killing the enemies of Allah. Also, the new-born child of Rukayyat is a potential participant in terrorism based on filial and cognate circumstances.

The film *Sambisa* affirms that children, especially the girl child play a major role in the advancement of terrorism in Nigeria. Fatima is a vivid example of how the girl child is fashioned for the mission of deceiving unsuspecting victims of terrorism, convincing other naïve children to join the group, and even inflicting pain and violence directly, either as a suicide bomber, explosive planter or shooter as in the case of Fatima. Unfortunately, not only does the girl child participate as a personality alone, but she is also responsible for birthing future terrorists. Thus, the girl child is made to play multiple roles of procreating, personal participation, culinary responsibilities for the group, etc., to sustain the group. This explains the preference of the terrorists in abducting the girl child as in the case of the female students at the Government Girls Secondary School, Chibok.

Conclusively, *Sambisa* decolonizes a crude epistemology. The philosophy of founding Boko Haram on the framework of Islam is disrupted by the girls led by Rukayyat, who refutes that the incessant killing, rape, and kidnappings by Boko Haram are not stipulated by the Prophet Muhammad and Allah in the Qur'an. It also sets up an argument for and on the misinterpretations of religious texts. While some believers interpret violence in their religious understandings, the character Rukayyat is a metaphor for the adherent of Islam who upholds peace. The film therefore goes beyond merely presenting issues on terrorism, advocating peace building and child protection. Child protection and cognizance are serious businesses that channel into social reconstruction, balance, and security.

REFERENCES

Agberia, J. (2006). Aesthetics and ritual of the *Opha* ceremony among the Urhobo People. *Journal of Asian and African Studies, 14*(3), 249–260. https://doi.org/10.1177/0021909606063880

Aguh, U. (2016). *Sambisa* (Ejiro Okorodudu, Joshua Okusanya and Shardiya Ssagala). 55 Media.

Arvin, J. (2021). *How kidnap for ransom became the most lucrative industry in Nigeria*. Boko Haram-inspired gangs are kidnapping hundreds of students in Nigeria | Vox. https://www.vox.com/22596198/students-nigeria-profit-kidnapping

Chika, D., & Joseph, C. (2019). A critical appraisal of Boko-Haram insurgency and the criminal topography of Sambisa Geosphere. *International Journal of Academic Research in Business, Arts and Science, 1*(1), 32–48. https://doi.org/10.5281/zenodo.3362967

Cissoko, V. (2022). Forms of initiations in the Mandinka world: A case study of the Pakao (Sedhiou and Marsassoum). *Akofena, 2*(5), 391–404. https://www.revue-akofena.com/wp-content/uploads/2022/01/35-T05-89-Vieux-Demba-CISSOKO-pp.391-404.pdf

Durkheim, E. (1951). *Suicide: A study in sociology*. Free Press.

Haley, A. (1976). *Roots*. Doubleday Publishing.

Hasham, M. (2007). *Suicide bombers: Tactics and mindset*. Royal United Service Institute.

Ike, T., Antonopoulos, G., & Singh, D. (2022). Community perspectives of terrorism and the Nigerian Government's counterterrorism strategies: A systematic review. *Criminology and Criminal Justice*, 1–30. https://doi.org/10.1177/17488958221110009

Jolie, A. (2017). *First they killed my father* (Srey Moch Sareum, Kompheak Phoeung and Socheata Sveng). Jolie Pas.

Lansdon, G., & Vaghri, Z. (2022). Article 1: Definition of a child. In Z. Vaghri, J. Zermatten, G. Lansdown, & R. Ruggiero (Eds.), *Monitoring state compliance with the UN Convention on the rights of the child. children's well-being: Indicators and research* (Vol. 25, pp. 407–412). Springer. https://doi.org/10.1007/978-3-030-84647-3_40

Laye, C. (1953). *The African child*. Fontana Press.

Maiangwa, B., & Agbiboa, D. (2014). *Why boko haram kidnaps women and young girls in North Eastern Nigeria*. The African Centre for the Constructive Resolution of Disputes (ACCORD).

Mbajiorgu, K. (2023). *UNODC and Nigeria join hands to protect children from terrorism*. Strive Juvenile Nigeria Factsheet.

O'Connor, R., Btancourt, T., & Elenamah, N. (2021). Safeguarding the lives of children affected by Boko haram: Application of the SAFE model of child protection to a rights-based situation analysis. *Health and Human Rights Journal, 23*(1), 27–41. https://www.ncbi.nlm.nih.gov/pmc/articles/PMC8233023/pdf/hhr-23-01-027.pdf

Ogunmekan, D. (2024). *Personal interview with teachers in Maiduguri in Borno state, Nigeria*.

Okpadah, S. (2024). Femi Osofisan or Ahmed Yerima? *Theatre and Performance Notes and Counternotes, 1*(2), 23–40.

Oriola, T. (2023). The exploitation of Nigeria's Chibok Girls and the creation of a social problem industry. *African Affairs*, 1–32. https://doi.org/10.1093/afraf/adac042

Piaget, J. (1937). *La Construction du réel chez l'enfant*. Delachaux and Niestlé.

Rauf, I. (2015). *Defining Islamic statehood: Measuring and indexing contemporary Muslim states*. Palgrave Macmillan.

Riaz, H. (2011, September 27). *9/11: Why suicide bombers blow themselves up*. https://theconversation.com/9-11-why-suicide-bombers-blow-themselves-up-3256

Sauvaire, J.-S. (2008). *Johnny mad dog* (Christophe Minie, Joseph Duo and Daisy Victoria Vandy). MNP Enterprise.

Shah, T. M. (2021). *Women as "Sites of Gendered Politics"*. Misogyny Across Global Media.

US Joint Publication. (2016). *Counterterrorism*. Department of the NAVY, United States Marine Corp. https://www.globalsecurity.org/military/library/policy/dod/joint/jp3_26_2009.pdf

Ward, V. (2018). What do we know about suicide bombing? Review and analysis. *Politics and The Life Sciences*, *37*(1), 88–112. https://doi.org/10.1017/pls.2017.31

Yenwong, U., & Osagie, C. (2016). *Nigeria's child terror suspects: No easy answers*. Institute for Security Studies. https://issafrica.org/iss-today/nigerias-child-terror-suspects-no-easy-answers

Zwick, E. (2006). *Blood diamond* (Leonardo Di Carpio, Djimon Hounsou, and Jennifer Connelly). Warner Bros.

CHAPTER 12

RESISTANCE IN YOUTH LITERATURE

Omama Al-Lawati

Sultan Qaboos University, Oman

ABSTRACT

In 1966, Palestinian writer Ghassan Kanafani coined the term "literature of resistance" through his seminal work "Resistance Literature in Occupied Palestine 1948–1966" (Harlow, 1987). This genre focuses on depicting experiences of resistance and resilience amidst colonization, often investigating the personal struggles of writers within contexts of injustice and oppression. When created for children and youth, the literature of resistance diverges from that intended for adults due to many reasons. Eventually, this genre aims to engage children with significant societal issues such as patriotism, liberty, disdain for injustice, and the fundamental importance of justice. This chapter explores examples within the realm of children's literature of resistance, encompassing both stories and novels tailored for young and teenage audiences. The chapter comprises four main sections. Firstly, a comprehensive introduction will elucidate the concept of resistance literature and underscore its scholarly significance. The second part will examine existing literature, highlighting thematic foundations and prevalent discourse within this genre. Subsequently, the third part will outline criteria used to ensure chosen narratives align with the overarching theme of resistance, followed by an examination of selected stories in terms of their literary and narrative aspects. Lastly, the fifth part will detail the dual analytical approach employed to offer a comprehensive understanding of how resistance is conveyed in the chosen narratives and the extent to which these stories fulfill their intended objectives.

Keywords: Resistance; youth storybook; Children Literature; Palestinian Literature; occupation; war; Palestinian authors

INTRODUCTION

The study on resistance in youth literature holds significant relevance in contemporary discourse, particularly within the context of social justice and advocacy. By exploring how narratives aimed at young readers depict themes of resistance, justice, and triumph over oppression, the research sheds light on the potential of literature to shape the values and beliefs of the next generation. Understanding how authors raise awareness among youths about the concept of resistance not only informs literary analysis but also provides valuable insights into strategies for engaging and empowering young audiences on social issues.

Moreover, the focus on resistance narratives within the specific cultural context of Palestine adds depth and specificity to the study. Given the ongoing socio-political challenges faced by Palestinian communities, examining how literature addresses themes of resistance and occupation carries particular significance. These narratives serve to reconnect Palestinian young readers in the diaspora with the tales of their homeland, particularly their cultural heritage, and the stories of their ancestors who were compelled to depart, whether by force or by choice. They offer a poignant portrayal of the ongoing reality faced by Palestinian youth living in Palestine, fostering a deeper connection to their roots and a heightened awareness of their cultural identity. By focusing on Palestinian narratives and authors, the research contributes to amplifying voices from marginalized communities and highlighting their struggles and resilience in the face of adversity.

The selection of study samples, limited to five stories due to time, resources, and scope constraints, ensures a focused and in-depth analysis within the limitations of the research. By prioritizing recent publications and considering diverse content and styles, the study aims to offer a comprehensive understanding of the strategies employed by authors to convey themes of resistance to young readers. Through careful examination of these narratives, the research seeks to uncover insights into their effectiveness in shaping cultural perspectives, fostering critical thinking, and promoting empathy among youth.

From this study, one can expect to gain a better understanding of the ways in which youth literature can influence cultural perspectives and foster critical thinking among young readers. Insights into the effectiveness of storytelling in shaping attitudes toward resistance and social justice issues can inform educational practices, curriculum development, and literary interventions aimed at youth empowerment. Ultimately, the research serves as a testament to the power of storytelling in inspiring resilience, fostering empathy, and empowering the next generation to challenge injustice and strive for a more equitable world.

RESISTANCE LITERATURE: FROM IDENTITY TO STRUGGLE

Rabiea (2008) articulates resistance literature as an expression that encapsulates the collective self-awareness of a community, aspiring to freedom while confronting external aggression. It serves as a channel for preserving community values and heritage, striving for collective redemption, and restoring usurped rights. According to Rabiea, this literature serves as a bridge between freedom and aggression, documenting historical events while embodying humanitarian values. Resistance literature emerged historically within the context of the Palestinian cause during the Arab-Israeli conflict. Its importance grew through the works of novelist Ghassan Kanafani (1936–1972), who distinguished between "occupation literature" and "exile literature," elucidating the societal ties linking individuals to their land and common cause (Harlow, 1987; Kanafani, 1966).

The concept of resistance literature prospered with the rise of Palestinian resistance movements in the late 1960s and 1970s, becoming emblematic of literature produced by Palestinians across different territories and in exile. However, its roots trace back to earlier periods, with Palestinian folk poets and writers embedding resistance themes in their works since the early 20th century (Kanafani, 1966).

In Egypt, after the October 1973 war, a surge of this literary genre surfaced in the novels of Egyptian writers such as Ihsan Abdel-Quddous and Youssef El-Sibai. However, its prominence waned with the conclusion of the war, only to resurface more prominently in Palestine. Poetry became the cornerstone of this literary expression, transforming into anthems that instilled determination and called for resistance, venerating martyrs and fighters as symbols of righteousness (Salwa, 2022).

The narrative of resistance literature underwent a significant transformation with the outbreak of resistance in Lebanon following the Zionist invasion in 1982. Subsequently, after the departure of the Palestinian resistance from Beirut, there was a notable shift from predominantly poetic expressions to a greater emphasis on narrative and storytelling. Writers like Abdel-Majeed Zaraqat and Ali Hajazi followed in the footsteps of Ghassan Kanafani, writing short stories, novels, and children's tales (Abu Madi, 2009).

Al-Sayed (1995) distinguishes between war literature and resistance literature, highlighting the latter's focus on collective struggle and identity preservation. He underscores the pervasive nature of resistance themes in Palestinian literature, where even fiction books invariably confront the realities of occupation and displacement.

The emergence of an Islamic Lebanese resistance ushered in a distinct style of writing that became central to Islamic resistance literature; although it has yet to fully integrate into the broader arena of resistance literature (Salwa, 2022). It is worth noting that resistance literature, with its roots in historical struggles against injustice and occupation, transcends geographical and cultural boundaries. Thus, it encompasses a broader spectrum of societal resistance movements, making it a more inclusive term than war literature (Salwa, 2022). In essence, resistance literature encapsulates the enduring struggle for justice and liberation, resonating across cultures and eras as a testament to the indomitable human spirit.

WRITING AND UNDERSTANDING RESISTANCE LITERATURE

Writing for children and youth presents a unique set of challenges, especially when tackling controversial and sensitive topics that may affect their psychological well-being. Issues such as harassment, divorce, bullying, death, loss, and the grim realities of war pose significant challenges for authors. Selecting language that effectively communicates the harsh realities of war, particularly to child readers who may have firsthand experience of it, is a delicate task.

Moreover, determining the conclusions of stories depicting war and death raises important questions: Should they adhere to the traditional happy-ending conclusion expected in children's tales, or should they reflect the stark realities of loss, displacement, and homelessness? The portrayal of war-related tragedies on television and social media platforms vividly exposes the profound devastation caused by conflicts, directly confronting children with these harsh realities.

The complexity deepens when stories revolve around themes of occupation or the daily realities of children living under occupation. For these children, war isn't merely an event with a clear start and finish; instead, it's an enduring struggle characterized by terms like imprisonment, captivity, house arrest, demolished homes, restricted movement, and checkpoints. Within this context, children face a stark reality that shapes their daily experiences and outlook.

When addressing stories of war and loss, children's literature writers hold varying perspectives. While some emphasize the importance of honestly depicting the harsh realities of conflict, others prioritize nurturing children's resilience and hope for a better future. Shahinaz Aleuqbawiu (2023) explains that in times of war, children undergo unique challenges that demand special attention and care. During such periods, literature targeted toward them should prioritize addressing their essential needs for security, peace, reassurance, and happiness.

She argues that some writers depict the harsh realities of conflict honestly; psychological studies emphasize the importance of nurturing children's resilience and hope for a better future. The most effective children's literature in wartime guides them toward healing instills optimism, and reinforces values of patriotism and sacrifice, all while avoiding explicit violence and horror.

When asked about the necessity of "war literature" aimed at children and its significance, Syrian writer Maria Dadoush elaborates, stating,

> Wars have proliferated, and conflict zones have erupted in various parts of the world. War literature, on the one hand, represents the children suffering in conflict zones, so they do not feel forgotten and marginalized alone. On the other hand, it helps other children in safe areas to appreciate peace and not consider it one of the gifts available to all children in the world. (Aabdaleazimi, 2023)

While children's literature has traditionally tackled themes of defying injustice and oppression, offering narratives that inspire resilience in the face of adversity, this can be conceptualized as a form of educational literary resistance aimed at children. However, its characters have mostly been forest animals or pets, with an oppressive villain targeting a weak group. A hero emerges to confront the villain, rallying their companions and ultimately achieving victory by defeating the aggressor. There have also been stories where a king rules over his people and deprives them of their rights, and opposition arises, "resisting" this tyranny and oppression, with the will of the weak prevailing and justice and harmony prevailing (Salwa, 2022).

The circumstances experienced by the Arab world in recent years and the succession of wars have imposed urgent necessities for discussing these wars, whose effects have directly or indirectly impacted children and youths. The old approaches, such as animal stories, are no longer effective with older age groups, especially when the child is at the heart of this war. Palestinian children's stories have addressed this conflict with the enemy and the retrieval of Arab heroic history, drawing inspiration for heroism and strength from the lives of fathers and ancestors, and criticizing defeated models in society or dealing with the occupier (Salwa, 2022).

Resistance literature directed at children serves not only to inspire a spirit of resistance through tales of heroism and triumph but also to expose the atrocities perpetrated by the enemy against humanity, the environment, and all living beings. It aims to cultivate a sense of resistance to combat tyranny and crime and to prevent their reoccurrence. However, depicting these atrocities in texts for children can be a delicate balance, as it may evoke fear and anxiety, potentially leading to unsettling nightmares. Therefore, it is crucial to handle the portrayal of the enemy's atrocities with sensitivity and skill, ensuring they are accompanied by a message of deterrence to prevent their repetition (Salwa, 2022).

Salwa (2022) refers to a story by Ghassan Kanafani for children depicting the killing of a girl and her mother. The killing here, as she indicates, may not have positive educational value, but Ghassan managed to gradually and indirectly present the concept of resistance when the hero of the story, *Abu Othman*, avenges the killing of his daughter and wife by bringing explosives hidden in his clothes. The escalation of the injustices experienced and witnessed by the child narrator serves as a profound lesson, teaching that combating injustice and reclaiming rights often requires immense sacrifices.

CHALLENGES AND OPPORTUNITIES IN CHILDREN'S LITERATURE

In this research on resistance literature in children's stories, I aimed to compile bibliographies documenting writings in children's literature, with a particular focus on Palestine and resistance. The lack of a comprehensive bibliography presented challenges in cataloging the wide range of publications aimed at children and youth within resistance literature.

From my perspective, these challenges span various categories: genre, subject matter, language, authorship, and target audience. Works may range from poetry, novels, and short stories to folktales, plays, and songs. In terms of subject matter, they may cover themes of resistance in general or specifically to Palestine. Authorship can include Palestinians or non-Palestinians, and the target audience may vary from Palestinian children living under occupation to those in exile and diaspora, Arab children in general, or non-Arab children. Additionally, literature in languages other than Arabic or English, such as French, may also contribute to this body of work.

While navigating these complexities, I observed significant differences in accessibility to Arabic children's literature produced in the Arab Levant compared to those originating from the North African region. This observation was based on monitoring publishing houses' releases, authors' social media pages, and a compiled list of books gathered primarily through online search engines during my study. Challenges escalate further when content is in languages other than Arabic or English, such as French. Despite the difficulties in categorization and classification, it remains imperative to acknowledge and document existing literary works. Hence, an appendix (Table A12.1) has been incorporated into this study, comprising a compilation of publications issued in the Arabic language, centered on Palestine, from the lens of resistance, identity, and belonging literature, with a particular focus on content suitable for children and youth readers.

Additionally, in the course of this study, my exploration of children's literature and Arab publishing houses' productions, as well as tracking literary awards spotlighting resistance literature, revealed several noteworthy entities interested in supporting and awarding resistance literature. While the chapter's scope and limitations permit only a brief overview of these organizations, they serve as potential avenues for future studies. The first entity is *Dar El-Fata El-Arabi* (The Arabic Boy), founded in 1974 in Beirut, and it stands as one of the oldest publishing houses specializing in children's literature in the Arab region. Notably, it dedicated efforts to raising awareness about the Palestinian issue through visually captivating children's books, a ground-breaking initiative during its inception (Ellabbad et al., 2020).

Another significant institution is the Tamer Institution for Community Education, founded in Jerusalem in 1989. It is a national, non-profit organization dedicated to community education for children and youth, with a particular focus on the West Bank and Gaza Strip. The institution has received numerous awards, including the Etisalat Award for Children's Books and the Astrid Lindgren Memorial Award (Tamer Institution, n.d.).

The Soleimani International Prize for Resistance Literature, established in 2021 by the Asfar Association for Culture, Arts, and Media in Lebanon, acknowledges exceptional works of resistance literature, now encompassing narratives aimed at youth and children. Named after Iranian commander Qasem Soleimani, the award honors works embodying the spirit of resistance against oppression (Asfar Organization, 2021; Crowley et al., 2020).

The Palestine International Prize for Literature, established in 2019, spotlights literary works worldwide addressing the Palestinian cause, resistance, and the liberation of Jerusalem, with a recent emphasis on liberation themes (AlMayadeen.net, 2024). Lastly, the Palestine Book Awards, initiated in 2012, annually celebrate outstanding new books in English exploring various aspects of Palestine. Although lacking a specific category for children's literature, many winning books highlight Palestinian resistance and struggle against occupation across diverse genres (Hussein, 2024).

These entities collectively enrich the landscape of resistance literature, providing platforms for recognition and celebration of the works of marginalized communities and promoting awareness of their struggles, rights, and histories.

EXPLORING RESISTANCE IN CHILDREN'S STORIES: AN ANALYTICAL FRAMEWORK

The analysis of the chosen texts will proceed through the following steps: Firstly, an examination of the literary and narrative elements present in each story will be conducted. This involves identifying the main themes, ideas, and symbols associated with resistance, as well as exploring how resistance is portrayed within the characters of the story. Character representation will be scrutinized to discern how characters are depicted and whether they contribute to reinforcing resistance values. Additionally, symbols within the stories will be examined to assess their impact on the reader.

Furthermore, the narrative structure of each story will be evaluated to understand how it guides the reader in interpreting resistance values. This will include an analysis of the language and style used in the stories to determine their effectiveness in conveying concepts related to resistance. Additionally, consideration will be given to the impact of the stories on children to ascertain whether they achieve the intended goals of resistance. The cultural context surrounding the stories will be taken into account, as it may influence the understanding of resistance. Finally, the role of the author and their perspective on resistance will be explored. While this study primarily focuses on the text itself, it is important to acknowledge the influence of the authors, particularly given that they are Palestinians who have experienced war, exile, or imprisonment, lending significant insight and depth to the written text.

These stories exhibit both commonalities and distinctions worthy of examination. Predominantly authored by Palestinian or Palestinian-origin writers, with one exception from a Lebanese writer acquainted with displacement due to conflict, these narratives primarily target youth aged 14–17. However, they possess versatility suitable for readers as young as 10 and potentially resonate with older audiences as well. Published by three prominent Arab publishing houses, including the Palestinian Tamer Foundation and the Jordanian Dar Al-Salwa, these stories span the years 2014 to 2022, maintaining consistent themes despite temporal disparities.

Before commencing the study, a selection of books was reviewed, from which 15 novels were examined. However, only five of these novels were chosen for deeper analysis, as previously mentioned. The list of the 15 books I reviewed is provided in Appendix Table A12.2 for reference. The selected authors are notable figures in children's literature, recognized for their significant literary contributions and regional accolades. Careful consideration was given to avoid duplicative content, resulting in the selection of one book per author. Furthermore, personal judgment played a role in the selection process, considering factors such as the relevance of the content, style of writing, narrative fluidity, avoidance of excessive detail to maintain reader engagement and potential for insights or findings.

Among these narratives, The Hen of the House that Departs by Hassan Abdullah employs symbolism within a framework depicting recurrent real-life events along the Lebanese borders, eschewing specific temporal or spatial references and refraining from identifying the adversaries, using an animal protagonist instead. Conversely, "Dragon of Bethlehem" by Huda Al-Shawa blends fantasy elements with reality, spotlighting life in camps and crossings in the West Bank through a predominantly male perspective. "The Tale of the Secret Oil" by Walid Daqqa delves into the ordeal of prisoners and their families, merging realism with imaginative components. In contrast, "Lady of All" by Taghreed Al-Najjar portrays a starkly realistic portrayal of life in Gaza City, portraying it as an expansive open prison. Lastly, "Thunderbird" by Sonia Nimr intertwines fantasy with historical elements, chiefly unfolding in locales such as Jerusalem and Jericho.

THE FIRST STORY: *THE HEN OF THE HOUSE THAT DEPARTS*

Storybook Profile

Among the stories examined, *The Hen of the House that Departs* stands out as uniquely focused on the aftermath of war, contrasting with others centered on daily life among Palestinian youth and resistance to occupation (Table 12.1). This story prompts reflection on how to broach discussions about prolonged conflicts with young audiences, including the difficult themes of mortality, injury, and resilience. The narrative deftly navigates the physical and emotional tolls of war through the symbolic lens of a hen, illustrating the multifaceted hardships endured by humans. By portraying the hen's disrupted existence after the village's assault, the author creates a story rich in allegory and depth. While drawing from animal allegories to depict human struggles, the narrative transcends age barriers, offering profound insights into resilience and perseverance.

Plot and Characters

The narrative opens sharply with the onset of war, plunging the *Abu Kareem* family into chaos as they flee their village amidst falling shells. The family, comprising *Abu Kareem*, his wife, and their children *Kareem*, *Hani*, and *Maha*, navigates the perilous landscape with a grim familiarity, hinting at a history of recurrent

Table 12.1. The Hen of the House that Departs.

Title of the Story	"Dajajat Al-Beit Al-Lathi Rahal," *the Hen of the House that Departs*.
Author	Hassan Abdullah (1943–2022): Lebanese poet and writer, one of the pioneers of writing for children in the Arab world. He has published 4 poetry collections for adults and more than 50 works for children and youth, including poetry.
Illustrations	Leena Ghaiba is a Professor of drawing and design at the American University in Beirut. She has published children's storybooks and animated films.
Publisher	Dar Academia, 2014, Beirut.
Number of Pages	46
Number of Chapters	24
Brief Summary	A story about war, destruction, and the psychological, social, and environmental effects it leaves behind. Through the story of a hen remaining alone in the house during the war, the owners return after the war, which lasts for more than a year. The owners find the chicken, but it is in a different condition than when they left it.
Age Group	10–14

conflict. The absence of explicit identification of the enemy adds to the sense of pervasive threat, amplifying the family's sense of vulnerability.

Amidst the turmoil, the author introduces a rich tapestry of characters, both human and animal, each emblematic of the broader struggles of war. The spotted hen emerges as a central figure, embodying innocence shattered by conflict and transformed into resilience. Through encounters with antagonistic creatures like the rat, the falcon, and the neighbor's dog, the hen's journey mirrors the harrowing experiences of civilians caught in the crossfire of war.

As displacement disrupts the fabric of village life, the narrative delves into the hen's struggle for survival, navigating a treacherous landscape fraught with danger and uncertainty. Symbolically, the animal adversaries represent the faceless forces of war, indifferent to the suffering they inflict. Yet, amidst the chaos, moments of compassion emerge, underscoring the innate capacity for empathy even in the bleakest of circumstances. The hen's evolution from a timid creature to a fierce survivor parallels the transformative effects of conflict on individuals and communities. As she confronts physical and psychological traumas, the hen embodies the resilience of the human spirit, tempered by the crucible of war. Her journey serves as a poignant reminder of the enduring impact of violence on both the body and the soul.

Through vivid descriptions of war-torn landscapes and poignant reflections on loss and displacement, the narrative paints a haunting portrait of the human cost of conflict. The hen's Odyssey becomes a lens through which to explore themes of trauma, resilience, and the enduring quest for peace amidst the ravages of war.

Resistance in the Story

Despite the initial scene of villagers fleeing the village in response to aggression, some instances highlight the necessity of staying, returning, and resisting. When the mother reassures her young daughter about the hen's fate, she emphasizes the hen's intelligence and strength, symbolizing resilience, and the will to survive. Collective resistance is depicted when villagers respond with shouting and applause as military vehicles pass by, indicating solidarity in the face of aggression. This scene likely draws from the author's observations and experiences, given their connection to a village with a history of resistance against external forces.

The author's background further enriches the theme of resistance, with parallels between the temporary displacement in the story and the author's hometown, which endured similar hardships. Despite not explicitly naming the enemy, the narrative reflects the transformation of the hen from a fearful creature to a fierce defender, mirroring the journey of individuals confronting adversity. Despite physical injuries, the hen persists in seeking life, ultimately finding solace in the return of her family, particularly the supportive role of the children.

Educational Aspects

The narrative illustrates how adults provide psychological reassurance to children amid the uncertainties of war. The mother's reassurance to her children about the hen's survival serves to implant hope in young readers, offering them a sense of security in the face of potential loss. This theme of reassurance is further reinforced by the passing soldiers, whose presence offers additional comfort to both the characters and readers alike. The parents' differing perspectives on the duration of the war – expecting it to last days versus weeks – underscore the uncertainty surrounding conflict and its impact on individuals and families. This ambiguity may serve as a mechanism for parents to shield their children from the harsh realities of prolonged conflict while also clinging to hope for a swift resolution and a return to normalcy.

The author's choice of chapter titles, such as "The First Day" and "The Second Day," reflects the initial stages of adaptation to change, highlighting the gradual process of adjustment amid upheaval. Additionally, the extended duration of the war, lasting 14 months instead of mere days or weeks, underscores the resilience of individuals and communities in the face of prolonged adversity.

The story offers a powerful testament to the resilience of the human spirit amidst the complexities of war's aftermath. Through the lens of the Abu Kareem family and their steadfast hen, the narrative vividly portrays the continuing struggle against adversity, illuminating the universal human longing for peace and security. The hen's journey, from symbolizing innocence to embodying resistance, serves as a touching metaphor for the transformative power of resilience in the face of conflict. As the characters grapple with the physical and psychological wounds of war, they reflect the innate human desire for a sense of home and belonging.

By delving into themes of hope, loss, and compassion, the narrative provides valuable insights into the psychological toll of war on both individuals and communities. This story teaches us the importance of sensitively engaging with difficult subject matter while nurturing hope and resilience in young minds. As we confront the harsh realities of war, this story stands as a beacon of hope, affirming the enduring power of the human spirit to overcome even the darkest of times.

THE SECOND STORY: *THE DRAGON OF BETHLEHEM*
Storybook Profile

Table 12.2. The Dragon of Bethlehem.

Title of the Story	"Tennin Beit Lahm," *The Dragon of Bethlehem*
Author	Hooda Shawa Qaddumi is a Palestinian-Kuwaiti writer acclaimed for her work in children's and young adult literature. Winner of the Sheikh Zayed Award for Children's Literature in 2008 and the State of Kuwait Encouragement Award in 2017. She is also active in theatrical production; she leads a company producing performances in Kuwait.
Illustrations	There are no illustrations in the story.
Publisher	Tamer Institution for Community Education, 2017, Ramallah, Palestine.
Number of Pages	76
Number of Chapters	17
Brief Summary	This is the story of Khader, a teenager in a Palestinian refugee camp, facing bullying, unfairness, and family challenges. Amidst the hardships of occupation, his encounter with a mythical dragon sparks a journey of resilience and self-discovery.
Age group	14–16

Introduction

This narrative diverges from discussions of the past or future, delving instead into the daily struggles of a teenage boy living under occupation (Table 12.2). He grapples with school assignments, the constraints of occupation, life in a refugee camp, his family's hardships, and his own diminishing confidence. Imagination becomes his solace amidst these challenges. Rooted in reality, the story incorporates elements of the city's history, revered figures, landscapes, cuisine, crafts, and folklore, presenting them as integral to Bethlehem's cultural heritage.

While the past depicted holds vibrancy, the present reality is somber. To educate the young reader about this vibrant past, the author introduces a mythical entity, a kind dragon linked to the city's Christian heritage. Through fantastical journeys with the dragon, the boy finds strength to resist his circumstances, echoing the narrative's call for resistance in all its forms as a pathway to a better future.

Plot and Characters

In the Palestinian town of Bethlehem,[1] in the Al-Dheisha[2] camp, resides Khader – a name steeped in historical and religious significance.[3] His struggles resonate with those of teenagers worldwide, notably his disdain for school, which he likens to a dreary prison, and the bullying he endures due to his father's confinement. Injustice from teachers, coupled with a pervasive sense of melancholy, drives him toward solitude. Yet, within the broader context of an enduring occupation, his challenges take on added complexity. The present reality is marked by decades of occupation, with the town itself separated from neighboring cities by walls and watchtowers. The camp is a congested enclave marked by poverty and a lack of basic services.

Khader's father, tormented by torture, languishes in hospital detention, his memory stripped bare. In contrast, his mother works tirelessly to make ends meet. Khader's constrained existence within the camp's dilapidated confines is juxtaposed against the omnipresent specter of war and death.

A fantastical intervention disrupts Khader's reality as a dragon enters his life, aiding him in his studies. Together, they traverse his homeland,[4] unfettered by barriers, offering Khader newfound insights into his town's history. Through his studies, Khader learns of resistance against occupation, culminating in a poignant reconnection with his father.

The novel's characters, spanning the living and the deceased, include Khader's family, friends, and local figures. Their lives intertwine amidst the backdrop of occupation and resistance, echoing the resilience of the Palestinian people in the face of adversity.

Resistance in the Story

Khader engages in a profound dialogue with the bishop of St. George's Church, delving into themes of courage and determination. Their exchange emphasizes the importance of resisting personal challenges, symbolized by the metaphorical "dragon" each person must confront. During a visit to the Church of the Nativity, a tragic episode from history underscores the imperative of resisting oppression, even in the face of violence targeting the innocent.

The narrative underscores the theme of conflict and resistance throughout. Khader's journey begins with an internal struggle against despair and anger, leading to a rediscovery of self-assurance and a commitment to defend others. As Khader realizes his town's history, he shines in his studies. When he studies the history of figures who resisted the occupation, he succeeds in saving his friend *Marwan* from the fire of the occupation. His efforts to reconnect with his father through storytelling become acts of resistance, restoring dignity in the face of adversity. Bethlehem's significance as the birthplace of Christ serves as a potent symbol of hope and resilience against occupation.

Art, literature, and faith converge to reinforce the ethos of resistance. Graffiti by *Aref* and Banksy,[5] along with the writings of *Ghassan Kanafani*, embodies the spirit of freedom and struggle against oppression. The figure of Saint George, revered by both Muslims and Christians, symbolizes defiance and endurance in the face of tyranny. The narrative underscores the collective struggle against oppression, emphasizing the need to confront and overcome injustice despite the sacrifices endured.

Educational Aspects

This novel offers a rich tapestry of moral and educational values that resonate deeply with young readers. It introduces them to real historical figures, significant landmarks, and religious customs, immersing them in Palestinian culture. From vivid descriptions of villages and sites to beloved culinary delights and traditional crafts, the narrative provides a window into Palestinian heritage and history. For Palestinian children in exile, this connection to their cultural roots amidst displacement can be incredibly enriching and captivating. Similarly, it offers valuable insights into Palestinian culture and history for children worldwide.

On the moral front, the story condemns bullying and sheds light on the plight of prisoners in occupation prisons, including children. It promotes religious faith and underscores common values shared between Islamic and Christian traditions, fostering unity amidst diversity. The portrayal of women lighting candles in church serves as a poignant reminder of shared suffering, transcending religious divides and highlighting the resilience of Palestinian mothers.

In sum, this narrative serves as a powerful testament to the theme of resistance, portraying it not only as a physical act but also as a mindset and a form of cultural preservation. Through the protagonist's journey, we witness the resilience of the human spirit in the face of adversity, inspiring readers to confront their own challenges with courage and determination. This portrayal of resistance can encourage critical thinking and empathy in young readers, encouraging them to stand up against injustice and oppression in their own lives and communities.

THE THIRD STORY: *THE TALE OF THE SECRET OIL*
Storybook Profile

Table 12.3. *The Tale of the Secret Oil.*

Title of the Story	"Ser Al-Zeit," *The Tale of the Secret Oil*
Author	Walid Daqqa (1961–2024) spent 38 years in Israeli occupation prisons and died on April 9, 2024, at the age of 62, because of prison conditions and medical negligence after he was diagnosed with cancer. During his arrest, he obtained a Master's degree in Political Science and wrote many studies, articles, and political and cultural texts. The novel won the Etisalat Children's Book Award for the year 2018, organized by the UAE Council on Books for Young People.
Illustrations	Fouad Al-Yamani. Book cover and the six interior drawings.
Publisher	Tamer Institution for Community Education, 2018, Ramallah, Palestine.
Number of Pages	97
Number of Chapters	NA
Brief Summary	This novel tells the story of the child "Jude," who, with the help of his animal friends and the magic energy in the olive tree of the village, penetrates the prison of his captive father, who has been deprived of seeing him since his birth.
Age group	14–16

Introduction

At the onset of his novel, the author declares, "I write to be freed from prison, in the hope of liberating the prison from myself" (Table 12.3). This statement unveils the intimate connection between the narrative and the author's life, marked by struggles against occupation, imprisonment, torture, and illness. Like the protagonist's father in the novel, the author himself is a prisoner. *Jude*, the 12-year-old boy, embarks on a quest to visit his imprisoned father, mirroring the author's longing to reunite with his own 4-year-old daughter, born under similar circumstances of occupation-induced separation. Both children were conceived through smuggled sperm due to bans on conjugal visits. In addition, Jude sneaks a phone to his father, echoing the author's own act. As punishment, the author faced a two-year extension of his prison term for smuggling phones to fellow inmates.[6]

Plot and Characters

As Jude navigates his adventure with the aid of animal companions, he encounters the plight of Palestinian farmers facing the Israeli occupation's destruction of ancient olive trees.[7] Seeking refuge in the hollow of a millennia-old tree, Jude uses its magical oil to conceal himself and visit his father in prison. Through Jude's journey, the novel sheds light on the struggles faced by Palestinians in navigating permits, bans, and sudden transfers of prisoners.

The animal characters, including the cautious rabbit, wise donkey, loyal dog, cunning cat, and empathetic birds, mirror human diversity in their perspectives and actions. Some, like the dog coerced into collaboration with American and

Israeli forces, suffer injustice under occupation; yet ultimately unite with Jude to defy the apartheid wall dividing families and animals alike. The author underscores the wall's role in driving cooperation with the occupier due to poverty. Throughout, characters, including the ancient olive tree named *Umm Rumi*, convey the author's language and opinions, complemented by footnotes translating the Palestinian dialect into classical Arabic for wider comprehension.

Resistance in the Story

The theme of resistance shines through the darkness of the protagonist's life behind prison walls, underscored by the humor that permeates dialogues within the story. It reflects the author's firm belief in his cause, highlighting the epidemic of the era as the "loss of freedom." Despite captivity, the author refuses to surrender, continuing to study and write and even finding a unique way to procreate – a testament to his determination to preserve his lineage in the face of oppression. This form of resistance holds particular significance in Palestinian society, where the continuation of family names and memories is seen as crucial for survival amidst ongoing struggles.

The novel encapsulates the suffering of Palestinians robbed of their childhood innocence in prison, emphasizing the premature maturity forced upon young children like Jude, who emerges as the future of resistance. His journey begins with a personal goal to reunite with his father but evolves into a broader mission, demonstrating his commitment to aiding others and investing in research and development to liberate the future. This defiance against oppression symbolizes a challenge to the occupier's decisions and serves as a beacon of hope for the Palestinian people.

Educational Aspects

The most significant values that both adults and children learn from this story include aiding others, considering their needs, avoiding selfishness, embracing morals, aspiring for freedom, and instilling confidence in children. The narrative underscores the belief that freedom and justice are attainable through ethical conduct and scientific inquiry.

The story also explores the multifaceted nature of freedom, distinguishing between its physical and inner dimensions. While prisons and barriers represent external manifestations of oppression, the loss of reason, morals, and ignorance symbolize its internal aspects. Children are encouraged to confront challenges beyond their abilities, mirroring the protagonist's resilience in the face of adversity.

Instead of using it for personal gain, Jude decides to assist children who have been deprived of visiting their imprisoned fathers. Through the magic oil, these children can journey to coastal cities in occupied Palestine, where they can experience the sea – a simple pleasure denied to many Palestinian children due to separation walls. The sight of their children on Israeli television brings joy to their imprisoned fathers. Additionally, Jude chooses to invest the remaining oil in scientific research and development, symbolizing a link between the past and the future, akin to connecting roots with branches.

The narrative intricately weaves together personal struggles and acts of resistance, offering profound insights into the Palestinian experience under occupation. Through the protagonist's journey, we witness the enduring spirit of resistance that transcends physical confinement and external barriers, symbolizing the unwavering determination of the Palestinian people to preserve their identity and fight for freedom.

The results of the story highlight the resilience of individuals amidst oppression, emphasizing the importance of empathy, morality, and the pursuit of justice. By navigating the complexities of occupation and imprisonment, the protagonist emerges as a beacon of hope, inspiring readers to confront adversity with courage and compassion.

THE FOURTH STORY: *LADY OF ALL*
Storybook Profile

Table 12.4. Lady of All.

Title of the Story	"Sett Al Kull," *Lady of All*
Author	Taghreed Al-Najjar: A Jordanian writer of Palestinian origin, she founded Dar Al Salwa, a publishing house specializing in children's literature. After graduating from the American University of Beirut, she initially worked in education before transitioning to children's literature. She has won numerous regional awards, including the 2019 Etisalat Award in the Young People's Literature category. Her novels for young readers often center on the Palestinian issue.
Illustrations	Gulnar Hajo
Publisher	Al Salwa, third edition, 2017, Jordan.
Number of Pages	154
Number of Chapters	27
Brief Summary	The novel portrays the hardships faced by Yusra and her family in Gaza, including the loss of her brother in an Israeli attack and her father's paralysis while trying to procure a boat motor. Despite societal resistance, Yusra takes up fishing to support her family. With the help of her late brother's friends and her father's friend, she becomes a successful fisher, documenting their struggles on her blog, "Sitt al-Kull" (Lady of All). The novel also addresses gender stereotypes and the need for psychological support for girls in difficult situations.
Age group	13–17

Introduction

This novel sheds light on the struggles faced by Palestinians living in the Gaza Strip, which has been under siege for many years (Table 12.4). It portrays the fishing community and the difficulties they encounter due to the ongoing occupation. Despite societal norms restricting women's participation in fishing, Yasra's circumstances drive her to pursue this occupation. Alongside grappling with the challenges of blockade, oppression, and poverty, she faces various social obstacles. The author concludes by stating that the novel draws inspiration from the real-life story of Madleen Qalab, a young girl from Gaza who, at 14, became Gaza's first female fisher. However, it's important to note that the events and characters in the story are fictional creations of the author.

Plot and Characters

The narrative centers on Yusra's family, who endure challenging circumstances. The novel vividly portrays the harsh realities of the Israeli occupation through tragic events. Yasra's older brother Saleh is killed in an Israeli attack, and her father is left paralyzed while trying to procure a motor for their boat through Gaza's secret tunnels, which Israeli forces had destroyed. These events underscore the extent of control wielded by the Israeli occupation over the flow of goods into Gaza, profoundly impacting the lives of its residents.

Yusra makes the bold decision to pursue fishing rather than depend on charity. However, she encounters resistance from her family and society, unaccustomed to the notion of a female fisher among men, especially in the face of threats from Israeli forces. With the support of her late brother's friends and her father's loyal companion, she overcomes these challenges and earns respect as a skilled fisherman. After a harrowing encounter with gunfire from the Israeli navy, she is interviewed by a Western journalist who gifts her a camera.

Yusra begins documenting their lives through photographs and writing on a blog she names "*Sitt al-Kull*" (Lady of All), symbolizing Gaza's importance to Palestinians and Palestine's significance among Arabs (Abu Jarour, 2020). Additionally, the novel addresses various social issues, including the need to rectify society's perceptions of women and the importance of providing psychological support to girls from their families, relatives, and friends.

Resistance in the Story

Hanan Abu Jarour (2020) posits that this novel delves into the existential struggles and the Palestinian resistance, encompassing the blockade, bombings, tunnels, and socio-economic conditions, as well as the intricate dynamics of international relations. She raises the question of whether exposing youth to such political complexities is appropriate. However, Hanan argues that presenting this "complex" content is essential as it fosters self-awareness of their shared identity. Palestinians, spread across various regions including Gaza, the West Bank, within the "Green Line" (Arab 48), and in exile, share a collective identity shaped by occupation and influenced by both Arab and foreign international interests and treaties.

Thus, the story serves to keep the youth abreast of current political events. It references real-life occurrences like the "Freedom Flotilla" maritime convoy in 2010, aimed at breaking the siege on Gaza, offering the Gazans' perspective on the event, and instilling a sense of remembrance from the world. Furthermore, the novel underscores the role of social media and the younger generation's innovation in defending their cause, as exemplified by the rap songs crafted by Yasra's brother Saleh and his peers. These songs, themed around freedom, resilience, and attachment to their homeland despite the occupation, face societal rejection, revealing a generational gap in expressing their ideas and concerns.

Educational Aspects

The novel vividly portrays a deep sense of solidarity and mutual support among community members, enabling them to persevere through their challenges despite facing a suffocating siege imposed on them by land, sea, and air. It serves as a call to youth beyond occupied Palestine to empathize with the lives of those under such a blockade, fostering a deeper understanding of their social and economic conditions.

Furthermore, the story presents a positive role model for children, regardless of gender, as Yasra demonstrates perseverance, courage, and ethical behavior in seizing opportunities and helping her family. Her sense of responsibility drives her success in her work and her discovery of multiple talents, not only in fishing but also in writing and photography, allowing her to convey her surroundings to the outside world. Despite this, Yasra experiences feelings of admiration toward her late brother's friend, based on mutual understanding and shared interests rather than conforming to traditional marriage expectations in society.

In conclusion, "Sitt al-Kull" illuminates the profound challenges faced by Palestinians in Gaza due to the ongoing occupation and siege, which have made daily life immensely difficult. The narrative underscores how the Israeli occupation, with its restrictions on movement, trade, and access to basic necessities, has compounded the struggles of families like Yusra's. The story vividly depicts the impact of the siege on Gaza's economy, social fabric, and collective psyche, portraying a community resilient yet profoundly affected by the harsh realities imposed upon them. It serves as a reminder of the urgent need for international attention and action to alleviate the humanitarian crisis in Gaza and address the root causes of the conflict.

THE FIFTH STORY: *THUNDERBIRD*
Storybook Profile

Table 12.5.   Thunderbird.

Title of the Story	"Tayr Al-Ra'd" *Thunderbird*
Author	Sonia Nimr: Palestinian writer and a Professor of Cultural Studies at Birzeit University in Palestine. She earned her Ph.D. in History from the University of Exeter in Britain. Her journey into children's literature began during her time in an Israeli prison. She has been nominated for various regional and international awards, including the Hans Christian Andersen Award and the Astrid Lindgren Memorial Award. This particular novel won the Sharjah Children's Book Award in the Young Adult Books category in 2018.
Illustrations	Abdullah Qawareeq
Publisher	Tamer Institution for Community Education, First edition 2016, Second edition 2019, Ramallah, Palestine.
Number of Pages	151
Number of Chapters	18
Brief Summary	"Thunderbird" follows Noor, a 13-year-old orphan in Jerusalem who discovers her ability to control fire. With the help of a mysterious ring inherited from her father, Noor uncovers her mother's research on the legendary thunderbird, a mythical creature crucial for maintaining balance between realms. To save the world, Noor embarks on a quest across different historical periods to find four feathers from the thunderbird before it perishes. Along the way, she confronts challenges and learns the importance of courage and resilience. The novel delves into themes of identity, heritage, and the power of storytelling.
Age group	16+

Introduction

This novel falls under the fantasy literature aimed at young adults. It follows the journey of an orphaned girl named "Noor," who engages in a fantastical quest centered on Jerusalem, traversing various historical periods with each leap sending her five hundred years into the past (Table 12.5). Through this adventure, readers are introduced to Jerusalem's tumultuous history under occupation, yet consistently rising to resist and regenerate itself, like the mythical bird thunderbird, which is known by different names, including the *Al-Anqa'* in Arabic and the phoenix. These legendary birds symbolize the cycle of life, living for about five hundred years before immolating and then being reborn from their ashes. The novel is divided into three parts released in different years, with this study focusing solely on the first part.

Plot and Characters

The story revolves around Noor, a 13-year-old girl who lost her parents in a plane crash two years prior. She moves in with her uncle Zaid, his stern wife Widad, their indulged daughter Wafa, and their affectionate grandmother. However, Noor finds herself implicated in minor fires occurring at school and home, with only her grandmother supporting her against the accusations. Before her grandmother's passing, she bequeaths Noor a golden ring adorned with a mysterious bird symbol, a precious inheritance left behind by her father. Noor discovers she can unintentionally ignite fire when angered and learns to control this ability.

While exploring her mother's computer, she stumbles upon her research regarding the ancient mythical bird, commonly known as the phoenix or thunderbird. Family friend Dr Samir believes in the bird's existence based on archaeological findings and ancient Islamic manuscripts. A peculiar cat, originally a genie, informs Noor that the thunderbird will not renew itself in their time, endangering the balance between the genie and human worlds. It becomes Noor's task to save this balance by obtaining four feathers from the mythical phoenix across different eras, preventing its complete incineration, and thereby saving the world.

Resistance in the Story

Thunderbird introduces us to the concept of resistance through the character of Noor, an orphaned girl who discovers her unique abilities. While the story is fantastical, it symbolizes the inner strength and determination we all possess. Despite facing adversity, Noor chooses to continue her mother's legacy, embarking on a journey to save the world. Through her adventures, we witness the injustices suffered by the people of Jerusalem under occupation, shedding light on the struggles Palestinians face at checkpoints and under Israeli oppression. By traveling through different historical periods, the novel emphasizes the common enemy of oppression and the importance of preserving the Arab identity that unites various religious groups in the region. The author compares Jerusalem to mythical creatures like the phoenix, which symbolizes resilience and the ability to rise again despite challenges.

Educational Aspects

The novel teaches us about the complexity of human personalities, from the negative traits exemplified by some characters to the positive qualities displayed by others. It encourages empathy and the rejection of negative behaviors, particularly among the young. Noor's character embodies kindness, altruism, and bravery, evolving throughout the story. Despite the risks and sacrifices she faces; Noor learns the value of protecting her homeland. Additionally, the novel blends real historical events with fantasy elements, making it an engaging educational tool for children to learn about their city, country, and shared identity beyond traditional history lessons.

Thunderbird presents a valuable tool for teaching children about historical and cultural heritage, encouraging empathy, and fostering a sense of solidarity with oppressed communities. Incorporating discussions about resistance and social justice into educational curricula can help deepen students' understanding of complex geopolitical issues and promote critical thinking skills. Additionally, recommending the novel to young readers can stimulate interest in learning about their own identity and heritage beyond traditional classroom settings. Overall, *Thunderbird* stands as a testament to the enduring power of hope, courage, and resilience in the face of adversity.

RESULTS AND RECOMMENDATIONS

The analysis of resistance literature in children's stories sheds light on the profound impact of occupation and conflict on individuals, families, and communities. Crafted to resonate with both adults and children, these narratives offer poignant depictions of the harsh realities endured by teenagers living under occupation. They paint a picture of a landscape scarred by death, mutilation, poverty, deprivation, arrests, hazardous employment, depression, educational disruption, and profound psychological effects, all of which impede the healthy development of personality.

Furthermore, these stories highlight the premature loss of childhood and youth experienced by children growing up in such environments. The novels resonate with a central theme of resilience amidst conflict. Despite the daunting challenges they face, the characters tap into their inner strength to navigate their circumstances and persist in pursuit of their goals and values. The narratives vividly depict the daily struggles, trauma, and injustices experienced under occupation, underscoring the pervasive impact of political conflict.

Solidarity is a recurrent motif, displaying how characters lean on their relationships with family, friends, and community networks for support and strength. These bonds underscore the importance of solidarity in times of hardship. The novels illuminate the complexities of identity formation amid upheaval, offering insights into how individuals navigate their cultural heritage and sense of self. The novels shed light on violations of human rights, restrictions on movement, access to resources, and the erosion of basic freedoms, highlighting the urgency of addressing humanitarian crises.

Overall, these narratives compel young readers to confront the complexities of conflict and oppression, fostering empathy, understanding, and a call to action. The authors in these stories play a pivotal role in raising awareness of these issues, primarily because they are part of a society that suffers from long occupations.

Below are some suggested directions for future research in the field of resistance literature in children's stories, offering opportunities for deeper exploration and analysis. First, conducting interviews with children's story writers can yield valuable insights into the creative process, motivations, and intended messages behind these narratives. Second, surveys with teachers or parents may shed light on the impact of these stories on children's understanding of conflict, resilience, and social justice. Third, employing case studies by selecting specific stories for in-depth analysis can unveil the depth of their impact and thematic nuances. Furthermore, expanding the study's scope to include resistance literature written in languages other than Arabic, as well as exploring resistance literature in other cultures under occupation and colonialism, can provide comparative perspectives and enrich our understanding of this genre. By embracing these future directions, researchers can conduct a comprehensive examination of resistance literature in children's stories, thereby enhancing our comprehension of its cultural and educational significance.

NOTES

1. Located between Jerusalem and Hebron, it covers an area of 575 square kilometers. It is renowned for its Christian churches and monuments, including the Church of the Nativity, the oldest church in the world, as well as some Islamic monuments. The city has been under Israeli occupation since 1967. https://info.wafa.ps/ar_page.aspx?id=3299

2. Al-Dheisheh Refugee Camp is one of three camps in the city of Bethlehem, along with the Aida Camp and the Azza Camp. Established in 1949, it is home to 13,000 refugees whose origins trace back to 46 villages in Jerusalem and Galilee. The camp faces numerous challenges, including overcrowded schools. https://www.bethlehem-city.org/%D9%85%D8%AE%D9%8A%D9%85%D8%A7%D9%84%D8%AF%D9%87%D9%8A%D8%B4%D8%A9

3. Al-Khader, admired in Islam, is equated with Saint George in Christian tradition. According to legend, a dragon terrorized the city, demanding sacrifices. When the lot fell on the governor's daughter, she prayed, and Saint George appeared. He slew the dragon, and in gratitude, a church was built on the site. https://rb.gy/eud7si

4. Bethlehem is about 30 kilometers away from the Dead Sea, and its Palestinian residents are not allowed to visit the sea.

5. Banksy, a British street artist, creates socially critical works condemning war. He visited Gaza in 2015, painting murals on bombed houses depicting the tragedy. Banksy operates anonymously, visiting areas without revealing his presence. https://shorturl.at/lAFQ0

6. Daqqa was set to be released after 37 years, but his sentence was extended by 2 years for providing mobile phones to prisoners. His death is the 14th among Palestinian political prisoners in Israeli custody in the past 6 months, due to practices like torture and medical neglect. https://www.reuters.com/world/middle-east/amnesty-international-urges-israel-return-body-ailing-palestinian-who-died-2024-04-08

7. Since the start of the Israeli occupation in 1948, about 2 million olive trees have been uprooted, with some dating back as far as 5,500 years. https://shorturl.at/isxRX

REFERENCES

Aabdaleazimi, R. (2023). الكاتبة السورية ماريا دعدوش: الحروب أصبحت جزءا من أدب الطفل [Syrian writer Maria Dadoush: Wars have become part of children's literature]. https://rb.gy/8h8a59

Abu Jarour, H. (2020). توصية على أدب الناشئة[Recommendation on emerging literature]. https://rb.gy/y6x1mo

Abu Madi, M. (2009). أدب المقاومة بين الثبات والتغير[Resistance literature between stability and change]. *Afnan Magazine* (15), 115–125.

Aleuqbawiu, S. (2023). أدب الطفل والحروب [Children's literature and wars]. مجلة فرقد الإبداعية. https://fargad.sa/?p=28712

AlMayadeen.net. (2024). "جائزة فلسطين العالمية للآداب" تمدد مهلة المشاركة بدورتها الثانية [The Palestine International Prize for Literature extends the deadline for participation in its second session]. AlMayadeen.net. https://rb.gy/ajej4z

Al-Sayed, N. (1995). أدب الحرب (الحرب: الفكرة. التجربة. الإبداع) *[War Literature (War: Idea, Experience, Creativity).* مصر: الهيئة المصرية العامة للكتاب.

Asfar Organization. (2021). *"About us"*.

Crowley, M., Hassan, F., & Schmitt, E. (2020, Jan 3). U.S. Strike in Iraq Kills Qassim Suleimani, Commander of Iranian Forces. *The New York Times*, p. 1. https://www.nytimes.com/2020/01/02/world/middleeast/qassem-soleimani-iraq-iran-attack.html

Ellabbad, M., Traboulsi, N., & Khan, H. (2020). Revolution For Kids: Dar El Fata El Arabi, Recollected. *BIDOUN, Winter* (19). https://bidoun.org/issues/19-noise#revolution-for-kids website

Harlow, B. (1987). *Resistance literature*. Methuen Press.

Hussein, M. (2024). *Palestine Book Awards 2023 winners announced during night of solidarity with Gaza.* https://www.middleeastmonitor.com/20240118-winners-of-palestine-book-awards-2023-announced/

Kanafani, G. (1966). أدب المقاومة في فلسطين المحتلة [Resistance Literature in Occupied Palestine]. *Al-Adab Magazine*, *14*(7), 1–3.

Rabiea, H. (2008). أدب المقاومة تراجع في المشهد الثقافي الفلسطيني *[Resistance literature has declined in the Palestinian cultural scene]/Interviewer: G. Abdulhamayd*. Al-Raya Newspaper.

Salwa, S. (2022). المفاهيم التربوية في أدب الأطفال[Educational concepts in children's literature]. Al Maaref Center for Cultural Studies.

Tamer Institution. (n.d.). *"About Tamer"*. https://www.tamerinst.org/en/pages/about-tamer

APPENDIX

Table A12.1. Arabic Language Publications Targeted at Youth and Children.

No.	Title In English	Author	Original title in Arabic
1.	Trees for absent people	Ahlam Bsharat	أشجار للناس الغائبين
2.	Coming Home: Stories of Captive Cubs	Ahlam Bsharat	عائدون إلى البيت: قصص الأسرى الأشبال
3.	The boy searches for his name	Ahlam Bsharat	الولد يفتش عن اسمه
4.	The sun will rise, even after a while	Taghreed AL-Najjar	ستشرق الشمس ولو بعد حين
5.	The Mystery of the falcon's eye	Taghreed AL-Najjar	لغز عين الصقر
6.	why not ?	Taghreed AL-Najjar	ما المانع ؟
7.	My father is a prisoner	Taghreed AL-Najjar	أبي السجين
8.	A strange, strange adventure	Taghreed AL-Najjar	مغامرة عجيبة غريبة
9.	In my City, there's war	Fatima Sharafeddine	في مدينتي حرب
10.	Aunti Zayoun and the Zaytoun tree	Fatima Sharafeddine	العمة زيون وشجرة الزيتون
11.	Whose olives?	Fatima Sharafeddine	لمن الزيتون؟
12.	If I were a bird	Fatima Sharafeddine	لو كنت طائرا
13.	Mansour's Memory	Mohamed Khaled	ذاكرة منصور
14.	Small but champions	Sally Khaled Zaki	صغار ولكن أبطال
15.	Doors and stories	Sally Khaled Zaki	أبواب وحكايات
16.	My right is my right	Lamis Khadija Asali	حقي من حقي
17.	From a country called Palestine	Dima Al-Alami	من بلد اسمه فلسطين
18.	Birds between the walls	Yasmeen Atieh	عصافير بين الجدران
19.	Lilac girl	Ibtisam Barakat	الفتاة الليلكية
20.	Me and my donkey friend	Mahmoud Shuqayr	انا وصديقي الحمار
21.	Ghassan Kanafani forever	Mahmoud Shuqayr	غسان كنفاني إلى الأبد
22.	The skinny boy's Dreams	Mahmoud Shuqayr	أحلام الفتى النحيل
23.	Archive	Amal Naser	ارشيفيا
24.	The house	Mahmoud Darwish	البيت
25.	My mother's bread	Mahmoud Darwish	خبز أمي
26.	Think about others	Mahmoud Darwish	فكر بغيرك
27.	So said the neglected tree	Mahmoud Darwish	هكذا قالت الشجرة المهملة
28.	Behind the wall	Muhammad AlHamwi	خلف الجدار
29.	The boy, the girl and the wall	Olaf Stark	الصبي والصبية والجدار
30.	Jaber's cakes	Fayhaa Nabesli	كعك جابر
31.	Purple bird	Samar Barghouti	طائر الأرجوان
32.	The return of the hoopoe	Alessandra Amorello	عودة الهدهد
33.	Samia's Colored Sky	Huda Al-Shawa	سماء سامية الملونة
34.	Emergency leave	Mays Dagher	إجازة اضطرارية
35.	I want to be a turtle	Amal Farah	أريد أن أكون سلحفاة
36.	The smiling crescent of Jerusalem	Shawqi Hijab	هلال القدس البسام
37.	The secret of Jerusalem	Hala Sawas	سر القدس
38.	The Plane	Zakaria Muhammad	الطائرة
39.	Stories from Palestinian folklore	Sharif Kenana	قصص من التراث الشعبي الفلسطيني
40.	My country	Nahed Shawa	بلدي
41.	Not to forget	Fayrouz Baalbaki	كي لا ننسى
42.	Hantoush	Salha Hamdeen	حنتوش
43.	Do you feel warmth in your eyes now?	Anas Abu Rahma	هل تشعر بالدفء الآن في عينيك؟
44.	Where did she disappear?	Rania Kilani	أين اختفت ؟
45.	Memoirs of Children of the Sea	Children from Gaza	مذكرات أطفال البحر
46.	Sawdust	Mohammed AlNabulsi	نشارة خشب
47.	Baddawi	Leila Abdelrazaq	بداوي

Resistance in Youth Literature 223

Table A12.2. Novels Analyzed for the Study.

No.	English Title	Author	Illustrations/book cover	Publication Year	Publication House	Age group	Original title in Arabic
1.	A Girls' Memories from the Lowest Spot on Earth	Ahlam Bsharat	Mahmoud Jahallah	2014	Tamer Institution for Community Service, Ramallah, Palestine	+13	شجرة الموظفين: مذكرات فتاة من أخفض بقعة في العالم
2.	Memories Factory	Ahlam Bsharat	Yasmin Abu-Al Majd	2018	Al-Salwa	+13	مصنع الذكريات
3.	Ginger	Ahlam Bsharat	Maya Fadawi	2017	Tamer Institution for Community Service, Ramallah, Palestine	10–14	جنجر
4.	My Code Name is Butterfly	Ahlam Bsharat	Bashar Al-Hurub	2009	Tamer Institution for Community Service, Ramallah, Palestine	+13	اسمي الحركي فراشة
5.	Whose Doll is this?	Taghreed Al-Najjar	NA	2019	Al-Salwa, Jordan	+13	لمن هذه الدمية؟
6.	The lady of All	Taghreed AL-Najjar	Gulnar Hajo	2017 (3rd edition)	Al-Salwa, Jordan	13–17	ست الكل
7.	Mystery of the Falcon's eye	Taghreed AL-Najjar	Ammar Khatab	2017	AL-Salwa, Jordan	+13	لغز عين الصقر
8.	The Tale of the Secret Oil	Walid Daqqa	Fouad Al-Yamani	2018	Tamer Institution for Community Service, Ramallah, Palestine	14–16	حكاية سر الزيت
9.	The Dragon of Bethlehem	Huda Al-Shawa	Hanane Kai	2017	Tamer Institution for Community Service, Ramallah, Palestine	14–16	تنين بيت لحم
10.	Apollo on the beach of Gaza	Huda Al-Shawa	Iyad Sabah	2015	Tamer Institution for Community Service, Ramallah, Palestine	+9	ابولام على شاطئ غزة
11.	Asaad's Secret	Najlaa Ataallh	Lara Salous	2017	Tamer Institution for Community Service, Ramallah, Palestine	14–16	سر أسعد
12.	We are going to..	Anas Abu Rahma	Hassan Manasrah	2016	Tamer Institution for Community Service, Ramallah, Palestine	14–16	ذاهبون إلى
13.	Thunderbird (Part1)	Sonia Nimr	Abdullah Qawareeq	2016 (1st edition) 2019 (2nd edition)	Tamer Institution for Community Service, Ramallah, Palestine	+16	طائر الرعد (الجزء الأول)
14.	The Hen of the House That Departs	Hassan Abdullah	Leena Ghaiba	2014	Dar Academia, Beirut	10–14	دجاجة البيت الذي رحل
15.	Massa	Hani AlSalmi	Kamla Basyoni	2015	Dar Kalemat, UAE	10–14	ماسة

PART III

EMOTIONS AND TECHNOLOGY

CHAPTER 13

HEALING THROUGH EMPATHY: MACHINE LEARNING FOR ADAPTIVE THERAPY FOR CHILDREN AND YOUTH IN ARMED CONFLICT

Javed M. Shah[a] and Tamanna M. Shah[b]

[a]*University of Illinois, Chicago, USA*
[b]*Ohio University, USA*

ABSTRACT

This chapter introduces EmoGenPath, an innovative machine learning-based model designed to deliver adaptive therapy to children and youth affected by the trauma of armed conflict. The model synthesizes advanced artificial intelligence (AI) techniques, including convolutional neural networks for emotion recognition and an advantage-actor critic-trained reinforcement learning model for therapeutic content tailoring toward goal achievement, to provide a dynamic and personalized therapeutic experience. Recognizing the importance of empathetic and culturally sensitive interventions, EmoGenPath offers a unique approach by prioritizing the emotional states and individual narratives of its users. In regions where conflict has impeded traditional mental health services, this model aims to bridge the gap, facilitating resilience and recovery through a virtual therapeutic environment that can be accessed via low-bandwidth internet connections, ensuring broader reach and impact. This chapter emphasizes the ethical implementation of AI in sensitive settings.

It discusses the imperative of privacy, security, and inclusive design, ensuring that the model is responsive to diverse emotional expressions across different ethnicities and backgrounds. Additionally, it outlines the potential of such a model to scale therapeutic resources effectively, delivering tailored interventions with a compassionate approach.

Keywords: Children; youth; artificial intelligence; resilience; NLP; cognitive therapy

INTRODUCTION

UNICEF (2021) reports that one in seven children and youth between the ages of 10 and 19 years are affected by some form of mental disorder. Among them, 27.5% suffer from anxiety disorders, and 12.7% experience depression, which can be debilitating to the extent that it functions as a disability, leading to an increased incidence of suicide among children and youth. Hong et al. (2015) note the limited availability of data on the global prevalence of behavioral issues among children and youth, as well as an equally limited understanding of their long-term consequences. Solmi et al. (2022) argue that around 50% of these mental health conditions originate early, before the age of 14, and 75% by the mid-20s. An important aspect of these findings is the fact that the mental health of children and youth is a direct reflection of their environments, which create experiences (Shah, 2020). It is molded not only by the family and community but also by conflict and violence in society (Jokinen et al., 2021; Shah, 2013). A traumatic experience such as the loss of a loved one, bodily injury, and witnessing will have different outcomes (Masten & Narayan, 2012). These experiences do not occur in isolation; they often compound and accumulate, posing a greater risk to mental health (Masten & Narayan, 2012). The result is a dose effect: the greater the exposure, the greater the risk to mental health. Indeed, chronic exposure to conflict has been associated with higher levels of mental health and psychosocial conditions (Slone & Shiri, 2016).

Therefore, it is imperative to reduce and prevent mental health issues arising from conflict among children and youth. It is essential to advocate for the holistic recovery of children and young individuals who undergo neglect, abuse, degrading treatment, or punishment, as well as those impacted by armed conflicts. Yu et al. (2023) contend that the majority of literature and research emphasize treatment rather than prevention, suggesting that current research tends to be more reactive than proactive when addressing mental health concerns (p. 2). Yu et al. (2023) also argue for research on digital mental health interventions in humanitarian settings, and initiatives specific to children and youth. Despite acknowledging the potential of digital interventions to overcome challenges such as "stigma, geographical limitations, and time constraints" (Yu et al., 2023, p. 22), this field of research remains insufficiently explored.

Artificial intelligence (AI)-assisted therapy and cognitive training possess the potential to assist children and adolescents in acquiring skills and strategies to cultivate resilience, as well as to develop the capability to effectively navigate and overcome adversities (Lansford & Banati, 2018). While most literature reports focus on treatment, prevention, and promotion, we recommend apps that heal. Intervention as healing refers to the process of implementing strategies or actions aimed at addressing and alleviating a person's physical, emotional, or psychological distress. These interventions are designed to address immediate concerns and to promote healing and recovery over time. They may include therapeutic approaches, medical treatments, counseling, support services, and other forms of assistance tailored to the individual's needs. The goal is to facilitate healing, restore well-being, and improve overall quality of life.

This chapter expands on the area of therapeutic learning pathways with a proposed model for machine learning (ML) and goal-oriented interaction experiences to achieve therapeutic outcomes. This approach is particularly beneficial for children from conflict zones who experienced trauma, as it augments humanitarian approaches and traditional therapy techniques. We propose *EmoGenPath*, an adaptive therapy model tailored to the unique needs of children emerging from the shadows of conflict. The model's design is inherently sensitive to the subtle nuances of emotional expressions, enabling a nuanced understanding that guides the interactive elements of our model.

HEALING AND RESILIENCE BUILDING

Healing can be understood as "the personal and institutional responses to perceived disease and illness" (Weiss & Copelton, 2020, p. 2). Healing among children and youth takes place within the social context, which consists of social forces and structures that exhibit common patterns in experiences and attitudes during conflicts. Robertson (1987, p. 6) suggests that,

> a pattern is sufficiently regular for us to be able to make generalizations – statements that apply not just to a specific case but to most cases of the same type…Generalizations are crucial to science because they place isolated, seemingly meaningless events in patterns we can understand. It then becomes possible to analyze relationships of cause and effect and thus to explain why something happens and to predict that it will happen again under the same conditions in the future.

AI can analyze patterns in communication to detect and intervene at an early stage, recognizing potential indicators of distress or mental health difficulties. This proactive methodology facilitates prompt support and intervention for individuals who are at risk (Ewelina, 2023). These virtual support networks can prove especially beneficial for individuals who may experience isolation in their offline surroundings (Akinsulure, 2020).

Transitioning to a discussion on innovative support methodologies, Parruca (2022) presents an interdisciplinary approach that incorporates AI, game theory, psychology, and counseling. One such approach is the utilization of a transcultural game as a tool within the MGS Methodology, integrating gaming principles and strategies to facilitate resilience-building and therapy sessions. The MGS Methodology consists of regular sessions held either daily or weekly, lasting approximately 45 to 90 minutes each, with a small group of 6 to 12 children. These sessions focus on movement (M), games (G), sports (S), and creative arts, aiming to foster trust, unity, participation, and integration among the participants. By emphasizing physical movement, the methodology seeks to rehabilitate and enhance children and youth's mental and psychosocial capacities, contributing to their overall well-being and resilience, particularly during catastrophic events and armed conflicts.

Additionally, Parruca (2022) mentions the incorporation of psychosocial approaches and concepts from Positive and Transcultural Psychotherapy (PPT), which highlights a focus on psychological well-being and cultural sensitivity in the intervention. The game is designed to address the mental health consequences of armed conflicts, forced displacement, and migration, with an emphasis on the holistic health of affected individuals. By integrating primary and secondary capacities and addressing unmet needs and potential conflicts, the approach aims to mobilize participants and support their recovery from trauma.

The integration of AI as a conversational agent into internet-based treatment platforms, whether as a virtual psychoeducational coach or as a psychotherapist, has the potential to significantly aid children and youth in assessing negative thoughts and beliefs (Morris et al., 2018). AI represents a means of enhancing automated treatments, akin to the early Eliza program developed as far back as the 1960s. Carlbring et al. (2023) argue that when effectively implemented, these AI applications could enhance internet-based treatments and streamline clinicians' workflows.

Although there is a lack of trauma interventions specifically designed for children and adolescents in general (Tishelman & Geffner, 2011), this research gap is even more pronounced when it comes to trauma experienced in armed conflict settings. Previous studies have provided evidence supporting the use of trauma-focused cognitive behavioral therapy (TF-CBT) (Mavranezouli et al., 2020), which is a structured approach involving sequential phases aimed at equipping children and young people with coping mechanisms, facilitating the construction of a trauma narrative, and promoting treatment consolidation and closure. While TF-CBT has demonstrated effectiveness in reducing symptoms of post-traumatic stress disorder (PTSD), depression, anxiety, and behavioral issues among traumatized children and adolescents (Cohen et al., 2011; Mannarino et al., 2012), its accessibility remains limited for those living in conflict-affected regions.

Researchers have explored the efficacy of neurofeedback interventions delivered through gaming platforms. For instance, Antle et al. (2015, 2018) investigated the effectiveness of the Mind-Full tablet application, which utilizes EEG headsets and features two relaxation games and one attention game. Similarly, another study by Antle et al. (2019a, 2019b) examined a different version of the *Mind-Full* app, which included three breathing-relaxation games and three sustained relaxation games. In addition to the Mind-Full app, Schuurmans et al. (2020, 2021) conducted two studies employing the *Muse* tablet application, which incorporates relaxation tutorials resembling components of Cognitive Behavioral Therapy (CBT), followed by meditation sessions. Moreover, Schuurmans et al. (2020) investigated the use of the *DayDream* meditative laptop game in conjunction with the Muse application, while also exploring Wild Divine, a biofeedback-based laptop game featuring relaxation tutorials that monitor heart rate through biofeedback hardware.

In a recent study conducted by Qasrawi et al. (2023), machine-learning techniques were employed to investigate the implications of conflict on the mental health and cognitive development of Palestinian children. The utilization of ML algorithms allowed for the identification of cognitive abilities that significantly influence children's emotional and psychological well-being. Moreover, the study revealed novel patterns of associations that may have been overlooked by traditional statistical models. Specifically, the research demonstrated a "significant correlation between cognitive ability scores and variables such as gender, place of residence, father's education, mother's education, physical activity, leisure time activity, parents' support, and school type" (Qasrawi et al., 2023, p. 9). ML has proven valuable in estimating mental health concerns and exploring the potential advantages and challenges associated with this approach, including the ability to analyze substantial amounts of data from various sources, enhance identification accuracy, and maintain cost-effectiveness (Tate et al., 2020).

EMPATHY OVER PRESCRIPTION: LISTENING BEFORE TREATMENT

Most studies have been conducted in controlled settings, underscoring the lack of a universally accessible online version of such interventions for children and youth in varied contexts. The absence of a mass-accessible digital intervention is evident. On a global level, what is needed is a model that can be trained with limited data but applies to all children and youth, placing healing as the top priority rather than prescribing specific treatments (Shah, 2024). Specifically, we suggest a change in perspective and direction for the future of adaptive therapy.

The first core principle of a renewed perspective is *nurture/empathy over prescription*. A model is needed that prioritizes children's emotional and cognitive well-being through an empathy-driven methodology. This immediate, sensitive response system allows for a personalized therapeutic experience that addresses each child's unique needs and emotional landscape. We propose *EmoGenPath*, which reflects a shift toward more holistic, empathetic approaches to therapy. It champions the idea that true healing comes from understanding, connection, and tailored support, offering a beacon of hope for children who have faced unimaginable challenges. Through this model, we envision a future where therapy is not just about managing symptoms but about nurturing resilient, emotionally healthy individuals.

The second aspect is *listening over treatment*. Healing must begin with listening and interaction without any preconceived notion of treatment, which is what the current techniques like the TF-CBT are based on. In the context of adaptive therapy and AI, the concept of "listening over treatment" takes on a new dimension that leverages technology to enhance therapeutic interactions and outcomes. Rather than relying solely on predefined treatment protocols, the emphasis is on creating dynamic and responsive therapy experiences tailored to each child's individual needs and preferences. The model learns and adapts the therapy to each child uniquely. In traditional therapeutic approaches like TF-CBT, therapists typically follow structured intervention plans based on established protocols and guidelines. While these approaches can be effective for many individuals, they may overlook subtle nuances and variations in the way children respond to therapy. Moreover, they may not fully account for the complex interplay of factors that contribute to a child's mental health and well-being.

Adaptive therapy, on the other hand, embraces a more flexible and personalized approach that prioritizes active listening and engagement with the child. By integrating AI-driven tools and technologies into the therapeutic process, therapists can gather rich data on the child's behaviors, emotions, and responses in real-time. These data can then be analyzed to identify patterns, trends, and preferences that inform personalized treatment strategies. For example, AI algorithms can analyze speech patterns, facial expressions, and other nonverbal cues to gauge the child's emotional state and level of engagement during therapy sessions. Natural language processing (NLP) techniques can also help to identify key themes, concerns, and triggers expressed by the child during verbal interactions. The adaptive therapy model learns from these interactions over time, continuously refining and adapting the therapeutic approach to better meet the child's evolving needs. This iterative process ensures that therapy remains responsive and tailored to the individual child, maximizing the potential for positive outcomes.

Furthermore, the use of AI-enabled therapeutic tools can facilitate remote therapy delivery, overcoming barriers related to accessibility, affordability, and geographic distance. This enables children to access high-quality therapy services from the comfort of their own homes, increasing the reach and impact of mental health interventions.

A third aspect stresses the importance of *healing through presence, not pills*. This aspect takes on a transformative meaning, emphasizing the importance of therapeutic presence and engagement over traditional pharmacological interventions. Traditionally, mental health interventions often relied on medication as a primary treatment modality, emphasizing the prescription of pharmaceuticals to manage symptoms. While medications can be beneficial for certain conditions, they may not address the underlying psychological or emotional factors contributing to mental health challenges.

Adaptive therapy, on the other hand, prioritizes the therapeutic relationship and the power of human connection in promoting healing and well-being. By leveraging AI technology, therapists can engage with clients in virtual spaces, offering real-time support, guidance, and intervention, regardless of geographic location. The Internet serves as a gateway to these virtual therapeutic environments, providing a platform for individuals to access support and resources from anywhere with an Internet connection. Through AI-driven chatbots, virtual reality simulations, and teletherapy platforms, individuals can engage in therapy sessions, participate in cognitive training exercises, and receive personalized feedback and guidance tailored to their unique needs.

Moreover, the flexibility of AI-powered models allows therapy to adapt to the evolving needs and preferences of each individual. By collecting and analyzing data on client interactions, behaviors, and responses, AI algorithms can dynamically adjust the therapeutic approach to better align with the client's goals and objectives.

In areas affected by armed conflicts, access to the internet may be limited or even non-existent, posing a significant challenge to the implementation of digital therapeutic interventions. In such contexts, the idea of *healing through presence, not pills* needs to be adapted to accommodate the unique circumstances and challenges faced by individuals. Alternative approaches to therapeutic support may involve deploying mobile clinics or outreach programs staffed by trained mental health professionals who can provide in-person counseling, support, and intervention to children and families affected by conflict. Additionally, community-based interventions and psychosocial support initiatives can play a crucial role in promoting healing and resilience among displaced populations. These programs often involve local community leaders, volunteers, and peer support networks who are familiar with the cultural context and can provide culturally sensitive and contextually relevant support to those in need.

Furthermore, innovative approaches such as teletherapy via satellite or mobile networks can be explored to deliver remote counseling and support services to areas with limited internet access. While these methods may not provide the same level of connectivity as traditional internet-based interventions, they can still facilitate meaningful therapeutic interactions and support the mental health and well-being of individuals in conflict-affected areas.

THE SPOKEN WORD – A STARTING POINT

With the foundation established on the importance of prioritizing the victim's experiences and healing, we suggest beginning with exploratory analysis to uncover the significance of spoken words in therapy sessions. We used NLP techniques to meticulously examine the distribution of emotionally charged words within a simulated chat.[1] Through the development of specialized scripts, we created dispersion plots, with each dot marking the presence of an emotion-laden word within a particular analytical unit of the chat text. This visual representation helped surface the emotional undercurrents of the conversation and provided a dynamic map of emotional ebb and flow throughout the dialogue.

Utilizing Sklearn's CountVectorizer for sophisticated feature extraction, we transformed our correspondence text corpus into vectorized sentences. This process enabled us to quantify the emotional resonance of each sentence, thereby offering a novel lens through which to view the emotional landscape of the dialogue. By treating each sentence as a distinct entity, our emotion-vocabulary-based vectorizer shed light on the dispersion of emotions, offering a preliminary yet insightful approximation of emotional distribution across the corpus.

Next, we divided the therapy session into five distinct segments, assuming each segment might have a different emotional tone or focus. We wanted to model the changes in the frequency of emotionally charged words (depicted on the Y-axis) across these time segments in response to **anchors, or interventions**, inserted at the end of each segment to determine the effectiveness of these interventions in modulating the emotional tone of the conversation (see Fig. 13.1).

By analyzing the shifts in emotional word frequency before and after each anchor point, we aimed to uncover patterns that would indicate whether certain types of anchors or *interventions* could lead to a positive change in the emotional dynamics of the dialogue.

LEARNINGS FROM NLP RESEARCH FOR ADAPTIVE THERAPY

This approach validated the impact of strategic interventions within therapeutic conversations and helped refine our understanding of how to navigate and influence the emotional trajectory of children from conflict zones in a way that promotes healing and resilience. Through this modeling, our research seeks to offer a nuanced, data-driven method for tailoring therapy and support, ensuring that each interaction is aligned with the child's emotional journey and therapeutic goals, thereby maximizing the potential for positive outcomes. Using several simulation runs, we mapped out emotional state transitions, as shown in Fig. 13.2.

Mapping out emotional state transitions using the concept of a finite state machine offers a unique and valuable perspective on understanding human emotions. By *conceptualizing emotions as states within a finite state machine*, we can systematically analyze how one emotion transitions to another and identify potential triggers and outcomes of these transitions. This structured approach allows

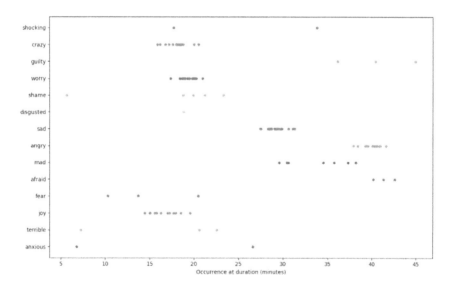

Fig. 13.1. Tracking In-Session Anxiety Triggers.

Healing Through Empathy

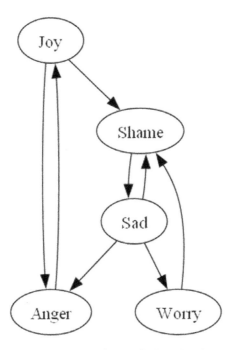

Fig. 13.2. Emotional State Changes in Sample Therapy Session.

for a clearer visualization and understanding of emotional dynamics, making it easier to pinpoint areas where *interventions* could be most effective. For children with trauma, it promotes greater self-awareness by revealing repetitive emotional patterns, while for therapists, it provides a framework for developing targeted therapeutic strategies. Ultimately, viewing emotional processes through the lens of a finite state machine aims to demystify the complexity of human emotions but also enhances our ability to manage and navigate them with precision and insight.

These state transitions represent the fluidity and interconnection between human emotions, and how one emotion can lead to another in response to external or internal stimuli. The most concerning loop was found to be of shame to sadness to worry and back to shame. This cycle underscores the potential for a more prolonged episode for the child unless meaningful interventions are created. Shame, with its roots in social judgment and self-evaluation, can make children feel isolated or unworthy, leading to profound and lingering sadness. Sadness can naturally evolve into worry as children ruminate on missed school time, homework, and lost connections with friends. Worrisome anxiety can lead back to shame when children blame themselves for their perceived inability to change their situation. This situation reinforces feelings of helplessness and is particularly debilitating because it traps the child in a cycle of negative self-evaluation and a pessimistic view of the future, making it impossible to break free and move toward healing.

We believe that breaking the cycle requires strategic *interventions* using adaptive therapy techniques that employ mindfulness and resilience-building scripts. We confirmed with the first stage of the research that anchors or interventions do cause some of these state changes but also that we could not control for the outcomes. The shame-sadness-worry-shame loop effectively demonstrates our conundrum in the absence of a trained goal-oriented model for adapting the therapy to building resilience through interaction.

MACHINE LEARNING FOR ADAPTIVE THERAPY

This preliminary research leveraged NLP techniques for analyzing the distribution of emotional activity and anchor-driven emotional state changes in controlled chat sessions with our own children. We had some crucial insights that ultimately guided our pivot toward using Convolutional Neural Networks (CNNs) for emotion recognition through facial expressions rather than relying solely on spoken text. This strategic shift was informed and inspired by several key benefits and revelations unearthed during the exploratory phase:

1. **Non-Verbal Emotional Cues**: Research indicates the profound role of non-verbal cues in conveying emotions, especially in therapy sessions (Lin & Anderson, 2024, Rocco et al., 2013). While NLP offered valuable insights into verbal expressions, it became evident that a significant portion of emotional communication remained unaddressed, despite the use of anchor points, prompting a need to capture the full spectrum of emotional expressions, including those beyond words.
2. **Immediate and Unfiltered Expressions**: Facial expressions provide immediate, unfiltered windows into a child's emotional state, often preceding the child's ability to articulate feelings verbally. Recognizing the power of these instantaneous expressions encouraged the exploration of CNNs, which excel in interpreting visual data and capturing subtle emotional nuances that spoken words might not fully convey.
3. **Enhanced Engagement and Understanding**: By integrating facial emotion recognition, we aim to foster a deeper engagement with the children, ensuring that every child feels seen and understood, irrespective of their verbal articulation capabilities. This approach aligns with the empathetic core of the model, prioritizing nurturing over prescription.
4. **Data-Driven Insights for Tailored Therapy**: The dispersion plots and analyses of emotionally charged words provided a rich dataset that highlighted the variability and complexity of emotional expressions in therapeutic contexts. These insights underscored the need for a model that could dynamically adapt to the child's changing emotional state, whether expressed verbally or non-verbally.

This adaptation of our approach from an initial focus on NLP to incorporating CNNs for facial emotion recognition exemplifies the iterative nature of innovation in therapeutic interventions (Swaminathan et al., 2023). By bridging the gap between verbal expression and non-verbal emotional cues, the model became more adept at fostering meaningful therapeutic interactions, ultimately enhancing the emotional well-being and cognitive development of children from conflict zones. This particular CNN architecture can be chosen to recognize and classify the emotional state from the facial expressions of children, serving as the entry point for the adaptive therapeutic journey.

This foundational work set the stage for an ambitious endeavor: the creation of *EmoGenPath*, an adaptive therapy model tailored to the unique needs of children emerging from the shadows of conflict. The model's design is inherently sensitive to the subtle nuances of emotional expressions, enabling a nuanced understanding that guides the interactive elements of *EmoGenPath*. Envisioned as a beacon of hope and healing, *EmoGenPath* aspires to recognize a child's emotional state and intelligently generate therapeutic content that fosters positive emotional and cognitive development. At the heart of *EmoGenPath* lies the convergence of our initial findings with cutting-edge ML technologies, including deep neural networks and reinforcement learning (RL), driving forward a new era of empathetically driven, adaptive therapy.

EMOGENPATH: MACHINE LEARNING FOR RESILIENCE

EmoGenPath is designed to recognize a child's emotional state to generate adaptive therapeutic content and guide the virtual therapy session toward beneficial goals. *EmoGenPath* offers a personalized and effective support system. It is conceived to be accessible over a low-speed internet connection with low computing requirements. This research, although in its initial stages, is a step forward in leveraging AI for mental health and well-being, promising a new horizon in therapeutic interventions. The name, *EmoGenPath,* can be further broken down to:

- **Emo** – Stands for "Emotion," highlighting the model's core capability of recognizing and interpreting emotions through CNN.
- **Gen** – Represents "Generation," pointing to the Large Language Model's (LLM) role in generating adaptive textual content responsive to the identified emotions.
- **Path** - Refers to "Pathway Learning," encapsulating the RL component's function of steering the interaction toward predefined therapeutic goals based on the emotional context.

We incorporate an LLM model to process emotional feedback and guide therapeutic continuation is an innovative approach. LLMs excel in handling sequential data and can be particularly adept at understanding the context and nuances of emotional states over time. We demonstrated this in a lab setting, using a therapy script, and then added a RL model to adapt the session for goal-oriented outcomes. The fusion of RL with CNNs to forge *EmoGenPath* represents a step forward in therapeutic interventions. By harnessing the capabilities of RL to adaptively respond to the shifting emotional landscapes of traumatized children and coupling it with the precise emotion recognition ability of CNNs,

EmoGenPath attempts to deliver personalized therapeutic experiences. This model aspires to make a difference and holds the potential to set a new standard of care, offering a path to healing for those who have endured the unthinkable. This approach leverages the strengths of both ML paradigms to provide a personalized therapeutic experience, crucial for addressing the diverse and complex emotional needs of affected children.

We improve upon the use of dispersion of emotionally charged words as discussed earlier. A pivot to using facial expressions, we trained a CNN to recognize positive, negative, and neutral facial expressions that each represent unique emotions a child experiences as they read or hear a virtual therapist. In our bootstrap of the model, we used images from the EMOTIC database (Kosti et al., 2019, 2017a, 2017b). To create a system where an LLM model generates or modifies text output based on emotions classified as positive, negative, or neutral, we used a conditional generation approach. This involved conditioning the generation process of the LLM on the emotional codes, which act as signals to steer the content of the generated text. We used GPT-2, a popular LLM model known for its text generation capabilities. We simulated the process of generating a therapeutic script segment based on the emotional code provided by the CNN model. We want to note that appropriate data augmentation techniques will be needed in the field to help the model generalize across diverse ethnicities and lighting conditions, which is crucial for working with children from various backgrounds.

The CNN model proposed needs to be used in a feedback cycle to classify facial expressions from children's live video feeds, sampled at a fixed rate during the session, as either positive, negative, or neutral. This real-time emotion detection and therapy loop provides a continuous feedback mechanism, assessing the child's responses to the therapy content. We plan on creating custom software to format the images for lower computational overhead in the future. The GPT-2 model generates text based on the provided emotion-codified prompt. We added a parameter to control for the length of the generated text and another to control for the randomness of the generation. The generated text, conditioned on the emotional code, is intended to provide a script segment that a virtual therapist could use in response to the child's emotional state.

ACHIEVING PATHWAY LEARNING OUTCOMES

The model described in the previous examples primarily focused on emotion recognition and classification using a CNN, followed by text generation conditioned on emotional states using an LLM model. While this setup provides an adaptive response mechanism based on the detected emotional states, it does not inherently include a component for progressing toward fixed therapeutic goals such as "learning to trust again," "making new friends," or "boosting self-esteem." By intertwining therapeutic goals with the concept of "pathways learning," *EmoGenPath* facilitates a structured yet flexible progression through various stages of emotional understanding, resilience, and social skills enhancement.

This approach is particularly effective for children with intellectual and developmental disabilities (IDD) and those from conflict zones, offering them tailored routes toward achieving significant milestones.

In the emotional pathway, therapists can help design customized activities to help children navigate their emotions, leading them on a path that enhances their ability to understand and manage feelings. Resilience-building exercises can be used where children learn to traverse adversity, developing inner strength and coping strategies that serve as foundations for overcoming challenges. Social Skills Development through interactive scenarios and simulations offers routes for practicing communication and social engagement, essential for fostering meaningful relationships and community integration. Self-esteem enhancement using positive feedback loops and achievements within *EmoGenPath* reinforces self-worth, guiding children along a journey that elevates their confidence and self-esteem. Mindfulness, focus exercises, and focus-enhancing activities direct children toward improved concentration and presence, essential for academic and personal success.

Cognitive flexibility via problem-solving and perspective-taking tasks that challenge and expand cognitive boundaries will help promote adaptability and creative thinking. Emotional Intelligence can be achieved through recognizing and responding to emotional cues in themselves and others, leading children down a path that cultivates empathy and deeper interpersonal connections. Stress and anxiety reduction techniques such as guided relaxation and breathing exercises provide routes to tranquility, equipping children with tools to navigate stressors more calmly. Behavioral modification, although not a direct target for *EmoGenPath*, can be a suitable area for future research using the goal-reward system for creating behavior change, reinforcing positive actions, and discouraging negative ones. Most importantly, *EmoGenPath* can help create the trauma healing pathway, where specialized content and activities offer gentle guidance for processing and healing from trauma, facilitating emotional recovery through expressive and therapeutic means.

We integrated RL into the model to empower its use for achieving the above-mentioned therapeutic pathways. We used the Advantage Actor Critic (A2C) learning algorithm for training a virtual agent to learn goal-oriented actions that guide the overall interaction strategy (Mnih et al., 2016; Schulman et al., 2015). In RL, value-based methods focus on estimating the value of each state (or state-intervention pair), with decisions made by selecting interventions that lead to the highest estimated value. The aim is to learn a value function that predicts the expected return from a given state or intervention. Policy-based methods, on the other hand, directly learn a policy that maps states to interventions without explicitly estimating values. These methods optimize the policy to maximize the expected return by adjusting the probabilities of selecting interventions in each state.

Each approach has its strengths, with value-based methods excelling in stability and policy-based methods in their ability to handle high-dimensional action spaces and continuous actions (Nachum et al., 2017). The A2C algorithm is a sophisticated approach in RL that combines the strengths of both value-based and policy-based methods to create a balanced model capable of learning optimal policies while accurately evaluating the value of environmental states. This method is particularly suited for applications like *EmoGenPath*, where the goal is to adaptively provide therapeutic support based on a child's emotional state and contextual factors.

IMPLEMENTATION OUTLINE

Algorithm 1 outlines the steps for training the *EmoGenPath* system using the A2C method (see Fig. 13.3). It emphasizes the iterative process of action selection based on the actor's policy, execution in the environment, and updates to both the actor (policy) and critic (value function) based on observed outcomes. The algorithm is designed to iteratively refine the system's ability to select the most beneficial actions (interventions) for children, based on their current emotional state and the contextual information provided, leading toward the ultimate goal of improving emotional well-being.

The core principle behind *EmoGenPath* aligns with the Markov Decision Process (MDP), where the future state depends only on the current state and action, not on the sequence of events that preceded it. We built two neural networks, called the actor-network and the critic network. The actor-network is responsible for policy approximation. It decides on the best action (intervention) to take in a given state by outputting a probability distribution over actions. The actor's goal is to select actions that maximize the expected return. The critic network estimates the value function, which assesses how good a particular state is for an agent. The critic helps the actor adjust by evaluating the chosen actions

```
1: Input: S: current state, A: set of possible actions, R: reward, γ: discount factor.
2: Require: V_final: final value function accuracy, A_policy: actor's policy, V_critic: critic's value estimation, T_episodes: total number of episodes, α_actor: learning rate for actor, α_critic: learning rate for critic.
3: Procedure 1: Main
4:      Initialize actor's policy A_policy randomly.
5:      Initialize critic's value function V_critic randomly.
6:      for episode = 1 to T_episodes do
7:          Initialize S with the initial state of the environment.
8:          while S is not done do
9:              Select action A from S using policy derived from A_policy.
10:             Take action A, observe reward R, and next state S'.
11:             Calculate temp. diff. error δ = R + γ * V_critic(S') - V_critic(S).
12:             Update critic by minimizing loss: δ^2.
13:             Calculate advantage A(S, A) = δ.
14:             Update A_policy with gradient of expected return weighted by A(S, A).
15:             S ← S'.
16:         end while
17:         if V_critic accuracy ≥ V_final then
18:             Break and return final policy and value function.
19:         end if
20:     end for
21: return {Final A_policy and V_critic}
```

Fig. 13.3. Algorithm 1: Training EmoGenPath Using A2C.

and indicating whether they're likely to lead to positive outcomes. In the context of *EmoGenPath*, the **actor** represents the model's decision-making component, choosing digital interventions based on the child's current emotional and contextual state. The **critic** evaluates these decisions, providing feedback on the potential effectiveness of an intervention in advancing toward therapeutic goals. The state space includes the detected emotional states and possibly other contextual information (e.g., time spent on the current topic, previous topics covered). The action space comprises different script segments or therapeutic activities. The reward function is designed to prioritize the child's emotional well-being, with higher rewards for transitions to positive states and lower (or negative) rewards for transitions to negative states (Hafner & Riedmiller, 2011).

1. **State**: The state could include the current emotional state of the child (as detected by the CNN), the context of the conversation (provided by the LLM model), and any relevant historical information about the child's progress toward the therapy goals.
2. **Actions**: Actions would be the possible responses or interventions the virtual therapist can choose from at any given state. This might include selecting specific script segments, virtual mindfulness exercises, or questions designed to encourage progress toward the therapy goals.
3. **Rewards**: Rewards would be defined based on the child's response to actions taken by the virtual therapist. Positive feedback, signs of engagement, or progress toward the therapeutic goals would yield positive rewards. The system could use direct feedback from the child, therapist assessments, or progress markers identified in the conversation to assign rewards.
4. **Policy**: The policy dictates how the system decides on the next action based on the current state. The goal of the RL model is to learn a policy that maximizes the cumulative reward, thereby guiding the child toward achieving the therapy goals.

The actor and critic networks are trained in tandem. The critic assesses actions taken by the actor by estimating state values and calculating advantages, which measure how much better an action is compared to the average. The actor's training involves adjusting its policy to favor actions that lead to higher advantages, effectively learning to choose interventions that are predicted to improve the child's emotional state. The critic's loss is computed based on the squared advantage, pushing it to make accurate state value predictions. The learning rates for the actor and critic optimizers require tuning separately to balance the learning dynamics between policy improvement (actor) and value estimation (critic).

MODEL ARCHITECTURE

Applying the A2C model within *EmoGenPath* presents an advanced method for adaptively selecting therapeutic interventions. It allows the system to learn from complex emotional and contextual states, making decisions that are grounded in both immediate feedback and long-term therapeutic goals. However, deploying such a model in practice requires careful consideration of ethical implications, robust safety mechanisms, and ongoing oversight by therapy professionals. Next, we describe the key concepts integral to understanding the mechanics and optimizing the performance of the *EmoGenPath* model. In particular, we introduce the concept of episodes that are sequences of state-action-reward interactions that terminate at a defined endpoint. Using the A2C algorithm, each episode contributes to training both the actor, which decides actions (interventions), and the critic, which evaluates their outcomes, iteratively refining the policy and value estimations toward optimal therapeutic goal-achievement. We present conceptual formulations of the returns of episodes, the losses incurred by the critic and actor networks, and the concept of entropy, which plays a critical role in ensuring sufficient exploration.

In the context of RL, the return of an episode is the total accumulated reward received by the agent from the start to the end of an episode. For *EmoGenPath*, this could represent the cumulative positive change in a child's emotional state throughout a therapy session, as facilitated by the digital interventions. The return is typically calculated as the sum of rewards for each step of the episode, often discounted by a factor to prioritize immediate rewards over distant ones. Understanding the returns helps in evaluating the effectiveness of chosen actions and in guiding the learning process toward strategies that enhance the child's emotional well-being. The critic network in A2C estimates the value function, which predicts the expected return from each state. The critic loss measures the difference between these predictions and the actual returns (computed from the episodes). It is typically calculated using Mean Squared Error (MSE), aiming to minimize the discrepancy and improve the critic's accuracy. The actor's job is to choose actions based on a policy that maximizes expected returns. The actor loss is calculated to encourage actions that lead to higher advantages, which are defined as the difference between the action value and the value of the state as estimated by the critic. This was done through policy gradient methods where the loss is defined to maximize the expected reward. To prevent premature convergence to a suboptimal policy and encourage exploration, an entropy bonus was added to the actor loss. Entropy measures the randomness of the policy's action distribution; higher entropy means more exploration.

Entropy in the context of RL is a measure of the unpredictability or randomness of the actions taken by the policy. A higher entropy value suggests a more explorative policy, while a lower entropy indicates a more deterministic policy. By incorporating an entropy term into the actor's objective function, the A2C algorithm ensures that the policy maintains a degree of randomness. This discourages the policy from becoming too deterministic too quickly, allowing the agent to explore a wider range of actions and potentially discover more effective strategies. While entropy encourages exploration, it is crucial to balance it against exploiting known good strategies. As training progresses, the entropy term is often reduced to allow the agent to exploit the best strategies it has learned while still maintaining some level of exploration.

TRAINING *EMOGENPATH*

To achieve goal-oriented outcomes, we set out with a sample objective to improve the child's ability to deal with anxiety. The RL model selects actions from a list of therapeutic interventions based on the current emotional response to maximize the likelihood of achieving the goal. Since RL training involves interactions with the environment, our example training setup is suitable for a therapy session. We present a state figure below (see Fig. 13.4) that incorporates the context of using detected emotional states and other contextual information as part of the state space and considers a reward system that prioritizes emotional well-being. This figure reflects a nuanced approach where interventions are dynamically selected based on comprehensive state assessments, and rewards are adjusted according to the emotional outcome of each intervention.

Each session's initial state includes both the emotional state and contextual information related to the therapy process, such as topic engagement or preceding activities. This dual consideration allows for a more personalized and situation-aware intervention strategy. The interventions are digital and AI-powered, designed to be both engaging and therapeutic, catering to the child's current needs and emotional readiness. The reward system is designed to reflect the effectiveness of each intervention in reducing anxiety. A significant reduction in anxiety levels yields a higher reward, while interventions that may inadvertently increase anxiety receive negative rewards. The choice of intervention is crucial and depends on the current emotional state. Some interventions might be more effective for certain states than others, highlighting the need for personalization. The goal is to guide the child toward a state of calm and RL training helps to identify the most conducive interventions to achieve this. We choose a learning algorithm that navigates through emotional states from extreme agitation to peacefulness using strategic interventions. Each episode simulates a session aiming to soothe and calm the child's emotional state, with the model progressively learning the most effective words to achieve a peaceful state. The modeling process includes tracking a moving average of the episode returns to smooth out fluctuations and reveal trends in the agent's ability to solve the environment. Increasing episode returns over time would indicate that the agent is learning to maximize its cumulative rewards, suggesting improved performance and decision-making in navigating the environment. Also important are the entropy values as the number of updates increases. A higher value indicates a more explorative policy, whereas lower entropy suggests the policy is becoming more deterministic. Together, these metrics might provide insights into the learning process and performance of the agent. We will work on visualizing these trends in a future research paper that will help in diagnosing issues, understanding the effects of algorithmic choices, and guiding further tuning to enhance the agent's capabilities. In training *EmoGenPath* with A2C, managing the dynamics between the returns of episodes, the calculation and optimization of critic and actor losses, and the strategic use of entropy to balance exploration and exploitation are critical for developing an effective adaptive therapy model. These elements work together to refine the model's policy and value estimations, aiming to maximize the therapeutic outcomes for children through personalized, adaptive interventions.

Session ID	Pseudo-anonymized Initial Emotion	Intervention	CNN recognized Resulting Emotion	Reward
1	(Very Anxious, New Topic)	Customized Breathing Instructions	(Moderately Anxious, Breathing Exercise Completed)	+10
2	(Moderately Anxious, Following a Difficult Topic)	Virtual Mindfulness Meditation	(Slightly Anxious, Mindfulness Completed)	+10
3	(Slightly Anxious, After Positive Visualization)	AI-Generated Encouraging Story	(Calm, Story Engagement)	+10
4	(Very Anxious, High Engagement Time)	Scripted Relaxation VR Scenario	(Slightly Anxious, VR Engagement)	+15
5	(Calm, Recent Success)	Digital Journaling Prompts	(Very Calm, Reflection on Success)	+5
6	(Moderately Anxious, Physical Inactivity)	Interactive Exercise Video	(Calm, post-exercise)	+15
7	(Calm, Seeking Distraction)	Therapeutic Music Playlist	(Very Calm, Engaged with Music)	+10
8	(Very Anxious, Revisiting Trauma)	Cognitive-Behavioral Therapy (CBT) Dialogue	(Moderately Anxious, CBT Insights)	+20
9	(Moderately Anxious, Social Isolation)	Virtual Peer Interaction	(Slightly Anxious, Social Engagement)	+10
10	(Slightly Anxious, Lacking Motivation)	LLM-selected Humor Clips	(Very Calm, Laughter Therapy)	+15
11	(Very Calm, Engaged with Music)	Guided Imagery Meditation with Nature Themes	(Extremely Calm, Continued Engagement)	+5
12	(Extremely Calm, Continued Engagement)	Gratitude Reflection Script	(Extremely Calm, Deepened Tranquility)	DONE

Fig. 13.4. Sample EmoGenPath State-Action-Reward.

TESTING OUTLINE

Initial Interaction:
The virtual therapist begins the session with a standard script designed to engage the child gently, covering broad topics with neutral emotional content.

Emotion Recognition Feedback Loop:
As the child interacts with the content, the CNN continuously analyzes their facial expressions and feeds the codified emotion into an LLM that generates a new script better designed to manage the emotional state of the child. The generated dialogue is used by the RL model, serving as the state information for deciding the next best action (i.e., which part of the script to follow next or when to introduce specific therapeutic exercises).

Therapeutic Goal Achievement:
The RL model, trained with the objective of maximizing positive emotional responses and minimizing negative ones, dynamically adjusts the therapy dialogue and intervention construct. It selects the next piece of content based on the child's current emotional state and the historical effectiveness of various scripts in eliciting positive emotional states. The RL model's output is rendered in the therapy session and the cycle begins again, where the RL model receives rewards based on the emotional outcomes of its script selections, encouraging, and reinforcing strategies that lead to more positive or neutral emotional states and discouraging those that result in negative responses.

VIRTUAL THERAPY EPISODE WITH *EMOGENPATH*

A narrative of a trial run of EmoGenPath is presented in Fig. 13.5 using sample emojis that represent the emotion states as input to the model. We describe how *EmoGenPath's* interventions impact a simulated emotional journey with the goal of achieving a predetermined therapeutic outcome. This trial run showcases an episode as a sequence of state-action-reward interactions that terminate at the achievement of the desired therapeutic learning pathway.

Session 1: Introduction to Mindfulness

Initial Emotion: The subject starts the session feeling moderately anxious due to a difficult topic discussed earlier.

Intervention: EmoGenPath introduces a virtual mindfulness meditation designed to ground the subject's thoughts and reduce anxiety.

Resulting Emotion: After the session, the subject feels slightly anxious, indicating a reduction in anxiety levels thanks to the mindfulness exercise.

Reward: +10 for the positive shift toward calmness.

Session 2: Engaging with Stories

Initial Emotion: Building from the slightly anxious state post-mindfulness, the subject is now more open to engagement.

Session ID	Pseudo-anonymized Initial Emotion	Intervention	CNN recognized Resulting Emotion	Reward
1	😟 (Moderately Anxious, Following a Difficult Topic)	Virtual Mindfulness Meditation	(Slightly Anxious, Mindfulness Completed)	+10
2	😟 (Slightly Anxious, After Positive Visualization)	AI-Generated Encouraging Story	(Calm, Story Engagement)	+10
3	🙂 (Calm, Story Engagement)	Therapeutic Music Playlist	(Very Calm, Engaged with Music)	+10
4	😌 (Very Calm, Engaged with Music)	Guided Imagery Meditation with Nature Themes	(Extremely Calm, Continued Engagement)	+5
5	😊 (Extremely Calm, Continued Engagement)	LLM-selected Humor Clips	(Extremely Calm, Deepened Tranquility)	DONE

Fig. 13.5. EmoGenPath Trial Episode Run.

Intervention: An AI-generated encouraging story is presented, possibly tailored to the subject's interests and emotional needs.

Resulting Emotion: The subject becomes calm, fully engaged in the story, showing signs of relaxation and reduced anxiety.

Reward: +10 for successfully engaging the subject and further alleviating anxiety.

Session 3: Musical Journey

Initial Emotion: Now calm, the subject is ready for deeper emotional nurturing.

Intervention: A therapeutic music playlist is activated, featuring soothing melodies that resonate with the subject.

Resulting Emotion: The subject transitions to a very calm state, deeply engaged with the music, further enhancing their emotional well-being.

Reward: +10 for elevating the subject's mood to a very calm state through music.

Session 4: Exploring Imagery

Initial Emotion: In a very calm state, the subject is immersed in therapeutic music.

Intervention: Guided imagery meditation with nature themes is introduced, inviting the subject to visualize peaceful, natural settings.

Resulting Emotion: The subject reaches an extremely calm state, continuing their engagement and finding deeper tranquility in the guided imagery.

Reward: +5 for maintaining and deepening the subject's tranquil state.

Session 5: Maintaining Tranquility

Initial Emotion: The subject is now in a state of deep tranquility, fully relaxed and at peace.

Intervention: To maintain this serene state, EmoGenPath selects humor clips ensuring light-heartedness without disrupting the calm.

Resulting Emotion: The subject remains in the state of "Extremely Calm, Deepened Tranquility," enjoying the humor clips while maintaining their serene state. No additional reward is needed as the subject has reached and sustained the optimal emotional outcome.

This trial demonstrates how a sequence of personalized digital interventions can effectively guide a child from a state of moderate anxiety to one of profound calmness and tranquility, each step thoughtfully designed to address the child's current emotional state and encourage progression toward emotional well-being.

REAL-WORLD CONSIDERATIONS

Translating this conceptual model to real-life therapy would involve much more granularity in recognizing emotional states and tailoring interventions. Additionally, direct input from experienced therapists and continual adaptation based on individual responses are crucial to ensure the model's effectiveness and sensitivity to each child's emotional journey.

While the model's output can guide the adaptive therapy tool to tailor activities that suit the child's current emotional needs, the detection of emotions involves capturing several features of facial expressions from the images of the children during a live therapy session. The image capture can be accomplished using a smartphone with sufficient lighting. The image can be represented as a simple two-dimensional matrix in grayscale and then passed through a filter to produce a series of different edge detectors, both vertical and horizontal, that make up a facial expression.

ETHICAL AND TECHNICAL CONSIDERATIONS

The development and deployment of *EmoGenPath*, especially the emotion detection component, are underpinned by stringent ethical considerations. Given the sensitive nature of the target demographic – children from conflict zones – the model is trained on a diverse and inclusive dataset, ensuring a broad understanding of emotional expressions across different ethnicities and backgrounds. Moreover, data privacy and security are paramount, with rigorous protocols in place to protect the personal information of the users. From a technical standpoint, the choice of architecture, optimization algorithms, and loss functions are aligned to achieve high accuracy in emotion recognition while maintaining computational efficiency. The model's adaptive learning capabilities are central to its effectiveness, enabling it to respond dynamically to the evolving emotional states of the children, thereby facilitating a personalized and impactful cognitive training experience. Additionally, the following considerations are integral to the refinement of EmoGenPath and aim to maximize its benefit while minimizing harm.

Do No Harm: More research is necessary to ensure bias mitigation that prevents unequal or harmful treatment of certain groups. This includes biases in emotion recognition due to cultural, racial, or individual differences in expression. While personalization is a strength of *EmoGenPath*, it requires careful state, action, and reward design to avoid over-personalization that might lead to dependency or avoidance of necessary but potentially distressing therapeutic topics. The system must be designed to recognize when human intervention is needed and facilitate this handover seamlessly.

Data Privacy and Ethical Use: Given the sensitive nature of the application, ensuring the privacy and security of the children's data is paramount. Adherence to ethical guidelines and possibly seeking oversight from psychological professionals are essential steps.

Cultural Sensitivity: The model must be trained on a diverse dataset to recognize expressions across different cultural contexts accurately, acknowledging that the manifestation of emotions can vary widely.

Adaptive Interventions with Safety Nets: *EmoGenPath's* interventions, while adaptive, must have built-in safety nets to prevent harm. This includes limiting the scope of AI-generated advice to areas where it has been thoroughly vetted and proven safe and ensuring that the system can identify and escalate cases that require human intervention.

Continuous Learning and Adaptation: The system should incorporate mechanisms for continuous learning, allowing it to refine its approach based on accumulating data on the most effective strategies in supporting the children's emotional health. Implementing mechanisms for continuous monitoring of the system's impact on children's emotional well-being allows for the early detection of any adverse effects. Feedback from therapists, caregivers, and the children themselves is invaluable for adjusting the model to ensure it remains supportive and non-harmful.

Professional Oversight: AI cannot replace human therapists but should act as a complement to traditional therapy. Professional oversight ensures that the therapeutic content generated by *EmoGenPath* is clinically sound and that any critical decisions are made or reviewed by qualified professionals.

CONCLUSION

At the age of 20, the author had a harrowing experience navigating communal violence during the Godhra riots in 2002. The journey of recovery and healing could have used a compassionate embrace from AI-assisted support. Through this work, the author has imagined a virtual space where his story is met with empathetic understanding, gently guided by ML to explore the depths of the traumatic emotions experienced while escaping conflict. We would like the audience to picture a therapeutic journey in a virtual world, carefully designed to help children and youth from conflict zones reclaim a sense of safety and peace. Let ML assisted therapy be a companion in their recovery, recognizing the resilience within each individual. Visualize a community of survivors brought together by shared narratives, fostering a collective healing that transcends the boundaries of language and culture. Ethical AI and ML, infused with compassion, can contribute to their restoration, reminding them that strength and support surround them on this courageous journey of healing.

We proposed *EmoGenPath* as a RL model that uses the detected emotional state and dialogue context to manage the conversation toward predetermined therapeutic outcomes. During training, the model learns to select the intervention that is most likely to achieve therapy objectives. This model has the potential to scale therapeutic resources and deliver personalized, effective interventions, addressing the acute need for mental health support in conflict-affected regions. Integrating RL into the therapy model adds a goal-oriented layer, enabling the virtual therapy system to adaptively guide interactions. This approach requires careful consideration of the state representation, action space, and reward structure to ensure that the system effectively supports the child's emotional and therapeutic journey. The modeling technique we used provides continuous longitudinal monitoring of the child's progress using predefined markers or milestones. An increase in positive emotional expressions or a decrease in negative expressions during or after certain interventions can serve as markers for progress, even if the model is unable to achieve a given therapeutic pathway. We recommended using CNNs for continuous emotion recognition to gauge the child's immediate response to the therapeutic content. This provides a real-time measure of engagement and emotional impact and engages the current state, action, and reward mechanism of the RL model.

However, future research could pivot to using transformer architecture for visual RL, which can explicitly model short-term state, action, and reward representations in a Markovian-like inductive bias system (Shang et al., 2022). Transformers, initially developed for NLP tasks, have shown remarkable capability in handling sequential data due to their attention mechanisms, which allow them to weigh the importance of different parts of the input data differently. Their self-attention mechanism can effectively determine the relevance of past events to the current state, mimicking the Markovian property in a more flexible, data-driven manner. *EmoGenPath* can be enhanced to track changes in the child's emotional responses over time to assess longer-term progress toward therapy goals. This involves comparing emotional response patterns from session to session. The models could be adjusted based on this progress, focusing on areas that require more attention. The same training procedures could be used with modification to the session outcomes with adjoining rewards for outcomes achieved. We realize that carefully designing the reward system is critical to encourage AI-assisted actions that are genuinely beneficial toward achieving the therapy goals. This must involve collaboration with child psychologists to identify effective markers of progress and engagement.

NOTE

1. We built a simulation chat application using an Large Language Model (LLM).

REFERENCES

Akinsulure, A. (2020). The rise of drug abuse in internally displaced persons' camps in Nigeria: A literature review. *Journal of Addiction & Prevention, 8*(1), 1–9.

Antle, A. N., Chesick, L., Levisohn, A., Sridharan, S., & Tan, P. (2015). Using neurofeedback to teach self-regulation to children living in poverty. In M. Bers (Ed.), *Proceedings of the 14th International conference on interaction design and children* (pp. 119–128). Association for Computing Machinery.

Antle, A. N., Chesick, L., Sridharan, S. K., & Cramer, E. (2018). East meets west: A mobile brain-computer system that helps children living in poverty learn to self-regulate. *Personal and Ubiquitous Computing, 22*(4), 839–866.

Antle, A. N., McLaren, E., Fiedler, H., & Johnson, N. (2019a). Design for mental health: How socio-technological processes mediate outcome measures in a field study of a wearable anxiety app. In TEI'19 (Ed.), *Proceedings of the thirteenth international conference on tangible, embedded, and embodied interaction* (pp. 87–96). Association for Computing Machinery.

Antle, A. N., McLaren, E., Fiedler, H., & Johnson, N. (2019b). Evaluating the impact of a mobile neurofeedback app for young children at school and home. In CHI'19 (Ed.), *Proceedings of the 2019 CHI conference on human factors in computing systems* (pp. 1–13). Association for Computing Machinery.

Carlbring, P., Hadjistavropoulos, H., Kleiboer, A., & Andersson, G. (2023). A new era in Internet interventions: The advent of Chat-GPT and AI-assisted therapist guidance. *Internet Interventions, 32*.

Cohen, J. A., Mannarino, A. P., & Murray, L. K. (2011). Trauma-focused CBT for youth who experience ongoing traumas. *Child Abuse & Neglect: The International Journal, 35*(8), 637–646.

Ewelina, K. (2023). Trauma and well-being: Understanding demographic differences in the impact of COVID-19 on mental health. *Journal of Happiness Studies, 25*(3), 10051023.

Hafner, R., & Riedmiller, M. (2011). Reinforcement learning in feedback control. *Machine Learning, 84*(1–2), 137–169.

Hong, J. S., Tillman, R., & Luby, J. L. (2015). Disruptive behavior in preschool children: Distinguishing normal misbehavior from markers of current and later childhood conduct disorder. *The Journal of Pediatrics, 166*(3), 723–730.

Jokinen, T., Alexander, E. C., Manikam, L., Huq, T., Patil, P., Benjumea, D., Das, I., & Davidson, L. L. (2021). A systematic review of household and family alcohol use and adolescent behavioural outcomes in low- and middle-income countries. *Child Psychiatry & Human Development, 52*(4), 554–570.

Kosti, R., Alvarez, J. M., Recasens, A., & Lapedriza, A. (2017a). Emotion recognition in context. In *Proceedings of the IEEE conference on computer vision and pattern recognition*, pp. 1667–1675.

Kosti, R., Alvarez, J. M., Recasens, A., & Lapedriza, A. (2017b). EMOTIC: Emotions in context dataset. In *Proceedings of the IEEE conference on computer vision and pattern recognition workshops*, pp. 61–69.

Kosti, R., Alvarez, J. M., Recasens, A., & Lapedriza, A. (2019). Context based emotion recognition using emotic dataset. *IEEE Transactions on Pattern Analysis and Machine Intelligence, 42*(11), 2755–2766.

Lansford, J. E., & Banati, P. (2018). *Handbook of adolescent development research and its impact on global policy*. Oxford University Press.

Lin, T., & Anderson, T. (2024). Reduced therapeutic skill in teletherapy versus in-person therapy: The role of non-verbal communication. *Counselling and Psychotherapy Research, 24*(1), 317–327.

Mannarino, A. P., Cohen, J. A., Deblinger, E., Runyon, M. K., & Steer, R. A. (2012). Trauma-focused cognitive-behavioral therapy for children. *Child Maltreatment: Journal of the American Professional Society on the Abuse of Children, 17*(3), 231–241.

Masten, A. S., & Narayan, A. J. (2012). Child development in the context of disaster, war, and terrorism: Pathways of risk and resilience. *Annual Review of Psychology, 63*, 227–257.

Mavranezouli, F., Megnin-Viggars, O., Daly, C., Dias, S., Stockton, S., Meiser-Stedman, R., Trickey, D., & Pilling, S. (2020). Research review: Psychological and psychosocial treatments for children and young people with post-traumatic stress disorder: A network meta-analysis. *Journal of Child Psychology and Psychiatry and Allied Disciplines*, *61*(1), 18–29.

Mnih, V., Badia, A. P., Mirza, M., Graves, A., Lillicrap, T., Harley, T., ... Kavukcuoglu, K. (2016, June). Asynchronous methods for deep reinforcement learning. In *International conference on machine learning* (pp. 1928–1937). PMLR.

Morris, R. R., Kouddous, K., Kshirsagar, R., & Schueller, S. M. (2018). Towards an artificially empathic conversational agent for mental health applications: System design and user perceptions. *Journal of Medical Internet Research*, *20*(6).

Nachum, O., Norouzi, M., Xu, K., & Schuurmans, D. (2017). Bridging the gap between value and policy-based reinforcement learning. *Advances in Neural Information Processing Systems*, *30*.

Parruca, E. (2022). Psychosocial transcultural games as tools in group counselling, therapy and training for dealing with crisis and trauma from war, armed conflict, and forced displacement. *The Global Psychotherapist*, *2*(2), 32–41.

Qasrawi, R., Vicuna Polo, S., & Abu Al-Halawa, D. (2023). Machine learning techniques for identifying mental health risk factor associated with schoolchildren cognitive ability living in politically violent environments. *Frontiers in Psychiatry*, *14*, 1071622.

Robertson, I. (1987). *Sociology* (3rd ed.). Worth Publishers.

Rocco, D., Mariani, R., & Zanelli, D. (2013). The role of non-verbal interaction in a short-term psychotherapy: Preliminary analysis and assessment of paralinguistic aspects. *Research in Psychotherapy: Psychopathology, Process and Outcome*, *16*(1), 54–64.

Schulman, J., Moritz, P., Levine, S., Jordan, M., & Abbeel, P. (2015). High-dimensional continuous control using generalized advantage estimation. *arXiv preprint arXiv:1506.02438*.

Schuurmans, A. A. T., Nijhof, K. S., Popma, A., Scholte, R., & Otten, R. (2021). *The effectiveness of game-based meditation therapy for traumatized adolescents in residential care: A randomized controlled trial*. (PREPRINT).

Schuurmans, A. A. T., Nijhof, K. S., Scholte, R., Popma, A., & Otten, R. (2020). A novel approach to improve stress regulation among traumatized youth in residential care: Feasibility study testing three game-based meditation interventions. *Early Intervention in Psychiatry*, *14*(4), 476–485.

Shah, T. M. (2013). Chaos and fear: Creativity and hope in an uncertain world. *International Sociology*, *28*(5), 513–517.

Shah, T. M. (2020). Children of Kashmir and the meaning of family in armed conflict. In S. Frankel, S. E. McNamee, & L. E. Bass (Eds.), *Bringing children back into the family: Relationality, connectedness, and home* (pp. 213–216). Emerald Publishing Limited.

Shah, T. M. (2024). Emotions in politics: A review of contemporary perspectives and trends. *International Political Science Abstracts*, *74*(1), 1–14.

Shang, J., Kahatapitiya, K., Li, X., & Ryoo, M. S. (2022, October). Starformer: Transformer with state-action-reward representations for visual reinforcement learning. In *European conference on computer vision* (pp. 462–479). Springer Nature Switzerland.

Slone, M., & Shiri, M. (2016). Effects of war, terrorism and armed conflict on young children: A systematic review. *Child Psychiatry and Humanitarian Development*, *47*(6), 950–965.

Solmi, M., Radua, J., Olivola, M., Croce, E., Soardo, L., Il Shin, J., Kirkbride, J. B., Jones, P., Kim, J. H., Kim, J. Y., Carvalho, A. F., Seeman, M. V., & Correll, C. U. (2022). Age at onset of mental disorders worldwide: Large-scale meta-analysis of 192 epidemiological studies. *Molecular Psychiatry*, *27*(1), 281–295.

Swaminathan, A., López, I., Mar, R. A., Heist, T., McClintock, T., Caoili, K., Grace, M., Rubashkin, M., Boggs, M. N., Chen, J. H., Gevaert, O., Mou, D., & Nock, M. K. (2023). Natural language processing system for rapid detection and intervention of mental health crisis chat messages. *Npj Digital Medicine*, *6*(1), 1–9.

Tate, A. E., McCabe, R. C., Larsson, H., Lundström, S., Lichtenstein, P., & Kuja-Halkola, R. (2020). Predicting mental health problems in adolescence using machine learning techniques. *PloS One*, *15*(4), e0230389.

Tishelman, A. C., & Geffner, R. (2011). Child and adolescent trauma across the spectrum of experience: Research and clinical interventions. *Journal of Child & Adolescent Trauma*, *4*(1), 1–7.

UNICEF. (2021). *The State of the World's Children 2021: On my mind – promoting, protecting, and caring for children's mental health*. UNICEF.

Weiss, G., & Copelton, D. (2020). *The Sociology of health, healing, and illness*. Routledge.

Yu, R., Perera, C., Sharma, M., Ipince, A., Bakrania, S., Shokraneh, F., ... Anthony, D. (2023). Child and adolescent mental health and psychosocial support interventions: An evidence and gap map of low- and middle-income countries. *Campbell Systematic Reviews, 19*(3), e1349.